THE A. W. MELLON LECTURES IN THE FINE ARTS

DELIVERED AT THE

NATIONAL GALLERY OF ART, WASHINGTON, D.C.

1952. CREATIVE INTUITION IN ART AND POETRY *by* Jacques Maritain

1953. THE NUDE: A STUDY IN IDEAL FORM *by* Kenneth Clark

1954. THE ART OF SCULPTURE *by* Herbert Read

1955. PAINTING AND REALITY *by* Etienne Gilson

1956. ART AND ILLUSION: A STUDY IN THE PSYCHOLOGY OF PICTORIAL REPRESENTATION *by* E. H. Gombrich

1957. THE ETERNAL PRESENT: I. THE BEGINNINGS OF ART II. THE BEGINNINGS OF ARCHITECTURE *by* S. Giedion

1958. NICOLAS POUSSIN *by* Anthony Blunt

1959. ON DIVERS ARTS *by* Naum Gabo

1960. HORACE WALPOLE *by* Wilmarth Sheldon Lewis

1961. CHRISTIAN ICONOGRAPHY: A STUDY OF ITS ORIGINS *by* André Grabar

1962. BLAKE AND TRADITION *by* Kathleen Raine

1963. THE PORTRAIT IN THE RENAISSANCE *by* John Pope-Hennessy

1964. ON QUALITY IN ART *by* Jakob Rosenberg

1965. THE ORIGINS OF ROMANTICISM *by* Isaiah Berlin

1966. VISIONARY AND DREAMER: TWO POETIC PAINTERS, SAMUEL PALMER AND EDWARD BURNE-JONES *by* David Cecil

1967. MNEMOSYNE: THE PARALLEL OF LITERATURE AND THE VISUAL ARTS *by* Mario Praz

BOLLINGEN SERIES XXXV · 11

Title page of *Jerusalem* (1804–1820)

The soul is depicted under the classical emblem of Psyche, the butterfly. The natural universe of sun, moon, and stars is represented as "dust on the Fly's wing" of the soul, with whose life they live. The figure at the top of the plate is, following another traditional emblem, bee-winged.

THE A. W. MELLON LECTURES IN THE FINE ARTS · 1962

THE NATIONAL GALLERY OF ART · WASHINGTON, D. C.

Blake

and Tradition

Volume I

KATHLEEN RAINE

BOLLINGEN SERIES XXXV·11
PRINCETON UNIVERSITY PRESS

711961

THIS TWO-VOLUME WORK IS THE ELEVENTH VOLUME
OF THE A. W. MELLON LECTURES IN THE FINE ARTS,
WHICH ARE DELIVERED ANNUALLY
AT THE NATIONAL GALLERY OF ART, WASHINGTON.
THE VOLUMES OF LECTURES CONSTITUTE NUMBER XXXV
IN BOLLINGEN SERIES, SPONSORED BY AND PUBLISHED FOR
BOLLINGEN FOUNDATION

Library of Congress catalogue card No. 66–16235

DESIGNED BY ANDOR BRAUN
PRINTED BY KINGSPORT PRESS, INC.
KINGSPORT, TENNESSEE
COLOR PLATES PRINTED BY CLARKE & WAY, INC.
NEW YORK, N.Y.
MANUFACTURED IN THE U.S.A.

The perfection of the highest virtue and the opening of the real spiritual senses constituted the highest degree of the Mysteries; another and most important part of the discipline was the training in the interpretation of myth, symbol, and allegory, the letters of the mystical language in which the secrets of nature and the soul were written, so plainly for the initiated, so obscurely for the general.

G. R. S. Mead, *Orpheus* (1896)

Acknowledgments

IN THE COURSE of the many years over which I have been working on Blake's sources I have received help, courtesy, and encouragement from many persons and more than one organization. When the work was begun it was with no thought that it would ever form part of so distinguished a series as the A. W. Mellon Lectures in the Fine Arts, or indeed that it would be given in the form of lectures at all. The present volume is (with additions and amendments) the manuscript as I submitted it for publication to the Bollingen Foundation in 1961; from it, six lectures were extracted to deliver at the National Gallery of Art, at Washington, D.C., in the spring of 1962. For the honor of this invitation I wish to thank Mr. Paul Mellon and the Trustees of the National Gallery.

Next I wish to thank the Bollingen Foundation, whose award of a fellowship for two years, generously extended to three when the work showed no signs of being finished, enabled me to undertake a prolonged and serious study of Blake's sources. When at the end of this time the book was still unwritten, Girton College took back a prodigal, who after half a lifetime as a poet had never thought to be received into a city of learning. I especially thank Professor M. C. Bradbrook, whose idea it was that I should return to my old College, where as a research fellow, and with further help from the Bollingen Foundation, I was able to complete my task. I am a debtor, also, to the London Library and to the Trustees of the British Museum, where for many happy days I read strange books in the North Library.

More specific thanks are due to Blake scholars who have in several ways helped me. First, to Sir Geoffrey Keynes, whose scholarly and beautiful editions and bibliography must be the foundation of all Blake studies. Textual references are to his 1957 Nonesuch variorum edition of Blake's writings. Besides this general indebtedness I have to add my personal thanks for help and counsel. Mr. H. M. Margoliouth's edition of *Blake's Vala* (Oxford, 1956) has been another invaluable text, studied with profit and delight. The beautiful facsimile volumes issued by the Blake Trust have added an element of aesthetic pleasure to hard work; and here I must thank Mr. Kerrison Preston, not only for much help, advice, and criticism, but for lending for reproduction two colored plates from *Jerusalem* here reproduced for the first time. Mrs. W. B. Yeats has kindly allowed me to copy and quote marginalia from Yeats's Blake library, and also to quote passages from Yeats's published works; for these and other marks of kindness, I wish to thank her.

Dr. J. Bronowski kindly read several long sections of my work in progress, early friendship outweighing a difference in point of view. To Dr. Philip Sherrard I am indebted also for reading my manuscript, for making me rewrite a great deal of it, and for holding me to traditional orthodoxy. Mr. John Holloway also read my manuscript; and Mr. Marco Pallis I also have to thank for instruction in traditional doctrine. Dr. F. A. C. Wilson helped me with the task of correcting and checking; Mr. Francis Warner gave me similar help at a later stage.

I am grateful also to Mr. Martin Bell and to Mr. John Heath Stubbs for recondite and relevant pieces of information both were kind enough (knowing I was engaged on this work) to volunteer; to Dr. R. J. Zwi Werblowsky, of Hebrew University, Jerusalem, for information on the cabalistic symbolism of "the garden of Eden"; and above all to the late Mr. Alan Glover, to whom I owe my thanks for his wonderful patience in the editing of this work for publication, and for his advice on matters of scholarship in so many of the fields covered by this book.

Mr. Ruthven Todd, a distinguished pioneer in Blake scholarship, has made the drawing of *Anemone pulsatilla* on p. 105, a mark of friendship. Professor I. A. Richards, Professor Bernard Blackstone, and Mr. T. R. Henn have all in some tangible way helped.

Among those who have helped in ways less tangible I would like especially to thank Sir Herbert Read, and to record my debt to the late Helen Sutherland, in whose house much of my work was done.

More generally, I gladly acknowledge my debt to scholars whose works are listed in the Bibliography.

If one may thank discarnate spirits, there are three above all whose thought has companioned me like a living presence: Blake, of course; W. B. Yeats, whom in life I never saw; and Thomas Taylor, the Platonist, ancestor of my grandchildren.

My thanks to Sir Geoffrey Keynes and the Nonesuch Press for permission to quote from Blake texts; to the Macmillan Company for quotations from

Gilchrist's life of Blake and from the works of Yeats; and to the Oxford University Press for permission to use the text of H. M. Margoliouth's *Vala*.

Sections of this book have appeared in different form as the following articles:

"Who Made the Tyger?" *Encounter*, II, No. 9 (June 1954), 43–50.
"Tiriel." *The Huntington Library Quarterly*, Nov. 1957.
"Blake's 'Cupid and Psyche.'" *Listener* (Nov. 21, 1957), 832–35.
"The Little Girl Lost and Found and The Lapsed Soul." Pp. 17–63 of *The Divine Vision*. Ed. V. de S. Pinto. London, 1957.
"The Sea of Time and Space." *Journal of the Warburg and Courtauld Institutes*, XX (1957), 318–37.
"Blake's Debt to Antiquity." *The Sewanee Review*, LXXI, No. 3 (Summer 1963), 352–450.

The last of these is a somewhat abridged version of the lectures I gave in 1962. Condensed versions of one or two other chapters have been broadcast on the B.B.C.'s Third Programme. All have been revised, some very extensively, since they first appeared.

K. R.

October 1964

Contents

VOLUME I

Part IV: The Zoas of Energy

VOLUME II

Part V: The Zoas of Reason

Part VI: The Zoas of Perception

Part VII: What Is Man?

Contents

List of Illustrations

An asterisk indicates a color reproduction. For a note on sources, see p. xxiii. Unless otherwise noted, the *Jerusalem* pictures are from the Mellon copy.

Sources and Credits

The illustrations reproduce drawings, paintings, prints, book illustrations, etc., from the sources listed below. Acknowledgment is gratefully made for permission to publish these.

Boston Museum of Fine Arts: 20a, 136, 174, 192
British Museum: 11, 13, 44, 79, 82, 83, 88, 95, 100, 101, 155
Ferrara Museum: 107
Fitzwilliam Museum, Cambridge, England: 19, 20b, 51
Coll. George Goyder: 129
Henry E. Huntington Library and Art Gallery, San Marino, California: 74, 175
Library of Congress, Washington, D. C., Rosenwald Collection: 1, 2, 3, 4, 6, 8, 9, 14, 17, 27, 32, 48, 49, 52, 53, 56, 57, 59, 60, 63, 64, 65, 67, 68, 69, 71, 73, 75, 80, 90, 93, 97, 110, 111, 112, 113, 114, 115, 118, 119, 135, 137, 139, 140, 142, 144, 145, 146, 147, 148, 153, 154, 156, 158, 168, 170, 183
City of Manchester Art Galleries: 108
Coll. Sir John Stirling Maxwell, Bt.: 66
Coll. Paul Mellon: frontispiece, 18, 31, 39, 46, 55, 81, 86, 87, 89, 94, 96, 103, 106, 128, 133, 164, 166, 171, 173, 180, 181, 188, 191
National Gallery of Art, Washington, D. C., Rosenwald Collection: 38, 124, 143, 176, 189
The National Trust, Arlington Court: 23, 26, 30
New York Public Library: 12, 15, 77, 91, 92, 104, 105, 122, 126, 131, 132, 149, 157, 160, 165, 167, 184, 190, 193
Pierpont Morgan Library, New York: 161, 162
Coll. Kerrison Preston: 85, 187
Coll. Kathleen Raine: 10, 34, 35, 36, 37, 41, 43, 58, 61, 62, 70, 72, 76, 78, 84, 98, 99, 102, 117, 134, 141, 152, 169, 172, 185
Coll. Graham Robertson: 22, 120
Tate Gallery, London: 24, 40, 116, 123, 125, 127, 130, 151, 159, 177, 179, 182
Ruthven Todd: 45
Victoria and Albert Museum, London: 29
Yale University Library: 33, 121

The photographs were in general provided by the owning institution.
The following subjects were photographed by John R. Freeman and Co., London: 5, 7, 10, 16, 19, 21, 22, 23, 24, 25, 26, 30, 34, 35, 36, 37, 41, 42, 43, 50, 51, 54, 58, 61, 62, 66, 70, 72, 76, 78, 84, 85, 88, 98, 99, 102, 117, 129, 134, 141, 150, 152, 155, 163, 169, 172, 178, 182, 185, 186, 187

Introduction

IT IS NOW NEARLY TWENTY YEARS since I began to study Blake. Like others before and since, I was overwhelmed first by his lucidity, then by his obscurity. The little I could understand of him so held me that I could not but believe that in the great *terra incognita* of the Prophetic Books there must lie veins of the same gold—not a few isolated fragments only but an entire vision, equal to, if not surpassing, the revelation of the *Songs*. The German painter Götzenberge said, after a visit to England in the 1820s, that he had seen many men of talents but only three of genius—Coleridge, Flaxman, and Blake—and of these, Blake was the greatest.[1] If the Prophetic Books seemed incomprehensible, the fault was more likely to lie with the ignorance of the reader than with the poet of *The Tyger*, who called himself "a Mental Prince," and whom his disciples called "the Interpreter."

I began to read books on Blake, and by a lucky chance came first upon one of the best of them, *Blake's Circle of Destiny*, by Milton O. Percival. From this I was led to Foster Damon's *William Blake, His Philosophy and Symbols* and Joseph Wicksteed's *Blake's Vision of the Book of Job*. There must be few books on Blake, good or bad, which I have not since read, including Ellis and Yeats's monumental commentary, as obscure to me at first reading as Blake himself. Yet I then sensed, and have since come to be certain, that, for all its inaccuracies in those mechanical matters to which the modern academic world attaches such inordinate importance, of all his commentators Ellis and Yeats (or was it above all Yeats?) most nearly shared Blake's essential premises. The psychological themes detected by Wicksteed and others since, the historical and political subject-matter upon which Erdman, Bronowski, and their school have thrown much light, are not in themselves unifying principles; mythology, not history, is Blake's cosmos. What these premises might prove to be, I had little idea; for Blake himself, no less than Ellis and Yeats, seemed to have a knowledge whose sources were not divulged, as knowledge of the ancient Mysteries was kept secret among initiates. I began to understand that in those Mysteries was to be found the ordering principle. I know now that the key for which many have sought is traditional metaphysics with its accompanying language of symbolic discourse.

Those for whom Blake's symbols are of more than academic significance have been, on the whole, followers of some one or another of the modern schools of psychology. Kerrison Preston was the first to discern in Blake's myths elements that strikingly resemble Jung's archetypes, as well as the four functions, the anima, and the rest. But what all psychological elucidations of Blake's work tend to overlook is the objective and traditional nature of his spiritual knowledge; Blake would not be the great prophet that he is if his work were no more than a projection of his own psychological states. As to that common ground of all souls which Jung calls the collective unconscious, no poet can go far in that region without discovering that all mythologies are its language and its realizations embodied in whatever symbolic inheritance he may himself possess. Tradition is the record of imaginative experience, and its myths and symbols provide a language in which such knowledge may be expressed and transmitted. Sublime art does not speak a private language. Jung's psychology has its roots in this tradition, and a very great part of Blake's affinity with Jung may be explained without recourse to analytical psychology: Blake and Jung had both studied the Neoplatonists, the Gnostics, and the alchemists. In restoring meaning to myth and symbol, Jungian psychology has indeed reopened for my generation a lost world of thought and experience; but Jung has, at the same time, been in certain ways misleading or ambiguous. As Bernard Blackstone says, "the attempt to interpret art in terms of psychology must necessarily fail because it ignores the hierarchical disposition of things"—what Blake calls "the body of Divine Analogy." [2] This is not to deny that the psychological plane is one among others upon which "analogy" is valid; but Blake's myths describe a cosmic process enacted upon all the planes of being. Blake claimed to teach the Everlasting Gospel, and it is only in the light of this doctrine that he can be understood. I have attempted to relate his thought to the basic texts known to Blake, in which this doctrine is embodied. Foster Damon first suggested Blake's debt to the Neoplatonists and, in particular, to the writings and translations of Thomas Taylor; Milton O. Percival followed him, and there have been others since I wrote the greater part of this book. No doubt more will be discovered, but this,

I believe, can only strengthen and confirm the main conclusions of this work.

Traditional metaphysics is neither vague, personal, nor arbitrary. It is the recorded history of imaginative thought and has, in every civilization, an accompanying language of symbol and myth in which such knowledge is preserved and transmitted: the royal language of poetry and the other arts. Such knowledge cannot be reduced to terms of mere scholarship; for it is not only one more field of special study in which a poet may happen to be interested, but rather the necessary basis and unifying principle of all knowledge. That is why the study of its records, neglected no less by the learned than by the vulgar in a profane society, has at all times been the occupation of precisely those poets who claim to be "inspired." The singing school of the soul, as Yeats knew, is the studying of "monuments of its own magnificence"; and Milton indicated in what school the poets have at all times gone to study what we may call the learning of the imagination:

> *Or let my lamp at midnight hour*
> *Be seen in some high lonely Towr*
> *Where I may oft out-watch the* Bear
> *With thrice great Hermes, or unsphere*
> *The spirit of* Plato *to unfold*
> *What Worlds, or what vast Regions hold*
> *The immortal mind that hath forsook*
> *Her mansion in this fleshly nook.*[3]

The schools do not teach this learning, but the poets find it out; for imaginative insight at once illuminates its records, and demands its language of symbolic discourse as a necessary means of expression. To quote C. S. Lewis: "Giants, dragons, paradises, gods, and the like are themselves the expression of certain basic elements in man's spiritual experience. In that sense they are more like words." [4]

In an age whose dominant philosophy is some one or another of the several current forms of materialism, the arts cease to perform their normal function. In ignorance of the language of cosmic analogy (and what else is true poetry but such a language?) some form of humanism or naturalistic "realism" usurps every field of thought. Works of the past are misread in the light of this novel opinion, with a consequent distortion of judgment that necessarily leads to the deposing of what has been thought high and an exaltation of what was formerly thought low. If, for example, Shelley's symbolic language of analogy be read (as, at the present time, is often the case) as descriptive merely of natural appearances, Shelley becomes scarcely distinguishable from Swinburne. Blake, so read, grandly defies comprehension altogether. But poets who in humanist terms are condemned because they neither describe natural appearances nor express personal feelings prove, in terms of this lost symbolic language, to be making statements of quite another kind. Much in their work that, as image, seems forced or vague is seen, in the light of tradition, to be most strict and, in C. S. Lewis' sense, most "grammatical" as symbol. These poets are found to be least personal where they have been thought most so, and greatest when least "original." For those very elements of their thought and symbolic language in which they are least personal and most orthodox, Yeats has been called eccentric and Blake mad.

Modern criticism too often concentrates on the means of art, while mistaking its ends. The purpose of a work of art is—to quote Coomaraswamy—effective communication; and "in order to answer the question, Has the thing been well said? it will evidently be necessary for us to know what it is that was to be said. It is for this reason that in every discussion of works of art we must begin with the subject-matter." [5] "The Nature of my Work is Visionary or Imaginative," Blake wrote; and "the Nature of Visionary Fancy, or Imagination, is very little Known, & the Eternal nature & permanence of its ever Existent Images is consider'd as less permanent than the things of Vegetative & Generative Nature." [6] Blake's subject matter is not to be evaded, and his symbolic language has to be learned. "Some, perhaps all, of those readers I most value," Yeats wrote in his Introduction to *A Vision*, "will be repelled by what must seem an arbitrary, harsh, difficult symbolism. Yet such has almost always accompanied expression that unites the sleeping and waking mind." Yeats mentions the cabala, the complicated mathematical tables of the magicians, and "the diagrams in Law's *Boehme*, where one lifts a flap of paper to discover both the human entrails and the starry heavens." What the "flap of paper" (Blake, too, had lifted it) revealed is "Divine Analogy." He then goes on to speak of Blake: "William Blake thought those diagrams worthy of Michael Angelo, but remains himself almost unintelligible because he never drew the like." [7]

Since Blake never did draw his diagram or provide notes to his Prophetic Books, it has remained for others to do so; for the "symbolic bones" are there, as Yeats was in a position to know.

It may be asked of what use is poetry whose symbolic language does not communicate its meaning immediately to the reader. The answer is that such a poetry is not meant simply to stimulate the emotions; it summons to an understanding. It therefore makes demands on the reader's intelligence similar to those made on the poet himself. If we do not respond to these demands, the fault is ours and does not lie in the poetry. The traditional language of symbols remains always intrinsically intelligible. Frithjof Schuon has well stated the reason for this: "The science of symbols—not simply a knowledge of traditional symbols—proceeds from the qualitative significances of substances, forms, spatial directions, numbers, natural phenomena, positions, relationships, movements, colours and other properties or states of things; we are not dealing here with subjective appreciations, for the cosmic qualities are ordered both in relation to Being and according to a hierarchy which is more real than the individual." [8] Whether an individual person or a whole society is able to receive what the symbol communicates does not affect the question at all. One hears that the symbols of, for example, Christianity are "dead." It may be true that the symbolic forms have been monstrously abused, but the essences signified by the Cross, the Virgin, the rite of baptism, and the rest remain what they always were.

Blake certainly believed that a work of art speaks directly to the imagination; but few retain into adult life the capacity for an intellectual response that transcends "corporeal understanding." Modern education at all levels, instead of, as within traditional societies, providing us with the means toward this, makes it virtually impossible. It is therefore necessary at this time to relearn both traditional doctrine and its symbolic language, before poetry like that of Dante or of Blake can be more than superficially understood. At least we may be encouraged to discover that the same key unlocks all: each poet may have his chosen symbolic themes, but all speak one language.

Sources as such have always a certain interest. Livingston Lowes's *The Road to Xanadu* delighted my generation by the light it cast upon the processes by which what Coleridge calls "the hooks and eyes of memory" bring together by association ideas and images of diverse origins. But what such material may be before it is recombined into the poem may be of little importance. Images are accidental: the organizing idea is what makes the poem. It is necessary to follow Blake back to his origins not because these are "sources" but because of the nature of those origins; for Blake is among those poets who has "set his soul to study in a learned school"; and what distinguishes his learning is that he everywhere and at all times followed, in art, poetry, and philosophy, the traces, now clear, now almost lost, of tradition.

Considered discursively, it would be easy to find differences, even contradictions, between the various systems upon which Blake drew. Much of the incomprehensibility of his work does in fact arise from the impossibility (given the premise "All Religions Are One") of making the parts taken from many systems fit into a coherent whole. But there may well be essential unity of thought where there are formal differences; and even these will appear much less to those who, like Blake, have apprehended their essences, than to the critic who approaches them by way of their formal terms.

Unfortunately for his commentators, Blake's practice was dictated by a belief in eclecticism for its own sake, because "All Religions Are One." He proceeded to draw in, to fuse and identify, gods and myths, symbolic terms and themes, from every source known or half-known to him. Yeats admits himself defeated in his attempt to find order in Blake's system, by its unbounded nature. New elements are continually added; Blake is, as Yeats says, forever attempting to master, by "some single shining image," the incoherence, the "overflowing and bursting of the mind." He was fanatically eclectic. For Dante the symbolic framework of medieval Christianity sufficed; but Blake lived in a world aware of many myths, many religions, and he could not fail to realize that all tell of the same reality. Eclecticism in the modern world can scarcely be evaded; at most it may be disguised or included within a Christian (or other) framework. Blake did weld his pantheon within a Christian framework; and he is perhaps the single instance of a poet who has succeeded in creating a Christian polytheism.

Blake was an enormous reader not only in literature but in all subjects that engaged his contemporaries and in many that did not. Samuel Palmer recalled for his biographer, Gilchrist, visits to Blake's rooms in Fountain Court, when the old Interpreter would show to his young disciples his wonderful collection of prints and antique gems. Dürer and Michelangelo, Fra Angelico and Claude, and, if Palmer's memory is true, even many of those painters he elsewhere criticizes were, with Homer and Vergil, Plato and Ovid, Shakespeare and Milton, the constant companions of his thought. "He was anything but sectarian and exclusive," Palmer recollected, "finding sources of delight throughout the whole range of art; while as a critic, he was judicious and discriminating." Palmer especially remembered Blake's "stores of classical imagery." What nature was to Wordsworth, works of art and literature were to Blake, the raw material of his poetry.

As an engraver Blake formed the habit of studying works of art with an attention far closer than any amateur. "Copy for ever is my way," he said of his practice as an artist. He is both learned and allusive. Sir Anthony Blunt, in an important series of articles published in the *Warburg Journal*, describes a number of remarkable instances of Blake's visual borrowings from classical, Italian, Gothic, Hindu, Persian, and other sources. His visual memory of words was no less exceptional; and the study of his sources is made easier, as all Blake scholars must have discovered, by the "minute particulars" of his allusions.

In my reconstructions I have tried to avoid drawing conclusions from general resemblance, which can be misleading, especially where a basic similarity of thought and symbol is axiomatic. I may sometimes be mistaken in my attribution of sources, the more so since traditional symbolism is not confined to any one author or period, and there are symbols and themes that might have reached Blake in several ways—as, for example, the Divine Names of cabalism. But he constantly introduces from his reading phrases and images so precise that it is impossible to doubt that he intended these to evoke, like quotations, this or that work or body of knowledge, and to give scope and resonance of a certain kind in a particular context. This has been the normal practice of poets at all times, including our own, and needs no justification. The only grounds for complaint against Blake might be that no one has read the works to which he alludes. Surprisingly enough—for Eliot, Saurat, and others have presumed that Blake's sources must be disreputably obscure—most of these prove to be the same texts from which all the imaginative schools of European art and thought have always drawn, because they are the only ones available. He rightly supposed that those learned in the kind of thought of which his own poetry is an expression would have read Plato and Plotinus, the Hermetica and the alchemists, the Bible and the Bhagavad-Gita. The basic studies of the Florentine School of Athens,[9] of the English romantic poets, and, in our own time, of the Irish Renaissance differ very little: for "Supreme art is a traditional statement of certain heroic and religious truths, passed on from age to age, modified by individual genius, but never abandoned." [10]

Of one important body of European thought Blake really was ignorant —Catholic theology. His only acquaintance with the Catholic mainstream seems to have come through Fénelon and Mme. Guyon (popular with the Methodists of the eighteenth century, and in many ways akin to them), through St. Teresa (whom as an old man he loved to quote to his disciples), through his favorite school of painting (the Florentine), through Gothic architecture, and above all through Dante, to whom he devoted his last years. Gilchrist admits, with evident reluctance, Blake's "sentimental" liking for the Roman Church. It was probably very far from sentimental, and most likely reflects a growing realization that here in Europe, if anywhere, is preserved what St. Augustine calls "Wisdom, that was not made, but is now what it always was, and ever shall be." Blake defended ecclesiastical government (so Gilchrist records), and attacked Gibbon. Perhaps his proclamation that "All Religions Are One" would at any time and in any place have set him at odds with ecclesiastical orthodoxy; but he was in reality a defender of tradition in a nontraditional society. Yet if we believe that every soul is sent into the world to fulfill its appointed destiny, we will not say that Blake was born out of his time because he lived in an age when prevalent values were least compatible with his vision. If Blake had one moral virtue above all others, it was courage, and no prophet has ever so luminously reaffirmed, with the voice of the rebel, the wisdom of ages.

I have tried to indicate the degree of certainty or doubt as to whether Blake had read this or that work. This comes with practice and cannot be altogether conveyed in short quotations; but every student of some special field knows it, and I must ask those not familiar with the works quoted to take something—though not too much—on trust, until opportunity comes to verify my claims. Evidence is cumulative; and if in one context it seems slight, I would ask the reader to refrain from judgment until the whole has been considered. My findings, such as they are, will not, in any case, surprise scholars who have been in the field before me. I have found very little that was not foreseen by my distinguished predecessors Yeats, Damon, Percival, Frye, Saurat, Todd, and others who have studied or are at present studying Blake's sources. This book was completed, and the present introduction written, in 1958; in order that an abridgment of certain parts of it should be given as the A. W. Mellon Lectures, and by reason of delays since, it has been held back; now some of the arguments it contains are, through my own publications in journals, and the publications of others (I think in particular of F. A. C. Wilson's books on Yeats and of George Mills Harper's quite independent studies, in America, of Blake's Neoplatonic sources), less novel than they were then. But the works of Blake's masters have stood the test of more centuries than the years taken in the writing of this book; and I hope that there may be some who will come, as I have done myself, to a deeper understanding of Blake through knowledge of his traditional roots, or who, through Blake, may discover that tradition itself.

Part I

The Northern Sun

We shall consider not Blake's early literary influences but the first clear evidence of his debt to what Yeats calls "the heterodox tradition." M. R. Lowery's *Windows of the Morning* is a study of Blake's *Poetical Sketches* and the evidence of Blake's reading there revealed. From the point of view of his symbolism, however, Blake's work tells a rather different story; the great change comes with his discovery of the philosophy and symbols of Neoplatonism. It is revealing to look closely at his symbolic framework as it was before this powerful transforming influence began; and here we most clearly see Blake as a Swedenborgian, not in his thought only but also in his imagery. Swedenborg's influence was never to disappear; but it was gradually overlaid and blended with other elements. It is only in his earliest writings that we see Blake's style and symbolism as it was before the impact of the Greek Revival.

CHAPTER 1

The Swedenborgian Songs

How came Blake, in the late eighteenth century, to emerge, from his earliest writings, as a symbolist poet? Something, certainly, must be allowed to his innate gifts: he was a natural visionary, who as a child saw angels walking among the harvesters and screamed in terror when God put his head in at the window. But how was such a gift preserved when the young poet began to experience the literary and philosophic influences of his time? The influence of Collins and Gray, Rowley and Ossian, Thomson and Spenser and Shakespeare, whose literary traces are easy to discover in the early *Poetical Sketches*, could not, singly or collectively, have given Blake the necessary training in the use of symbols. But his sudden emergence as a symbolist need not be explained by literary influences at all; Blake with his young wife, and Flaxman and his wife, were early members of the newly founded Swedenborgian Society in London. If we suppose that Blake was from his early years saturated in the atmosphere of Swedenborgian symbolism, the picture will begin to clarify. Blake was a symbolist before he was a poet, just as any man of pagan antiquity or the Christian Middle Ages inherited a symbolic way of thought as part of his environment.

We know from the best authority—his own—that Blake used Swedenborgian themes in both his paintings and his poems. In his *Descriptive Catalogue*, Number VIII, *The Spiritual Preceptor* (now lost) is described: "The subject is taken from the Visions of Emanuel Swedenborg, Universal Theology,[1] No. 623. . . . The works of this visionary are well worthy the attention of Painters and Poets; they are foundations for grand things."[2] This was written many years after *The Marriage of Heaven and Hell*, with its robust satirizing of the founder of the New Church. That satire was neither the beginning nor the end of Blake's deep interest in Swedenborgian thought. No lapsed Catholic thinks like a Protestant, still less like a positivist, and in the same way, while Blake's attitude to Swedenborg may have changed—perhaps more than once—the mark of Swedenborgian doctrine and symbolism went deep.

There is no literary value in Swedenborg's symbolism, and nothing could be less poetic than the "visions" of that sage. It is merely raw material. But to a mind naturally gifted, the Swedenborgian doctrines of influx and correspondence present a world symbolic in its whole and in its parts, not by some literary choice but in its very nature, a world informed throughout with imaginative meaning and beauty.

In common with the Platonic schools and the Hermetic, Gnostic, cabalistic, and alchemical traditions (and indeed with Christian doctrine) Swedenborg taught that "natural cause only seems." The world of nature and of man himself are but the lowest terms in a series of dependent spiritual causes. Natural forms and appearances of all kinds are the outward manifestation of a spiritual life and energy whose effects we see as the phenomena of nature. This Swedenborg calls "influx." The divine influx alone upholds the universe; and man, as Blake says, is only "a form and organ of life" that flows into him from a divine fountain.

Together with influx we have the related idea of correspondence: that is, everything in the physical world is symbolic in its very nature; it is the sensible representative of a spiritual essence. Correspondence is related to the older alchemical doctrine of signature and goes back to the Platonic view of the temporal world as an image of the eternal. Boehme—whom Blake held to be far greater than Swedenborg—speaks of the "vegetable glass" of nature—that is, as it were, a mirror in which spiritual realities are reflected; and again, the image of the glass goes far back into antiquity to the glass of Isis, the mirroring pool that drowned Narcissus and the dangerous toy of the child Dionysus—dangerous because in the mirror shadows take on the appearance of substance. In Swedenborg's words, then, "the whole natural world corresponds to the spiritual world, both in the whole, and likewise in its several parts; and what exists and subsists in the natural from the spiritual, is called correspondence; now the whole natural world exists and subsists from the spiritual, as an effect from its efficient cause." [3]

Place a young poet in such a world and he has no need to learn his symbolism from literary sources. Indeed, the decision to be a symbolist cannot be a literary one; symbolism, given any of the variants of the Platonic philosophy (of which Swedenborg's teaching must be accounted a degenerate descendant), becomes inevitable, for no image can be separated from its intelligible or spiritual meaning and content. Given, on the other hand, a philosophy that denies such a dependence of physical nature upon spiritual cause, symbolism is impossible. There can be no symbolist poetry produced by a materialist culture, since "divine analogy" is precluded.

The symbol is far from abstract: it is most concrete;[4] and no naturalism in poetry can be more concrete than the symbolism of a poet who sees the whole of manifested nature as a language that, as Coleridge says, "enunciates the whole" of an inseparable union of spiritual essence and physical existence.

Had this been all, the influence of Swedenborg would have been wholly good. But the symbolic language has at all times been more precise and more arbitrary than this universal and undifferentiated sacramentalism—which is, nevertheless, an underlying basis of all Blake's thought and of all symbolist systems. The most enduring and universal symbols have been evolved and have survived by reason of their natural fitness; and Swedenborg himself was often consciously or unconsciously using such traditional symbols, whose validity is intrinsic. His solar symbolism, his orientation to the four points of space, and many other elements of his symbolic vocabulary are of this kind. But in the Swedenborgian commentaries on the Scriptures we also find much that is arbitrary and, so far as one can see, personal. Every natural image, every town, country, and person named in the Bible, is taken to signify some spiritual state; and Blake at his worst follows Swedenborg into this profitless and unimaginative misuse of the Bible. When Blake lists "Moab & Ammon & Amalek & Canaan & Egypt & Aram" as spiritual states, he is incomprehensible without the key: "by Ægypt is signified what is scientific, by Ashur what is Rational, by Edom what is Natural, by Moab the Adulteration of Good, and by the Children of Ammon the adulteration of Truth, by the Philistines Faith without Charity."[5] This kind of pseudo-symbolism—for it cannot be said to correspond to Coleridge's requirement that the symbolic term form "a living part in that unity of which it is the representative"—is as disastrous in Blake as it is in Swedenborg. Fortunately, it is much less frequent.

As a rule the Swedenborgian correspondences—at least those that Blake selects—are somewhere between the two extremes of the total sacramental vision implied by the doctrine of influx and the arbitrary. Vine and oak, rose and myrtle, thorns, thistles, brambles, and nettles—all the vegetation of Blake's contrasting worlds of Innocence and Experience—belong to this language, half fitting, half arbitrary; and we often find more illumination of Blake's meaning in Swedenborg's commentaries than in the Bible itself. Thistles and thorns, for example, are constantly mentioned together in both the Old and the New Testaments—as, for example, "Ye shall know them by their fruits. Do men gather grapes of thorns, or figs of thistles?" But Swedenborg is more specific: "*Thorns and thistles* signify a curse and vastation." [6] Thorn, thistle, briar, bramble, and nettle all have a similar significance; and thorns, in particular, "denote the falsities of concupiscences." So that when Blake went

> *To the thistles & thorns of the waste*
> *And they told how they were beguil'd,*
> *Driven out, & compel'd to be chaste* [7]

the plants told him precisely what, within the Swedenborgian convention, they ought to say: they have been "driven out" of Paradise by God's curse and vastation; and they symbolize unsatisfied desires—"concupiscences," as Swedenborg less charitably says.

In all the spiritual vegetation of Innocence and Experience we nowhere find a plant named that does not prove to be derived from some already established symbolic tradition. Not one is an observed image, elaborated into a poem. Blake might have used his rushes, sunflowers, thistles, and vines without having ever seen a living specimen of any of them. This was certainly not the case; we know that he had a real vine in his Lambeth garden that he loved too much to allow it to be pruned. For the real vine, to the symbolist, is informed by that divine life of which it is the symbol. Wordsworth found his symbols in nature—the image came first, a lesser celandine, a violet, a tree in a field—but Blake saw nature through symbol, not symbol through nature.

The Swedenborgian idiom has left its mark on the designs as well as on the poems. The colors red, blue, and golden-white signify, respectively, love, wisdom, and the celestial state that is above both. When these colors are clear and radiant, the states of the soul to which they belong are likewise of a high order. The colors of hell are murky and dark. Yeats thought that Blake's colors were taken from Boehme, and he may be right. In any case Swedenborg's color equivalents are similar to Boehme's. The rainbow, says Boehme, is the type, in its three colors, of the three principles of the Divine Being. These colors of hell, heaven, and earth do, in general, correspond to Blake's usage—above all his murky reds and browns, as these are to be found in the *Marriage* or *The Book of Urizen*, and that exquisite light-filled

1 Frontispiece to *Songs of Experience* (1789–94)   2 Frontispiece to *Songs of Innocence* (1789)

yellowish white that seems to emanate, as Blake uses it, from the very essence of heaven.[8] Blake preferred love to wisdom (since "thought alone can make monsters, but the affections cannot")[9] and in nearly all copies of the *Songs*, in *Experience*, the blue of reason and the murky colors of hell [1, 2] tend to predominate. It is not possible to generalize absolutely about Blake's use of symbolic color, for every copy of his illuminated books is different; but the Piper of *Innocence* is rosy-clad in many copies; and the similar figure of the *Experience* wears blue. Wicksteed makes much of the advancing of the right or left foot of the figures of the Job illustrations and other works; but this, also, almost certainly derives from Swedenborg, for whom whatever is on the right pertains to wisdom, on the left to love. So we find the rose-clad Piper of *Innocence* advancing his left foot and the blue-clad figure of *Experience* his right, for the first is guided by affection, the second by reason.[10] Too much may be made of this symbolism if it is taken too far; in the processions of tiny dancing figures the posture is obviously determined only by the demands of composition.

The very first poem of *Songs of Innocence* introduces, in the image of the child on a cloud, a Swedenborgian commonplace transmuted by Blake into an image so perfect that to suggest that it has behind it a convention may seem little better than to cast doubt upon miracle. The encounter with the child-spirit who tells the poet first to "Pipe a song about a lamb" and then to write "In a book, that all may read" has its prosaic counterpart in a dozen of those Swedenborgian *Memorable Relations* that form dry oases in the still drier deserts of his theology. Some spirit descends from heaven or ascends from hell, enters into conversation with the Seer, often instructs him to report this or write that in the world of men, and at the end of the interview vanishes. Visionary though Blake was, interviews with angels and devils (especially when so named) in his writings have less to do with vision than with this borrowed convention. This is more obvious in his failures than in his successes. The first draft of *The Human Abstract* has a Swedenborgian framework:

> *I heard an Angel singing*
> *When the day was springing,*
> *"Mercy, Pity, Peace*
> *Is the world's release."*
>
> .   .   .
>
> *I heard a Devil curse*
> *Over the heath & the furze,*
> *"Mercy could be no more,*
> *If there was nobody poor."* [11]

The typical Swedenborgian angel also appears in *I Asked a Thief to Steal Me a Peach* and *The Angel;* but only in the last does the Angel find his way into the published version. The Swedenborgian structure was removed from the finished version of *The Human Abstract*, and the fragment *I Asked a Thief* was not included. No doubt Blake felt that these angels and devils were lacking precisely in visionary immediacy.

It is impossible, however, to doubt that the child on a cloud was

3 New-born Orc in flames: *Urizen* (1794), plate 20, detail

perceived by Blake's imaginative eye. Certainly he was not perceived in nature; for from the "valleys wild" to the hollow reed which Blake made his pen, as Prometheus stole fire from heaven in the same plant, all is symbolic. The "valley" is a symbol of the natural world or the body – or, in Swedenborg's words, "The Divine Natural and Sensual principle." The wild valley is the free and joyful world of nature and the senses of the bodily life of childhood, or perhaps of the young poet himself. In the later Prophetic Books the phrase "dark valley" is used, following, perhaps, Boehme rather than Swedenborg, for whom, nevertheless, the meaning is the same: "the whole *Body* of Man . . . is a dark Valley, as the Body of the Deep of this World is." [12] So in *Jerusalem* Blake writes that ". . . the perturbed Man away turns down the valleys dark." [13] The "vale of Leutha," similarly, signifies sexuality. There is a consistency of meaning between the happy "valleys wild" of innocence and the "valleys dark" of the fallen man, which confirms the view that the basic meaning of valley was already intended in the early poem.

There are innumerable spirits in clouds in the writings of Swedenborg. Angelic societies, good or evil, appear in clouds more or less radiant according to the nature of the spirits they comprise; and the Lord himself is described as appearing in a cloud of multitudes of spirits. Every spirit has its "ambient Sphere" – "in Heaven sometimes under the Appearance of atten-

uated Flame, in Hell under the Appearance of crass Fire; and sometimes in
Heaven under the Appearance of a thin and white Cloud, and in Hell under
the Appearance of a thick and black Shower." [14] Blake makes frequent use
of both these forms of ambient sphere, and spirits in or on clouds are no less
frequent in his designs than in the text. Spirits surrounded by flames and
clouds meet and embrace on the pages of the *Marriage;* in *Urizen* Orc is
characteristically enveloped in his own fires; Oothoon is cloud-born. In the
Marriage there is the deliberate satire of "Once I saw a Devil in a flame of
fire, who arose before an Angel that sat on a cloud." Blake here is laughing
at the "ambient sphere" imagery that he uses elsewhere with much
beauty.

[3, 113,
119, 120]

Swedenborg thinks habitually in pairs of opposites, angels and
devils, dark clouds and bright clouds. So in Blake the laughing child on the
cloud is opposed to the child of *Experience:*

> *Into the dangerous world I leapt:*
> *Helpless, naked, piping loud:*
> *Like a fiend hid in a cloud.* [15]

In Blake's most completely—and most successfully—Swedenborgian
poem, *The Little Black Boy* (the poem that Coleridge loved most of all the
Songs), we discover something more about the meaning of the cloud
symbol. Swedenborg's "ambient spheres" are probably the aura or etheric
body, but Blake's black and white clouds are the physical bodies of the
children:

> *"And these black bodies and this sunburnt face*
> *Is but a cloud . . ."* [16]

In Blake's symbolic language a cloud is always the body, which will
"vanish" when the soul has learned to look upon the face of God unveiled.
Perhaps we have here the first indication of Blake's reading of Paracelsus,
and it may be that the latter's remarkable comparison of the body to smoke
helped to form Blake's symbol:

> Briefly, whatsoever hath a body is nothing but curdled smoke,
> wherein a particular predestination lyeth hid . . . For all bodies
> shall passe away and vanish into nothing but smoke, they shall all
> end in a fume. This is the end of things corporeall both living and
> dead . . . Man is a coagulated fume. . . . We see nothing in our

own selves but thickned smoke made up into a man by humane predestination.[17]

Only the spirit that animates the "cloud" or "smoke" can be said to possess human lineaments; for "a Spirit and a Vision are not, as the modern philosophy supposes, a cloudy vapour, or a nothing: . . . Spirits are organized men." [18] In other words, soul is form. It is the body that is a cloudy vapor possessing, as Plotinus says of matter, no inherent entity or form. The child in his cloud is the living soul that animates the body: in the world of

4 *The Little Black Boy* from *Songs of Innocence* (1789), detail

Innocence, riding *on* his cloud, in Experience, densely enveloped and hidden *in* it.

The black boy and the white boy are evidently related to Swedenborg's good and evil angels, each in his ambient sphere; but already Blake is calling in question Swedenborg's moral dualism, for it is the black child who teaches the white, a foreshadowing of his later full-scale defense of the "devils" in the *Marriage*, where again the black spirits are wiser than the white, and devils preach to angels the wisdom of hell. But from Swedenborg comes the African, who is wiser than his European brother in spiritual matters. The Africans are represented by Swedenborg as having a natural understanding of the central doctrine of the New Church—one that Blake not only accepted but so far made his own that the very name of the Divine Humanity is now more strongly associated with Blake than with Swedenborg, from whom it originates. In the New Age, so Swedenborg taught, the worship of God as man will supersede the worship of an invisible God; and only those who can understand the nature of this Divine Humanity will

5 "Europe supported by Africa & America": engraving by Blake for Stedman's *Narrative* (1796)

This plate, made some years later than *The Little Black Boy*, expresses the climate of opinion in which the questions of color and slavery were at that time being considered, and which Blake's writings reflect. Stedman was a personal friend of Blake.

partake in the new revelation. In 1757—the year of Blake's birth—the New Age was declared in the heavens, and a church began on earth that was to be "the Crown of all Churches that have heretofore existed on this earthly Globe, because it will worship one Visible God, in whom is the invisible God, as the Soul is in the Body; and the . . . Conjunction of God with Man is thus, and in no other Way possible." [19]

 It is for their natural understanding of this doctrine that the Africans are praised:

[5] The Gentiles, particularly the Africans, who acknowledge and worship one God the Creator of the Universe, entertain an Idea of God as of a Man, and say that no one can have any other Idea of God: When they hear that many form an Idea of God as existing in the Midst of a Cloud, they ask where such are; and when it is said that there are such among Christians, they deny that it is possible; but in Reply it is shewn, that some Christians conceive such an Idea from this Circumstance, that God in the Word is called a Spirit, and of a Spirit

they think no otherwise than of a thin Cloud, not knowing that every Spirit and every Angel is a Man.[20]

We know that Blake was struck by this passage, for he wrote in the margin of his copy of *Divine Love and Wisdom:* "Think of a white cloud as being holy, you cannot love it; but think of a holy man within the cloud, love springs up in your thoughts, for to think of holiness distinct from man is impossible to the affections." [21]

In the natural state, however (so Swedenborg affirms), God is seen, but "afar off," as a sun shedding his "beams of love." "The Worship of the Sun is the lowest of all Kinds of Worship of a God"; [22] and it is this form of worship that is taught to the black boy by his *mother* (that is, nature) "underneath a tree"—the tree of life, the natural world. In this world of innocent nature the teaching of the "mother" earth is the right and true worship: [4]

> *Look on the rising Sun: there God does live*
> *And gives his light, and gives his heat away.*

These two lines are packed with Swedenborgian allusion. The *rising* sun is by no means a naturalistic image; for to angelic spirits the sun is always rising. The angels "constantly turn their Faces to the Lord as the Sun," [23] and the sun "constantly appears in it's Place, and where it appears is the East." [24] Thus the blessed spirits are constantly oriented toward the *rising* sun. Let them turn as they will, the sunrise is always before their faces. This is "eternity's sun rise," [25] in which the angels always dwell. *Light* and *heat* are also specified with clear symbolic intention; for they are correspondences of the two attributes of God: "[He] appears before the Angels in Heaven as a Sun, and . . . from the Sun proceedeth Heat and Light, and . . . the Heat thence proceeding, in it's Essence, is Love, and the Light thence proceeding in it's Essence is Wisdom." [26] What God "gives away" in Blake's poem is therefore, in terms of divine analogy, love and wisdom.

The higher knowledge of God as "uncreated man" is only possible for souls at a higher stage of development; only when freed from their "clouds" do the boys, who learned their first lessons from their mother nature, "lean in joy upon our *father's* knee." This teaching Blake summed up in the lines

> *God Appears & God is Light*
> *To those poor Souls who dwell in Night,*

6 *The Little Boy Lost* and *The Little Boy Found* from *Songs of Innocence* (1789), details

> *But does a Human Form Display*
> *To those who Dwell in Realms of day.*[27]

To the two children under the earthly tree of life, God is the sun; but when both come to spiritual maturity, they will know their spiritual father in his divine-human form.

Perhaps our understanding of *The Little Black Boy* is not essentially changed by the knowledge that its symbolic structure is Swedenborgian. But with *The Little Boy Lost*[28] and *Found*[29] the case is different.

In these two poems, and their accompanying designs, we can see Blake's imagination at work, transforming story to myth and illustration to vision. The story of *The Little Boy Lost* Blake owed, it seems, to Mary Wollstonecraft, whose part as the inspirer of *Songs of Innocence* was perhaps very great. Mary, a true daughter of Rousseau, was much concerned with the education of children, with guiding their natures rather than forming them, with allowing what in them is innately good to unfold. This was a way of thought altogether in keeping with Blake's own. He himself designed and engraved the plates for Mary Wollstonecraft's own book, *Original Stories from Real Life*, and we may be sure that in writing *Songs of Innocence* he must have felt that he was working with Mary in a cause dear to a woman he admired and loved.

In 1790 and 1791 Johnson the publisher, Mary's employer and Blake's friend, published a little book, translated by Mary herself from the German of the Rev. C. G. Salzmann, *Elements of Morality, for the Use of Children*, a moral narrative, showing real imaginative sympathy with the joys and fears of childhood—a much better work than Mary's own *Original Stories*. Blake engraved many of the plates, and in doing so must have given much thought to the problems of literature for children, to Mary's cause, and to the stories themselves. The best of these tells of a Little Boy Lost. In Chapter III, little Charles wanders away into a strange wood.

> Then it came into his head that he had lost himself, and was wandering still further out of his way. At this thought he felt a cold shivering run over his body, and he could hardly draw his breath, his heart was so dull. *What will become of me, thought he*, if I am obliged to remain in the wood with nothing to eat or drink! Must I—oh, must I lie in the dark; perhaps, a serpent or some bad man, may come and kill me while I slumber.[29a]

Night falls, the moon rises, the child thinks he sees phantom shapes, and he "wanted his father's advice to teach him how to think, as much as his strong arm to support a poor tired boy, whose legs tottered under him." The poor lost child "at last . . . recollected his father's advice, and fell on his knees and prayed to God to have pity on him." Almost immediately he "saw a tall black figure approach him, with a white cap on its head, and a milk white pigeon flew before it." The figure is a kind clergyman in a white wig, carrying a white handkerchief, which the boy mistook for a pigeon. This detail is described with a vividness suggesting that Salzmann is recollecting an adventure of his own childhood, for it is, in its way, strikingly true to life. [7] The episode is illustrated by two charming plates, one of the little boy lost, the other of Charles found by the clergyman; and here, surely, is the raw material of Blake's poems and of his two designs, and of God who appears [6] like his father "in white"—a most curious detail in the poems which can easily be understood if we suppose that he is thinking of Charles's adventure with the tall figure with the wig and handkerchief. It is not certain that Blake was the engraver of the two plates in question, though it is very possible that he was. Keynes is doubtful; but Ruthven Todd, on grounds of style and technique, supports my own inclination to think that he was. In any case this is not the crucial point, for as one of the engravers employed on the book, and as a friend of the translator, he would have read the story, and no doubt have seen the other plates.

But Blake's two poems are much more than narrative; his little boy is "lost" in quite another sense than little Charles in the wood; and every image in the poem is symbolic. There is, in Salzmann's story, no "vapour," or "mire," or "dew"; the child was not pursuing a will-o'-the-wisp. It is true that his prayer to God was answered by the appearance of a man to save him; and in this detail Blake found the symbolic starting-point of a story which, as the poet has told it, may be seen as an illustration of the central doctrine of the Swedenborgian New Church, that God can only be known in human form.

Wicksteed [30] long ago observed that the adventures of little boys in the *Songs* are religious or philosophical, those of little girls romantic; and the story of the little boy lost is a philosophical adventure. If we turn back to the passage from *Divine Love and Wisdom* about those who think of God as "a little cloud in the midst of the universe," we have the key. The two poems describe the spiritual state of those who think of God as a Spirit, and "of a Spirit they think no otherwise than of a thin Cloud, not knowing that every Spirit and every Angel is a Man." Blake's phrase about a spirit not being "a cloudy vapour" leads us back again to Swedenborg, who used the word "vapour" for this false conception of the nature of a spiritual being. It is an error, he says, to suppose that after death "Man will then be like a Vapour, or like Wind, or like Æther, or like Something floating in the Air." "Lay aside," he says, "the Idea concerning the Soul as being a Vapour or Breath." [31] As for Blake, so for Swedenborg, "spirits are organized men." [32]

The Little Boy Lost is in just this condition of error. For him God is "a cloudy vapour." Attempting to follow this will-o'-the-wisp, he loses God

7 Engravings probably by Blake from Salzmann's *Elements of Morality* (1791), plates 4 and 5

and strays in a dark night, far from the sun of the spiritual world. He falls into the deep "mire" of materialism:

> *The night was dark, no father was there;*
> *The child was wet with dew;*
> *The mire was deep, & the child did weep,*
> *And away the vapour flew.*

It is clear that when Blake wrote these poems, he was already familiar with the Neoplatonic symbolism of matter as mire, clay, and water, and materialist thought as immersion in mire. *The Little Boy Lost* appears first in *An*

Island in the Moon, dated approximately 1787.[33] If Foster Damon is right in his identification of Sipsop the Pythagorean as Thomas Taylor the Platonist, we may conclude that Blake already knew Taylor, and is likely to have read his translation of Plotinus' *Concerning the Beautiful*, which appeared in that year. In this essay it is said that the soul becomes impure through its preoccupation with sensible forms: "it is covered with corporeal stains, and wholly given to matter, contracts deeply its nature, loses all its original splendor"[34] through its "total immersion in mire and clay." This is the darkness, the mire, and the "lonely fen" (a landscape of mire and water) that the lost child finds on every side when he follows the "vapour," the will-o'-the-wisp of an abstract god. The "dew"[35] with which the child is wet is another symbol of immersion in matter, whose symbol is water—again taken from Plotinus. When man loses his spiritual vision and becomes immersed in materialist thought, spirit (the father) is exchanged for a cloudy vapor; but he also loses the "mother," nature. According to Swedenborg everything in nature is upheld in being by the divine "influx," a doctrine that gives it substance and meaning, by its insistence that it exists "from the Divine Humanity of the Lord."[36] Without this influx, matter is "mire" and not a loving "mother." Blake is preaching the doctrine of the New Church, "the true god is the Divine Humanity." "Finite things are the Recipients of Infinite,"[37] Swedenborg wrote, and "A Man is an organ of life, and God alone is life: God infuses his life into the organ and all its parts; and God grants man a sense that the life in himself is as it were his own"; and "Man is a Recipient of life from God."[38] Blake uses Swedenborg's very words, when he writes:

> . . . *thou art but a form & organ of life, & of thyself*
> *Art nothing, being Created Continually by Mercy & Love divine.*[39]

"God only Acts and Is in created beings and men," he also writes; God's fatherhood is expressed toward earthly children in human fatherhood and not otherwise:

> *Man liveth not by Self alone, but in his brother's face*
> *Each shall behold the Eternal Father . . .*[40]

and again,

> . . . *General Forms have their vitality in Particulars, & every*
> *Particular is a Man, a Divine Member of the Divine Jesus.*[41]

It is possible that the pursuit of the will-o'-the-wisp into a miry fen came to Blake from a finely imagined passage of Plotinus, the more so as this theme gave him the symbolism of a later myth (described in Chapter 11, below). The pursuit of matter, he says, is the pursuit of "non-entity," "avoiding the desire of him who wishes to perceive its nature. . . . So that it is a phantom, neither abiding, nor yet able to fly away. . . . Hence, too, in each of its vanishing appellations, it eludes our search . . . as it were a flying mockery." [42] Plotinus refers to the myth of Narcissus, whose legend was interpreted in the Neoplatonic schools as a myth of the death by drowning of the soul that falls in love with the "watery image" or material form, mistaking the shadow for the substance:

> For he who rushes to these lower beauties, as if grasping realities, when they are only like beautiful images appearing in water, will, doubtless, like him in the fable, by stretching after the shadow, sink into the lake, and disappear. For, by thus embracing and adhering to corporeal forms, he is precipitated, not so much in his body, as in his soul, into profound and horrid darkness; and thus blind, like those in the infernal regions, converses only with phantoms, deprived of the perception of what is real and true. It is here, then, we may more truly exclaim, "Let us depart from hence, and fly to our father's delightful land." [43]

In Plotinus also, it is the "father" (spirit) who is able to save the lost soul from the mire. It is tempting to imagine that behind Blake's *Little Boy Lost*, symbol of the intellect of man pursuing the phantom of matter, is the shadow of that less fortunate boy, Narcissus.

To this group of Swedenborgian poems we must add *The Divine Image*,[44] whose meaning is so clear as to require no exegesis. The poem illustrates the doctrine "that Esse and Existence in God-Man are Distinctly one." The qualities have their divine essence and their human existence:

> *For Mercy, Pity, Peace, and Love*
> *Is God, our father dear,*
> *And Mercy, Pity, Peace, and Love*
> *Is Man, his child and care.*
>
> .   .   .

Then every man, of every clime,
That prays in his distress,
Prays to the human form divine,
Love, Mercy, Pity, Peace.

There could be no more simple and orthodox statement of the central doctrine of the New Church.

Blake's "Religion of Jesus" was never at any time confined by the frontiers of Christendom. Swedenborg was not narrow in this matter; for he praises the Africans for their understanding of God, and cites several other instances, from the world of spirits, of those who know "the Lord" although not by the name of Jesus. Mohammedans and heathens, he says, are "soon brought to the knowledge of and belief in the Lord through the means of instruction; and the more so, as it is a fundamental of their creed, that God is visible in a human form. These are the greater number [of the appointed for heaven]; and the best of them are from Africa." [45]

Had Blake also at this time begun to read the works of Boehme? Near the beginning of *Aurora*, the first book in Volume I of the famous four-volume edition known as Law's Boehme, which Blake praised so highly, is the passage:

> Most certainly *there is but One God;* but when the Veil is put away from thy Eyes, so that thou seest and knowest *him,* then thou wilt also see and know *all* thy Brethren, whether they be *Christians, Jews, Turks,* or *Heathens.* Or dost thou think that God is the God of you *Christians* only? Do not the *Heathens* also live in God, *whosoever doth* Right or *Righteousness, God* loves and *accepts him.* . . . Is he only *thy* King? Is it not written, *He is the Comfort of all the Heathen?* [46]

It is easy to argue that such poems as *The Little Boy Lost* and *Found* are symbolist in intention, for read as realistic they are unintelligible. *The Chimney Sweeper* [47] is entirely satisfactory as a poem about real London chimney sweepers (as of course it is), full of human sympathy and of social indignation. But this poem, also, can be read on several levels. It necessarily follows from the doctrine of influx and correspondence that every happening of earth has its counterpart in the world of spirit; and it is easy to see in the chimney sweepers—boys forced into a despised and oppressed class, just as the Africans are an enslaved and outcast race—yet another group belonging to the Blakean conception of the devils, the unjustly outcast spirits whose cause he was presently to embrace. Like the black African, the sweep (the wage slave) may say, "And I am black, but O my soul is white." These seemingly black sheep are really innocent lambs:

> *There's little Tom Dacre, who cried when his head,*
> *That curl'd like a lamb's back, was shav'd: so I said*
> *"Hush, Tom! never mind it, for when your head's bare*
> *You know that the soot cannot spoil your white hair."*

8 *The Chimney Sweeper* from *Songs of Experience* (1789–94), detail

The "soot" is the earthly mire and clay that cannot defile the spirit:

And as the gold is deformed by the adherence of earthly clods, which are no sooner removed than on a sudden the gold shines forth with its native purity; and then becomes beautiful when separated from natures foreign from its own, and when it is content with its own purity for the possession of beauty: so the soul, when separated from the sordid desires engendered, by its too great immersion in body; and liberated from the dominion of every perturbation, can thus and thus only, blot out the base stains imbibed from its union with body.[48]

Whether or not Blake had in mind these words of Plotinus concerning the incorruptibility of the soul, this is the essential meaning of the poem; and moreover the symbolic language of Neoplatonism is in this poem unmistakable in the symbol that Blake here uses for the body, a denser envelope than Swedenborgian cloud or Paracelsus' smoke; here it is for the first time called a "coffin," the first of many such homonyms in Blake's later works, as funeral urn, grave, or shroud. This symbol he probably knew from several sources. Everard's translation of the Hermetica, *The Divine Pymander*, contains a striking passage in which the body is called "the Sepulchre carried about with us." Taylor in his *Dissertation on the Mysteries* explains the symbol and the doctrine in a passage that gives also some idea of its widespread use:

> And to begin with the obscure and profound Heraclitus, speaking of souls unembodied: "We live," says he, "their death, and we die their life" . . . And Empedocles, blaming generation, beautifully says of her [i.e. material nature]:
>
> > *The species changing with destruction dread,*
> > *She makes the* living *pass into the* dead.
>
> And again, lamenting his connection with this corporeal world he pathetically exclaims:
>
> > *For this I weep, for this indulge my woe,*
> > *That e'er my soul such novel realms should know.*
>
> Plato, too, it is well known, considered the body as the sepulchre of the soul; and in the *Cratylus* consents with the doctrine of Orpheus, that the soul is punished through its union with body. . . . The Pythagorean Philolaus [writes] "that the soul is united with body for the sake of suffering punishment, and that it is buried in the body as in a sepulchre." And lastly, Pythagoras himself confirms the above sentiments, when he beautifully observes . . . "that whatever we see when awake, is death; and when asleep, a dream." [49]

Such is the condition of the "thousands of sweepers" all locked up in "coffins of black," for whom life in this world is no better than a living death.

It is a saying of Heraclitus that the waking are illuminated from dreams, and dreamers from the dead (that is, from those whose death we live); in Tom Dacre's dream the chimney sweepers enter the spiritual world, where their bodies are no longer coffins but clouds that ride on the wind:

> *Then naked & white, all their bags left behind,*
> *They rise upon clouds and sport in the wind.*

Blake, however, may not have gone to Heraclitus for the belief that dreams give access to the world of spirits, for Swedenborg's visions of other worlds were often revealed in dreams or in trance. The value of dreams as revelations of some order of reality is, after all, older and more normal than the myopic concentration upon waking experience as the only reality, characteristic of the concrete mind, of which Watts, the hymn writer, is so typical a representative. Watts's Sluggard is a dreamer: "You have wak'd me too soon, I must slumber again."

For Watts virtue was industry in the tasks of this world. Blake's chimney sweeper he would not have encouraged to tell his dream, but sent him about his business. Blake knew otherwise:

> *Father, O Father! what do we here*
> *In this Land of unbelief & fear?*
> *The Land of Dreams is better far,*
> *Above the light of the Morning Star.*[50]

The difference between the child dreamer and the adult dreamer is that the child naturally accepts the Land of Dreams as a plane of reality. Children come and go freely, and because they do not question the truth of their visions, the dreams of the night give comfort for the day. In the poem *The Land of Dreams* the child does not doubt that he has really walked with his dead mother in the Elysian fields—as Swedenborg, no less than Heraclitus and Pythagoras, taught:

> *Among the Lambs, clothed in white,*
> *She walk'd with her Thomas in sweet delight.*
> *I wept for joy, like a dove I mourn;*
> *O! when shall I again return?*

But the father can no longer come and go so freely:

> *Dear Child, I also by pleasant Streams*
> *Have wander'd all Night in the Land of Dreams;*

> *But tho' calm & warm the waters wide,*
> *I could not get to the other side.*

The sweeps, poor half-starved slaves in working life, are in spirit still gifted with the prerogative of childhood; their "angels behold the face of their heavenly Father" and are not wholly confined to this world. The world of Innocence includes the Land of Dreams. Some might say that Blake realized the nature of dreams in somewhat the same way as did Freud, who interprets dreams as the fulfillment of the vain desires of waking life. In fact he meant much more and saw dreams as states of real insight into the world of imagination, of "what eternally exists, really and unchangeably."

The world into which the chimney sweepers are freed suggests very strongly the landscape of Vergil's Elysium; and it is possible that Vergil had part in the inspiration of the lines,

> *Then down a green plain leaping, laughing, they run,*
> *And wash in a river, and shine in the Sun.*

If *The Chimney Sweeper* was written after Blake had read Thomas Taylor's *Dissertation on the Eleusinian and Bacchic Mysteries* [51] (we have evidence in the two *Lyca* poems of the deep impression made on him by that work), it is likely that his attention would have been drawn by Taylor to Vergil's description of Elysium:

> *Nulli certa domus. Lucis habitamus opacis*
> *Riparumque toros, et prata recentia rivis*
> *Incolimus. . . .*

translated by Dryden:

> *In no fix'd place the Happy Souls reside.*
> *In Groves we live; and lye on mossy Beds*
> *By Crystal Streams, that murmur through the Meads.*[52]

Taylor comments on this passage in terms that might well have suggested to Blake the freeing of the chimney sweepers from their "coffins" into Elysian existence: "By the blessed being confined to no particular habitation, the liberal condition of their existence is plainly implied; since they are entirely free from all material restraint, and purified from all inclinations to the dark and cold tenement of the body." The opening lines of *London* suggest very strongly Vergil's account of the damned in Hades:

> *Nor Death itself can wholly wash their Stains;*
> *But long-contracted Filth ev'n in the Soul remains.*
> *The Reliques of inveterate Vice they wear;*
> *And spots of Sin obscene in ev'ry Face appear.*[53]

Not like the chimney sweepers who "wash in the river" and are cleansed of the soot that has never defiled their souls, the people of London are spiritually defiled:

> *I wander thro' each charter'd street,*
> *Near where the charter'd Thames does flow,*
> *And mark in every face I meet*
> *Marks of weakness, marks of woe.*[54]

Vergil describes the gradual purgation of the souls as a washing; and "To cleanse the Face of my Spirit . . ." and "To bathe in the Waters of Life, to wash off the Not Human" [55] is a return to an image that Blake first used of the chimney sweepers.

A passage in Swedenborg suggests an additional meaning that is not immediately apparent in this poem. Swedenborg in one of his "memorable relations" writes the following strange account of chimney sweepers:

There are also Spirits amongst those from the Earth Jupiter, whom they call Sweepers of Chimnies, because they appear in like Garments, and likewise with sooty Faces. . . . One of these Spirits came to me, and anxiously requested that I would intercede for him to be admitted into Heaven; he said, that he was not conscious of having done any Evil. . . . He was likewise of a black Colour in the Light of Heaven, but he himself said that he was not of a black Colour, but of a darkish brown. I was informed that they are such at first, who are afterwards received amongst those who constitute the province of the Seminal Vessels in the Grand Man or Heaven.[56]

This unlooked-for link between the chimney sweepers and the sexual instinct would have seemed singularly apt to Freud. The symbol, for Swedenborg, seems to have no social significance; it is, so far as we can judge, purely personal. There is all the difference in the world between Swedenborg's use of the chimney-sweeper figure and Blake's far more human sympathy with the real London boys, to whom he gives names—Tom, Dick, Joe, Ned, and Jack—lest we should forget that it is in these "minute particulars" that alone universal life is expressed. But that Blake made use of Swedenborg's *Relation*, even that this provided the initial impulse of the poem, seems beyond doubt, for the passage continues:

> He came again to me, in vile Raiment, and again said, that he had a burning Desire to be admitted into Heaven . . . At that Instant the Angels called to him to cast off his Raiment, which he did immediately, with inconceivable Quickness from the Vehemence of his Desire; whereby was represented what is the Nature of their Desires, who are in the Province to which the seminal Vessels correspond. I was informed that such, when they are prepared for Heaven, are stripped of their own Garments, and are clothed with new shining Raiment, and become Angels.

Is this the source of the angel in Blake's poem,

> *And by came an Angel who had a bright key,*
> *And he open'd the coffins & set them all free;*

calling to them, like the Angel in Swedenborg, to strip off their foul garments and to rise free, "naked & white, all their bags left behind"?

There is, if this be so, a direct link between the chimney sweepers and Orc, who is Blake's Eros. He, too, chained to his rock and burning in his own flames, is set free in dreams, and the images used are the same ones we have already found in *The Chimney Sweeper:*

> *Yet thou dost laugh at all these tortures, & this horrible place:*
>   .   .   .
> *. . . feeding thyself*
> *With visions of sweet bliss far other than this burning clime.*
> *Sure thou art bath'd in rivers of delight, on verdant fields*
> *Walking in joy, in bright Expanses sleeping on bright clouds* [57]

There is nothing improbable in the suggestion that the figure of Orc-Eros has its beginning—or one of its beginnings—in this strange and uncouth fable of the erotic figure of the sweeper of chimneys.

When we come to *Songs of Experience*, Swedenborg is giving place to more powerful influences, which were by now at work. But his influence is still present; in *The Clod & the Pebble*, *The Garden of Love*, and perhaps *The Human Abstract* and *The Angel* we may still find the mark of Swedenborgian symbolism.

The Clod & the Pebble [58] seems to have been suggested by a passage in *Divine Love and Wisdom* (though there are similar passages elsewhere), a book upon which Blake had drawn freely for several of the *Songs of Innocence*. The passage is one of Swedenborg's habitual black and white contrasts between the angelic and diabolic points of view. This characteristic Swedenborgian presentation has certainly left its mark upon Blake. One might say that the very conception of *Innocence* and *Experience* as "contrasting states of the human soul" is essentially Swedenborgian, as is the structure of the *Marriage*, with its angels and devils. In this case the theme is love:

> Love consists in this, that what it hath may be another's, and that it may feel his Delight as Delight in itself; this is to Love; but for a Man to feel his own Delight in another, and not the other's Delight in himself, is not to Love, for in the latter Case he loves himself, but in the former he loves his Neighbour: These two Kinds of Love are diametrically opposite to each other: They both indeed effect Conjunction, and it doth not appear, that for a Man to love his own, that is, himself in another, disjoineth, when nevertheless it so disjoineth, that in Proportion as any one hath thus loved another, so much does he afterwards hate him. [59]

Blake's poem follows the pattern closely, clod and pebble symbolizing Swedenborg's two kinds of love:

> *"Love seeketh not Itself to please,*
> *Nor for itself hath any care,*
> *But for another gives its ease,*
> *And builds a Heaven in Hell's despair."*
>
> *So sang a little Clod of Clay*
> *Trodden with the cattle's feet,*
> *But a Pebble of the brook*
> *Warbled out these metres meet:*
>
> *"Love seeketh only Self to please,*
> *To bind another to Its delight,*

Joys in another's loss of ease,
And builds a Hell in Heaven's despite." [60]

Hell and Heaven are strictly Swedenborgian in this context. What Blake has
added is the poetic vision—the murmuring cold voice of the brook, the
magical coldness of the vowels, "Warbled out these metres meet." There is
nothing peculiar to Swedenborg in the symbol of a stone for hardness of
heart, although one may point to plenty of examples of objects that turn to
stone in the hands of those who have "removed themselves from the good of
love." But the little Clod of Clay is a more interesting figure. She first
appears in *The Book of Thel* as matron Clay, and later as Enion the Earth
Mother (matter), one of the most beautifully characterized figures of
Blake's mythology. I believe she has her genesis in an image in the *Universal
Theology*, whose animation might well have delighted Blake. Swedenborg
is expounding the spiritual and indeed human nature of every expression of
life, and thus describes a particle of mold: "The Internal of a Particle of
mould, whereby its External is impelled, is its Tendency to make the Seeds
of Plants vegetate, exhaling somewhat from its little Bosom, which insin-
uates itself into the inmost [Parts] of the Seeds, and produceth this wonderful Effect." [61]

Blake's Clod of Clay in *Thel*, who nourishes the worm, is surely
based upon this humblest of things. Blake's use of the word "exhale" in this
context makes it almost certain:

The Clod of Clay heard the Worm's voice & rais'd her pitying head:
She bow'd over the weeping infant, and her life exhal'd
In milky fondness: then on Thel she fix'd her humble eyes.

"O beauty of the vales of Har! we live not for ourselves.
Thou seest me the meanest thing, and so I am indeed." [62]

Her action and her words are altogether in keeping with the Clod of Clay
and with Swedenborg's mold.

Among the several influences traceable in *The Garden of Love*, Swedenborg's predominates. Blake is following the Swedenborgian formula for
constructing a symbolic landscape in terms of correspondences. The two
states of the garden correspond respectively to the freedom of love in

9 *The Garden of Love* from
Songs of Experience (1789–94)

childhood and its suppression, in the name of religion, in the sexual expression that it naturally takes on in adult life. Or one might read the poem without a specifically sexual meaning, as a simple contrast between the freedom of a religion of love and the restraints of a religion consisting only of moral laws; for this is all that is implied in the passage of Swedenborg upon which it seems to be based:

> Faith separate from Charity deadens all Things, and Faith joined with Charity enlivens all Things. The nature of such Deadening, and Enlivening, may be seen visibly in our spiritual World. . . . for where Faith is joined with Charity, there are paradisaical Gardens, flowry Walks, and verdant Groves, gay and delightful, in Proportion to such Conjunction; but where Faith is separate from Charity, there doth not grow so much as a blade of Grass, nor any green Thing, except it be on Thorns and Briers.[63]

That the garden of love must obviously bear sweet flowers, and the garden of cold faith only thorns and briars, follows by the logic of correspondence. The "priests in black gowns" are evidently taken from the same *Memorable Relation*, which continues: "There were standing at a little Distance from us, some of the Clergy, whom the Angel called Justifiers and Sanctifiers of Men by Faith alone, and also *Arcanists*, that is, Dealers in Mysteries." These clergy refused to listen to the teaching that "Faith without Charity Kills all things," and turned away so as not to hear it.

There is also a strong dig here at Isaac Watts, who describes the Sluggard's garden as overgrown with "nettles and briars" because its owner is an idle dreamer. Blake sees the matter otherwise: on the spiritual plane it is the moralistic clergy like Watts himself who make a wilderness of thorns, where the happy play of childhood plants bright gardens.

By a natural association of images, a passage from Boehme possibly comes into the complex whole of Blake's garden of love: "the Devil has built his Chapel close by the Christian Church, and has quite destroyed the Love of Paradise, and has in the Stead of it set up mere covetous, proud, self-willed, faithless, sturdy, malicious Blasphemers, Thieves and Murderers," [64] a description of the clergy quite after Blake's own heart.

[9]   The "graves" in the garden, Gothic as imagery, have obvious Neoplatonic overtones. They are the bodily sepulchers of souls who have lost all access to eternity. They are, by the logic of the symbol, the graves of the children who once played in the garden, but are now its dead.

Appendix

One unmistakable influence on the *Songs*, as Professor Pinto has shown in an article published in the *Divine Vision*, is Isaac Watts's *Divine Songs for Children* and more especially his *Moral Songs*, whose title page Blake must have read as a personal challenge: "A slight Specimen of Moral Songs," so Watts wrote,

> Such as I wish some happy and condescending Genius would undertake for the Use of Children, and perform much better. The Sense

and Subjects might be borrowed plentifully from the *Proverbs of Solomon*, from all the common Appearances of Nature, from all the Occurrences in the Civil Life, both in City and Country: (which would also afford Matter for other Divine songs). Here the Language and Measures should be easy and flowing with Chearfulness, and without the Solemnities of Religion, or the sacred Names of God and Holy Things; that Children might find Delight and Profit together.[65]

Watts's poems certainly influenced Blake, but the influence was a negative one. Watts's titles—*Innocent Play, The Rose, The Ant* or *Emmet, A Summer Evening, A Cradle Hymn*—were Blake's starting points for poems very unlike those of Watts. Yet let none underrate the importance, to Blake at all events, of the bracing effect of a violent antagonism, to which he owns in the aphorism "Damn braces, bless relaxes." He managed—this, Professor Pinto, in kindness perhaps to Watts, does not say—to differ with Watts at every point.

Isaac Watts also plays his part in the inspiration of *The Divine Image* as a negative influence. Watts's *Praise for the Gospel* opens unashamedly with these lines:

> *Lord, I ascribe it to thy Grace,*
> *And not to Chance, as others do*
> *That I was born of* Christian *race*
> *And not a* Heathen *or a* Jew.[66]

To this Blake's lines,

> *And all must love the human form,*
> *In heathen, turk, or jew* [67]

are an answer. Watts's Sluggard (*Moral Songs*, No. I) refuses to work and asks for

> *A little more Sleep, and a little more Slumber,*
> *Thus he wastes half his Days, and his Hours without Number.*[68]

It is the false nurse of the world of *Experience* who preaches to her child-charges the morality of Watts, "Your spring & your day are wasted in play."

The nurse of *Innocence*, on the other hand, loves to hear her children's laughing voices as they play on the hill until the last moment of the day. Watts's Sluggard, because he is not industrious, has a garden full of weeds:

> *I past by his Garden, and saw the wild Bryar,*
> *The Thorn and the Thistle grow broader and higher;*

but Blake's garden of love becomes full of thorns because joyless moralists kill the flowers of delight:

> *And Priests in black gowns were walking their rounds,*
> *And binding with briars my joys & desires.*[69]

Watts's Sluggard is a character after Blake's own heart; for

> *He told me his Dreams, talk'd of Eating and Drinking;*
> *But he scarce reads his Bible, and never loves Thinking.*
>
> *Said I then to my Heart, "Here's a Lesson for me,*
> *That Man's but the Picture of what I might be.*
> *But Thanks to my Friends for their Care in my Breeding,*
> *Who taught me betimes to love Working and Reading.*[70]

Blake's Innocents tell their dreams, like Tom the chimney sweeper, and love eating and drinking, "When the table with cherries and nuts is spread."

For Watts, professed Christian though he was, this world is the reality; Blake, following a more philosophic tradition, understood that it is a dream. In *A Dream* Blake seems to be answering Watts's poem *The Ant* or *Emmet:*

> *They don't wear their time out in sleeping or play,*
> *But gather up corn in a sun-shiny day,*
>   *And for winter they lay up their stores:*
> *They manage their work in such regular forms*
> *One would think they foresaw all the frost and the storms.*[71]

This taking thought for the morrow Blake saw as to be not admired but deplored. Blake saw these anxiety-ridden creatures as objects of the kindest compassion. For the careworn timid anxiety of the industrious poor, forever fearful of the future because they have lost all sense of the eternal, Blake felt not admiration but pity; for what to them seems the only reality—this world—is, in truth, only a dream of the fallen soul. In *A Dream* he is speaking to the bewildered poor, filled with cares as they struggle through life,

> *Troubled, 'wilder'd, and forlorn,*
> *Dark, benighted, travel-worn,*
> *Over many a tangled spray.*[72]

To the emmet Watts gives worldly advice—to pinch and save for this world; Blake gives the message of eternity to the soul who has strayed: "Little wanderer, hie thee home." The friends who teach the child "betimes to love working and reading" are not, as Watts supposed, improving, but destroying the young life; and if the buds of life are nipped and the joys stripped from childhood,

> *. . . how shall we gather what griefs destroy,*
> *Or bless the mellowing year,*
> *When the blasts of winter appear?* [73]

Play is the expression of the freedom of life, the natural activity of joy and imagination; in the world of *Innocence* children do not work, they play. Watts praises the rose not for its beauty, but because it preserves its scent when it is dead; the ant, for its parsimonious care for its own future wants, because it takes thought for the morrow, and thanks God that he was not born a heathen or a Jew. It is true that Watts's simple diction has a certain charm, and this Blake must have recognized; but his chief part in inspiring Blake to write the *Songs* was that he formulated and, in his own person, represented all that to Blake seemed most wrong with the religious morality of the time in its special relation to childhood.

10 Emblem (unsigned) from Darwin's *Botanic Garden* (1789)

CHAPTER *2*

Tiriel

What will be the result if into a world of Swedenborgian, Ossianic, and Nordic myth there breaks the "Grecian light and glory" that was in such works as Stuart's and Revett's *Antiquities of Athens* and Winckelmann's *Reflections on the Painting and Sculpture of the Greeks*, culminating in 1804 in the bringing to England of the Elgin marbles? Many translations from the Greek were made during the last quarter of the eighteenth century, a strong new influence upon Blake's generation during the late eighties and early nineties.

Blake's earliest formative influences—other than the mild main-stream of English poetry—were pre-eminently "gothic": Ossian; the Norse myths, popularized by Gray and translated from Mallet's French by Percy (whose *Reliques of Ancient English Poetry* introduced yet another North-ern current); Chatterton's imitations of ballads; as well as Swedenborg, whose fantasy is as Nordic as the fairy tales of his own country, abounding in fens and mists, toads, underground houses entered by the roof, mills, caverns, troll-like devils among the rocks, fragile flower-gardens, and, ruling over all, the pale hyperborean sun.

Into an imagination intoxicated by these various Nordic dreams, familiar with Swedenborgian speculation upon the state of spirits after death and perhaps other works on the "psychic" level of the supernatural, we now see a new element introduced. *Tiriel* is the product of a strange blending of Gothic fantasy and a Grecian theme—a hybrid, unrecognizable in character, unlike any work of English poetry before or since—which is perhaps just as well.

Tiriel, written about 1789, is the first of the Prophetic Books and Blake's first essay in myth-making. This phantasmagoria on the theme of the death of an aged king and tyrant-father may be—indeed, must be—read at

34

several levels. Ellis and Yeats call it "a treatise on Old Age written in the form of a myth, with the purpose of showing the decline of life as it appears in the mirror of symbolic poetry, and of using senility in its turn, as itself a symbol." [1] At the opposite extreme, David Erdman [2] reads *Tiriel* as an historical allegory upon the English kingship, with George III as the model of Tiriel, the king who has lost his kingdom in the "West," the American Colonies. But Blake's interest in politics and history was of a peculiar kind; in history, as in other fields, he was a symbolist. History is subject to the Swedenborgian law of correspondence; or perhaps Blake should more justly be compared to the Hebrew Prophets, for he saw all human events, private or public, as the effects of supernatural causes. The peculiar value of this kind of symbolic narrative is that it makes possible an implicit affirmation that the same forces are manifesting themselves on multiple levels.

Tiriel, then, we may regard as the state of senility as it may be found in a human individual — that in man which selfishly resists its own dissolution; or we may see him as tyrannous kingship in decadence; or beyond both these, as the principle of a blind materialism — "the mental error of belief in matter," so Ellis and Yeats define Tiriel's nature. Blake seems to have found the name in Cornelius Agrippa's *Three Books of Occult Philosophy*, where Tiriel is given as the name signifying "the intelligence of mercury." [3] Erdman ingeniously points out the aptness of mercury as a symbol of English trade and commerce; but the more obvious significance of mercury in alchemical tradition is the crude untransmuted *prima materia*, a meaning that well fits Ellis and Yeats's definition of Tiriel's nature.

In form *Tiriel* resembles nothing so much as Swedenborg's "memorable relations" of happenings seen in the spiritual worlds. In those worlds each mental state creates its appropriate surroundings; and a change of state changes these surroundings. This insubstantial and shifting texture of images which correspond to their symbolic content is precisely what we have in dreams. The landscape of *Tiriel* is dreamlike: the forests and deserts over which he passes, the animals, personages, and events which he encounters, are all appropriate to his mental state, by correspondence. The logic of *Tiriel* is dream logic, inconsequent in terms of natural cause and effect, but not so if we accept a sudden change of scene as a necessary accompaniment of a change of thought. Thus understood, there is nothing particularly obscure about the sequence of events in *Tiriel*. Considered as an illustration of the doctrine of correspondence, *Tiriel* is masterly; as a work of literature, it lacks structure, and the language moves from the overviolent and Ossianic to clumsy flatness. But this discrepancy is just what we might expect from a practicing Swedenborgian who had never been to school.

Blake's first readings in Greek literature seem to have been the tragedies of Sophocles and Aeschylus; and from the Theban legend he has taken the story of *Tiriel*. There is no trace in this work of the Neoplatonic symbolism that was so soon to transform Blake's imaginative world. *Tiriel* is a Greek story transposed into the symbolic terms of Swedenborg.

Oedipus is the prototype of Tiriel—not Freud's Oedipus, the young man who murdered Laius and married Jocasta, but the banished tyrant of Thebes who from the edge of the grave curses his sons and calls down ruin upon his kingdom.

The many resemblances, both in general and in minute particulars, between *Tiriel* and *Oedipus* are so obvious and so striking that it is surprising they have so long remained unnoticed.

Tiriel, as Blake has represented him in the drawings that accompany the text, wears a classical cloak, and the garments of Hela and Myratana also suggest Greek garments. Blake at about this time was becoming interested in Greek art, and made a number of drawings after Stuart's and Revett's *Antiquities of Athens*, a key work at that time, above all for Flaxman, who learned from the Greeks his characteristic linear style and treatment of drapery. One drawing might almost serve as a stage set for *Oedipus Rex*. Tiriel stands on the portico of his palace, the dead queen in his arms and his three sons before him, dressed in Greek tunics and crowned respectively with bays, vine, and a golden circlet. Three pillars of the classical order describe the palace; in the background is a pyramid.[4]

[11]   Tiriel makes his entry as an old blind king before his "once delight-ful palace," supporting in his arms his dying queen; a deleted second line of the poem reads "Dark were his once piercing eyes," so that it is made to appear that Tiriel is not only blind, but has been blinded. He raises his voice to curse his sons, who are called "sons of the Curse" and said to be "in their gates." It must be that the immediately striking resemblance to Lear's entry with Cordelia in his arms has obscured the far closer parallel with Oedipus. If we see in the dying queen a parallel not only with Cordelia but also with Jocasta, the appearance of Tiriel can be seen as closely following the appearance of the blinded Oedipus, about to be banished from Thebes (so far from *Oedipus Tyrannus*) cursing his sons, as he does in the later play

11 Tiriel with palace in background and three sons: illustration for *Tiriel* (c. 1789)

Oedipus at Colonus. The sons are called "Sons of the Curse" even before Tiriel curses them; and the phrase is several times repeated in the course of the poem with an emphasis that cannot be overlooked.

Blake does not trouble to explain what the "curse" is of which they are sons; and this is typical of his allusive style, for to himself it was perfectly clear: it is the curse which lay upon the House of Cadmus, condemning Oedipus to the murder of his father and a marriage with his own mother, from which were born the sons whom he himself curses with such terrible passion before his death, and who perish under the double curse of fate and Oedipus himself, fighting in the gates of Thebes.

Tiriel's eldest son retaliates by calling Tiriel "thou accursed man" – again, some curse is to be understood, which rests alike upon Tiriel and his sons, as the curse upon the house of Cadmus rested alike on Laius, Oedipus, and the sons of Oedipus. No doubt Blake was also thinking of the curse that rests upon Adam and his sons; and the power of the symbol lies in its general truth; for every man is, in the words of the Christian rite of baptism, "conceived and born in sin." But Tiriel's and his sons' reiteration of this curse suggests a particular as well as a general significance.

Aeschylus' *Seven against Thebes* [5] tells of the champions gathered by the sons of Oedipus, each fighting in one of the gates of the city. In *Tiriel* there are repeated allusions to the sons "in the gates." In the opening passages the sons of Tiriel are "in their gates"; and in his final cursing, Tiriel says:

> *. . . may the heavens rain wrath*
> *As thick as northern fogs around your gates, to choke you up!* [6]

He then wishes that they may lie unburied, as Polynices lay unburied outside the gates of Thebes, in the *Antigone* of Sophocles:

> *. . . like dogs cast out,*
> *The stink of your dead carcases annoying man & beast.* [7]

He alludes twice to the unburied stinking carcasses of his sons, and we cannot but think of the powerful image in the speech of the Messenger in the *Antigone:*

> *. . . we swept the dust away,*
> *The dead which cover'd o'er, and laying bare*
> *The putrid body, on the higher ground*
> *In the free wind sate down, th' infectious smell*
> *Avoiding . . .* [8]

It is by no means clear how Tiriel has come to be an exile from his palace, and he himself blames his sons; but the sons say that he has refused to accept shelter from them. A situation in which sons could be in a position to offer or refuse food and shelter to a king in his own palace requires some explanation. Lear's daughters were in such a position by the King's abdication, as were Oedipus' sons because of the King's banishment. Blake is evidently assuming one or the other of these situations; but his failure to explain strikes the reader strangely. His eldest son says:

> *Thou hast refus'd our charity, thou hast refus'd our food,*
> *Thou hast refus'd our clothes, our beds, our houses for thy dwelling,*
> *Chusing to wander like a Son of Zazel in the rocks.* [9]

Polynices, in *Oedipus at Colonus*, offers his father shelter, but is indignantly refused; Polynices sees his father:

> *But how attired! his mean and squalid garb,*
> *Worn bare by length of time, his aged limbs*
> *Contaminates; and on his eyeless head*
> *His matted locks by each rude gale are waved;*

> *And to his garb akin his wretched food*
> *But ill supports him. Late, too late I know*
> *The ruin I have caused. . . .*
> *I come with wholesome food to cherish thee,*
> *And lighten thy accumulated woes.*

Polynices pleads for forgiveness; but Oedipus accuses him of having driven him out:

> *For thou, vile wretch, the sceptre and the throne*
> *Holding, which now thy brother holds at Thebes,*
> *Didst drive thy father out, by thee constrain'd*
> *An exile from my country far to rove,*
> *And wear these loathsome weeds . . .*[10]

He proceeds to denounce him and his brother Eteocles:

> *Death will o'ertake you, when thy forces come*
> *To Thebes, which shall not fall before thy arms,*
> *There soon shalt thou, and thy vile brother, die:*
> *Long since my curses did declare thy fate,*
> *Which here I do repeat, that you may learn*
> *The rev'rence due to parents, and no more*
> *Reproach a sightless father . . .*[11]

He calls upon Erebus, Mars, and the Eumenides to bear witness to his curse, and dismisses his son with the unforgiving and terrible words:

> *. . . go,*
> *Tell all the Thebans, tell thy faithful friends*
> *Confederate in thy cause, that Oedipus*
> *Confers this meed of merit on his sons.*[12]

We have only to fill into the background of *Tiriel* the story of Oedipus for much that is unexplained to become clear. Without this background we can only guess and wonder what story Blake has chosen to leave untold.

In *Tiriel*, however, the sympathy is so entirely reversed that in the senile tyrant we are reluctant to recognize the travel-weary noble figure of Oedipus; yet it is perfectly possible to see in the unforgiving Oedipus just such a venomous death-dealing tyrant as Tiriel. If Blake had read *Oedipus at Colonus* not in Potter's but in Francklin's translation, *Oedipus Coloneus*, he would have found this view put forward by the translator, who writes that

"nothing can be more artful, tender, and pathetic than this speech of
Polynices . . . his modest and humble supplication, clothed in terms that
must have moved any but the implacable Oedipus." Antigone pleads for
forgiveness, a part she herself is later to play in her noble resolution to bury
her brother, showing mercy as against Creon's justice. To her father she
pleads:

> *Others like thee have base unworthy children,*
> *And yet their minds are soften'd to forgiveness*
> *By friend's advice, and all their wrath subdu'd.*
> *Think on thy own unhappy parent's fate,*
> *Thence may'st thou learn what dreadful ills have flow'd*
> *From anger's bitter fountain; thou, alas!*
> *Art a sad proof; those sightless eyes too well*
> *Bear witness to it . . .*[13]

This contrast between relentless vengeance and forgiveness Blake echoes in
the dialogue between Tiriel and Har, whose sons have also left him, but who
has forgiven them. Har (who is the ancestor of Tiriel) is a realization of the
situation described by Antigone:

> *"If thou dost go," said Har, "I wish thine eyes may see thy folly.*
> *My sons have left me; did thine leave thee? O, 'twas very cruel!"*
>
> *"No! venerable man," said Tiriel, "ask me not such things,*
> *For thou dost make my heart to bleed: my sons were not like thine,*
> *But worse. . . ."*[14]

(That "But worse" expresses the very essence of egoism; what happens to
ourselves is always "worse" than the same event experienced by others.) To
Blake forgiveness is the supreme glory of Christianity; and its absence in the
character of Oedipus evidently impressed Blake more than the nobler
aspects of the suffering exile.

Insofar as *Tiriel* can be said to have a plot, that plot is based upon
Oedipus at Colonus. An old blind and dying king, banished from his palace
by his usurping sons, wanders long and far, and comes at last to a sweet
valley of refuge. There he conceals his identity, fearing that if it is made
known, he will not be received; he leaves, but later returns, led by his
daughter, reveals his identity, is kindly received, and dies. Apart from
Blake's duplication of Tiriel's wanderings and return to the vales of Har,
this is Sophocles' plot. Blake's inability to manage the structure of any poem

longer than a lyric is glaringly apparent if we realize that this was the best he could do with the prototype of classical dramatic form. But the description of Tiriel's wanderings, compressed by Blake into four lines, captures the very essence of Oedipus' travels which lead him at last to the grove of the Eumenides:

> *He wander'd day & night: to him both day & night were dark.*
> *The sun he felt, but the bright moon was now a useless globe:*
> *O'er mountains & thro' vales of woe the blind & aged man*
> *Wander'd, till he that leadeth all led him to the vales of Har.*[15]

So Oedipus tells that Phoebus himself has led him at last to Colonus and

> *. . . foretold that here at last*
> *I shou'd have rest, within this hallow'd grove*
> *These hospitable shades, and finish here*
> *A life of mis'ry.*[16]

He prays to the Eumenides and Athena to receive him, and the people of Colonus, who at first seek to drive him away as a man under a curse, at last summon Theseus, who receives Oedipus in obedience to Athena herself.

In *Tiriel* the strange figures of Har, Heva, and Mnetha play a similar part. At first Har and Heva shrink in fear from Tiriel; but he persuades them that he is a "harmless man," and they then receive him. The Greek belief that an accursed man carries his infection of evil with him seems to be echoed in Har and Heva's suspicion of Tiriel and his reluctance to declare himself to them. He is ashamed, and equivocates:

> *"I am not of this region," said Tiriel dissemblingly,*
> *"I am an aged wanderer, once father of a race*
> *Far in the north; but they were wicked & were all destroy'd,*
> *And I their father sent an outcast. I have told you all.*
> *Ask me no more, I pray, for grief hath seal'd my precious sight."* [17]

So Oedipus is also reluctant to declare himself:

> Chorus: *Now, wretched stranger, tell us who thou art,*
>   *Thy country, and thy name.*
> Oedipus: *Alas! my lords*
>   *A poor abandon'd exile, but O! do not—*
> Chorus: *What say'st thou?*

Oedipus: *Do not ask me who I am;*
       Enquire no farther.
Chorus: *Wherefore?*
Oedipus: *My sad race*—[18]

Oedipus at last reluctantly reveals his identity; Tiriel does so only on his second encounter with Har, Heva, and Mnetha, in his last speech before his death.

Tiriel, after his first fruitless visit to the vales of Har, returns to his palace, where for the last time he curses his sons and daughters and calls down ruin on the palace. He then leaves, led, as Oedipus was by Antigone, by his youngest daughter, Hela. There is so much of the imagery of *Oedipus at Colonus* in this speech that no one with the two texts before him could doubt that Blake is here inspired by Sophocles. Tiriel's speech is indeed an eloquent gloss, almost a paraphrase, of that grand scene in *Oedipus* that begins with the sounding of thunder and flash of lightning from the Grove of the Eumenides—the sign of Oedipus' imminent death—and ends with the blind king's departure into the grove, while the chorus invokes the gods of the underworld. Oedipus himself recognizes the omens, and forbids his daughters to follow him, saying:

> *Let me find out the tomb where I must hide*
> *My poor remains; that way my journey lies;*
> *Away: thou god of shades, great Mercury,*
> *And Proserpine, infernal pow'rs, conduct me!* [19]

The Chorus declare that horror has made their hair to stand on end with fear; and as the blind king sets off into the grove, they call upon Proserpina queen of the dead, Pluto, and the Eumenides themselves. Mention is made of the barking of Cerberus:

> *Goddess invisible, on thee we call*
> *If thee we may invoke, Proserpina, and thee*
> *Great Pluto, King of Shades . . .*
>
>   .   .   .
>
> *Ye goddesses rever'd, who dwell*
> *Beneath the earth deep hid, and thou*
> *Who barking from thy gloomy cave,*
> *Unconquer'd Cerberus, guard'st the ghosts below,*

What, night eternal—but a frown from thee?
What, heaven's meridian glory—but thy smile?
And shall not praise be thine? not human praise?
While heaven's high host on hallelujahs live?
    O may I breathe no longer than I breathe
My soul in praise to HIM who gave my soul
And all her infinite of prospect fair;
Cut through the shades of hell, great love! by THEE,
Oh most adorable, most unadored!
Where shall that praise begin, which ne'er should end?
Where'er I turn, what claim on all applause!
How is night's sable mantle labour'd o'er!
How richly wrought with attributes divine!
What wisdom shines! what love! this midnight pomp,
This gorgeous arch with golden worlds inlaid,
Built with divine ambition, nought to THEE!
For others this profusion: THOU apart,
Above, beyond: oh tell me, mighty mind!
Where art thou? shall I dive into the deep?
Call to the sun, or ask the roaring winds
For their creator? shall I question loud
* The thunder, if in that the ALMIGHTY dwells?
Or holds HE furious storms in streighten'd reins,
And bids fierce whirlwinds wheel his rapid car?
    What mean these questions?—trembling I retract;
My prostrate soul adores the present GOD:
Praise I a distant DEITY? HE tunes
My voice, if tuned; the nerve that writes, sustains;
Wrapp'd in his being I resound his praise:
But though past all diffused, without a shore

12 The thunder: plate designed and engraved by Blake for Young's *Night Thoughts* (1797), p. 80

> *On thee, O son of Tartarus we call,*
> *For thou art ever wakeful, lead, O! lead*
> *To thy dark mansion this unhappy stranger.*[20]

Presently a messenger returns to describe how the infernal powers made the earth miraculously open to receive Oedipus.

Every one of Sophocles' images is repeated in Tiriel's speech – thunder, earthquake (the king of the underworld), the Eumenides, the dogs of Erebus:

[12]
> *. . . Where does the thunder sleep?*
> *Where doth he hide his terrible head? & his swift & fiery daughters,*
> *Where do they shroud their fiery wings & the terrors of their hair?*
> *Earth, thus I stamp thy bosom! rouse the earthquake from his den,*
> *To raise his dark & burning visage thro' the cleaving ground,*
> *To thrust these towers with his shoulders! Let his fiery dogs*
> *Rise from the center, belching flames & roarings, dark smoke!* [21]

The earthquake's "dark and burning visage" is reminiscent of Ossian, where apparitions with eyes like "meteors" of fire in a dark face are often described – as, for example, the spirit of Loda, the Norse god of the dead:

> *He came to his place in his terrors, and he shook his dusky spear.*
> *His eyes appear like flames in his dark face; and his voice is like*
> *   distant thunder* [22]

The description of the "swift and fiery daughters" with shrouded wings and "the terrors of their hair" suggests that Blake had also read Aeschylus' *Eumenides:*

> *. . . not women,*
> *But Gorgons rather, nor the Gorgon form*
> *Exactly representing. . . .*
> *These have not wings; but cloath'd in sable stoles,*
> *Abhorr'd and execrable; as they sleep*
> *Hoarse in their hollow throats their harsh breath rattles* [23]

So far is Blake unlike the "classics" as conceived by the eighteenth century that this living re-creation of the very spirit of Greek antiquity (so far also from the "classical") has gone undetected.

Thus invoking the Gorgon-like Eumenides by "the terrors of their hair," their snaky tresses, Tiriel summons to him Hela, his youngest

13 Tiriel led by Hela: illustration for *Tiriel* (c. 1789)

daughter, to lead him. The parallel with Antigone, who leads her father to Colonus, is obvious; but more fundamental is the parallel with Oedipus' summoning of Persephone to conduct him; for Hela, like Persephone, is a goddess of death and queen of the dead, so named in the Norse mythology. Persephone is to lead Oedipus to his grave; and Hela, in Blake's poem, is to play the same part. Goddess of death by her name, Gorgon-fury in her snaky tresses, she resembles Antigone in her daughterhood.

As compared with Sophocles' great statement on the theme of old age, *Tiriel* is superficial. The reconciliation of Oedipus with the Furies, who for him at last become in truth "the benevolent ones," has no parallel in *Tiriel*, nor is there anything like the heart-rending pathos of Oedipus' parting with his daughters or the majesty of his death. Formally, Sophocles is incomparably Blake's superior; and yet there are moments of pure poetry in Blake that make the shade of Oedipus walk in Gothic dress.

It is impossible that in planning his poem Blake should not have considered *King Lear;* and there are passages that clearly suggest that he did so. But even such a king-hater as Blake could scarcely have drawn, from Lear alone, so fierce and unsympathetic a tyrant-father as Tiriel. Like Oedipus, Tiriel curses, above all, his sons rather than, like Lear, his daughters; he is not a mad but a blind king, although indeed symbolically there is no difference,

14 Blind Urizen: *Urizen* (1794), plate 11

[14]   for both states symbolize spiritual darkness. It is true that Gloucester is blinded, and by his sons; and there is much in *Lear* that Shakespeare himself doubtless derived from Sophocles and that Blake might have taken from either. There are, however, many verbal echoes. Zazel's taunt "where are now thine eyes," addressed to Tiriel, clearly echoes Lear's speech:

> *Do's any heere know me?*
> *This is not* Lear:
> *Do's* Lear *walke thus? Speake thus? Where are his eies?*
> *Either his Notion weakens, his Discernings*
> *Are Lethargied. Ha! Waking? 'Tis not so?*
> *Who is it that can tell me who I am?* [24]

Tiriel, like Lear, "hath ever but slenderlie knowne himself"; Zazel's "Where are now thine eyes? . . . Where are you going?" [25] recalls not only Lear's "Where are his eyes?" but also blind Gloucester's "I have no way, and therefore want no eyes," as also does Tiriel's "pathless way." Har's "I wish thine eyes may see thy folly" [26] defines Tiriel's "aged ignorance." the Fool's words to Lear, "Thou shouldst not have bin old, till thou hadst bin wise," are of the very essence of Tiriel's character. Oedipus, like Lear, is described, both by Tiresias and by Creon, as characterized by the same dangerous absence of self-knowledge.   [15]

It is likely that in Tiriel's invocation of the earthquake and the thunders there are reverberations not only of Sophocles' Erebus but of Lear's "You Sulph'rous and Thought-executing Fires"; [27] and Tiriel's ". . . Pestilence, that bathest in fogs & standing lakes" [28] echoes Lear's

> *. . . Infect her Beauty,*
> *You Fen-suck'd Fogges, drawne by the powrfull Sunne*
> *To fall, and blister.*[29]

It would have been impossible to draw a Tiriel from a Lear; nevertheless Blake's philosophy is one in whose light even Lear does not appear as a figure altogether deserving our sympathy. A moral that has seemed obvious to the least sensitive readers of Shakespeare is that the old should not give away their property to their children while they are still in need of it. Blake reverses the moral and shows us the folly of a refusal of one generation to give place to the next. Tiriel curses his children for succeeding him: "Ye worms of death, feasting upon your aged parent's flesh!" [30] The old man who cannot relinquish worldly power and possessions, and indeed temporal life

15 "Aged Ignorance": *For Children: The Gates of Paradise* (1793), plate 11

itself, is, for Blake, a figure not of tragedy but of selfish folly. The human selfhood, the "worm of sixty winters," is but an encrustation over the immortal spirit, and death is its portion as certainly as life is the portion of "the immortal man that cannot die." Blake's certainty of the immortality of the soul was such that he could not enter sympathetically into that part of Shakespeare's tragedy whose power to move us lies in the dark uncertainty of the world beyond death.

Lear comes to terms with death only as he dies; Oedipus at Colonus, from the beginning of the action of the play, is glad to have reached sanctuary in the grove of the Furies, who for him are truly, and not by mere euphemism, the Eumenides. His acceptance of death gives him at last a stature almost divine. William Empson points out that when King Lear calls upon the gods, the prayer is answered only by some new catastrophe. "Every time Lear prays to the gods, or anyone else prays on his behalf, there are bad effects immediately." [31] He might have added that catastrophe following prayer to the gods is so regular a feature of Sophoclean tragedy as to be almost a convention. But Blake would not have seen in this an irony of heaven; it is for man to understand the gods and to know what to pray for. Lear ought to have been praying as Oedipus prayed, not to the gods of the living but to the "blessed gods of the underworld." Lear's moving appeal to the gods "If you do love old men . . ." has a negative answer, unless old age can recognize, as Oedipus recognized, that death is the blessing of age.

Lear's last hope from life is that, with Cordelia, he may live in the world yet not of it, as a spectator. Was Har's "cage" in which the old man sings suggested to Blake by Lear's "Come, let's away to prison, / We two alone will sing like Birds i' th' Cage"? [32] It is altogether characteristic of Blake's imaginative processes that where Shakespeare gives a simile, Blake at once visualizes and personifies, and presents us with a complete piece of myth, the strangely shocking picture of an old witless man singing in a "great cage." In this image Blake is implicitly rejecting Lear's hoped-for happiness as a fool's paradise.

This implied criticism of Lear's great speech occurs on the first encounter of Tiriel with Mnetha, Har, and Heva. Under the care of Mnetha are two ancestral figures, Har and Heva,[33] also very old:

Mnetha, now aged, waited on them & brought them food &
clothing;
But they were as the shadow of Har & as the years forgotten.[34]

They are living in the past, and senile—inevitably so, since the food that Mnetha gives them is that of memory and can nourish only second childhood: "Playing with flowers & running after birds they spent the day." Perhaps this is an echo of Lear's entry, crowned with flowers, pursuing a field mouse with his glove, fancying that he is hawking. Har catches birds, and keeps them in his cage, where he, too, sings. Heva pleads with Tiriel to remain with them,

> *"For we have many sports to shew thee & many songs to sing,*
> *And after dinner we will walk into the cage of Har,*
> *And thou shalt help us to catch birds & gather them ripe*
> *cherries."*

.   .   .

> *"Thou shalt not go," said Heva, "till thou hast seen our singing*
> *birds,*
> *And heard Har sing in the great cage & slept upon our fleeces."* [35]

To Blake the notion of singing birds in a cage was horrible and unnatural:

> *A Robin Red breast in a Cage,*
> *Puts all Heaven in a Rage.* [36]

We have only to remember this and two lines from *The School Boy*, to be left in little doubt that we are meant to regard Har's cage with horror:

> *How can the bird that is born for joy*
> *Sit in a cage and sing?* [37]

The temporal world is but a cage and prison of the soul, and Lear's attempt to elude death by singing in the prison-cage, Blake seems to imply, is vain.

Har and Heva remain mysterious figures; but something may be surmised of them from their later appearances. Their final metamorphosis into serpents suggests that they are earthborn. This episode links them again with the Theban legend, for here Blake is basing the episode upon the metamorphosis of Cadmus and Harmonia into two harmless serpents. The story is told in Ovid's *Metamorphoses*, with much pathos; and it is certainly Blake's model in *The Song of Los:*

> *. . . like a dream, Eternity was obliterated & erased.*

.   .   .

> *Since that dread day when Har and Heva fled*

Because their brethren & sisters liv'd in War & Lust;
And as they fled they shrunk
Into two narrow doleful forms
Creeping in reptile flesh upon
The bosom of the ground;
And all the vast of Nature shrunk
Before their shrunken eyes.[38]

Cadmus [39] founded his city with the help of the earthborn men who grew
from the teeth of the dragon of Ares, whom he slew. The metamorphosis into
serpent form is again repeated in *Europe* – without mention of Har and Heva
by name, however – and said to have come about

. . . when the five senses whelm'd
In deluge o'er the earth-born man . . .[40]

[16, 17]   There is a great deal about Cadmus in Stukeley's *Abury, A Temple of the
British Druids*, a work certainly known to Blake, for, as Ruthven Todd has
[18]   shown, the last page of *Jerusalem* shows the "serpent-temple" of Avebury,
copied from Stukeley's reconstruction. From this plate and Blake's use of the
term "serpent-temple," we may be sure that he knew and approved Stukeley's theory. Cadmus, according to Stukeley, was a founder of serpent
temples: he was a Hivite, as Bryant also says, and Bryant, too, describes
Cadmus and the Hivites as serpent worshipers. Is the name Heva derived
from this Hivite association? Stukeley informs us that in the Syriac language "Hevaeus signifies a snake." [41] If Heva is Har's snake bride, her

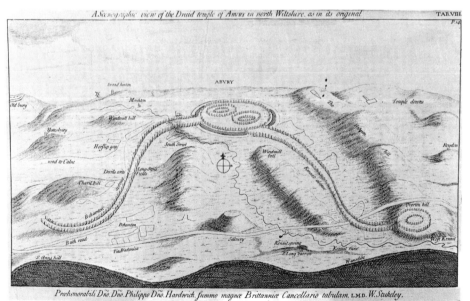

16 Serpent temple:
Stukeley,   *Abury*
(1743)

17 Men metamorphosed into serpents: *Urizen* (1794), plate 25, detail

See also [II, 146].

"earth-born" nature is implied in her name. Given Blake's interest in Stukeley's serpent temples, this explanation is by no means farfetched.

The same name, similarly associated with the snake, could also have been reached through Bryant, who writes that "Clement acknowledges, that the term Eva properly aspirated" is the same as Ophis, a serpent. In the orgies of Bacchus "the persons, who partook of the ceremony, used to carry serpents in their hands, and with horrid screams call upon Eva, Eva." [42] Heva may simply be Eva, "properly aspirated."

If Har and Heva are akin to Cadmus and Harmonia, Tiriel (Oedipus)

18 Serpent temple: *Jerusalem* (1804–1820), plate 100

The figures are Urthona, Los, and Enitharmon, with solar and lunar emblems of their labors at the "furnaces" and "looms" of generation.

visits his own ancestors; and this is implied by Heva's greeting, "Then Heva came & took old Tiriel in her mother's arms." [43] Heva seems to be in some doubt as to whether she is embracing Tiriel or his father; for her the generations have become confused with the passage of time, and she can no longer distinguish them:

> *Bless thy poor eyes, old man, & bless the old father of Tiriel!*
> *Thou art my Tiriel's old father; I know thee thro' thy wrinkles* [44]

but presently she calls him *Tiriel:* "How didst thou lose thy eyes, old Tiriel?" [45] Oedipus is the son of Laius, son of Labdacus, the great-grand-son of Cadmus and Harmonia. Some such long ancestral retrospect is implied in Tiriel's relationship with Har and Heva. There may be, in the figure of Har, an overtone also of Theseus, to whose kingdom and protection Oedipus wanders.

Mnetha owes her name to a combination of *mnemosyne* (memory) and perhaps *Manethon*, the Egyptian chronologist, and *Athena*. She is one of the "Daughters of Memory," who are the Greek Muses; and perhaps Athena, as patron goddess of Athens and its learning, plays some part in her composition. Blake had but small regard for the Daughters of Memory, who are his false muses, not being the "authors of such sublime conceptions" as his own "Daughters of Inspiration," who draw not upon the memories of temporal tradition but upon memory of the kind Plato called anamnesis, recollection of the eternal forms or ideas. Blake doubtless found the name Manethon in Stukeley's works on Avebury and Stonehenge, as "a valuable piece of antiquity, call'd Manethon, the Egyptian Dynasties." [46] Now Blake neither valued nor venerated such pieces of antiquity as Manethon's Chronology. "Public Records! As if Public Records were True!" Blake wrote indignantly in the margin of Watson's *Apology*. "Nothing can be more contemptible than to suppose Public RECORDS to be True." [47] Lear's telling of "old tales" and "court news," and the wearing out of "packs and sets of great ones" belong to Mnetha's world of recorded memory; but a retreat into the vistas of the past can give no enduring refuge from dissolution; Lear's hope was never realized, nor could it have been; and neither can Tiriel remain with Mnetha, nourished on her food of memories.

There is a very beautiful water-color drawing [48] of Har, Heva, and [19] Mnetha, entitled "Har and Heva bathing." What is illustrated, of course, is

19 Har and Heva bath-
ing: illustration for *Tiriel*
(c. 1789)

nothing so naturalistic as a bath, but the nature of Har and Heva: they are
immersed in the waters of *hyle* – matter – for their philosophy is unspiritual.
The spiritual world is a true childhood, ageless, and this spirituality is as
unknown to the inoffensive Har and Heva in their senile second childhood as
to the raging Tiriel.

The name Har appears in Stukeley [49] in a chronology where he is associated
with Haran, the place of Abraham's sojourn after his departure from Ur.
But the Har who seems undoubtedly to be the source of Blake's Har appears
in the Icelandic Edda, translated by Percy from Mallet's *Northern Antiquities*.[50] Har is an important figure in this work, and appears as the narrator of
ancient wisdom to a king, Gangler, who travels to Asgard from the west
(Tiriel is also a "king of the west") and who conceals his true name from
Har (as Tiriel also does) in order to learn the myths of creation and the
corpus of wisdom as embodied in the Norse traditions. Therefore, this Har,
also, is an educator:

> "He who sits on the lowest Throne is the king, his name is Har, or
> the lofty one: the second is Jafnhar, i.e. equal to the lofty one: but he
> who sits on the highest throne is called Thridi, or the third." Har
> perceiving Gangler, desired to know what business had brought him
> to Asgard: Adding, that he should be welcome to eat and drink

without cost, along with the other guests of his court. Gangler said,
He desired first to know whether there was any person present who
was famous for his wisdom and knowledge. Har answered, If thou
art the more knowing, I fear thou wilt hardly return safe: But go,
stand below, and propose thy questions; here sits one will be able to
answer thee.[51]

This Har, like Blake's, offers to the wanderer hospitality and instruction.
Tiriel's last speech denounces Har for the false system of education he has
received from him—a purely materialistic philosophy. What evidence is
there that the teaching of the Norse Har was of this kind?

Gangler was taught by *three* kings, who speak in turn; Tiriel was
taught only by Har—the lowest of the three. The statement that Har is the
lowest of three potencies Blake would certainly interpret in terms of the
traditional threefold division of elementary, celestial, and intellectual orders,
familiar to him through Swedenborg, Agrippa, and other sources. Har, then,
would be a king of the elementary or natural world, "earth-born." He could
teach, therefore, only the lowest form of wisdom, that of natural philosophy.
That this is in fact the meaning of the Norse myth appears from the answers
of the three kings to a question concerning the nature of God:

> Har replies: He lives for ever; he governs all his kingdom; and
> directs the great things as well as the small. Jafnhar adds: He hath
> formed the heaven, the earth, and the air. Thridi proceeds, He hath
> done more; he hath made man, and given him a spirit or soul, which
> shall live, even after the body shall have mouldered away. And then
> all the just shall dwell with him in a place named *Gimle*. But wicked
> men shall go to Hela, or death.[52]

Har teaches only a natural religion, for only Thridi knows of an
eternal world. Har does not teach it because he, by his very nature, does not
know it; and Mnetha (the wisdom of Blake's Har) is also surprised to know
that there are other men besides the sons of Har. Har, Heva, and Mnetha live
in the good faith of their ignorance. The earthborn Cadmus and the
elementary Har have this in common.

From Mallet's *Northern Antiquities* also comes the name of Hela, Tiriel's
youngest daughter. She is the Norse goddess of death, described not only in
the Eddas but in several other works accessible to Blake—Gray's poems, for

one. Not only is Hela the goddess of death; she is specifically the goddess of death through old age. Only those go to her hells who die disgracefully (so the Norsemen saw it) of old age or sickness, and not in battle. This is evidently why Blake substitutes Hela for Persephone, who leads the aged Oedipus to his grave.

The Norsemen honored those who died in battle, and willingly sought what Blake was later to call "Self-annihilation" [53] (albeit in a barbaric form), believing that only by so casting aside all selfish clinging to life could they reach Valhalla, a place of immortal happiness. As for Hela, "Her hall is Grief; Famine is her table; Hunger, her knife; Delay, her valet; Slackness, her maid; Precipice, her gate; Faintness, her porch; Sickness and Pain, her bed; and her tent, Cursing and Howling." [54] Blake's Hela is snake-locked like a Gorgon, a trait that she seems to derive from the Eumenides. But the Norse Hela is also associated with snakes; and if Blake had read—as seems likely in view of his great admiration for Macpherson—the *Introduction to the History of Great Britain and Ireland*, he would have found there a long section devoted to "The Regions of Hela": "On the shores of dead bodies, remote from the sun, there is a spacious and dismal hall, with its gate wide open to the northern winds. The walls are wattled with snakes, whose heads look inward and vomit poison. Rivers of this poison rush through the hall, which the unhappy are forced to ford." [55] Hela's aspect, Macpherson says, "is fierce and terrible; her temper unrelenting and cruel." Blake's Hela, howling and serpent-haired, reveals her mythological antecedents:

> "*Hela, my daughter, listen! thou art the daughter of Tiriel.*
> *Thy father calls. Thy father lifts his hand unto the heavens,*
> *For thou hast laughed at my tears & curst thy aged father.*
> *Let snakes rise from thy bedded locks & laugh among thy curls!*"
>
> *He ceast; her dark hair upright stood, while snakes infolded round*
> *Her madding brows: her shrieks apall'd the soul of Tiriel.*
>
> .   .   .
>
> *She, howling, led him over mountains & thro' frighted vales.*[56]

Macpherson explains at some length that only those who die, like Tiriel, of old age or sickness fall into the power of Hela. What follows throws light upon the attitude of contempt expressed by Tiriel's sons, who address their father as "Old man! unworthy to be call'd the father of Tiriel's race!" [57] This taunting of old age is shocking to our morality, but it was not

so by Norse standards. Blake, with his enthusiasm for Ossian,[58] no doubt
found much to admire in the Norse heroes:

> As valour was the only virtue among the northern nations, cow-
> ardice was the only vice. The first intitled them to the joys of the
> Valhalla; the latter subjected them to an uncomfortable eternity in
> the regions of Hela. . . . The coward who suffered himself to be
> taken off by disease, or to be extinguished by age, brought disgrace
> on his friends as well as misery upon himself. The relations of the
> aged often prevented the reflections, which otherwise might have
> fallen upon themselves, by putting them to a violent death. Children
> have been known to precipitate their parents from rocks, whilst the
> devoted persons exhibited every demonstration of gladness and
> joy.[59]

To Tiriel's sons the very fact that their father is old and feeble proves
him a coward: he is afraid to die. This barbaric view of old age did not, to
Blake, seem either cruel or unjust, at least in a symbolic sense. The
Scandinavian heroes whom Mallet describes as laughing as they fell in
battle showed a kind of spiritual wisdom; for in their savage way they were
willing to renounce temporal selfhood in their joyous faith in an eternal
world. An instance of the opposite Blake would also have known from
Mallet: Aun, king of Sweden, "who devoted to Odin the blood of his nine
sons, to prevail on that god to prolong his life." This extreme example of old
age reluctant to die may be among the contributory sources of *Tiriel*.[60]

The atmosphere of phantasmagoria in *Tiriel*, from which landmarks of
classical drama rise as strangely as rocks out of swirling mist, comes from
Swedenborg and from Agrippa. Tiriel's brother Zazel is taken, like Tiriel
himself, from Agrippa's *Three Books of Occult Philosophy*. The demon
Zazel and his army (Blake changes "army" to "sons") are the consumers of
carcasses: "the flesh being forsaken, & the body being defunct of life, is
called a dead Carkass; Which as say the divines of the Hebrews, is left to the
power of the demon *Zazel*, of whom it is said in the Scripture, *Thou shalt eat
dust all thy daies;* and elsewhere, *The dust of the earth is his bread.* Now
man was created of the dust of the earth, whence also that Demon is called
the lord of flesh, and blood." [61] This is precisely the part played by Zazel in
Blake's poem. Myratana, Tiriel's queen, is dead:

> *. . . he began to dig a grave with his aged hands;*
> *But Heuxos call'd a Son of Zazel to dig their mother a grave.*[62]

No wonder that Tiriel, the natural man, blind to spiritual things, is mocked by Zazel and his sons, who "throw dirt at him" as he wanders blindly toward his grave, beset by all the terrors of bodily corruption that appal those who have no knowledge of "the immortal man that cannot die."

Less explicable is the statement that it is Tiriel himself who has "enslav'd the sons of Zazel." Tiriel's sons, addressing the tyrant, say:

> *Old Cruelty, desist! & let us dig a grave for thee.*
> *Thou hast refus'd our charity, thou hast refus'd our food,*
>
> .   .   .
>
> *"Chusing to wander like a Son of Zazel in the rocks.*
> *Why dost thou curse? is not the curse now come upon your head?*
> *Was it not you enslav'd the sons of Zazel? & they have curs'd,*
> *And now you feel it. . . ."* [63]

The same accusation is later repeated by Zazel himself: " 'Twas thou that chain'd thy brother Zazel." [64] The curse "dust shalt thou eat," etc., which condemns Zazel and his army to be consumers of corpses, was uttered in Eden by the God who cursed the serpent with the words "Upon thy belly shalt thou go, and dust shalt thou eat all the days of thy life." This curse immediately precedes the curse of death laid upon man: "In the sweat of thy face shalt thou eat bread, till thou return unto the ground; for out of it wast thou taken: for dust thou art, and unto dust shalt thou return." [65] It is not, according to esoteric tradition, the supreme God who declares that man is dust of the earth; "Adam is only The Natural Man & not the Soul or Imagination." [66] Blake, in saying that it was Tiriel who enslaved Zazel, is therefore implicitly identifying Tiriel with the tyrant demiurge who cursed the serpent in Eden—his brother, as Blake astonishingly affirms.

Blake is here venturing into the forbidden realms of demonology according to the magical tradition. Agrippa quotes Origen and other Christian authors, besides Hebrew sources, in support of the view that the fallen angels—at least certain of them—may at some time be saved. Blake has evidently seized eagerly upon this fruitful tradition, later expanded in *The Marriage of Heaven and Hell*, where he denounces the morality that has made outcasts of the devils, the Titans, and other spiritual forces not in themselves either good or evil. He develops the myth of the dust-eating serpent subject to the tyranny of the Demiurge in the relationship between Orc and Urizen, who does, literally, enslave his "brother" and force him into serpent form until he frees himself in the final regeneration of man. In Zazel we have the first appearance of this important and bold train of thought; and also a clue to its source—or one of its sources—in the writings of Agrippa and the magicians on the subject of demons. Jung has introduced the idea of the bipolarity of all archetypal energies; but this bipolarity was already understood in both the practice and theory of magic; and every one of Blake's gods, or Zoas, is likewise rendered good or evil by spiritual circumstances.

Tiriel, then, is the enslaver of Zazel; therefore he is the God of the Old Testament whom Blake identifies with Zeus and with the demiurge of Hermetic and Gnostic traditions, who is the creator of this world and of natural man, "a very cruel being." Tiriel is called "old Cruelty"; and he foreshadows the later figure of Urizen, whom he resembles in his "aged ignorance," his tyranny, his blindness,[67] his philosophy of scientific materialism, and his belief that "the spectre is the man. The rest is only delusion and fancy." The ruin and desolation that Urizen brings upon his world and his children by his errors is foreshadowed by the cursing of Tiriel, which brings catastrophe upon his sons and daughters.

As Tiriel, led by Hela, approaches his grave, the terrors of corruption beset him:

> She, howling, led him over mountains & thro' frighted vales,
> Till to the caves of Zazel they approach'd at even tide.
> Forth from their caves Old Zazel & his sons ran; when they saw
> Their tyrant prince blind, & his daughter howling & leading him,
> They laugh'd & mocked; some threw dirt & stones as they pass'd
> by;
>
> But when Tiriel turn'd around & rais'd his awful voice,
> Some fled away; but Zazel stood still, & thus begun:
> "Bald tyrant, wrinkled, cunning, listen to Zazel's chains!
>
> 'Twas thou that chain'd thy brother Zazel! where are now thine
> eyes?
> Shout, beautiful daughter of Tiriel! thou singest a sweet song!
>
> .   .   .
>
> Thy crown is bald, old man; the sun will dry thy brains away,
> And thou wilt be as foolish as thy foolish brother Zazel."

> *The blind man heard, & smote his breast, & trembling passed on.*
> *They threw dirt after them . . .*[68]

Zazel's "Where are now thine eyes?" and (two lines further on) "Where are you going?" are not the sadistic taunting of the mutilated Gloucester, but are spoken in just contempt for the selfhood blind to eternity that must go down to the grave it fears; for to the ego its own dissolution is the ultimate horror. Symbolic age and symbolic blindness cannot be occasions of pity, as can natural age or blindness; Zazel's taunts are not cruel but just. The figure of the Traveller in *The Gates of Paradise* is the contrasting figure; he "hasteneth in the Evening" because he knows where he is going:

> *But when once I did descry*
> *The Immortal Man that cannot Die,*
> *Thro' evening shades I haste away*
> *To close the Labours of my Day.*[69]

As Agrippa himself writes:

> The body returnes to the earth from whence it was, & the spirit returnes to God that gave it; which *Lucretius* hath expressed in these verses:

> *What came from earth to earth returnes again;*
> *What came from God, returnes from whence it came.*[70]

There is a dramatic chapter in Agrippa's work, entitled "What concerning man after death, diverse Opinions." [71] From this chapter Blake has taken so much of the landscape of *Tiriel* that it would be a not impossible theory that the wanderings of the tyrant after the ruin of his palace (the body) are a post-mortem phantasy. Such a notion would occur very naturally to Blake as a subject for a poem, for all Swedenborg's visions are of the illusory heavens and hells of souls in the world of the dead. But I do not wish to press this interpretation; it is of little importance whether Tiriel's wanderings in the realms of the subjective occur before, at, or after death. All that need be said is that Blake has drawn freely upon Agrippa's account of the post-mortem state. The evil soul, he says, is punished by the law of *Adrastia*, "viz, an inevitable power of divine laws, by which the courses to come, is recompensed to every one according to the reason and merits of his former life; so as he who unjustly ruled in the former life, in the other life should relapse into a servile state." So Tiriel the tyrant falls into the hands of Ijim, who uses the tyrant as a slave:

> *"Come! I will lead thee on thy way & use thee as a scoff."*
>
>   .   .   .
>
> *"Ay! now thou art discover'd, I will use thee like a slave."*
>
> *When Tiriel heard the words of Ijim, he sought not to reply:*
> *He knew 'twas vain, for Ijim's words were as the voice of Fate.*[72]

Tiriel recognizes the law of *Adrastia*, which decrees that the tyrant must become the slave.

Northrop Frye first traced Ijim to his source.[73] The reference is to Swedenborg's *True Christian Religion*, and Ijim personifies "the diabolical love of self":

> . . . the various Lusts [of this love of self] appear in Hell, at a Distance, like various Kinds of wild Beasts; some like Foxes and Leopards; some like Wolves and Tygers, and some like Crocodiles and venomous Serpents; and that the Desarts where they live consist solely of huge Heaps of Stone, or of barren Sand, with Bogs interspersed, full of croaking Frogs; and that dismal Birds fly, and make a mournful Skreeking over their miserable Abodes. These are the Ochim, Tziim, and Ijim, mentioned in the Prophecies of the Old Testament, where the Love of Dominion arising from the Love of Self is spoken of.[74]

This is, of course, Tiriel's spiritual state. However, there is another passage, describing "the hell which contained the emperors of emperors and kings of kings," which explains more precisely why Ijim is called Tiriel's "brother," who can yet in turn tyrannize over him. The inhabitants of these hells appear

> like various Kinds of wild Beasts with fierce and savage Eyes. In like Manner . . . there appeared terrible Birds of Night called *Ochim* and *Ijim*, flying about them, being the representative Images of their Phantasies. Hence was discovered the true Nature of political and ecclesiastical Self-love, that the former would make its

Votaries desirous of being Emperors, and the latter of being Gods; and that under the Influence of such Love Men wish and strive to attain the Objects of their Desires, so far as they are left free and unrestrained . . .[75]

If Tiriel is a figure of political tyranny, Ijim is his "brother," ecclesiastical tyranny, who has power even over a king. "Ijim shall rend thy feeble joints, thou tempter of dark Ijim!"[76] Ijim

> . . . *scorns*
> *To smite thee in the form of helpless age & eyeless policy*[77]

but uses him "as a scoff." If these passages have a specific reference to the mutual tyrannical hate existing between the two evils of kingly and ecclesiastical tyranny, the part played by Ijim as the exposer of Tiriel and his denouncer to his sons at his own palace becomes clear. The rebel sons themselves ". . . knew 'twas vain to strive with Ijim; they bow'd & silent stood."[78] His ecclesiastical character would also explain why the sons

> . . . *knew 'twas vain,*
> *Both spear & shield were useless & the coat of iron mail,*
> *When Ijim stretch'd his mighty arm . . .*[79]

What seems mere wordy fulmination proves to be quite specific.

A similar passage in Agrippa, in which is described the fate of the evil soul, wandering in hell, suggests the wanderings of Tiriel "over mountains and thro' frighted vales." The evil soul there becomes the prey of its own hallucinations:

Then are represented to the phantastick reason those species, which are so much the more turbulent and furious, by how much in such souls there lies hid an intellectuall spark more or lesse covered, or altogether extinct, into which are then by evil spirits conveyed species either most false, or terrible. . . . But they are most cruelly tortured in the irascible faculty with the hatred of an imaginary evil, into the perturbations whereof, as also false suspitions, and most horrible Phantasmes they then fall, and there are represented to them sad representations; sometimes of the heaven falling on their head, sometimes of being consumed by the violence of flames, sometimes of being drowned in a gulfe, sometimes of being swallowed up into the earth, sometimes of being changed into divers kinds of beasts, sometimes of being torn and devoured by ugly monsters, sometimes of being carried abroad, through woods, seas, fire, air, and through fearfull infernall places.[80]

Such are Tiriel's wanderings, and he is literally "carried abroad" through forests by the demon Ijim: "Ijim rais'd him up & bore him on his shoulders." [81] The souls, Agrippa continues, "are thereby tormented, as if these things did really happen to them, which truely are not reall, but only species of them apprehended in imagination: even so do horrible representations of sins terrifie those souls after death as if they were in a dream and the guilt of wickedness drives them headlong through divers places; which therefore *Orpheus* calls the people of dreams, saying, the gates of Pluto cannot be unlocked; within is a people of dreams." [82] These are the hells; and they are illusory, "States that are not, but ah! seem to be," as Blake later wrote in *Milton*.[83]

Such disincarnate souls may impress their fantasies upon the consciousness of the living, in the form of apparitions:

Such wicked souls therefore enjoying no good places, when wandring in an Aeriall body they represent any form to our sight, are called hags, and goblins, inoffensive to them that are good, but hurtfull to the wicked, appearing one while in thinner bodies, another time in grosser, in the shapes of divers animals, and monsters, whose conditions they had in their life time, as sings the Poet [84]

> *Then divers forms and shapes of brutes appear;*
> *For he becomes a tyger, swine, and bear,*
> *A skalie dragon, and a lionesse,*
> *Or doth from fire a dreadfull noise expresse;*
> *He doth transmute himself to divers looks,*
> *To fire, wild beasts, and into running brooks.*[85]

This passage echoes very closely the account given by Ijim of how Tiriel, as "the tormentor of dark Ijim," appeared to him in a series of apparitions that closely follow the list given by Agrippa. Undoubtedly the idea that Tiriel could be a "fiend" and haunt his brother comes from Agrippa; Ijim calls the sons from the palace with the words "Heuxos, come forth! I here have brought the fiend that troubles Ijim," [86] and he then describes the shape-shiftings of this protean goblin:

This is the hypocrite that sometimes roars a dreadful lion;
Then I have rent his limbs & left him rotting in the forest
For birds to eat; but I have scarce departed from the place,
But like a tyger he would come: & so I rent him too.
Then like a river he would seek to drown me in his waves;
But soon I buffetted the torrent: anon like to a cloud
Fraught with the swords of lightening; but I brav'd the vengeance
too.

Then he would creep like a bright serpent, till around my neck,
While I was sleeping, he would twine: I squeez'd his pois'nous soul.
Then like a toad, or like a newt, would whisper in my ears;
Or like a rock stood in my way, or like a pois'nous shrub.
At last I caught him in the form of Tiriel, blind & old,
And so I'll keep him! . . .[87]

These are the traditional metamorphoses of Proteus, with slight variation; and Proteus is matter, the same *prima materia* of all transformation that gives Tiriel his name. This symbol is not only alchemical but is given by Bacon in his tract *On the Wisdom of the Ancients*. An examination of Blake's list is revealing, and shows how deliberately he worked with his symbols. Blake's list of metamorphoses is: lion, tiger, river, lightning cloud, serpent, toad or newt, rock, poisonous shrub, Tiriel himself. This is not Agrippa's list, which contains tiger, swine, bear, dragon, lioness, fire, running water. The model of all later accounts of Proteus is, of course, to be found in the *Odyssey*, where Phorcys is captured by Menelaus after he has become, in turn, stream, fire, lion, leopard, boar, dragon, and tree.

Of Blake's list, the lion, river, lightning, and serpent (or dragon) are common to all; the tiger appears only in Agrippa; the tree or "poisonous shrub" appears in the *Odyssey;* this leaves the toad or newt unexplained, and the stone.

Let it not be supposed that Blake simply invented these additional metamorphoses; that would have been entirely contrary to his method of working. The stone comes from Ovid's account of Proteus in the *Metamorphoses*, which Blake had certainly read.[88] Ovid's list is lion, boar, serpent, bull, tree, stone, fire, and water, which contains all Blake's images except the tiger (this comes from Agrippa) and the toad.

Whence comes the toad that "would whisper in mine ears"? It is the form taken by Milton's Satan when he first tempts Eve with evil dreams:

20a Adam and Eve sleeping: illustration (c. 1808) for *Paradise Lost*
Notice the toad "close at the eare of Eve."

[20a]

> . . . *him there they found*
> *Squat like a Toad, close at the eare of* Eve;
> *Assaying by his Devilish art to reach*
> *The Organs of her Fancie, and with them forge*
> *Illusions as he list, Phantasms and Dreams.*[89]

The parallel with Agrippa's account of the operation of fantasy, and the form in which an evil spirit approaches a living man through his dream hallucinations, is striking; and we see that Blake's single departure from the classical list of the metamorphoses of Proteus was not made in accordance with any personal whim. He gives us a plain clue to the source of the toad by describing its whispering in the ear of Ijim as he slept. Blake's purpose was neither fanciful nor arbitrary: he wishes further to define Tiriel's nature by

64

20b Jesus and Satan, or "The First Temptation": illustration (1816?) for *Paradise Regained*

pointing to his affinity with Satan, who is, in all Blake's later writings, the selfhood itself—"Satan the selfhood" is no less an invariable term than "Jesus the Divine Humanity." This conception of Satan was already forming when he implicitly identified Tiriel, dominated by the love of self, with Milton's Satan.

Tiriel's identification with Satan (this time as the serpent) is again stressed in his last speech of self-realization. He has been formed into a distorted egoistic tyrant by his education,

> *Compell'd to pray repugnant & to humble the immortal spirit*
> *Till I am subtil as a serpent in a paradise.*[90]

This is Tiriel's single mention of "the immortal spirit," denied to the very point of death. With his belated realization of his own monstrosity, he curses Har the earthborn, and dies: "Mistaken father of a lawless race, my voice is past."

Blake was not a hater of old men. *Jerusalem* closes on a vision of

> *. . . the wonders Divine*
> *Of Human Imagination throughout all the Three Regions immense*
> *Of Childhood, Manhood & Old Age . . .*[91]

A few months before the end of his life he wrote: "I have been very near the Gates of Death & have returned very weak & an Old Man feeble and tottering, but not in Spirit & Life, not in The Real Man The Imagination which Liveth for Ever. In that I am stronger & stronger as this Foolish Body decays."[92] Job is an old man, illuminated by imagination; and so is the Traveller who hastens in the evening. But symbolically, old age stands for the temporal, which alone ages. In eternity nothing ages; the "eternal man" "cannot die." Only the temporal selfhood can grow old, for it alone is built up in time, nourished on memories, and its final fate—whether in man or institution, church or state—however long it may totter on the verge of dissolution, can only be death. The imaginative wisdom is ever young and its symbol is the child, whose eternal nature outlasts all the dynasties of old men and their amassed experience. The child, symbol of "the human existence itself," comes into the world with every man, before the amassing of memories and the construction of an aging selfhood begins. Angels appear [20b] in the form of a child; but Satan is only old and experienced, as in *Paradise Regained* Milton shows him as an old man. Thus Tiriel stands as the symbol of all the bodies of tradition, kingdoms, and institutions that seek perpetuity in Mnetha's kingdom, where records of the past are preserved like papyrus and mummies in the dry sands of the spiritual Egypt. But the long continuance of the temporal never leads to eternity, and is, indeed, only an obstacle to the realization of the world of Imagination, which can be entered only by becoming "as a little child."

Part II

The Myth of the Soul

This second part follows out a theme Blake learned from Neoplatonic sources: the myth of the soul which "descends" from an eternal world or state, undergoes experience and suffering in the world of generation, and returns at last to her native purity. The figure of the soul is symbolized in a series of female figures, each a little more complex than the last—Thel, Lyca, Oothoon, Vala, and Jerusalem. All these experience descent, suffering, and return. The first chapter describes Blake's last formulation of a myth that had held his imagination throughout his poetic life; for in 1821 he illustrated what was evidently, for him, a key work, Porphyry's treatise *On the Cave of the Nymphs*. The reversal of chronological order is justified by the fact that this treatise, published in Thomas Taylor's translation in 1788, seems to have been the first of the formulations of the myth through which Blake came to know the ancient Orphic teaching, so profound in its wisdom and so beautiful in the formal terms of its mythology.

In *The Book of Thel* we see Blake's first work written under Porphyry's influence; and in each of his successive returns to the theme we can trace some new tributary that enriched his thought and kindled his imagination. In *Jerusalem* the story of the soul is Christianized but retains traces of the earlier myths out of which grew this latest expression of Blake's mature spiritual insight and perfected artistry. Porphyry's myth of the cave likewise provides a symbolic structure for the theme of the descent and return of souls, expressed by Blake in the mythology of his specters generated through the agency of Los and Enitharmon.

CHAPTER 3

The Sea of Time and Space

Blake has not hitherto been regarded as belonging to the Greek Revival, even though several of his closest friends – Flaxman, Fuseli, and Cumberland – were among its moving spirits. There is nothing neoclassical in Blake's imagery; his love of Gothic sculpture and architecture is apparent in his early designs (for Blair's *Grave*, for Young's *Night Thoughts*, and in many of the pages of *Songs of Experience*), and his later writings and designs are increasingly Christian in theme. He did not name his gods from Greek mythology; and this fact has obscured the extent of his borrowing of their stories. There are a few early drawings after Stuart's and Revett's *Antiquities of Athens;* but neither from these nor from the handful of drawings on such conventional classical themes as the Judgment of Paris [21, 22] (1817) [1] or the Infant Hercules would it be possible to say that Blake shared Flaxman's enthusiasm for the Greek art that had so evidently formed him. But if we look more deeply, we shall find that Flaxman's debt to the Greeks, so apparent in his linear style, his preoccupation with drapery, his interest in Homer, is certainly no greater than Blake's. Flaxman's debt to Greece, however, can be seen at a glance, while Blake's, no less essential, is masked by a style (both of verse and of drawing) formed by other influences.

Foster Damon long ago suggested – and the suggestion has never been questioned – that Neoplatonism was a formative influence upon Blake's thought; he also surmised that Blake probably knew Thomas Taylor, the translator and exponent of Plato and the Neoplatonists, and that Taylor was Sipsop the Pythagorean, of *An Island in the Moon*. Indeed, there is reason to suppose Blake knew Taylor well and for a time shared his enthusiastic desire to see a revival of the philosophy of Plotinus and his disciples. From about 1789, when the Neoplatonic influence makes its first unmistakable appearance, for some six or seven years Neoplatonism is still a major influence. One may see reflected in Blake's work the successive publications of "the English Pagan." Taylor was a professed Platonist, polytheist, and anti-

Christian, and, in the cause of that philosophy, was fired with a proselytiz-
ing zeal often reminiscent of Blake's own.

Blake may have met Taylor through Cumberland, who knew both
men well, or through Flaxman, at whose house Taylor delivered twelve
lectures on Platonism, presumably before 1787, when Flaxman departed for
Italy, there to remain for several years. Another link—one that may, moreover, have led to Blake's later estrangement from Taylor—is Mary Wollstonecraft, whom Blake met at the hospitable house of the publisher Joseph
Johnson. Mary Wollstonecraft was Johnson's reader and French translator
during the years before her departure for Paris in 1792; and she was also, for
a time, a lodger in the household of Thomas Taylor. Taylor was shocked by
her avowed principles. Her *Vindication of the Rights of Woman* was
published in 1792, Blake's *Visions of the Daughters of Albion*—a far more
eloquent plea for those rights, and perhaps a personal tribute to Mary—in
1793. In the same year Taylor published his *Vindication of the Rights of
Brutes*. His championship of animals, in this answer to Thomas Paine's
Rights of Man, was probably sincere—his love of animals was such
that his friends whispered that he literally accepted the doctrine of metempsychosis (in view of the subtlety of his philosophic thought this is
unlikely)—but he introduced some harsh criticism of his former lodger.
Taylor's attitude to Mary Wollstonecraft is recorded also in a letter to

21 The Judgment of
Paris: design by Flax-
man (1805) for the
Iliad

George Cumberland.[2] Taylor criticizes Cumberland's novel, *The Captive of the Castle of Sennaar*, wherein is described a Utopia of "free" love, as

> more entertaining than instructive, more ingenious than moral. I will not, indeed I cannot suppose that you would undertake to defend lasciviousness publickly: and yet to me it is as much patronized by the conduct of your Sophisms as by the works of Mrs. Wollstonecraft. You will doubtless excuse the freedom of this Opinion, when you consider that as I am a professed Platonist, love with me is *true* only in proportion as it is pure; or, in other words, in proportion as it rises above the gratification of our brutal part.

(No doubt Taylor was the more irritated because Cumberland's Utopians are of Greek descent.) Mona Wilson further suggests that Blake had Taylor in mind when he, too, wrote to George Cumberland in quite the opposite vein. "Now you will, I hope, shew all the family of Antique Borers that Peace & Plenty & Domestic Happiness is the Source of Sublime Art, & prove to the Abstract Philosophers that Enjoyment & not Abstinence is the food of Intellect."[3] Sipsop has become an Antique Borer.

Taylor is to this day known and admired among students of the Perennial Philosophy; A.E. called him "the uncrowned king." For all their stiff and polysyllabic style, Coleridge delighted in his works;[4] Shelley

22 The Judgment of Paris: drawing by Blake (1805?)

Note the figure of Eris (strife). See p. 394, n. 34.

possessed a copy of his Plato; through the enthusiasm of Bronson Alcott and
Emerson, he became a formative influence on the New England school of
Transcendentalists; and Yeats was a student of his writings and translations. To these poets the fact that academic circles may have looked coldly
upon this self-taught scholar,[5] or that he was more concerned with the truth
of the philosophy of the hymns of Orpheus than with their date or their
authorship, had no importance. Taylor understood Platonic philosophy as
few in modern Europe have understood it. In his foreword to *A Dissertation
on the Eleusinian and Bacchic Mysteries* he wrote of "a philosophy of all
others most venerable and august":

> As to the philosophy, by whose assistance these mysteries are de-
> veloped, it is coeval with the universe itself; and however its continuity
> may be broken by opposing systems, it will make its appearance
> at different periods of time, as long as the sun himself shall con-
> tinue to illuminate the world. It has, indeed, and may hereafter, be
> violently assaulted by delusive opinions; but the opposition will be
> just as imbecil as the waves of the sea against a temple built on a
> rock, which majestically pours them back,
>> Broken and vanquish'd foaming to the main.[6]

It is the *philosophia perennis*. In 1788, while Taylor was no doubt preparing
his *Dissertation*, Blake was etching *All Religions Are One*. It is hard to
believe that these two dedicated servants of the one true religion had not
discussed matters of such central concern to both of them. Did Taylor for a
time make a convert of Blake to his Platonic polytheism? Of his proselytiz-
ing zeal there is no doubt: "Impetuous ignorance is thundering at the
bulwarks of philosophy, and her sacred retreats are in danger of being
demolished, through our feeble resistance. Rise, then, my friends, and the
victory will be ours. The foe is indeed numerous, but, at the same time,
feeble: and the weapons of truth, in the hands of vigorous union, descend
with irresistible force, and are fatal wherever they fall."[7] Is there in these
words an echo of the voice of Blake? Or was it Blake who was echoing
Taylor when in 1804 he wrote a countermanifesto that is at the same time a
recantation? Why should Blake renounce Plato (whom he names together
with Homer) unless he had at one time been of his party? "Rouze up, O
Young Men of the New Age! . . . We do not want either Greek or Roman
Models if we are but just & true to our own Imaginations, those Worlds of
Eternity in which we shall live for ever in Jesus our Lord."[8]

Meanwhile, Blake had derived from Taylor's works on Orphism and the Neoplatonists the foundations of his own system of what one may call Christian polytheism.

In 1787–the most probable year of *An Island in the Moon*–Taylor published the first edition of his *Mystical Hymns of Orpheus* and Plotinus' *Concerning the Beautiful*. His translation of Proclus' *Mathematical Commentaries*, containing his essay *On the Restoration of the Platonic Theology*, appeared the following year, and in 1790, the *Dissertation on the Mysteries*. During the years 1792–93 his *Phaedrus, Cratylus, Phaedo, Parmenides*, and *Timaeus* appeared. During the same years, 1787–93, Blake was no less active, having written the *Songs of Innocence* (1789), *Thel* (1789), the *Marriage* (1790), *Visions of the Daughters of Albion* and *America* (1793), and *Songs of Innocence and Experience* (1793–94). In 1794–95 Taylor published his *Five Books of Plotinus* and his translation of Apuleius' *Cupid and Psyche*. These works are the essential texts of Blake's Platonic studies.

As late as 1799 Blake's enthusiasm for the Greeks was still active; for he wrote in a letter that his "Genius or Angel" guided his inspiration in fulfillment of "the purpose for which alone I live, which is . . . to renew the lost Art of the Greeks." [9] These are very different words from his later diatribes against the classics in general and Plato in particular, as the source of the rational thought which has led to the materialist civilization of Western Europe, "The Stolen and Perverted Writings of Homer & Ovid, of Plato & Cicero, which all Men ought to contemn." [10] In his later years Blake seems to have recovered from this view of Plato, for Crabb Robinson reports the warmth with which he acknowledged that Socrates was "a sort of brother"; and Samuel Palmer told Gilchrist that Blake was "a Platonist in politics."

It is not possible that Blake's reaction against Plato was merely a secondary result of an estrangement from Taylor: this would be an absurd suggestion to make of a mind of Blake's quality. At most such an estrangement may have lent animus to judgment. The explanation probably lies rather in the fact that Blake read the Neoplatonists before he read Plato, and the *Phaedrus, Cratylus, Phaedo, Parmenides*, and *Timaeus* before he read the more purely discursive works. Neoplatonism stems from one side of Plato–all that he inherited, through Pythagoras and the Orphic tradition, from the "revealed" wisdom of antiquity. Blake is neither the first nor the last reader of Plato's works to have been bewildered by the presence of two, in many respects contradictory, aspects of his thought–*logos* and *mythos;*

23 The sea of time and space: the Arlington Court tempera painting (1821)

and he rejected the former with no less vigor than he continued to embrace the latter.

Taylor's interpretation of Plato was essentially that of the Neoplatonists and, above all, of Proclus; and in Blake's judgments of Plato, both favorable and adverse, we may see the result of an education in Greek philosophy received through the writings and probably the conversation of "the modern Plethon."

As Blake grew older, he moved toward a more explicit Christianity; but it was an inclusive, not an exclusive, conception of the Everlasting Gospel to which he held first and last. Already in *Milton* he had begun to Christianize his mythology, and in *Jerusalem* this tendency continues. But that he never became in an exclusive sense Christian there is remarkable evidence in one of the most beautiful of his late paintings, the tempera discovered at Arlington Court in 1949 and provisionally entitled "The Sea of [23] Time and Space" or "The Cycle of the Life of Man." The date is plainly written under Blake's signature—1821; it is, in fact, a fine example of Blake's late and mature style, the style of the Dante illustrations and the Job engravings.

All the symbols of the Arlington Court painting are familiar to Blake scholars: [11] there are the urns, the looms and furnace, the cave, the sea, the sun pulsing with the "innumerable company of the heavenly host." But in this painting we have clear evidence that Blake invented none of these; it is based upon Porphyry's treatise on Homer's *Cave of the Nymphs*, to which Blake has added details from the *Odyssey* and from Platonic sources. It is a profoundly considered representation of the essentials of Neoplatonism. This work, painted with such evident love, such wealth of symbolic detail, makes it plain that he never forgot a work which had given him his own essential myths.

Porphyry's treatise was first published in 1788, in the second volume of Taylor's translation of Proclus' *Mathematical Commentaries*. It forms part of an essay *On the Restoration of the Platonic Theology by the Later Platonists*—Taylor's own Platonic apologia. The *Cave of the Nymphs* was republished in 1823; but Blake must have read Taylor's *Porphyry* on its first appearance, for there are unmistakable allusions to its symbolism in *The Book of Thel* (1789).

The living spirits of light and water, reborn in their everlasting youth from Blake's imagination, are age-old. They enact the perpetual cycle of the descent and return of souls between an eternal and a temporal world, and the journey through life, under the symbol of a crossing of the sea. Of this journey, the voyage of Odysseus, his dangers and adventures, his departure and his home-coming to Ithaca, is the type and symbol. In Blake's painting the figure on the sea-verge is Odysseus, newly landed on his native shore, in the cove of the sea god Phorcys, close to the Cave of the Nymphs. His dark, clever face is a highly convincing "vision" of that wary-wise Greek. In the distance, sheltered by trees, we see the tall classical pillars of his house. Behind him, and still unseen by Odysseus, stands Athena, depicted not with helmet and gorgon-shield, but as the Divine Wisdom, a figure somewhat resembling the Beatrice of Blake's Dante illustrations. Odysseus is in the act [24] of throwing something out to sea, with his face averted. What has he

24 Beatrice in her car: illustration no. 88 (1826) for Dante's *Paradiso*

thrown? Out at sea a nymph or goddess has caught a scarf-like wreath that spirals upward above her head, dissolving into radiant cloud. She is Leucothea, or Ino, who lent Odysseus her sea-girdle by which he came safe ashore – not on the coast of Ithaca but on the shore of Phaeacia. Blake has combined the two accounts[12] of the hero's coming safe to land: from the landing on Ithaca (*Odyssey*, Book XIII) come Athena and Phorcys and the Cave of the Nymphs; from the Phaeacian landing (Book V) the episode of Leucothea's girdle. Odysseus had been shipwrecked, and alone survived in the tempest:

> *But Cadmus' beauteous daughter (Ino once,*
> *Now named Leucothea) saw him. . . .*[13]

Leucothea takes pity on the hero, and advises him to swim for the shore:

> *Thus do (for I account thee not unwise)*
> *Thy garments putting off, let drive thy raft*
> *As the winds will, then, swimming, strive to reach*
> *Phaeacia, where thy doom is to escape.*
> *Take this. This ribbon bind beneath thy breast,*
> *Celestial texture. Thenceforth ev'ry fear*
> *Of death dismiss, and, laying once thy hands*
> *On the firm continent, unbind the zone,*
> *Which thou shalt cast far distant from the shore*
> *Into the Deep, turning thy face away.*[14]

[25]

It is this throwing with averted face that Blake has represented in Odysseus' strange posture; for when he was safe on land,

> *. . . loosing from beneath*
> *His breast the zone divine, he cast it far*
> *Into the brackish stream, and a huge wave*
> *Returning bore it downward to the sea,*
> *Where Ino caught it. . . .*[15]

Guided by Leucothea and two lesser sea-spirits, male and female, are four dark-colored horses breasting the waves out at sea. Here again Blake is literally following Homer, who in a long simile compares the ship that carried Odysseus from Phaeacia to Ithaca to a team of four stallions:

> *She, as four harness'd stallions o'er the plain*
> *Shooting together at the scourge's stroke,*
> *Toss high their manes, and rapid scour along,*
> *So mounted she the waves. . . .*[16]

Whatever the significance in Greek mythology of Leucothea's girdle, Blake takes it to be the physical body, an integument "lent" by the goddess of the watery, or physical, world, which at death man must return to her. The girdle dissolves into cloud, for cloud is Blake's constant symbol of the physical body:

> *And these black bodies and this sunburnt face*
> *Is but a cloud . . .*[17]

25 "All radiant on the raft the Goddess stood": design by Flaxman (1805?) for the *Odyssey*
The theme Blake incorporated into his painting was current in his circle.

He depicts it as cloud because he took it to mean the body.

Behind Odysseus, Athena's hand reaches to the lowest steps of the staircase that ascends to the sun's shining realm. Both goddesses are pointing the way to the eternal world, though for the moment Odysseus sees neither of them—Leucothea by her own command, Athena because (as Homer tells) he has not yet recognized her. The body, like the soul, returns to eternity, the one as a dissolving cloud, the other as "the true Man."

Against the upward gesture of the two goddesses is balanced the violent descending energy expressed in the groups of figures on the right, who follow the course of the stream that issues from the cave and flows downward to enter the sea with the force of a river in spate. But here it is necessary to give the text of Homer's account of the strange cave near whose entrance Odysseus arrived at last upon his native shore:

> *High at the head a branching olive grows,*
> *And crowns the pointed cliffs with shady boughs.*
> *A cavern pleasant, though involv'd in night,*
> *Beneath it lies, the Naiades delight:*
> *Where bowls and urns, of workmanship divine*
> *And massy beams in native marble shine;*
> *On which the Nymphs amazing webs display,*
> *Of purple hue, and exquisite array.*
> *The busy bees, within the urns secure*
> *Honey delicious, and like nectar pure.*
> *Perpetual waters thro' the grotto glide,*
> *A lofty gate unfolds on either side;*
> *That to the north is pervious by mankind;*
> *The sacred south t'immortals is consign'd.*[18]

We find each detail of this strange and beautiful imagery reproduced in Blake's painting. The entrance of the cave stands high in a cliff face, on which grow tufted olive trees. Above are two groups of small figures, a naiad pouring water from an urn or water pot, and a pair of reclining lovers. In the deepest and highest recess stand winged female figures bearing on their heads "bowls or urns." Below this group other nymphs are weaving on a loom. Three hold shuttles in their upraised hands. On the left a reclining nymph holds up a coil of yarn upon her wrists, while a second winds it off to pass to the weavers at the loom. On the right two others are measuring off the finished fabric.

From the recesses of the cave flows a stream that trickles down over

26 The chariot of the sun: detail (upper left corner) of the Arlington Court picture
(1821)

the steps, but gathers force as it rushes below the lowest steps of the cave, to
the sea. In the very mouth of this rushing flood a last group of figures
consists of Phorcys, the "old man of the sea," and the three Fates, with
spindle, thread, and shears. The Fates are mentioned neither by Homer nor
by Porphyry – we shall presently consider why Blake introduces them
here – but the cove where Odysseus was put ashore in Ithaca is, according to
the Homeric story, dedicated to the sea god.

On the left, high above the sea and the clouds, there is yet another
sequence of distant figures. Here we see the radiant world of the immortals
that opens from the cave by its southern gate. The chariot of the sun is seen
surrounded by radiant spirits, scarcely distinguishable from the flames of
light that pulse from the creative fire. To the chariot four bright horses are
harnessed, groomed by female figures who seem to be restraining the "four   [26]
living creatures" – Blake's own Zoas, or energies of the soul – eager for their   [27]
journey; but in the car the god himself is sunk in sleep or deep drowsiness.
There are other significant figures, but here it is necessary to pass from
description to exposition.

Odysseus, for the Neoplatonists, symbolized man, whose progress
from birth to death, through material existence, is likened to the hero's
perilous adventures. The sea was universally taken in the ancient world as a
symbol of the material world, on account of its mutable flux. Blake's phrase
"the sea of time & space" [19] is therefore a traditional piece of Neoplatonic
symbolism:

> the person of Ulysses, in the Odyssey, represents to us a man, who
> passes in a regular manner, over the dark and stormy sea of genera-

27 The four starry ones represented at the top of Blake's illustration (1808) for *Paradise Lost:* Adam and Eve led by Michael out of Paradise

Here the four Zoas or angels are represented with horse vehicles.

tion; and thus, at length, arrives at that region where tempests and seas are unknown, and finds a nation, who

Ne'er knew salt, or heard the billows roar.

Indeed, he who is conscious of the delusions of the present life, and the enchantments of this material house, in which his soul is detained, like Ulysses in the irriguous cavern of Calypso, will, like him, continually bewail his captivity, and inly pine for a return to his native country.[20]

The stripping off of the ragged garments of mortality is an aspect of the symbol that Taylor often stressed; and the many instances in Blake's writings in which the body is compared to ragged or filthy garments, and that which is experienced in the body to "the rotten rags of memory," seem to echo Taylor's many allusions to the beggar's rags of which Odysseus divested himself when he returned to Ithaca: "a life in conjunction with body is contrary to nature, and is an impediment to intellectual energy.

Hence it is necessary to divest ourselves of the fleshy garments with which we are clothed, as Ulysses did of his ragged vestments, and no longer like a wretched mendicant, together with the indigence of body, put on our rags." [21] The discarding of the mortal rags is, in this composition, implicit in the throwing out to sea of the sea girdle.

This sea-crossing and its implicit parallel with the *Odyssey* Blake would also have found in Taylor's translation of *The Delphic Oracle upon Plotinus*.[22] Here it is Plotinus who has made the crossing of "Dire resounding Hyle's mighty flood":

> *Freed from those members that with deadly weight*
> *And stormy whirl inchain'd th[e]y soul of late:*
> *O'er lifes rough ocean thou hast gain'd that shore,*
> *Where storms molest, and change impairs no more;*
> *And struggling through its deeps with vig'rous mind,*
> *Pass'd the dark stream, and left base souls behind.*[23]

Plotinus, through his spiritual wisdom, has come in sight of the Islands of the Blessed, as Odysseus reached Ithaca through his courage; and it may well be that Blake himself, in 1821, chose this theme because he, too, felt that for him the buffetings of the long voyage were almost over, and that, guided by the Divine Wisdom, he had come within sight of the golden country

> *Where streams ambrosial in immortal course*
> *Irriguous flow, from Deity their source.*
> *No dark'ning clouds those happy skies assail,*
> *And the calm aether knows no stormy gale.*
> *Supremely blest thy lofty soul abides*
> *Where Minos and his brother judge presides;*
> *Just Aeacus, and Plato the divine,*
> *And fair Pythag'ras there exalted shine*
> *With other souls who form the general choir,*
> *Of love immortal, and of pure desire.*[24]

But it is the cave itself whose symbolism forms the main theme of Porphyry's treatise and of Blake's painting. Porphyry says that the cave is not an invention of Homer's, and that long before Homer's time such caves were sacred places, consecrated especially to the female powers, the nymphs: "the ancients, indeed, very properly consecrated a cave to the world," and later, he says, men established "temples, groves and altars to the celestial gods . . . and to the subterranean deities pits and cells; so to the world they dedicated caves and dens; as likewise to Nymphs, on account of the water which trickles, or is diffused, in caverns, over which the Naiades . . . preside." [25]

[28]
Ceres educated Proserpina and her nymphs in a cave; temples of Mithra, so Porphyry records, were caves watered by springs or fountains; and the Pythagoreans, and after them Plato, "showed that the world is a cavern and a den"—and here Porphyry quotes from the seventh book of the *Republic:* "Behold men as if dwelling in a subterraneous cavern, and in a den-like habitation, whose entrance is widely expanded to the admission

[76]
of the light through the whole cave."

The naiads preside over generation and dwell near perpetually flowing streams of water, "For we peculiarly call the Naiades, and the powers that preside over waters, Nymphs; and this term, also, is commonly applied to all souls descending into generation." [26] The cave is the place of generation. The river of life rises in the most secret depths of the world-cave, and like "Alph, the sacred river," runs through "caverns measureless to man, down to a sunless sea"—the sea of hyle,[27] remote from spiritual light.

The river-source of life in the depths of a cave is described in the Orphic Hymn to the Fates, who preside over the issuing flow. They, too, dwell where the waters of "the heavenly lake"

> *Burst from a fountain hid in depths of night*
> *And thro' a dark and stony cavern glide,*
> *A cave profound, invisible. . . .*[28]

It seems likely that it is by reason of this association of the Fates with the flow of waters from the world-cave that Blake felt it necessary to represent them in this composition, although Porphyry makes no mention of them. In Apuleius' legend Psyche's third task is to bring water from the sacred source of the river so that no mortal can approach.

Descending into her "bodily house," Psyche finds herself, on her first entry into the "valley" of earthly existence, "near the fall of a river"; [29] and

[29]
Blake represents Eve, in his illustration of the Genesis story, at her first creation, standing, like Psyche, by a waterfall whose remote source is invisible to us. Thus the Cave of the Nymphs and their fountains is an image both lovely and awe-inspiring, even terrible, since the river flows from inpenetrable darkness. "Through matter," Porphyry writes,

28 "The Soul exploring the recesses of the Grave": design for Blair's *Grave* (1808)

The cave or grave, following the Platonic philosophers, is this world. The male figure, above, appears to be (like Thel) "listening to the voices of the ground."

the world is obscure and dark; but through the connecting power, and orderly distribution of form, from which also it is called *world*, it is beautiful and delightful. Hence it may very properly be denominated a cave; as being lovely, indeed, to him who first enters into it. . . . but obscure to him who surveys its foundation, and examines it with an intellectual eye. So that its exterior and superficial parts are pleasant, but its interior and profound parts are obscure, and its very bottom is darkness itself.[30]

The small figure pouring water from an urn is an emblem of the female powers who pour out continually the waters of life. Water in itself is a symbol of the greatest possible significance. "What's water but the generated soul?"—and Yeats's definition sums up the teaching of Porphyry and his masters; for "souls descending into generation fly to moisture"—for

29 Eve, Adam, and the serpent (1799?)

Eve, encircled by the coils of the serpent matter, is represented "near the fall of a river."

which reason the water-loving naiads are not only the powers presiding over generation but the generated souls themselves. Heraclitus says that "moisture appears delightful and not deadly to souls," and that the lapse into generation (although this is in reality a death from eternity) is delightful to them. "Hence the poet calls those that are in generation *humid*, because they have souls which are *profoundly* steeped in moisture. On this account such souls delight in blood and humid seed; but water is the nutriment of the souls of plants." "It is necessary," Porphyry concludes,

> therefore, that souls, whether they are corporeal or incorporeal, while they attract to themselves body, and especially such as are about to be bound to blood and moist bodies, should verge to humidity, and be corporalized, in consequence of being drenched in moisture. . . . Souls that are lovers of body, by attracting a moist spirit, condense this humid vehicle like a cloud. . . .[31] But the pneumatic vehicle being condensed in these souls, becomes visible through an excess of moisture . . . But pure souls are averse from generation; so that, as Heraclitus says, *"a dry soul is the wisest."* Hence, here also, the spirit becomes moist and more aqueous through the desire of coition, the soul thus attracting a humid vapour through verging to generation. Souls, therefore, proceeding into generation, are the Nymphs called Naiades.[32]

To the Nymphs likewise, who preside over waters, a cavern, in which there are perpetually flowing streams, is adapted. Let, therefore, this present cavern be consecrated to souls, and, among the more partial powers, to nymphs, that preside over streams and fountains, and who, on this account, are called *fontal* and *Naiades*.[33]

So Porphyry concludes his exposition of the world-cave.

Two figures in the right foreground provide visible evidence that Blake was working not merely from Homer but from Porphyry. They illustrate Socrates' parable of the tubs, from the *Gorgias:*

the tubs are the desires. . . . the initiated, therefore, *i.e.* those that have a perfect knowledge, pour into the entire tub: for these have their tub full; or, in other words, have perfect virtue. But the uninitiated, viz. those that possess nothing perfect, have perforated tubs. For those that are in a state of servitude to desire always wish to fill it, and are more inflamed; and on this account they have perforated tubs, as being never full.[34]

In Hesiod, too, Porphyry says, "we find one tub closed, but the other opened by Pleasure, who scatters its contents everywhere." [35] These two conditions Blake has represented by two women. One, whose aspect is sober and resolute, has turned her back upon the swirling waters and begun to climb the steps of the cave, against the current of generation. In her right hand she carries a full bucket; and her left hand is raised toward the celestial world. She is the initiated soul, who is beginning her journey of re-ascent. Her upward progress is opposed, as Keynes observed, by the nymphs of the cave; for she is a "dry soul," and her progress is contrary to their nature and function.

In the extreme right of the foreground, the uninitiated soul dominated by desire lies deeply sunk in "deadly sleep," half immersed in the water, and reclining over her tub (or sieve) which lies on its side, the water lapping into it, forever unfilled. Her expression is one of bliss and unconsciousness, for the lapse into generation is delightful to the soul. She is a "moist soul" proceeding on her downward journey to the sea. She has summoned, like Lyca in *A Little Girl Lost*, the "sweet sleep," or death, of generation, and she is on the descending path.

These two figures are related very directly to the spiritual situation of Odysseus himself; for he has reached the point of return. He is no longer on the descending path, but about to take the upward way of the "dry soul," pointed out for him by Athena herself.

Porphyry's cave is the womb by which man enters life; but, seen otherwise, it is the grave in which he dies to eternity. However, for those who leave it by the southern gate, it is, conversely, the grave of this world, from which returning souls are born into the world of immortals. There could be no fitter symbol of this identity or ambiguity of womb and tomb than those [30] "bowls or urns of workmanship divine" that Blake has represented as carried, in the manner of water pots, on the heads of winged nymphs in the deepest recess of the cave. In these bowls, according to Porphyry's text, the bees deposit their honey. Now the bees are souls proceeding into generation; and the winged souls, about to descend into the cave, make their way first to these womblike urns—"the funeral urns of Beulah," as they become in Blake's myth—signifying that the descent of souls into the wombs of this world is a death from eternity. Porphyry quotes Sophocles, who says of souls:

> In swarms while wandering, from the dead
> A humming sound is heard.

Proserpina herself was called the "honied," and the moon, who presides over generation, is called a "bee." [36] Bees were thought an apt symbol of the descent and return of souls, because "this insect loves to return to the place from whence it first came," as souls that descend into generation will make their way home to the eternal world.

Are Blake's winged figures intended to suggest these bees? And are the figures woven into the looms souls who have lost their wings? Bee-[frontis- winged souls may also be seen on the title page of *Jerusalem* and elsewhere piece] in Blake's designs.

Descending from the highest recess, we come to a group of wingless nymphs at work about a loom. The looms of generation are to be found in many passages both in *The Four Zoas* and in *Jerusalem;* all Blake's female figures [32, 33] are weavers of garments. The Virgin Mary herself is shown with distaff and spindle, or with spinning wheel. Painting this composition in 1821, Blake had his own work behind him, and in these nymphs at their loom we can [31] recognize his own Daughters of Albion, whose shuttles are plied in cruel delight. Blake's looms of generation correspond exactly to Porphyry's description:

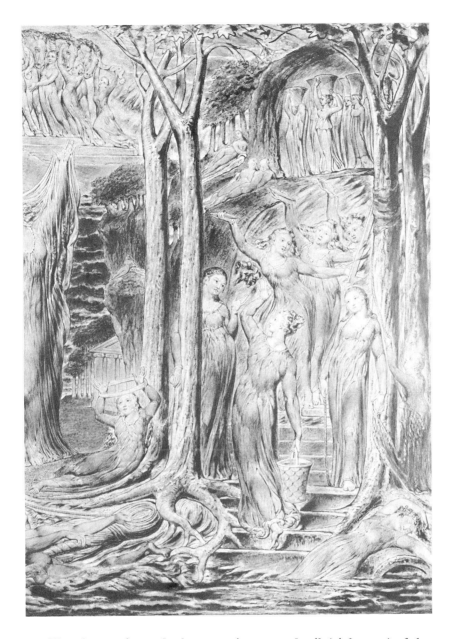

30 Nymphs weaving and others carrying urns: detail (right part) of the
Arlington Court picture (1821)

Note the olive trees on the promontory
above the Greek porticoed house on left;
in top center the nymph pouring water
from an urn and the reclining lovers; top
right, winged figures carrying urns; and
main group of weaving nymphs holding
shuttles, the little figure on left woven
into the garment, the reclining sleeping
figure sinking into the water, the arm
outstretched over a bucket or tub, and
the central ascending figure holding in
her hand a full bucket. Also the stone
beam of the "loom" behind the shuttles
held by nymphs.

And, in the North Gate, in the West of the North, toward Beulah
Cathedron's Looms are builded. & Los's Furnaces in the South
A wondrous golden Building immense with ornaments sublime
Is bright Cathedron's golden Hall, its Courts Towers & Pinnacles
And one Daughter of Los sat at the fiery Reel & another
Sat at the shining Loom with her Sisters attending round
Terrible their distress & their sorrow cannot be utterd
And another Daughter of Los sat at the Spinning Wheel
Endless their labour, with bitter food, void of sleep,
Tho hungry they labour: they rouze themselves anxious
Hour after hour labouring at the whirling Wheel

31 The daughters of Los at the wheel: *Jerusalem* (1804–1820), plate 59, detail

to souls that descend into generation, and are occupied in corporeal energies, what symbol can be more appropriate than those instruments pertaining to weaving? Hence, also, the poet [Homer] ventures to say, "that on these the Nymphs weave purple webs, admirable to the view." For the formation of the flesh is on and about the bones, which in the bodies of animals resemble stones. Hence these instruments of weaving consist of stone, and not of any other matter. But the purple webs will evidently be the flesh which is woven from the blood. . . . Add, too, that the body is a garment with which the soul is invested, a thing wonderful to the sight.[37]

The girlish figure is being enmeshed in what the three nymphs are weaving. Perhaps Blake here intends to represent the process of generation; the little girl is being woven into the "garment" of the body.

Gray found the same powerful symbol of weaving nymphs in a cave in the Orkney saga. A man from Caithness saw twelve weird women enter a hollow hill: "curiousity led him to follow them; till looking through an opening in the rocks, he saw twelve gigantic figures resembling women; they were all employed about a loom, and as they wove, they sang the following dreadful song"—and this, in the form of Gray's ode *The Fatal Sisters*, Blake had illustrated in 1793–94 (by which date he had also read Porphyry):

[34]

See the grisly texture grow
('Tis of human entrails made,)

And the weights that ply below
Each a gaping warrior's head.

Shafts for shuttles, dipt in gore
Shoot the trembling cords along,
Sword, that once a monarch bore,
Keep the tissue close and strong!

There may be a recollection of the group of three figures in Blake's illustration to Gray in the group of three who ply the shuttles in the later composition.

There are instances in Blake's writings of weaving "in a cave," which can only derive from the Homeric Cave of the Nymphs. In *The Gates of Paradise*,

When weary Man enters his Cave
He meets his Savior in the Grave
Some find a Female Garment there,
And some a Male, woven with care,
Lest the Sexual Garments sweet
Should grow a devouring Winding sheet.[38]

32 The Virgin Mary watched by two angels: illustration (1816?) to Milton's *Paradise Regained*

33 The Virgin Mary with a spinning wheel and distaff encircled by a vine: detail from illustration to the *Divine Comedy* (1827), No. 3 Roe

See the grisly texture grow!
('Tis of human entrails made,)
And the weights that play below,
Each a gasping warrior's head.

Shafts for shuttles, dipt in gore,
Shoot the trembling cords along.
Sword, that once a monarch bore,
Keep the tissue close and strong.

Mista, black terrific maid,
Sangrida, and *Hilda*, see!
Join the wayward work to aid:
'Tis the woof of victory.

Ere the ruddy sun be set,
Pikes must shiver; javelins sing,
Blade with clatt'ring buckler meet,
Hauberk crash, and helmet ring.
                                    (Weave

34 Woven entrails: design (early 1790's) for Gray's *The Fatal Sisters*

50   ODE ON THE DEATH

Her coat, that with the tortoise vies,
Her ears of jet, and emerald eyes,
     She saw; and purr'd applause.

Still had she gaz'd; but 'midst the tide
Two angel forms were seen to glide,

35 Fate severing the thread with shears: detail from Blake's water-color drawing (early 1790's) illustrating Gray's *Ode on the Death of a Favourite Cat* Compare with Atropos with shears in Arlington Court tempera, and figure with single shear in [40].

Here the world-cave is the grave "where the dead dwell" and where man finds his woven garments. This is Porphyry Christianized; the Saviour himself descended into this cave, the earth, and here, in the "grave" of souls dead to eternity, man meets his Saviour, who also puts on a "body of death." Blake has used the strange image of the stone looms:

> *. . . and they drew out from the Rocky Stones*
> *Fibres of Life to Weave, for every Female is a Golden Loom,*
> *The Rocks are opake hardnesses covering all Vegetated things;*
> *As they Wove & Cut from the Looms, in various divisions*
>
> .   .   .
>
> *They divided into many lovely Daughters, to be counterparts*
> *To those they Wove; for when they Wove a Male, they divided*
> *Into a Female to the Woven Male: in opake hardness*
> *They cut the Fibres from the Rocks: groaning in pain they Weave,*
> *Calling the Rocks Atomic Origins of Existence, denying Eternity* [39]

In another passage the "fibres of life" are cut from both "rivers" and "rocks," a piece of symbolism comprehensible only in terms of Porphyry's weaving nymphs, with their stone looms and ever-flowing source:

> *. . . they cut the fibres from the Rivers; he sears them with hot*
> *Iron of his Forge & fixes them into Bones of chalk & Rock.*
> *Conwenna sat above; with solemn cadences she drew*
> *Fibres of life out from the Bones into her golden Loom.*
>
> .   .   .
>
> *For the Male is a Furnace of beryll, the Female is a golden Loom.* [40]

The looms of generation passed, we reach the fourth and lowest stage of the descending series, the Stygian waters of the river's mouth, where the Fates [23, 35, control the entry upon "the Sea of Time & Space." With faces of savage 40] cruelty and joy, one unwinds the thread from a great distaff-like coil of flax presented by Phorcys, a second measures off the yarn with her fingers, and a third cuts it with her shears. Phorcys is the shape-shifter Proteus (matter) and is therefore appropriately shown working together with the Fates in determining mortal life: "according to Plato, the deep, the sea, and a tempest, are images of a material nature. And on this account, I think, the poet [Homer] called the port by the name of Phorcys. For he says 'It is the port of the ancient marine Phorcys.'" [41] There is something of Phorcys in Blake's "parent power" Tharmas, "demon of the waters." [42]

The seemingly strange combination of weaving and the sea found in *Milton*, Plate 29, falls into place when we consider the fall of the river from the looms of the cave into the waters of the bay of Phorcys:

> *. . . Tirzah & her Sisters*
> *Weave the black Woof of Death . . .*
>
>   ·   ·   ·
>
> *. . . they sing to the winged shuttle.*
> *The River rises above his banks to wash the Woof:*
> *He takes it in his arms; he passes it in strength thro' his current;*
> *The veil of human miseries is woven over the Ocean*
> *From the Atlantic to the Great South Sea, the Erythrean.* [43]

What of the flames that pour out of the cave, on the right of the painting, beside the looms? The symbol is a familiar one in Blake's own writings: "The Male is a Furnace of beryll, the Female is a golden Loom"; the furnaces of Los accompany the looms of Enitharmon, and both are symbols of generation. The "spectres," or generated mankind, pass through both looms and furnaces. Blake has not violated the traditional symbolism of the cave, but merely introduced a detail from another source.

Bryant's *Mythology* contains a chapter entitled "Of Worship Paid in Caverns." [44] Bryant has drawn extensively on Porphyry; but most of his material relates to the worship of Mithra, whose worship Porphyry also cites. Bryant has little to say of water in connection with worship in caves, but stresses instead the worship of fire practiced especially in the cult of Mithra. There are a number of very fine engravings of Persian cave-temples,

[36, 37]

36 Sacred cave in a fiery mountain (Mons Argaeus): Bryant's *Mythology*, vol. 1 (1774), plate I

Plate V.

37 Temple of Mithras: Bryant's *Mythology*, vol. 1 (1774), plate v, signed by Basire but possibly by Blake
Note the flames on the altar.

several of them indicating symbols of fire worship. Blake may himself have worked on these as Basire's apprentice. Bryant's *Mythology* was the *Golden Bough* of its day, and Blake cites it as authoritative in matters of mythology. From Bryant, Blake as a boy had first discovered the intoxicating possibilities of mythological eclecticism; what, then, could be more natural than to add, on the authority of Bryant, a significant detail of the symbolism of cave-temples that he did not find in Porphyry?

Homer speaks of the northern and southern entrances of the Cave of the Nymphs; and in explaining these, Porphyry passes to astronomical symbolism. For "a cavern is an image or symbol of the world," and there are two extremities in the heavens, viz. the winter tropic, than which nothing is more southern, and the summer tropic, than which nothing is more northern. But the summer tropic is in Cancer, and the winter tropic in Capricorn. And since Cancer is nearest to us, it is very properly attributed to the Moon, which is the nearest of all the heavenly bodies to the earth. But as the southern pole, by its great distance, is invisible to us, hence Capricorn is attributed to Saturn, the highest and most remote of all the planets. . . . Theologists therefore assert, that these two gates are Cancer and Capricorn.[45]

By the logic of astrological symbolism it follows that souls enter generation by the moon-governed gate of Cancer, since the moon is the ruler of generation and also of the waters. Conversely, souls leaving this world through the gate of Capricorn enter Saturn's golden country of eternity:

The northern parts . . . pertain to souls descending into generation. And the gates of the cavern which are turned to the north, are rightly said to be pervious to the descent of men; but the southern gates are not the avenues of the Gods, but of souls ascending to the Gods. On this account, the poet does not say that they are the avenues of the Gods, but of immortals; this appellation being also common to our souls, which are *per se*, or essentially, immortal. It is said, that Parmenides mentions these two gates in his treatise *On the Nature of Things;* as likewise, that they are not unknown to the Romans and Egyptians.[46]

These two entrances Blake has faithfully depicted in the vital downward current of generation and in the radiant staircase rising from the distant extremity of the cave into a golden world. Blake himself had long ago assimilated the northern and southern gates into his own system, attributing the northern gate, through which souls descend into generation, to Los, or Urthona. The first mention of the northern gate occurs in *The Book of Thel,* from which we must conclude that Blake read Taylor's *Porphyry* very soon after its publication in 1788.

Of the southern gate that leads upward out of the cave into the world of immortals, Porphyry's description is less detailed. Those who pass through the southern gate pass into the galaxy, outside the seven spheres of the planets that govern this world. "Capricorn and Cancer are situated about the galaxy. . . . According to Pythagoras, also, the 'people of dreams' [47]

38 "Then went Satan forth from the presence of the Lord": engraving for *Job* (1826), plate 5

Compare the drowsy figure of God with the sleeping god in car [23, 26; II, 181].

are the souls which are said to be collected in the galaxy, this circle being so called from the milk with which souls are nourished when they fall into generation." These "people of dreams" are the spirits departed from, or awaiting, incarnation; and we see a multitude of them about the chariot of the sun. They are scarcely distinguishable from the bright flames that emanate from the sun as it rests on its golden chariot. Porphyry says that "the Sun and Moon are the gates of souls, which ascend through the Sun, and descend through the Moon."

It is of these discarnate spirits that Heraclitus says, "We live their death, and we die their life"; and in these words we have the heart of the myth of the Cave of the Nymphs, the descent and return of souls in a ceaseless round of death and rebirth, suggested by Blake in the very composition of the painting. Taylor gives from the *Gorgias* Plato's quotation of Euripides' variant on the same paradox, "who knows whether to live is not to die, and to die is not to live"—for, says Socrates, perhaps in reality we are the dead. This is the heart, also, of Blake's philosophy; generated man is sunk in "deadly sleep," and he enters his cave, or grave, when he is born into this world. Something of this alternation of life and death is suggested by Blake in the difference of character in the people of the two worlds. In strange contrast with the fierce vitality of the descending spiral of generation, the sun-god in his chariot is sunk in profound sleep.[48] Blake is suggesting the contrasting states of life in this world as death in the other; or, in this case, the waking of the one as the sleep of the other, for the symbolic meaning of sleep and death is the same: the lost vision becomes, in [26, 28] psychological terms, the "unconscious."

The god in the chariot of the sun is a strange figure. He appears to be intended to resemble the traditional Apollo, although he has no "bow of burning gold"—and there is a striking resemblance to the figure of God in [38] the Job engravings,[49] the fifth plate, "Then went Satan forth from the presence of the Lord." There the drowsy God is not yet actually sleeping, as he appears to be here; yet the symbolic event, though stated in other terms, is parallel. The separation of Satan (the selfhood, as Blake invariably defines him) from God (the Divine Humanity) is about to initiate just such a cycle of Experience, a descent and return, in the sufferings of Job, as is here symbolized by the voyage of Odysseus across the stormy sea of time and space, and his final home-coming. One thinks also of the opening lines of *The Gates of Paradise:*

39 Eve rising from the sleep of Adam: detail from *Jerusalem* (1804–1820), plate 31

My Eternal Man set in Repose, [39]
The Female from his darkness rose.[50]

Again, the sleep of the Eternal Man—who is, for Blake, the divine in every man—initiates a descent into the "grave" or "cave" of this world, the putting on of a bodily garment in the cave of the female powers. The traveler at last returns to his native country:

But when once I did descry
The Immortal Man that cannot Die,
Thro' evening shades I haste away
To close the Labours of my Day.[51]

This cycle of descent and return, the journey of the traveler who leaves his native country to return again, is not Christian: it is Platonic; and even into his interpretation of Job, Blake is carrying that grand conception that re-echoes from Heraclitus down through the Greek philosophers and poets, "we live their death, and we die their life." Job is the traveler who enters Experience, the state in which the divine in man sleeps, or dies; when the lost traveler returns, the God awakes. The contrasting states of sleep and waking, a death into life and a reawakening into eternity, form the very substance of Blake's thought.

40 "The River of Life": water-color drawing (1805?)
Note shear in hand of stooping figure, and radiant figures surrounding sun.

The sun as the symbol of deity is one that unites Christian and classical symbols. Swedenborg's angels saw the Lord as the sun, in the midst of innumerable bright spirits; and so always did Blake himself. His painting [40] "The River of Life," illustrating a passage in the Book of Revelation, shows that river flowing toward just such a spirit-encompassed sun as this, and communicates the same truth in other terms, the return of all souls to

> . . . that sweet golden clime
> Where the traveller's journey is done.[52]

In this painting the woman with a single shear that cuts the thread of life is not fierce but beneficent.

41 Emblem from Bryant's *Mythology*, vol. 2 (1774), plate X

CHAPTER *4*

Thel

The first appearance of Porphyry's influence on Blake's poetry is to be found in *The Book of Thel*, written in 1787, thirty-two years before the Arlington Court tempera was painted. If we compare *Thel* with *Tiriel*, we find a clarity and formal beauty of symbol that is new. With his discovery of Neoplatonism, Blake found a structure able to express metaphysical meaning in symbolic terms both coherent and beautiful; and he could now enter the central tradition of European poetic and pictorial symbolism. His reading of Porphyry must have brought him the realization—one may say revelation—of the true nature of the symbols used by poets already known to him; and in *Thel* he has brought together thoughts from many sources, symbols distilled and enriched by the imagination of philosophers and poets. *Tiriel* is obscured by the Nordic poverty of imagination of Swedenborg and Agrippa; *Thel*'s symbolic landscape has the classical strength and delicacy of Botticelli.

The theme of the poem—one to which Blake was often to return—is a debate between the Neoplatonic and the alchemical philosophies. To Plotinus and Porphyry matter is evil and the soul's descent into body a death from eternity incurred by sin or by folly. "A dry soul is the wisest," and refuses the descent. But the Paracelsan philosophy is based upon the monism of the Smaragdine Table of Hermes, "That which is beneath is like that which is above." Which is the truth? *Thel*'s motto asks the question, but does not answer it:

> *Does the Eagle know what is in the pit?*
> *Or wilt thou go ask the Mole?*
> *Can Wisdom be put in a silver rod?*
> *Or Love in a golden bowl?* [1]

Like *The Tyger* the poem ends, as it begins, on an unanswered question; again and again Blake in his later writings returns to the inconsolable lament of Thel, of the soul imprisoned in a mortal body; but *The Marriage of Heaven and Hell* is a manifesto of the philosophy of Paracelsus and Boehme, of the "one thing" in which contraries are resolved, and this philosophy was the one Blake seems finally to have preferred, though not without vacillation.

The actors in the drama of *Thel* fall into two groups: the Neoplatonic Thel, and the dewdrop, lily, and matron Clay who teach the mysteries of alchemy.

Thel herself is a nymph from Porphyry's myth; she is looking down from the Galaxy into the cave or grave of generation: Shall she descend? Can she safely entrust herself to the cycle of generation? Proof that Blake already knew *The Cave of the Nymphs* may be found in the reference to the northern gate:

> *The eternal gates' terrific porter lifted the northern bar:*
> *Thel enter'd in & saw the secrets of the land unknown.*
> *She saw the couches of the dead . . .*[2]

The "terrific porter" comes not from Porphyry but from Spenser's Garden of Adonis. *Thel*, in mood, theme, and imagery, is close to Spenser. Mutability is *Thel*'s theme, as it was Spenser's; but the particular resemblances are even more striking. The Garden, where the souls await generation, has two gates:

> *It sited was in fruitfull soyle of old,*
> *And girt in with two walles on either side;*
> *The one of yron, the other of bright gold,*
> *That none might thorough breake, nor over-stride:*
> *And double gates it had, which opened wide,*
> *By which both in and out men moten pas;*
> *Th' one faire and fresh, the other old and dride:* [3]

These are Porphyry's gates of birth and death. Spenser makes no mention of their facing north and south, but his iron and gold signify the same, since the golden world of the Platonists is the eternal world, and the iron, this lowest of the four worlds, the world of the cave. So Blake also understood the golden gates:

42 Title page designed by Blake for Blair's
Grave (1808)
Compare the "Door of Death" with the "Gates
of Birth" [82].

The Door of Death is made of Gold, [42]
That Mortal Eyes cannot behold;
But, when the Mortal Eyes are clos'd,
And cold and pale the Limbs repos'd,
The Soul awakes; and, wond'ring, sees
In her mild Hand the golden Keys:
The Grave is Heaven's golden Gate [4]

The Garden of Adonis is "a joyous Paradise" which is "the first
seminarie of all things." There are stored the "originals" of generated forms.
It is the Galaxy, where the people of dreams await birth. The Galaxy,
Porphyry says, is so called because of the milk there supplied to the
incarnating souls; and these Spenser describes as "babes" waiting to be
clothed in bodies by Genius, the porter of the gates:

Old Genius *the porter of them was,*
Old Genius, *the which a double nature has.*[5]

43 *Janus Bifrons:* emblems from Bryant's *Mythology*, vol. 2 (1774), plate v

[43]   Genius is the daemon of generation; and like Janus and all gatekeepers, he looks two ways, both into time and into eternity. In "the eternal gates' terrific porter" we have at once a direct allusion to Spenser and the first foreshadowing of Los-Urthona in his aspect of keeper of the northern gate:

> *He letteth in, he letteth out to wend,*
> *All that to come into the world desire;*
> *A thousand thousand naked babes attend*
> *About him day and night, which doe require,*
> *That he with fleshly weedes would them attire.*
> *Such as him list, such as eternall fate*
> *Ordained hath, he clothes with sinfull mire,*
> *And sendeth forth to live in mortall state,*
> *Till they againe returne backe by the hinder gate.*[6]

The "thousand thousand naked babes" are the people of dreams, who assemble in the Galaxy by the gate of Cancer, through which they will presently descend.[7] Platonic also is Spenser's description of the bodily garments as "sinfull mire"—sinful because the soul's attraction downward toward moisture is a lapse from eternity. To the moist nature of generating souls Spenser alludes a few lines below:

> *Ne doe they need with water of the ford,*
> *Or of the clouds to moysten their roots dry;*
> *For in themselves eternall moisture they imply.*[8]

They are Heraclitus' "moist souls," who in descending into generation attract to themselves the moist envelope of a physical body.

Thel's lament for mutability is Spenserian in mood:

[46]   *O life of this our spring! why fades the lotus of the water,*
      Why fade these children of the spring, born but to smile & fall? [9]

She echoes the lament of Spenser's Venus, as immortal mother of the mortal creatures:

> *Yet pittie often did the gods relent*
> *To see so faire things mard, and spoyled quight:*
> *And their great mother* Venus *did lament*
> *The losse of her deare Brood, her deare delight:*
> *Her hart was pierst with pittie at the sight,*
> *When walking through the Gardin, them she spyde,*
> *Yet no'te she find redresse for such despight.*
> *For all that lives, is subject to that law:*
> *All things decay in time, and to their end do draw.*[10]

Thel, like Venus, is a weeping figure: "The daughter of beauty wip'd her pitying tears with her white veil," [11] and the cause of her grief is the same as that of Spenser's Venus—the mutability of generated forms.

Spenser's Venus is not the queen of pleasure, as she is presented by Apuleius or Ovid; she is, rather, the presiding goddess of vegetation and generation. She is the great mother of all creatures; and Adonis is her consort. Indeed, the link of Thel with Venus is closer than appears at first sight. She is not only a "daughter of beauty" but also a "daughter of Mne Seraphim." The expression "Bne Seraphim" (sons of the Seraphim) occurs in the writings of Cornelius Agrippa,[12] who defines the Seraphim as "the Intelligence of Venus," and elsewhere describes Venus as presiding over the processes of vegetation, and the Seraphim as "the fifth order of angels by which God Elohim Gibor [the cabalistic Geburah] . . . draweth forth the elements."

Her affinity with Venus extends to her mourning for Adonis: "by the river of Adona her soft voice is heard." Thel's lamentation is the traditional mourning for "Thammuz, yearly wounded," for the transience of mortal forms. Spenser's Adonis is the eternally renewed mortal parent of generated beings, as well as being himself the type of their transient mortality. Spenser, in his characterization of Adonis, is following the Orphic tradition, and the Hymn to Musaeus Blake also no doubt knew in Taylor's translation:

> *. . . Fair Adonis, never doom'd to die,*
> *End and Beginning he is all to all.*[13]

Thel's "river of Adona" is appropriate because of the flowing and hylic, or

44 Title page of *The Book of Thel* (1789)
Blake describes fairies as spirits of vegetation, here associated
with the pasqueflower of the vegetation-god Adonis.

watery, nature of generated life, and also because Thammuz was mourned by the river Adonis. Milton alludes to Adonis not as a youth but as the river itself:

> *Whose annual wound in* Lebanon *allur'd*
> *The* Syrian *Damsels to lament his fate*
> *In amorous dittyes all a Summers day*
> *While smooth* Adonis *from his native Rock*
> *Ran purple to the Sea. . . .*[14]

Another allusion to Adonis is concealed in the emblem upon the title page. The flowers, from whose centers spring little lovers in amorous pursuit and flight, are pasqueflowers, *Anemone pulsatilla.* In coloring the plates Blake usually makes them, correctly, purple or red; and the fernlike drooping leaves are also characteristic of that plant. The anemone is the flower of Adonis, into which he was, according to tradition, metamorphosed. Blake knew his Ovid and also, of course, Shakespeare's *Venus and Adonis;* the flowers on the title page of *Thel* are a plain allusion to the theme of the poem.[15] The association of the flower with Easter (*pasque*) is itself significant.

[44, 45]

There are other Spenserian echoes. Thel's Lilly is

> *. . . clothed in light, and fed with morning manna,*
> *Till summer's heat melts thee beside the fountains and the springs*
> *To flourish in eternal vales.*[16]

45 *Anemone pulsatilla* (pasqueflower)
Specially drawn for this book by Ruthven Todd. When the plant is fully grown, the drooping leaves resemble more the title page of *Thel* [44].

Every ornament of perfection. and every labour of love.
In all the Garden of Eden. & in all the golden mountains
Was become an envied horror. and a remembrance of jealousy:
And every Act a Crime. and Albion the punisher & judge.

46 Lovers in a water-lily: *Jerusalem* (1804–1820), detail from plate 28

Fairies or spirits of vegetation in a lily or "lotus of the water."

Spenser uses the same image of evanescence:

> *And that faire flowre of beautie fades away,*
> *As doth the lilly fresh before the sunny ray.*[17]

The "eternal vales" to which Blake's Lilly returns are the same as Spenser's garden of Platonic archetypes:

> *After that they againe returned beene,*
> *They in that Gardin planted be againe;*
> *And grow afresh, as they had never seene*
> *Fleshly corruption, nor mortall paine.*[18]

    In the Notebook [19] there is a pencil drawing showing a little female [47] figure with upraised arms, emerging from a flower, embraced by a little male fairy. The drawing illustrates Shakespeare's fifteenth sonnet:

> *[When I consider] every thing that growes*
> *Holds in perfection [but a little moment]*

The sonnet continues:

When I perceive that men as plants increase,
Cheared and checkt even by the selfe-same skie:
Vaunt in their youthfull sap, at height decrease

The flower itself is indeterminate – not, certainly, an anemone; but Thel, on the title page, is meditating upon two similar figures: the female with upraised arms, emerging from one of Adonis' flowers of mortality, the little lover from another. It is impossible that Blake should have used this visual theme without reference to its first inspiration; Thel is reflecting on the theme of mutability common to Spenser and to Shakespeare's sonnet.

47 Page 21 from Blake's Notebook, with flower drawing illustrating the first lines of Shakespeare's fifteenth sonnet

The theme of the sonnet is growth and decay; Blake has therefore introduced the "fairies" of vegetation.

The same little figures later appear in another flower, the "Sick Rose"; [20] and the flower of Adonis decorates the poem *Infant Joy*. Within its crimson womb-like petals the "Infant Joy," but two days old, is tended by a butterfly-winged spirit of vegetation. The Infant Joy is one of the "thousand thousand naked babes" sent forth to live in the world from Adonis' garden and appropriately sheltered within his flower—stylized now, and less like the actual flower and plant than the similar emblem on the title page of *Thel*.

The imagery of the poem is appropriate to the "watery" world of generation of the naiads and their ever-flowing streams, to the "moist" souls who attract to themselves the hylic envelope. Thel's lamentation "falls like morning dew." She speaks of "the lotus of the water," rainbow, and cloud; she converses with the Lilly, who calls herself "a watery weed," for like the Neoplatonic Narcissus, she is here a symbol of generated, hylic, or, as Blake would say (following Plotinus), "vegetated" life. Cloud and dewdrop, the moist "clay" of the body, the worm upon its "dewy bed," and the "dewy grave" are all images appropriate to the theme of generation. "Dewy bed" and "dewy grave" are by no means phrases descriptive only, or principally, of the physical appearance of dewiness; [21] but like Enion's "wat'ry Grave" [22]

48 *The Sick Rose* from *Songs of Experience* (1789–94)

49 *Infant Joy* from *Songs of Innocence* (1789)

they describe the moist envelope of the soul, the generated body, called a "grave" because in it the soul is dead from eternity, or a "bed," as the place of the soul's sleep. All is appropriate to the theme of the "moist soul." The whole poem is, in Porphyry's phrase, "drenched in moisture."

Plotinus, in *Concerning the Beautiful*, describes natural forms as "like beautiful images appearing in water." The book is full of the imagery of shadows, reflections, and water that we find in *Thel;* and a note from Proclus is particularly relevant:

> The forms which appear in matter, are merely ludicrous; shadows falling upon shadow, as in a mirror, where the position of a thing is different from its real situation; . . . But the things which enter and depart from matter, are nothing but imitations of being, and semblances, flowing about a formless semblance. They appear, indeed, to affect something in the subject matter, but in reality produce nothing: from their debile and flowing nature, being endued with no solidity, and no rebounding power. And since matter, likewise, has

no solidity, they penetrate it without division, like images in water, or as if any one should fill a vacuum with forms.[23]

The watery beings change perpetually from one form to another, but their matter is never destroyed. Thel, however, is fleeting in a different sense; she compares herself not to water but to light reflected on water (a rainbow), to "a reflection in a glass" and "shadows in the water," the very images Plotinus uses to illustrate his theme of the soul reflected in matter; like Thel, "they appear indeed to effect something, but in reality produce nothing." Her inability to effect anything is the burden of Thel's complaint: "without a use this shining woman lived."

> *"Ah! Thel is like a wat'ry bow, and like a parting cloud;*
> *Like a reflection in a glass; like shadows in the water;*
> *Like dreams of infants, like a smile upon an infant's face;*
> *Like the dove's voice; like transient day; like music in the air."* [24]

In his introduction to the *Parmenides* (1793) Taylor writes that "material species . . . on account of their apparently real, but at the same time delusive subsistences . . . are similar to images in water, or in a mirror, or a dream" (p. 256). Thel cannot reconcile herself to the "delusive subsistence" of the material world, the transience of a shadow or reflection whose reality is elsewhere. But matter, according to matron Clay, has its own kind of immortality in perpetual change from one thing to another, without loss of substance,

> *. . . eterne in mutabilitie,*
> *And by succession made perpetuall,*
> *Transformed oft, and chaunged diverslie* [25]

This is Spenser's theme, and doubtless his thought is reflected in the speeches of Blake's Lilly and Cloud, who explain to Thel that they "by their change their being doe dilate." Matter is changed without being destroyed:

> *The substance is not chaunged, nor altered*
> *But th' only forme and outward fashion;*
> *For every substance is conditioned*
> *To change her hew, and sundry formes to don.* [26]

Lilly is browsed by sheep; dew and rain nourish the flowers; clay nourishes

the infant worm; and the dead body, as "the food of worms," returns to the
endless happy life-cycle. Nothing ever dies; all lives in the one life. But Thel
knows that her nature is not like theirs; for she is the soul; not a part of the
mortal earth but the beauty of eternity reflected in the temporal world. As
the soul, she animates the body, but is not herself bodily. To the Lilly she
says:

> *"Thy breath doth nourish the innocent lamb, he smells thy milky*
> *garments,*
>
> *He crops thy flowers . . .*
>
> .   .   .
>
> *Thy wine doth purify the golden honey; thy perfume,*
> *Which thou dost scatter on every little blade of grass that springs,*
> *Revives the milked cow, & tames the fire-breathing steed.*
> *But Thel is like a faint cloud kindled at the rising sun:*
> *I vanish from my pearly throne, and who shall find my place?"* [27]

Thel's mistake is to identify herself with the image or reflection; she
has forgotten who she is—an immortal spirit—and believes that she, too, dies
like the plants. But the transient beauty she laments is only a shadow of the
eternal beauty of the soul. The "dewdrop"—the bodily envelope of "moist
souls"—is to the soul merely a "pearly throne," and the soul does not vanish
with the dewdrop; but Thel fears that in descending into generation, she will
lose her immortal nature:

> *And I complain'd in the mild air, because I fade away,*
> *And lay me down in thy cold bed, and leave my shining lot.*[28]

Why should the soul descend? The poem gives no answer; for having
envisaged her condition if she enters her "grave," Thel refuses to make the
descent:

> *. . . & with a shriek*
> *Fled back unhinder'd till she came into the vales of Har.*[29]

The conclusion of Thel is the conclusion of Plotinus; she follows the
advice of that philosopher to the soul who is precipitated "into profound and
horrid darkness . . . It is here, then, we may more truly exclaim, 'Let us
depart from hence, and fly to our father's delightful land.' " [30]

This is what Thel does, after "listening to the voices of the ground"
and wandering "through the land of clouds and valleys dark": she flees to

"the vales of Har"; but she is deluded still, for Har is ruler only of the earthborn kingdom.

The figure of Vala in *The Four Zoas*, IX, is in many ways identical with Thel; she continues the theme, but finds the answer to Thel's predicament. (This answer is discussed in Chapter 7, below, with reference to Blake's *Cupid and Psyche*, which should be read as a continuation and solution of the story of Thel.)

His symbolic landscape thus established, Blake could add details from other landscapes, not in themselves symbolic but capable of being so understood.

The plot—if one may so describe it—of *Thel* he seems to have taken from *Rasselas*.[31] Dr. Johnson's Prince of Abyssinia lives with his brothers and sisters in "the Happy Valley," situated in the south, where no cares or sorrows are permitted to enter. With his sister and her companion, he leaves this earthly paradise to explore the unknown world of men. He goes in search of experience, but at last returns to the innocence of the Happy Valley; so that the story of Rasselas is on the pattern of the soul's cycle of descent and return.

The earthly paradise of the Abyssinian princes was "a spacious valley in the kingdom of Amhara":

> The only passage, by which it could be entered, was a cavern that passed under a rock, of which it has long been disputed whether it was the work of nature or of human industry. The outlet of the cavern was concealed by a thick wood, and the mouth which opened into the valley was closed with gates of iron, forged by the artificers of ancient days, so massy that no man could, without the help of engines, open or shut them.[32]

The Happy Valley had a second exit; it contained a lake that "discharged its superfluities by a stream which entered a dark cleft of the mountain on the northern side, and fell with dreadful noise from precipice to precipice till it was heard no more." Once a year, when the Emperor paid a visit to his children, "the iron gate was opened to the sound of musick."

This paradise, whose two exits are a gate used only by the Emperor and a cavern to the north through which water descends from a lake, is on the plan of Porphyry's cave, with its two entrances and a descending stream flowing down through the northern gate. How far—if at all—*Rasselas* is intended as an allegory of the soul is not clear; but there are phrases that must have made it very easy for Blake to read it as such: "When he [Rasselas] looked round about him, he saw himself confined by the bars of nature which had never yet been broken, and by the gate, through which none that once had passed it were ever able to return." [33] In Blake's mind this must have struck an echo of Agrippa's quotation from Orpheus: "The gate of Pluto can never be unbarred; within is a people of dreams."

Rasselas, alone of his brothers and sisters, becomes melancholy and seeks solitude:

> The sons and daughters of Abissinia lived only to know the soft vicissitudes of pleasure and repose, attended by all that were skilful in delight, and gratified with whatever the senses can enjoy. They wandered in gardens of fragrance, and slept in the fortresses of security . . . Thus they rose in the morning, and lay down at night, pleased with each other and with themselves, *all but Rasselas,* who, in the twenty-sixth year of his age, *began to withdraw himself from their pastimes* and assemblies, *and to delight in solitary walks and silent meditation.*[34]

So Thel:

> *The daughters of Mne Seraphim led round their sunny flocks,*
> *All but the youngest: she in paleness sought the secret air* [35]

Like Thel, Rasselas takes his questionings to the natural creation. He "spent day after day on the banks of rivulets sheltered with trees, where he sometimes listened to the birds in the branches, sometimes observed the fish playing in the stream, and anon cast his eyes upon the pastures and mountains filled with animals." His question is akin to Thel's, for he asks wherein is the human lot different from that of the creatures, that he alone should be dissatisfied:

> What, said he, makes the difference between man and all the rest of the animal creation? Every beast that strays beside me has the same corporal necessities with myself; he is hungry and crops the grass, he is thirsty and drinks the stream, his thirst and hunger are appeased, he is satisfied and sleeps; he rises again and is hungry, he is again fed and is at rest. I am hungry and thirsty like him, but when thirst and hunger cease I am not at rest; I am, like him, painted with want, but am not, like him, satisfied with fulness . . . Man has surely

some latent sense for which this place affords no gratification, or he has some desires distinct from sense which must be satisfied before he can be happy.[36]

There is a paradisiacal quality about the early chapters of *Rasselas*, which must have charmed Blake, whose imaginative atmosphere in this poem is strangely akin to Johnson's.

[50] We have now to consider the philosophy of alchemy which is opposed to that of the Neoplatonists in the dialectic of the poem. Is the charming figure of Thel herself partly drawn from an alchemical allegory, itself akin to the Cave of the Nymphs, in Thomas Vaughan's *Lumen de Lumine?*

Vaughan's theme, likewise, is the feminine mystery of generation; and his Eugenius Philalethes "descends" into a cave that is both the grave and the womb of nature, the place where mutability recreates new life from death.

Philalethes is led by the sound of the humming of bees (Porphyry's generating souls?) into a thick grove of bays: "it was not a *wood*, but a *Building*. I conceived it indeed to be the *Temple* of *Nature*." [37] A feminine figure now appears, "her frame neither long nor short, but of a mean, decent stature. Attired she was in thin loose silk but so green that I never saw the like, for the colour was not earthly. In some places it was fancied with white and silver ribbons, which looked like lilies in a field of grass. Her head was overcast with a thin, floating tiffany . . . From her black veil did her locks break out, like sunbeams from a mist . . . To be short, her whole habit was youthful and flowery.[38] She presently reveals her name to Philalethes: "Thalia, for I am alwaies green." [39]

Thalia is the Greek Θαλία from Θάλλειν, "blossoming" or "the blossoming one." She is the earth, according to the Pythagorean tradition which Vaughan probably inherited by way of Agrippa, who so describes Thalia. Was the name Thel suggested by Thalia, with perhaps also an overtone of Lethe (reversed)?

Thalia, like Porphyry's nymphs of the cave, is a fontal goddess; for in Vaughan's allegory she leads Philalethes down a green path by the light of stars, until in a "deep bottom," or valley, they reach the mysterious "Mountains of the Moon," where Thalia shows the alchemist the secret source of Nilus, the river that in Vaughan's allegory is the *prima materia* of alchemy, the equivalent of Plato's Lethe (matter) and of the fontal waters of the naiads in their secret caves.

The Mountains of the Moon have a symbolic significance in this context, since the moon is the planetary ruler of generation. The northern gate of Porphyry's cave is in the sign of Cancer, and ruled by the moon. The river itself is thus described:

[From the mountains descends] a stupendous Cataract, or Waterfall. The streame was more large than any River in her full Chanell, but notwithstanding the Height, and Violence of its Fall, it descended without any Noyse. The Waters were dash'd, and their Current distracted by those Saltish Rocks, but for all this they came down with a dead silence like the still, soft Ayr . . . Thalia told me, it was the first Matter, and the very Naturall, true Sperm of the great World.[40]

Vaughan's Nile, the "first Matter" of this world, is the same as the

50 Engraving in Vaughan's *Lumen de Lumine* (1651)

The serpent or basilisk with its tail in its mouth is an emblem of matter often used by the alchemists. The seated figure inscribed in Vaughan's serpent may be compared with matron Clay [51] and the figure from *The Gates of Paradise* [57]. See p. 124. Cf. also [52, 53].

51 Matron Clay: *Thel*
(1789), plate 5

waters of the fontal goddesses of Porphyry's cave. Vaughan's account of this first matter may have been decisive in Blake's use of the feminine gender for the river of Adona, for he writes of this watery element as a virgin, in most anthropomorphic terms. It is the essential feminine substance of the universe.[41]

Thalia initiates Philalethes into the mysteries of the cave-grave. The "underworld" is entered through a "little portal" in "a rock of adamant figured as a just, entire cube"—the traditional alchemical symbol of earth. The Muse and her initiate now approach an altar dedicated "To the Blessed Gods in the Underworld." On this altar is inscribed an emblem, "the Trunck of an old rotten tree, pluck'd up by the Roots"—and from the decaying roots hatches a snake. "From this place we moved straight forward till we came to a Cave of Earth. It was very obscure and withall dankish, giving a heavy odour like that of graves."[42] This, Thalia tells her initiate, is the inmost sanctuary of nature's mysteries, where death perpetually gives place to regeneration.

Porphyry's cave is, above all, the place of generation, where the mortal garments are woven; Vaughan's cave is also the place of generation, for the newly hatched serpent signifies that from decay new life begins; but it is, more obviously, also the grave, and closer to Thel's vision of the mysteries of [51] the house of matron Clay:

116

Appear to the Americans upon the cloudy night.

Solemn heave the Atlantic waves between the gloomy nations
Swelling, belching from its deeps red clouds & raging fires.
Albion is sick. America faints! enrag'd the Zenith grew.
As human blood shooting its veins all round the orbed heaven
Red rose the clouds from the Atlantic in vast wheels of blood
And in the red clouds rose a Wonder o'er the Atlantic sea;
Intense! naked! a Human fire fierce glowing, as the wedge
Of iron heated in the furnace; his terrible limbs were fire
With myriads of cloudy terrors banners dark & towers
Surrounded; heat but not light went thro' the murky atmo-
⎯sphere

53 The dragon of the moon: Agrippa, *Three Books
of Occult Philosophy* (1651), Book II, p. 303

*Thel enter'd in & saw the secrets of the land unknown.
She saw the couches of the dead, & where the fibrous roots
Of every heart on earth infixes deep its restless twists* [43]

The "roots" of life are in death.

The serpent is the symbol of matter, both in the works of the alchemists and in Blake. It is also an emblem of immortality, because it can slough its skin and perpetually renew its youth. Perhaps by "newly hatched" Vaughan meant that the serpent had sloughed its skin. There is no mention of a serpent in the text of *Thel;* which makes it the more striking that the last [54] design shows children riding the serpent—safely and cheerfully, as Mona Wilson pointed out.[43a]

54 Serpent with children: *Thel* (1789), plate 6, detail

The Spectres of Albions Twelve Sons revolve mightily
Over the Tomb & over the Body: raining to devour
The Sleeping Humanity. Los with his mace of iron
Walks round: loud his threats, loud his blows fall
On the rocky Spectres, as the Potter breaks the potsherds;
Dashing in pieces Self-righteousnesses: driving them from Albions
Cliffs: dividing them into Male & Female forms, in his Furnaces
And on his Anvils: lest they destroy the Feminine Affections
They are broken. Loud howl the Spectres in his iron Furnace

55 Eagle-man: *Jerusalem* (1804–1820), plate 78, detail

The resemblance between this and [53] suggests Blake's familiarity with Agrippa's works. Cf. also the eagle-men described in *The Marriage of Heaven and Hell*, plate 15.

The great difference between the Neoplatonic and the alchemical philosophies lies in their opposed conceptions of the nature of matter.[44] For Plotinus and his school, matter is mere mire, the dregs of the universe, a philosophic "non-entity" because incapable of form except as it reflects intelligibles. To the alchemists spirit and matter, active and passive, light and darkness, above and below are, like the Chinese yin and yang, complementary principles, both alike rooted in the divine. The *deus absconditus* is hidden and operating in matter, no less than He is to be found in the spiritual order. Blake's own words summarize the philosophy of alchemy: "God is in the lowest effects as well as in the highest causes."[45] *The Marriage of Heaven and Hell* is written under the direct influence of this philosophy—explicitly so, for in it Blake acknowledges his debt to Boehme and Paracelsus—but in *The Book of Thel* also, lily, dew, and clay are the mouthpieces of the alchemical philosophy, which the Platonic Thel has to confess she "did not know."

Thel's motto, which prefaces the poem, is a calling in question of the central teaching of alchemy, the legendary Smaragdine Table of Hermes, which is repeated, commented upon, and paraphrased over and over again in alchemical writings, "That which is beneath is like that which is above: and that which is above, is like that which is beneath, to worke the miracles of one thing. And as all things have proceeded from one, by the meditation of one, so all things have sprung from this one thing by adaptation." [46] This Blake must have known from several sources, probably including Thomas Vaughan's paraphrase, as inscribed on "a stone erected neere Memphis":

> *Heaven Above, Heaven Beneath*
> *Starres Above, Starres Beneath,*
> *All that is Above, is also Beneath;*
> *Understand this, and bee Happy.*[47]

The conception of a "marriage" of heaven and hell Blake undoubtedly owes to the tradition of alchemy. What is often regarded as his most original contribution to thought is precisely this conception of a single existing principle operating through "contraries." [48] Thel's question is answered in *Visions of the Daughters of Albion*, and the answer is that of the alchemists:

> *Does not the eagle scorn the earth & despise the treasures beneath?*
> *But the mole knoweth what is there, & the worm shall tell it thee.*
> *Does not the worm erect a pillar in the mouldering church yard*
> *And a palace of eternity in the jaws of the hungry grave?* [49]

This is Thalia's revelation to Philalethes of the secrets of the grave, where   [56] the serpent matter renews itself in the vaults of decay.

But the inadequacy of the temporal body as the vehicle of the soul is still the burden of Thel's last speech:

> *Why cannot the Ear be closed to its own destruction?*
> *Or the glist'ning Eye to the poison of a smile?*

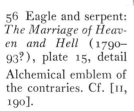

56 Eagle and serpent: *The Marriage of Heaven and Hell* (1790–93?), plate 15, detail Alchemical emblem of the contraries. Cf. [11, 190].

Why are Eyelids stor'd with arrows ready drawn,
Where a thousand fighting men in ambush lie?
Or an Eye of gifts & graces show'ring fruits & coined gold?
Why a Tongue impress'd with honey from every wind?
Why an Ear, a whirlpool fierce to draw creations in?
Why a Nostril wide inhaling terror, trembling, & affright?
Why a tender curb upon the youthful burning boy?
Why a little curtain of flesh on the bed of our desire? [50]

This is certainly the Platonic and not the alchemical view of the body. The fact of the soul's confinement in a temporal body was at all times terrible to Blake, and in this at least he was consistent in all his writings. He returns to this horror of incarceration in many passages, all written in the spirit of Thel. Why this limitation, this confinement, the "binding" of the immortal mind to a mortal vehicle? The child in the world of Experience struggles against its "swaddling-bands"; Rahab and Tirzah bind down the sons of Albion on the "stems of vegetation" with cruel fingers. The binding of Urizen is the terrible incarceration of man's "eternal mind" in the cave of the body. Thel's images are echoed over and over again, and always with a stressing of the restriction and cruelty of incarnation.

Incarnation ceases to be a "prison-house" when we realize that soul is the substance, and body the shadow. There is only "one thing"; so the alchemists believed—and the Platonists also, who saw the visible world as only a "moving image of eternity," as Plato says in the *Timaeus*. Blake could even see a danger in the alchemical view, if it results in supposing the material to have an equal substantial reality with the eternal; for in *Jerusalem* the Spectre (himself a Platonic figure, the "shadowy man" who is only an image or reflection of "the true Man"—intellect) refuses to believe in an eternal world "without demonstration." He uses the Smaragdine Table as a pretext for compelling Los to create temporal forms; for to the Spectre these seem more real than the eternal. This is not so; Blake was in no doubt as to which was shadow, which substance, "for tho' on Earth things seem Permanent, they are less permanent than a Shadow, as we all know too well": [51]

The Spectre builded stupendous Works, taking the Starry Heavens
Like to a curtain & folding them according to his will,
Repeating the Smaragdine Table of Hermes to draw Los down
Into the Indefinite, refusing to believe without demonstration

.   .   .

. . . erecting pillars in the deepest Hell
To reach the heavenly arches. . . .[52]

Matron Clay is, however, alchemical;[53] and accepts with joy the mutable cycle of matter in which she takes part:

Thou seest me the meanest thing, and so I am indeed;
My bosom of itself is cold, and of itself is dark;
But he, that loves the lowly, pours his oil upon my head,
And kisses me, and binds his nuptial bands around my breast,
And says: "Thou mother of my children, I have loved thee
And I have given thee a crown that none can take away."[54]

—crowned as the bride is crowned to this day in the Eastern Orthodox marriage ceremony. She is the "adamic earth" of the alchemists. This earth "answers to God the Father, being the foundation of every creature, as he is of the supernatural." Mother Earth, the lowest and humblest matter, is the bride of the Father, as matron Clay tells Thel. One can see Blake's theme of the matron Clay and the worm whom she nourishes already forming in an annotation to Lavater's *Aphorisms*[55] written in 1788. Lavater says: "A GOD, an ANIMAL, a PLANT, are not companions of man"; and Blake replies:

57 The worm in her winding sheet: *For Children: The Gates of Paradise* (1793), plate 16
Compare small female figure encircled by basilisk in [50], and the reference to the "fibrous roots," p. 117, l. 2, and [112] (bottom left). Note face of the dead in right foreground.

I have said to the Worm Thou art my mother & my sister

It is the God in *all* that is our companion & friend, for our God himself says: "you are my brother, my sister & my mother" . . . God is
in the lowest effects as well as in the highest causes; for he is become
a worm that he may nourish the weak. For let it be remember'd
that creation is God descending according to the weakness of man,
for our Lord is the word of God & every thing on earth is the word
of God & in its essence is God.

The emblem of the worm in her winding sheet, in *The Gates of Paradise*,[56] is
at once matron Clay and the worm she nourishes; for beneath the emblem
are the words, "I have said to the Worm: Thou art my mother & my sister."
Later the little humble woman becomes matron Clay in *Thel*, and the worm,
"image of weakness," her charge.

The same philosophy is expressed many years later in the line "God is
within & without: he is even in the depths of Hell!" [57] This is the philosophy
of Hermes Trismegistus, the legendary teacher of the alchemists. In the
eleventh book of the *Pymander* his son asks Hermes the nature of matter,
and is told: "there is not anything of all that hath been, and all that is, where
God is not . . . Whether thou speak of Matter or Body, or Essence, know
that all these are Acts of God . . . And in the whole, there is nothing that
is not God." [58]

Matron Clay speaks of herself as "cold" and "dark"; and these are
earth's traditional alchemical attributes. Paracelsus writes that "the element
of earth is so cold that it would bring all things to the ultimate matter, as
water into Chrystall, and into Duelech, living creatures into marble, trees
into gyants"; [59] and Vaughan, "in the Matter there was a horrible confused
Qualme, or stupifying spirit of Moysture, Cold and darknesse." [60] Blake on
his Laocoön group wrote that God made Adam (the natural man) "of the
Female, the Adamah"; and he evidently here also means the "Adamic earth"
of the alchemists. In the *Marriage* "Red clay brought forth" is linked with
the passage from Isaiah that describes how "the wilderness shall blossom as
the rose," and he was here, also, thinking in terms of the philosophy of
alchemy. The work of alchemy is, in essence, the bringing forth out of the
matrix of earth the divine riches latent in her, a process that takes place in
the course of nature, but that can be imitated and hastened by the Art:

The Earth you know in the Winter time is a dull, dark, dead Thing,
a contemptible frozen phlegmatick Lump. But towards the Spring,

and Fomentations of the Sun, what rare Pearles are there in this Dung-hill? what glorious Colours and Tinctures doth she discover? a pure eternall green overspreads her, and this attended with innumerable other Beauties: Roses red and white, golden Lilies, Azure Violets, the Bleeding Hyacinths, with their severall coelestiall odours, and Spices. . . . Behold I will tell you as plainly as I may. There are in the world two Extremes, Matter and Spirit: one of these I can assure you is earth.[61]

It is right, therefore, that the most eloquent statement of the harmony and marriage of heaven and earth should come from matron Clay, she being the anointed bride of the Most High. Vaughan is full of eloquent passages on this theme, and Blake seems to be echoing one or more of these: "Heaven here below differs not from that above but in her Captivitie, and that above differs not from this below but in her Libertie. The one is imprisoned in the Matter, the other is freed from the grossness and impurities of it; but they are both of one and the same Nature, so that they easily unite; and hence it is that the Superior descends to the Inferior to visit, and comfort her in this sickly infectious Habitation." [62]

"He, that loves the lowly," of whom the Clay speaks, is the heavenly Father considered as husband of the earthly Mother; the phrase is an exact epithet, descriptive of the mysterious marriage of heaven and earth: "Thou mother of my children, I have loved thee."

The love-gifts bestowed upon the matron Clay may have been suggested by another passage from Vaughan: "Consider what a vast Universall Receptacle this Element is. The Starrs and Planets over-look her, and though they may not descend hither themselves, they shed down their golden Locks, like so many Bracelets, and Tokens of their Love. The Sun is perpetually busie, brings his Fire round about her, as if he would sublime something from her bosom." [63]

"My bosom of itself is cold and of itself is dark" — so Blake's Clay speaks in the very character of Earth as conceived by the alchemists. Earth as the bride of heaven is one of Vaughan's favorite themes: "When God (saith Hermes) had filled his powerfull hands with those things which are in Nature, and in that which compasseth Nature, then shutting them close again, hee said: 'Receive from me, O holy Earth! that art ordained to be the Mother of all, lest thou shouldst want any thing; when presently opening such hands as it becomes a God to have, hee pour'd down All that was Necessary to the Constitution of things.' " [64] This is the earth, in itself cold and dark, impregnated with the seminal forms of all created beings.[65] The same mystery is visually expressed in Vaughan's *Non nisi Parvulis* and in the little figure who holds in her hand a necklace of "pearls" taken from the "dunghill" on which she is seated.

[50]

Images from Spenser and themes from Plotinus and Paracelsus, fraught with symbolic meaning, are disguised in the coloring of Ossian, still the strongest stylistic influence upon *The Book of Thel*. If verse cadence and imagery were all, we would have to say that Blake as a poet is very close indeed to Macpherson. The difference is the all-important one between an imagist and a symbolist poet. Macpherson's imagery is descriptive merely of natural appearances; Blake uses the same images as the vehicles of imaginative thought. Blake had used this imagery in the Ossianic fragments in *Poetical Sketches*, but without a pronounced symbolic dimension. These are full of such phrases as "he was like a cloud tossed by the winds, till the sun shine, and the drops of rain glisten, the yellow harvest breathes" or "All was still. The moon hung not out her lamp, and the stars faintly glimmered in the summer sky; the breath of night slept among the leaves of the forest; the bosom of the lofty hill drank in the silent dew." [66] Blake soon abandoned this poetic prose for verse; but in both diction and imagery *Thel* is very near to such passages as this from Ossian, here arranged as lines of verse:

> *Star of the descending night! fair is thy light in the west!*
> *Thou liftest thy unshorn head from thy cloud: thy steps are stately*
> *on thy hill.*
> *What dost thou behold in the plain? The stormy winds are laid.*
> *The murmur of the torrent comes from afar. Roaring waves climb*
> *the distant rock.*
> *The flies of evening are on their feeble wings, and the hum of their*
> *course is on the field.*
> *What dost thou behold, fair light? but thou dost smile and depart.*
> *The waves come with joy around thee, and they bathe thy lovely*
> *hair.*[67]

Such passages have set their seal on *Thel:*

> *"But Thel is like a faint cloud kindled at the rising sun:*
> *I vanish from my pearly throne, and who shall find my place?"*

> "Queen of the vales," the Lilly answer'd, "ask the tender cloud,
> And it shall tell thee why it glitters in the morning sky,
> And why it scatters its bright beauty thro' the humid air." [68]

or,

> The Cloud then shew'd his golden head & his bright form emerg'd,
> Hovering and glittering on the air before the face of Thel. [69]

Macpherson's characteristic imagery of water, cloud, dew, the pale radiance of the long Highland twilight, "golden-haired" stars and clouds hovering over a landscape of sea and mountain Blake has taken over, to all outward appearance unchanged; and if one were to ask in what country on earth one might find such a landscape as we find in *Thel*, the answer would be: the western Highlands. Macpherson's imagery of evanescent light, mist, and solitude is in itself very beautiful, and there seems no reason to apologize for Blake's liking for a poetic landscape that must have appealed so strongly to his visual imagination.

But though Macpherson might give golden hair to his stars, he could never animate them into heavenly powers; he gave them only physical attributes. His evanescent landscape of sky and water is the counterpart of a mood of thin sentimentality and of monotonous and unvarying nostalgia. Nostalgia is not a mood characteristic of Blake, but *Thel*'s theme is mutability, and Ossian's imagery is peculiarly appropriate to her nature. Such words as "faint," "fade," "vanish," "pale," "gentle," "clouds," "dew," "depart," "seen no more" may be found on any page of Ossian.

It could be said of Ossian's maidens that most, like Thel, are "born but to smile & fall." Thel has all the external attributes of the Ossianic heroines, and some of these may well have contributed to her lovely fleeting form. Vinvela's ghost laments her transience in language suggestive of Thel's: "He saw her fair-moving on the plain: but the bright form lasted not: the sun-beam fled from the field, and she was seen no more . . . She fleets, she sails away, as gray mist before the wind." [70]

Thel is the shepherdess of a landscape of "secret air," of pale, fading forms of beauty, faint cloud, and the "bright glittering" forms created by light on water. In her poetic dress she is entirely of her age. But beneath that surface of Ossianic imagery Thel, Leutha, and Oothoon have hard symbolic bones never to be found in their prototypes Vinvela, Malvina, Oithona, and the rest of Macpherson's gentle mournful ghosts.

CHAPTER 5

The Myth of the Kore

The currents and cross-currents of fashion that lead a poet to the choice of a certain subject at a certain time tend to be forgotten, leaving the work itself in isolation, as if produced by miracle alone. But the Eleusinian Mysteries were the fashion in and about 1790. In a letter dated February 5, [58] 1784, Flaxman wrote to Josiah Wedgwood urging him to come to London to "see Sir Wm. Hamilton's Vase, it is the finest production of Art brought to England."[1] Flaxman suggested that Wedgwood might be interested in making replicas of the much admired Barberini vase. It is possible that Blake may also have seen the urn at this time, and it is likely that Flaxman spoke of it with an enthusiasm that his friend would have been disposed to share. In 1786 the vase was purchased by the Duke of Portland; and in 1790 the Wedgwood pottery did in fact issue several replicas. One of these was exhibited at the Wedgwood showrooms in Greek Street in 1790; and Josiah Wedgwood lectured on the vase and on the reproduction. Did he, at that lecture, suggest the nature of the emblematic figures?

The view of the nature of the vase and the meaning of its figures current in the Wedgwood circle must be presumed to be that given by Erasmus Darwin (a close friend of the Wedgwoods) in the essay that he includes in Part I of his *Botanic Garden*, published in 1791. In this essay Darwin argues that the figures are emblems of the Eleusinian Mysteries, of the immortality of the soul, fittingly inscribed upon an urn made to hold the ashes of the dead. When we consider Flaxman's part in advising on the making of the replicas, and his close association with the Wedgwood activities on the one hand and with Blake on the other, we may guess that Blake knew all that there was to be known about the vase well in advance of the publication of Darwin's work.

Nor is this all: the vase itself—or perhaps one of the replicas—came

58 The Portland vase: engraving by Blake for Darwin's *Botanic Garden* (1791)

into Blake's hands in the autumn of 1791. This has been proved by Keynes,[2] who has shown that the engravings of the vase in Darwin's *Botanic Garden* were made by Blake himself. A letter from Johnson (Blake's friend and the publisher of the book) dated July 23, 1791, to Erasmus Darwin, speaks of arranging for the vase to be lent to Blake for this purpose. This was presumably done, and the beautiful engravings in Darwin's book are the result. Blake had already, in 1791, written the two "Lyca" poems; but he was engraving, if I am not mistaken, a work of art that had already captured his imagination and that of his circle.

The Grecian urn makes its entry into English poetry, then, with Blake. *The Little Girl Lost* and *Found* tell the story that Blake first learned from the Portland vase; Lyca is the *Kore*, whose death—or, as Blake says, "sleep"—is watched with such grave wonder by the man and woman on the urn.

If we may guess what, in Blake's imagination, his "Funeral Urns of Beulah" were like, we may not be wrong in supposing that they, too, were

59 Mourners weeping over effigies of the dead: title page of *Songs of Experience* (1794)

somewhat like the Portland vase. It is said of the Daughters of Beulah that

> . . . *the Eternal Promise*
> *They wrote on all their tombs & pillars, & on every Urn*
> *These words: "If ye will believe, your Brother shall rise again,"*
> *In golden letters ornamented with sweet labours of Love* [3]

They were, in this, following the classical tradition that inscribed on urns and sarcophagi emblems of the mysteries of the Resurrection.

The two poems, *The Little Girl Lost* and *Found*, at first formed part of *Songs of Innocence;* and Blake later transferred the plates to *Experience.* The date on the title page of *Songs of Innocence* is 1789; but we must remember that the dates on Blake's title pages are not publication dates.

They indicate no more than that Blake was at work on a particular book at that time. It was quite in character for Blake to begin work, in the energetic enthusiasm of a new inspiration, with the title page.[4] We may suppose that most of the *Songs of Innocence* were written by 1789, when the title page was made, but we cannot be sure that they all were. There is no fixed order assigned to the poems, and the two poems in question may very well have been among the last that Blake wrote before he set to work on *Experience*. The fact that he later transferred these two poems suggests that they belonged to the new series in spirit and in theme; the eight opening lines of *The Little Girl Lost*, expanded into the *Introduction* and *Earth's Answer* at the beginning of the second series of poems, serve as the enigmatic key to the mysteries of Experience—for Mysteries these are, in the religious sense of the word. *Experience*, as a whole, deals with the world of the soul that has "died," or "lapsed," from an eternal into a temporal state; and his readings of   [59, 60] the Neoplatonists, whose constant theme is death-in-life and life-in-death, must have helped Blake to define the state that he calls "Experience." On the title page of *Experience* two mourners bend over effigies of the dead, laid upon Gothic tombs which suggest, in style, the Royal Tombs of Westminster; the style disguises the Neoplatonic meaning of the emblem. The dead or sleeping figures are those lapsed from eternity; and all the poems that follow—we are to understand—concern the state of the living dead in the world-cave. There is no ground for the often expressed view that Blake regarded experience as a state of equal value with innocence, or indeed of any value at all; it is a state of delusion, "Error, or Creation," which originates with the fall of man and has no place in "Truth, or Eternity."

 The Little Girl Lost and *Found* are based upon the Mysteries of Eleusis; their actors are the emblematic figures on the Portland vase, interpreted in the light of Taylor's *Dissertation on the Eleusinian and Bacchic Mysteries*.[5] In the first compartment of the vase there is a reclining   [61] virgin figure beneath a tree. In the maiden's hand is an inverted torch, emblem of death. She is falling into the sleep of death; and Darwin, in his commentary, describes her as an hieroglyphic or Eleusinian emblem of mortal life. She and two attendant figures "sit on loose piles of stone beneath a tree, which has not the leaves of any evergreen of this climate, but may be supposed to be an elm, which Virgil places near the entrance of the infernal regions, and adds, that a dream was believed to dwell under every leaf of it."[6] The original Lyca, who invites death with the words:

Sweet sleep, come to me
Underneath this tree [7]

is the lovely recumbent figure of the Portland vase. The man and woman who so gravely watch her are the "father" and "mother" of Blake's poems. Darwin compares them to Adam and Eve.

[62]   The figures on the reverse side of the urn show the soul of the newly dead entering Hades, led by Love and greeted by a woman who holds a

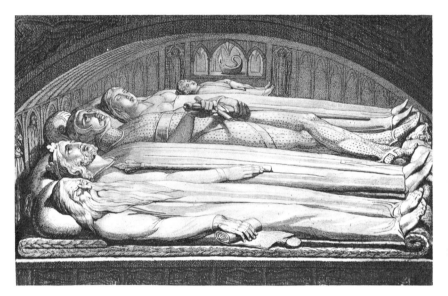

60 "The Counsellor, King, Warrior, Mother & Child in the Tomb": design by Blake for Blair's *Grave* (1808)

The Gothic style of this suggests the influence of the Royal Tombs in Westminster Abbey, of which Blake made drawings during his apprenticeship to Basire.

serpent upon her knees, and a man, presumably the god Hades. The youthful figure of the initiate discards, as he enters Hades, his garment (his "mortal dress," Darwin says)—the original, perhaps, of Lyca's "slender dress."

The story of Lyca in the two poems *The Little Girl Lost* and *Found* is, then, Blake's version of the myth of Persephone and Demeter. Blake's poems are symbolic on several levels, like the Mysteries themselves. The rape of Proserpina, as we know from Apuleius (whom Taylor quotes), was exhibited among the symbolic shows of the Mysteries; and to consider the myth first simply as a narrative, we may see that this story is the basis of Blake's story of Lyca. Taylor's version of the classical myth is as follows:

61 The first compartment of the Portland vase: engraving by Blake
for Darwin's *Botanic Garden* (1791)

62 The second compartment of the Portland vase

Proserpine, the daughter of Ceres by Jupiter, as she was gathering tender flowers, in the new spring, was ravished from her delightful abodes by Pluto; and being carried from thence through thick woods, and over a length of sea, was brought by Pluto into a cavern, the residence of departed spirits, over whom she afterwards ruled with absolute sway. But Ceres, upon discovering the loss of her daughter, with lighted torches, and begirt with a serpent, wandered over the whole earth for the purpose of finding her till she came to Eleusina; there she found her daughter, and discovered to the Eleusinians the plantation of corn.[8]

We are told in the two stanzas that preface the first poem that what is to follow is the story of "earth," her sleep and return to her "maker." Lyca, like Persephone, is a personification of the flowering earth:

> *In futurity*
> *I prophetic see*
> *That the earth from sleep*
> *(Grave the sentence deep)*
>
> *Shall arise and seek*
> *For her maker meek;*
> *And the desart wild*
> *Become a garden mild.*

Blake's Lyca, like the figure of Persephone, is at once the human soul and the soul of the earth. The sleeper is Lyca; but it is "earth" who will awake. This alone should tell us that we are to read what follows as myth. Persephone, as earth in spring, and Ceres, as earth in harvest, are considered by the Neoplatonists to be one and the same, just as the virgin Lyca and the aged Earth of *Earth's Answer* are one and the same. Blake has beautifully combined a classical and a biblical allusion in the flowering of the desert that is to follow the awakening of earth. The passage from Isaiah that foretells that the desert shall blossom as the rose is one to which Blake was to return in *The Marriage of Heaven and Hell*, whose theme is the condition of that new blossoming. The inner content of the biblical myth Blake took to be identical with that of the blossoming which heralds the return of Persephone.

The story of Lyca is of a wandering, a descent into a "cavern," a sleep; a search and discovery by her mother; and a foretold awakening and return.

The first of the two poems follows the action of the Lesser Mysteries of Eleusis, which celebrated the rape of the maiden Persephone by the god of the underworld; the second, that of the Greater Mysteries, which tell of the wanderings of Demeter. Blake closely follows both Taylor's account and his symbolic interpretation.

According to the Neoplatonists, the rape of Proserpina represents the descent of the soul and "its union with the dark tenement of the body." Taylor quotes Olympiodorus' commentary on the *Phaedo*, where it is said that "The soul descends Corically, or after the manner of Proserpine, into generation, but is distributed into generation Dionysiacally; and she is bound to the body Prometheiacally and Titanically; she frees herself from its bonds by exercising the strength of Hercules; but she is collected into one through the assistance of Apollo and the saviour Minerva, by philosophizing in a manner truly cathartic." [9] Taylor further says that Ceres represents "that self-inspective part of our nature which we properly denominate *intellect*," and Proserpina, "that vital, self-moving, and animating part which we call *soul*"; [10] Pluto "signifies the whole of a material nature," and the cavern, "the entrance, as it were, into the profundities of such a nature, which is accomplished by the soul's union with this terrestrial body." This seems to have been the passage that suggested to Blake his treatment of the theme of Lyca.[11]

Lyca's native home, like Persephone's, was

> *In the southern clime,*
> *Where the summer's prime*
> *Never fades away.*

The "southern clime" may be read as the vales of Sicily, the flowery island where the daughter of Demeter dwelt before her rape, or, to read the eternal through the temporal, the intelligible world of light, where death and mutability have no place. Earlier, in *Thel*, Blake had used Porphyry's symbol of the northern gate; and here he refers to the southern dwelling of the Immortals, the eternal world. Elsewhere Blake is more explicit in his identification of the South with the region of the Immortals; in *Vala* "many Eternal Men" sit at the feast of the gods in the "bright South":

> *The Eternal Man arose. He welcom'd them to the Feast.*
> *The feast was spread in the bright South, & the Eternal Man*
> *Sat at the feast rejoicing . . .*[12]

63 The second plate (upper half) of *The Little Girl Lost* from *Songs of Experience* (1789–94)

Compare the reclining figure of Lyca beneath the tree with the similar figure in [73], said to be dreaming in "the vale of Leutha" (sexuality).

Lyca is, in an unexplained way, overcome with drowsiness. She lies down under the branches of a tree, and she summons sleep:

[63]

> *Sweet sleep, come to me*
> *Underneath this tree.*

The apparent naïveté of the lines could not be more misleading: the symbol of the tree in Blake signifies always the natural universe, the vegetated condition of generation. The tree of Genesis is, of course, implied, but this is not the whole allusion. Trees and woods in classical mythology, Taylor argues, are symbols of material nature, "the word *silva*, as is well known, being used by ancient writers to signify matter"—from which we are to understand why Vergil makes Aeneas descend into the underworld "through a wood." Here he quotes the passage from Book VI of the *Aeneid* that describes the hero's descent into the infernal regions. At the entrance of Hades there stands an elm, beneath whose branches reposes the god of sleep himself:

> *In medio ramos annosaque brachia pandit*
> *Ulmus opaca, ingens; quam sedem somnia vulgo*
> *Vana tenere ferunt, foliisque sub omnibus haerent*

or in Dryden's translation (to which Blake would most likely have turned for an English version):

> *Full in the midst of this infernal Road,*
> *An Elm displays her dusky Arms abroad:*

> *The God of Sleep here hides his heavy Head;*
> *And empty Dreams on ev'ry Leaf are spread.*[13]

It is therefore entirely appropriate that Lyca should invoke sleep under the branches of the tree of dreams, of the maya of generated life.

Darwin, a year or two later, was to call the tree on the Portland vase an elm (against the plain evidence of his eyes and, what is more, in a work on botany), because he considered that symbolically this must be so. Darwin's authority was not Thomas Taylor but Warburton's *Divine Legation.* Warburton held that Aeneas' descent into Hades in *Aeneid* VI was an account of the mysteries of the Eleusinian initiation—a view that Taylor shared; and Warburton lays especial stress on the elm. Blake's:

> *Once a dream did weave a shade*
> *O'er my Angel-guarded bed* [14]

and his:

> *Sweet dreams, form a shade*
> *O'er my lovely infant's head* [15]

surely also suggest those dreams of mortal life hidden under the leaves of the tree of sleep.

It is by no means easy to identify the trees depicted in the accompanying designs. In the second illustration, in which Lyca is seen half-reclining under a tree, the black and white patches on the bark suggest rather the birch (the Celtic tree of death, as Blake might have known from Percy's ballads) than the elm. But that the tree shown in the third plate is an elm any naturalist can see. Only the great trunk is shown—*ingens*, as Vergil says— divided into two boles which enwrap one another as they ascend. This detail is symbolic, not naturalistic, indicating the duality of the tree of the knowledge of good and evil.[16] But Blake has been at pains to show the bark as heavily grained; and while no leafy boughs are shown, there are many slender twigs emerging from the trunk itself—a well-known characteristic of the elm and, in particular, of the pollarded hedgerow elms, once beautiful features of the landscape of the country around London.[17]

Lyca longs to sleep, and appropriately summons the god of sleep and dreams under his own tree; but she fears that her mother will not wish her to sleep. This seemingly inexplicable and unmotherly prohibition becomes understandable when we have realized under what tree it is that her daughter has invoked "sweet sleep." The sleep she has invoked is death; the

[64]

tree stands at the entrance to Hades. Here, for a moment, we are meant to be reminded, it seems, of the primary meaning of death; Lyca is dying, and although the soul has no fear of death, she sees that her parents weep for her:

> *Do father, mother weep,*
> *Where can Lyca sleep?*

Blake here seems to be thinking of the pathos of the group of three figures on the Portland vase: the "father" and "mother" who sadly watch the death-sleep of the virgin. But we are carried on, almost at once, to the second level of the symbol: death as the descent of the soul from the eternal to the temporal world.

Taylor defines Demeter as "the self-inspective part of our nature," intellect. Such a "mother" will never willingly consent to the soul's lapse into the sleep of Lethean forgetfulness that is consequent upon a descent into generation. The descending soul, sinking into *amnesis*, must somehow elude the vigilance of the intellect, or higher reason, as, in another myth, Adam and Eve must "hide" from God:

> *How can Lyca sleep*
> *If her mother weep?*

but:

> *If her heart does ake*
> *Then let Lyca wake;*
> *If my mother sleep,*
> *Lyca shall not weep.*

If the story were simply that of a lost little girl being sought by her parents, this would be nonsensical: no mother would refuse sleep to her weary child; and no child lost in a forest would give, as a reason for her inability to sleep, her mother's vigilance and sorrow. Fear might keep her awake, or the anxiety at *not* being found by her parents, but not, conceivably, the opposite fear here described – that of displeasing her mother by falling asleep. Nor would the daughter dry her tears at the thought that her mother has given up the search for her, and herself fallen asleep. Blake's poem is myth pure and simple.

If we read Lyca's sleep as death in the primary sense, we may understand the parents' reluctance to let Lyca sleep; but this explanation is inadequate to explain Lyca's positive desire, her invocation, of sleep, or the wish implied for her *mother* to sleep. But if we see the mother as the higher consciousness that opposes the lapse of the soul into its temporal dream, all becomes clear. She is about to "live the death" or, in Blake's symbolism, "wake to the sleep" of generated life, while the "mother" in eternity, conversely, sinks, like the god in the sun's chariot in the Arlington Court tempera, into a phase of unconsciousness.

Lyca has come to the place of the people of dreams, and will presently follow her desire to descend into the world of generation to which her drowsiness so strongly attracts her: "For to be plunged in matter, is to descend into Hades, and there fall asleep." Earthly existence as a *dream* is one of Blake's favorite symbols—the dream of the lost emmet, "the lost Traveller's dream under the hill," the "deadly dreams that the soul falls into when it leaves Paradise following the serpent"; and so with the symbol of sleep or "deadly sleep," which is used so powerfully to describe the condition of fallen Albion. The dreams under the leaves of the elm are mortal lives.

Blake would have been familiar, from Taylor's *Porphyry*, with the

64 The third page of *The Little Girl Found* from *Songs of Experience* (1789–94)

Compare the reclining figure of Lyca with similar figure of Vala [80], reclining beside not a lion but a ram; and the double trunk with [29].

view that it is pleasure which draws souls downward to generation. The goddess Night advises Jupiter to make use of honey as an artifice to ensnare the god Saturn.

> *When stretch'd beneath the lofty oaks you view*
> *Saturn, with honey by the bees produc'd,*
> *Sunk in ebriety, fast bind the God* [18]

. . . The theologists obscurely signifying by this that divine natures become through pleasure bound and drawn down into the realms of generation. This pleasure, symbolized as honey, is "the pleasure arising from copulation." In the same work Blake would have found quoted the passage from the *Phaedo* describing the souls drinking the waters of forgetfulness, "the new drink of matter's impetuous flood, through which the soul, becoming defiled and heavy, is drawn into a terrene situation." Lyca's desire for [65] sleep is of this order—the irresistible desire of sexual pleasure through which the "moist" soul comes to drink the honeyed cup of generation. Porphyry says that the lapse into generation, through the attraction toward moisture, appears "delightful and not deadly" to souls like Lyca or the little figure in [30] the right foreground of the Arlington Court tempera, in blissful sleep as she lies half-immersed in the river of generation. That Lyca's fall was also sexual is implied by the design to plate 34, which shows a maiden with her lover, pointing to the "sweet bird" whose song she hears. Leutha (who is sexuality) is called the "luring bird of Eden" (see below, p. 174). Blake [66] painted Eve in Paradise "naming the birds." [19]

Lyca, then, like Persephone, falls into danger through a temporary separation from her mother. Ceres had left her daughter unguarded in Sicily, and Persephone wandered out into the meadows, gathering flowers. Lyca, apparently without fear and, like Persephone in Enna, following only her own pleasure, had

> *. . . wander'd long*
> *Hearing wild birds' song.*

In the Greek myth the rape is unsought by Persephone; [20] but in Blake's telling of the myth it is the soul herself who wishes to descend. This is perfectly comprehensible if we consider his sources, in particular Porphyry, who, following Plotinus, stresses the voluntary nature of the soul's descent. Lyca, at the foot of the tree of sleep, summons the powers of darkness, night, and the moon, all traditionally associated with the entry of souls into generation:

> *Frowning, frowning night,*
> *O'er this desart bright*
> *Let thy moon arise*
> *While I close my eyes.*

Plato tells that the souls descend into incarnation at midnight, "this period being peculiarly accommodated to the darkness and oblivion of a corporeal nature; and to this circumstance the nocturnal celebration of the mysteries doubtless alluded"—so Taylor comments. The moon, according to Proclus,[21] "is the cause of nature to mortals," and her association with the descent of souls into birth and generation is described at length by Porphyry, who further tells us that the Tropic of Cancer is attributed to the moon, because this tropic—the northern gate—is that through which souls descend to earth. It is in the lunar house that the souls drink "the starry cup placed between Cancer and the Lion, a symbol of this mystic truth, signifying that descending souls first experience intoxication in that part of the heavens through the influx of matter. Hence oblivion, the companion of intoxication, there begins silently to creep into the recesses of the soul." [22]

65 The first plate of *The Little Girl Lost* from *Songs of Experience* (1789–94)

Note the "luring bird" which, with the "weeping" tree, is also shown in [80].

There is no mention of the northern gate in the poems of Lyca, nor of the sign of Cancer. Blake does, however, introduce the next sign of the Zodiac: the Lion. For the lion—as we ought to expect—makes his appearance just at that point in the narrative at which Lyca has sunk into oblivion in (presumably) the lunar house of Cancer. She has now passed the frontiers of generation, and a new existence awaits her. In the myth of Persephone it is Pluto who bears the virgin away to his subterranean palace; and why Blake chose to substitute a lion for Pluto will be made clear by a further quotation from Macrobius:

> Pythagoras thought that *the empire of Pluto, began downwards from the milky way*, because souls falling from thence, appear already to have recèded from the Gods. . . . On this account, since those who are about to descend, are yet in *Cancer*, and have not left the milky way, they rank in the order of gods. *But when by falling they arrive at the Lion; in this constellation, they enter on the exordium of their future condition.* And, because in the Lion, the rudiments of birth, and certain primary exercises of human nature commence.[23]

This is precisely the situation in which Lyca encounters the lion; she is at the beginning of her human incarnation—the "exordium of her future condition." She enters the empire of Pluto (that is, this world), *when she arrives at the lion;* for here she is no longer in the world of the gods but in generation. Lyca is, from this point on, throughout the remaining verses of the two poems, *asleep.* She has forgotten her former life, and is in the condition of those souls who in Plato's myth of Er have drunk the waters of Lethe. In her sleep she is conveyed by the lion and lioness to "caves"—the "caverns deep" of Pluto's kingdom.

An additional meaning of the lion and the lioness refers to a piece of information that Blake must have found in Warburton's *Divine Legation* (a work to which both Taylor and Darwin refer).[24] The priest and priestess of Mithra, whose duty it was to initiate adepts into the Mysteries of the sacred cave, were called the Lion and the Lioness. Their being so named is no doubt related to the information given by Macrobius about the significance of the Lion of the Zodiac. Lyca's lion is both king of the caves and dens—Pluto himself—and his priest, with his consort lioness.

With the carrying of Lyca into the cave, we have, again, a momentary re-emergence of the primary meaning of death:

66 "Eve Naming the Birds": water-color
drawing (1802)

> *While the lioness*
> *Loos'd her slender dress,*
> *And naked they convey'd*
> *To caves the sleeping maid.*

The soul, naked without its mortal body, entering the realms of the dead, is
the only possible reading of these lines. The generating souls, on the
contrary, are given woven garments by the nymphs of the cave:

> *Some find a Female Garment there,*
> *And some a Male, woven with care.*[25]

In Lyca's cave it seems as though Blake, in attempting to keep all his multiple meanings in mind simultaneously, has failed at this point. Those dying
from this world discard a garment; those who "die" from eternity assume
one. Yet the line is beautiful and imaginatively satisfying, if we do not insist
upon pressing every possible meaning of the symbol at every point in the
poem. In the total impression one would not wish this lovely quatrain
changed.

The lion-king finds Lyca on "hallow'd ground." Caves were, Porphyry says, the earliest shrines and, in Mithraism, places of initiation. It is into such a sacred place that the sleeping maid is carried by the lion, in whose house she enters upon her "future condition," which is at once that of a generated soul and of marriage; for "Souls proceeding into generation are the Nymphs called Naiades. Hence it is usual to call those that are married Nymphs, as being conjoined to generation." The soul descends; but that descent is itself a sacred mystery, and the place of that descent, the world-cave, "hallow'd ground." Lyca "descends" as a child, seven years old; but her married condition is shown by the children playing beside her. Taylor provides a hint here; for he says that "previous to the soul's merging into the dark receptacle of matter," its energies are in their "infantine state" [26] – thus plainly implying that the soul perfects itself only through experience.

In this nocturnal underworld, animal forms play about the sleeping Lyca:

> *Leopards, tygers, play*
> *Round her as she lay.*

It may be that Blake was here, again, thinking of Vergil's account of the descent into Hades, in whose cavernous entrance, once the elm tree is passed, monstrous forms encounter the traveler: "Multaque praeterea variarum monstra ferarum." Animal existences are, in the Neoplatonic symbolism, creatures of the world of generation–"omniform and terrific monsters," Taylor says.

Taylor's account represents this mystery of generation as one of double aspect–from the point of view of the eternals (represented by Demeter) a disaster, yet from the other side–that of Hades–the greatest blessing. The "descent of intellect into the realms of generation becomes, indeed, the greatest benefit and ornament which a material nature is capable of receiving: for without the participation of intellect in the lowest regions of matter, nothing but irrational soul and a brutal life would subsist in its dark and fluctuating abode." [27] Zeus, in the myth, overrules Demeter's protestations, and permits and enables the King of Hades to carry off the maiden. Taylor quotes Claudian's poem on the Rape of Proserpina, in which the holy significance of this marriage is stressed. The account seems to foreshadow the myths associated with Jesus in the harrowing of hell and the freeing of the imprisoned souls; for it is said that on the night of the marriage of Persephone all the souls in Hades rejoiced, that no souls descended into the underworld, and that Charon the ferryman rowed his empty boat on the river of Lethe, singing. The descent of Persephone, foreshadowing that of Jesus, brings hope to the place of darkness, which is illuminated by the presence of a heavenly nature.

Blake follows this traditional understanding of the mystery in describing the joy of the beasts at Lyca's presence. The lion gambols and weeps for joy, and no harm is offered to the sleeping maiden. Plato, also, in the *Timaeus*

> both praises the world and calls it a blessed god, and, asserts that soul was given to the universe by its beneficent artificer, that it might possess an intellectual condition; since it is requisite that the world should be intellectual, which cannot take place without the intervention of soul. Hence soul was infused into the universe by the demiurgus on this account; and each of our souls was in a similar manner inserted into body, as necessary to the perfection of the whole. For it is requisite that as many and similar genera of animals should be contained in the sensible, as abide in the intelligible world.[28]

The second of the two poems takes up the theme of the Greater Mysteries, in which were celebrated the Great Mother's search for her lost daughter. Demeter, inconsolable, sets out on her long wanderings in search of Persephone; and the search of Lyca's parents is but a paraphrase of the myth:

> *All the night in woe*
> *Lyca's parents go*
> *Over vallies deep,*
> *While the desarts weep.*
>
> *Tired and woe-begone,*
> *Hoarse with making moan,*
> *Arm in arm seven days*
> *They trac'd the desert ways.*[29]

The presence of two parents in Blake's poem might seem an obstacle to this view. But it is strikingly evident that only the mother counts. It is the mother's vigilance that prevents the virgin's falling asleep; and it is the mother's grief that is stressed in *The Little Girl Found*:

> *Rising from unrest,*
> *The trembling woman prest*
> *With feet of weary woe;*
> *She could no further go.*

This is the essence of the old story of the wandering mother-goddess of Eleusis, who refused all rest and comfort as she traveled the earth seeking for her child. Demeter's wanderings are the type of the journey of all the initiates of Eleusis, who, like the Great Mother, seek the dead in ignorance of the "eternal promise" whose revelation is the outcome of the search.

Just as Persephone descends into night (who, personified, presides over the nuptial couch of Pluto and his bride), so in her turn the mother—intellect—must descend into the night of this world to seek for her lost daughter, the incarnating soul: "According to the Fable the wanderings of Ceres commence after the rape of Proserpine; hence intellect descends posterior to the soul, and in a separate manner. The defection and revolt commences indeed from the soul, and afterwards takes place in intellect, yet not so as the former descends without the inescapable attendance of the latter." [30]

Lyca, in the first of the two poems, invokes "frowning, frowning, night," since (so Taylor comments on Claudian) "the soul through her union with a material body becomes familiar with darkness, and subject to the empire of night, in consequence of which she dwells wholly with delusive phantoms." These are the shades of Hades, the seeming realities of this world. Claudian describes Persephone's "appearing in a dream to Ceres, bewailing her captive and miserable condition, for such indeed is the wretched condition of the soul when profoundly merged in a corporeal nature." From the point of view of the immortal mother, the daughter's descent is so understood; Lyca's parents also

> *. . . dream they see their child*
> *Starv'd in desart wild.*
>
> *Pale, thro' pathless ways*
> *The fancied image strays*
> *Famish'd, weeping, weak,*
> *With hollow piteous shriek.*

Taylor does not make any mention of Persephone's refusal of food in Hades; but Blake's "famish'd" suggests that he also knew other versions of the myth, which tell the episode of the eating of the seven seeds of a pomegranate. (This he might well have added from Ovid's *Metamorphoses*.)

The number seven appears as a recurrent and inexplicable theme in the two Lyca poems. Lyca is "seven summers old" at the time of her descent into the caverns; and her parents sought her for seven days and nights:

> *Arm in arm seven days*
> *They trac'd the desart ways.*
>
> *Seven nights they sleep*
> *Among shadows deep,*

and on the eighth they meet the lion. The seven seeds might seem, from Ovid's [31] version of the myth, to be a measure of time, since they determine the partition of Persephone's year, above and below. But the number seven also occurs in Plato's mythology.[32] The souls returning to incarnation, having been allotted their lives, travel for "seven days" across a desert, hot and dry, and, at the end of this journey, reach the waters of Lethe (matter), whose oblivion they drink and immediately "descend" into generation. Lyca enters incarnation in the seventh sign; and the parents, also, seek for their daughter seven days, and on the eighth come, in turn, to the sign of the lion:

> *Till before their way*
> *A couching lion lay.*
>
> . . .
>
> *"Follow me," he said;*
> *"Weep not for the maid;*
> *In my palace deep*
> *Lyca lies asleep."*

The "palace deep" of Hades is described by Vergil in the sixth book of the *Aeneid;* it is a "golden" palace. The gold of the underworld has, in Blake's poem, transferred itself to the lion-king himself, who is

> *A Spirit arm'd in gold.*
>
> *On his head a crown,*
> *On his shoulders down*
> *Flow'd his golden hair.*
> *Gone was all their care.*

The King of Hades is not, after all, ironclad in the dress of the fallen world; he is—when seen with the eyes of vision—golden, divine. This epiphany is the climax of the poem, and its central meaning. So, according to some classical sources, the Zeus of the underworld is the same as the Zeus of Olympus, and Persephone's marriage, a marriage to the supreme deity himself.

This teaching is akin to the teaching of the alchemists, dear to Blake, "that which is beneath is like that which is above and that which is above is like that which is beneath." In *Thel* Blake had already described the alchemical "marriage" of the matron Clay with "He that loves the lowly." Here again the ruler of the underworld, the "spirit arm'd in gold," is surely conceived in terms of the *deus absconditus* of alchemy, appearing as he does in the "lowest effects" as in the "highest causes."

So in the "palace deep" (does not the worm "Erect a palace of Eternity in the jaws of the hungry grave?") the parents find Lyca sleeping safe among "tygers wild," and the immortal intellect must, according to divine providence, remain in the lower world in attendance on that child of heaven, the soul:

> *To this day they dwell*
> *In a lonely dell;*
> *Nor fear the wolvish howl*
> *Nor the lion's growl.*

Lyca is still in her sleep at the end of the poem. Blake made no question but that the generated soul is asleep, and the promised awakening is foreseen only in a remote future, when

> *. . . the earth from sleep*
> (*Grave the sentence deep*)
>
> *Shall arise and seek*
> *For her maker meek.*

Here one may stop to consider the poem as an essay in mythological composition. Blake is now using a far more subtle interplay of varied symbolic depths than is to be found in the Swedenborgian early period, or even in *Thel*. Jung and Kerényi see the essence of myth in the action and movement of symbolic personification.[33] In this sense myth is a poetic figure, more complex than metaphor or symbol; from an aesthetic point of view the movement and transformation of the symbolic event must be considered as a single whole. But if the formal structure of myth may be regarded aesthetically, it remains metaphysical in its essence; and it is impossible to judge a mythological composition by aesthetic standards without apprehending it in depth. The structure of the myth must be firmly grounded at all levels, and the meanings of the symbols at these different levels harmonized into a single and consistent whole; the images must have their harmonic resonances on all levels, as well as a melodic theme in themselves. These structural levels of myth were discussed by the philosophers from whom Blake was now learning; and Taylor in his *Dissertation* gives the gist of Sallust's account [34] of the structure of myth. There can be no doubt that Blake was deeply influenced, as a mythological poet, by Sallust's thought.

Fables, Sallust says, are of four kinds; some "are theological, others physical, others animastic (or relating to soul) others material, and lastly, others mixed from these." Taylor, in presenting Sallust's thought and in demonstrating by his own exegesis of the myth of the *Kore* "how infinitely superior the explanation which the Platonic philosophy affords of these fables is to the frigid and trifling interpretations of Bacon and other modern mythologists," certainly opened a door long closed, making it possible for the Romantic poets to use to the full the potential of myths long emptied of content. For whatever the "true" interpretation of myths may be (it is hard to know what criterion we can here employ), their greatest value is quite obviously to be discovered in those works (of philosophy or of art) in which they are made the vehicles of the fullest possible content. The moderns, says Taylor, "are able indeed to point out their correspondence to something in the natural or moral world, because such is the wonderful connection of things, that all things sympathize with all, but are at the same time ignorant that these fables were composed by men divinely wise, who framed them after the model of the highest originals, from the contemplation of real and permanent being, and not from regarding the delusive and fluctuating objects of sense." [35] Whatever may have been the earliest meaning of the Greek myths, the Neoplatonic philosophers may be said to have read into, or out of, them more truth than any other interpreters; and to this school, therefore, the artists and poets have turned and returned.[36]

The fable of Proserpina, Taylor says, "is properly of a mixed nature, or composed from all the four species of fables, the theological, physical, animastic, and material." One part (the life of Proserpina with the celestial gods) "relates to the supermundane establishment of the secondary cause of life [i.e. the *Kore*] and the other to the procession of life and soul to the extremity of things." He then analyzes the fable according to Sallust's four divisions; and there can be no doubt that Blake was at pains to write his two poems on the *Kore* with due attention to the four divisions of Sallust and Taylor's application of them.

First, there is the outward form itself, the fable. It is a story, a fairy tale, designed to capture our attention, while evoking a mood appropriate to its content by the very images it employs; little girl, night, and tree, the lion with his golden crown, the desert, and the cave cannot fail to hold our interest and our sense that "more is meant than meets the ear"—the necessary point of departure for any symbolic work. When a story is obviously nonsensical on the level of natural fact, the reader ought thereby to be shown that the meaning lies deeper. Blake sets the mood of wonder by the slow, subtle incantation of the meter, with its three-stressed, end-stopped lines, which seem to call upon us to pause and ponder an event whose nature is grave, significant, yet at the same time simple; for the verse form has an almost didactic clarity which is counterpointed, as it were, against the obscurity of the images and the narrative.

Considering Sallust's second—the physical—sense of the myth, Blake was certainly not unaware that the story of Proserpina is, on one level of meaning, that of the blossoming earth; the "desart wild" is to become a "garden mild"; and the personification of earth is strengthened in the sequels, *Introduction* and *Earth's Answer*, and in the later figure of Ahania, the "corn field" and "vegetater happy." But Blake seems to justify Sallust's opinion that the animastic level is "proper to poets," by his beautiful elaboration of the theme of the soul. Lyca is the dying soul; she has no fear of death, but sees the grief of her parents. The discussion of the parents' grief at Lyca's sleep becomes meaningful when we understand that the sleep is death; and in the second poem the "fancied image" of Lyca's ghost evokes the poignant and everlasting human grief for the dead by those who are unsure of their fate. The solemnity of the bearing of Lyca into the cave by the lion and the lioness is seen to be appropriate in mood to death and burial.

When we come to the third—the theological—level of meaning, and see the two poems as a discourse on the theme "who knows if to live is not to die, and to die to live?" the full weight of every episode and every image clearly emerges. A child lost in a desert is a symbol of the poor frail soul of the dead; and death itself is but another emblem of the mystery of man's condition in the cave-grave of this world. Beyond this meaning again, we are made to understand that the human condition is a manifestation of the divine nature, of the presence of the gods (the lion-king) "in the lowest effects as in the highest causes." Blake's poem is sustained on all the levels required by Sallust. His originality in writing such a poem in 1790 cannot be exaggerated; but in praising Blake, we must add a tribute to Thomas Taylor, who more than anyone made possible the Romantic poets' magnificent use of myths. It should now be clear that the story of Lyca is a composition of traditional symbolism worked upon in the light of traditional doctrine, and that it can by no means be read in the same terms as Wordsworth's *Lucy Gray*.[37]

Songs of Experience are all, in one way or another, concerned with the nature of things in the underworld into which the soul has, in Neoplatonic terms, "descended." The soul's sufferings in this world, the cruel laws to which she is here subjected, and her inextinguishable longing for eternity are the theme of all the poems; for Experience is Plato's cave, Plotinus' Hades. *Introduction* and *Earth's Answer* give their context to all the poems that follow; and the emblems that accompany them add further symbolic meaning to these two grand and somber poems. They are an expanded version of the two opening verses of *The Little Girl Lost*, and take up the story of Earth, or Lyca, where it is left in *The Little Girl Lost* and *Found*. She is now dwelling in a world of phantoms, "familiar with darkness, and subject to the empire of night," as Taylor writes of the soul; for "till she breaks her fetters she is deprived of the perception of that which is real and true." The accompanying design shows a starlit sky in which Earth rests on [67] her clouds; and the situation described in *Earth's Answer* (the first of the poems to be written, though now the second in order) might be a paraphrase of Taylor's account of the soul in Hades, or generation.[38]

Earth's Answer in the Notebook follows a poem that Blake discarded:

> *Thou hast a lap full of seed,*
> *And this is a fine country.*
> *Why dost thou not cast thy seed*
> *And live in it merrily?*
>
> *Shall I cast it on the sand*
> *And turn it into fruitful land?*

For on no other ground
Can I sow my seed,
Without tearing up
Some stinking weed.[39]

The image of the sower might itself have been suggested by Taylor's essay; for he describes the "sowing" of the souls into the earth by the *Demiurgus* as an aspect of the Eleusinian Mystery of the corn, the same to which St. Paul alludes in his epistle to the Corinthians, the grain that "dies" into the earth to be reaped as the harvest of immortality. Blake takes up the theme again in [68] *The Book of Ahania*, with Urizen as the husbandman. Urizen becomes also the reaper of souls in *The Four Zoas*. The fragment, as it stands, might not have been suggested by Blake's Neoplatonic studies, though it is quite consistent in symbolism with these; but *Earth's Answer* is full of the symbolic imagery of Neoplatonism.

The time has come for the return of the maiden Earth, who was some day to awake from sleep,

67 *Introduction* to *Songs of Experience* (1789–94)

68 Ahania in her youthful form: title page of *The Book of Ahania* (1795), detail

> *And the desart wild*
> *Become a garden mild.*

We left Lyca safe in the care of the lion-king; but is the alchemical text "as above, so below" borne out in experience? Earth declares that this is not so:

> *Earth rais'd up her head*
> *From the darkness dread & drear.*
> *Her light fled,*
> *Stony dread!*
> *And her locks cover'd with grey despair.*
>
> *"Prison'd on wat'ry shore,*
> *Starry Jealousy does keep my den:*
> *Cold and hoar,*
> *Weeping o'er,*
> *I hear the Father of the ancient men.*
>
> .   .   .
>
> *Break this heavy chain*
> *That does freeze my bones around.*
> *Selfish! Vain!*
> *Eternal bane!*
> *That free Love with bondage bound."* [40]

Earth's cry against the restrictions imposed upon the soul in the name of the body is taken up in a later poem, by Oothoon,[41] who like Persephone plucks a golden flower, and who like Earth finds herself, in consequence, raped and carried away to be "prison'd on wat'ry shore," in a cave.

The "starry floor," like the "deeps or skies" of *The Tyger*, suggests the "stars beneath" of the alchemists, and their teaching "as above, so below"; but the darkness, the watery shore, the fetters, and the den are all derived from Neoplatonism. Taylor's essay *On the Wanderings of Ulysses* [42] describes the lamentation of the hero held prisoner by Calypso as the type of soul held captive in the material world: "Indeed, he who is conscious of the delusions of the present life and the enchantments of this material house, in which the soul is detained, like Ulysses in the irriguous cavern of Calypso, will, like himself, continually bewail his captivity, and inly pine for a return to his native country." According to Plotinus, "Men are placed in body as in a certain prison, secured by a guard," [43] and Earth's strange landscape of a prison and a den on a watery shore, in darkness and fettered, is consistent – and consistent only – in terms of the symbolic vocabulary of the Platonists.

If Blake had seen Taylor's *Five Books of Plotinus*, or parts of it, one might be tempted to imagine that *Earth's Answer* was a paraphrase of Plotinus himself: "The soul therefore, falling from on high, suffers captivity, is loaded with fetters, and employs the energies of sense; because in this case her intellectual energy is impeded from the first. She is reported also to be buried, and to be concealed in a cave; but when she converts herself to intelligence, she then breaks her fetters and ascends on high, receiving first of all from reminiscence the ability of contemplating real beings; at the same time possessing something supereminent and ever abiding in the intelligible world." [44] From the same essay (*On the Descent of the Soul*) he might have found the text for his entire philosophy of Experience: "Souls are able . . . to rise from hence, carrying back with them an experience of what they have known and suffered in their fallen state; from whence they will learn how blessed it is to abide in the intelligible world." [45] The essence of Plotinus' thought is also paraphrased by Taylor in his *Dissertation*.

Concerning the Beautiful appeared in 1787. The title page of *Songs of Experience* is dated 1794, the year Taylor's *Five Books* appeared; [46] and the influence of this work is unmistakable on the later poem *Introduction*. The phrases "the lapsed Soul," "fallen light," and "the slumberous mass" can be found in Plotinus' *On the Nature and Origin of Evil*. In Blake's poem "the voice of the Bard" [47] (or "the Holy Word" – the syntax is ambiguous) reminds the soul of her native state:

Calling the lapsed Soul,
And weeping in the evening dew;
That might controll
The starry pole,
And fallen, fallen light renew!

"O Earth, O Earth, return!
Arise from out the dewy grass;
Night is worn,
And the morn
Rises from the slumberous mass." [48]

Plotinus argues that the soul's descent into the material world is the only source of evil; her true country is the world of "divine light," and falling into darkness and "the watery element," she must await in captivity the "break of day" that will restore her to her native place: "matter obscures by sordid mixture . . . *the light which emanates from soul;* by opposing the waters of generation she occasions the soul's entrance into the rapid stream, and by this means renders *her light, in itself vigorous and pure, polluted and feeble,* like the faint glimmerings from a watch tower beheld in a storm; for if matter was never present the soul would never approach to generation; *and this is the lapse of the soul, thus to descend into matter."* [49] A further quotation throws light on the phrase "the slumberous mass"; Blake has condensed into a single fine image a sentence of Plotinus: "the death of the soul is both while merged in body, to descend into matter and be filled with its darkness and deformity, and after it lays aside body, to return into it again, till after proper purgation it rises to things superior, and *elevates its eye from the sordid mass;* for, indeed, to descend into Hades, and *fall asleep* in its dreary regions, means nothing more than to be profoundly merged in the filth and obscurity of body." [50] The "dew" of evening, stressed by repetition in "dewy grass," is of course that "moisture" of the nymphs that forms the watery envelope of the generating soul, "vegetated," as Blake often says, into the "plantal condition" whose nourishment is moisture.

The darkness in both poems is, obviously, spiritual darkness; for "by thus embracing and adhering to corporeal forms, he is precipitated, not so much in his body, as in his soul, into profound and horrid darkness." [51] Taylor, in his enthusiasm for the genius of Plotinus ("full of intellectual light") calls to his readers to enlist under his banner to fight against the materialist philosophy in vogue, and "disperse the darkness of her baneful night." [52] Is Blake, in these poems which are so deeply influenced in their symbolic language by Plotinus, influenced also by Taylor's manifesto, his declaration of war against the current "barbarous ignorance" of "Material-ism, and its attendant Sensuality"? Blake, likewise, believed in the dawn of a new age; he found his hope prophetically sanctioned by Swedenborg; in Thomas Taylor had he at this time found a fellow soldier, "enlisted under the banners of Plotinus"?

The story of Earth is continued in the myth of Ahania, a figure whom we find only in the early Lambeth books. She appears, with little explanation, as the emanation and consort of Urizen; but Blake's seeming failure to explain her to us is easy to understand when we recognize her as Earth and as Lyca. This identity is easy to discover, for *The Book of Ahania* is an expansion of Earth's protest, and expands the Earth Mother's lamentation that her "eternal births" and "infant joys" have been condemned by the laws of Urizen (Starry Jealousy is now so named) to a birth that is spiritual death:

> *Selfish father of men!*
> *Cruel, jealous, selfish fear!*
> *Can delight,*
> *Chain'd in night,*
> *The virgins of youth and morning bear?* [53]

Ahania's last words are almost identical with those of Earth:

> *But now alone over rocks, mountains,*
> *Cast out from thy lovely bosom,*
> *Cruel jealousy! selfish fear!*
> *Self-destroying, how can delight*
> *Renew in these chains of darkness,*
> *Where bones of beasts are strown*
> *On the bleak and snowy mountains,*
> *Where bones from the birth are buried*
> *Before they see the light?* [54]

In *Vala*, Night VIII, Ahania is called "thou corn field! O thou vegetater happy!" She is the "furrowed field," the goddess of the corn harvest, fruitful mother earth. But there are elements of Zeus's other consort, Hera, in Ahania's regal figure. The Orphic Hymn to Hera names her "mother of clouds and winds," and describes her as "thron'd in the bosom of cerulian air." Ahania is often described in imagery associated with clouds—"Like a bright cloud in the harvest"; she wraps Urizen "in her bright skirts," and her casting out by her consort, Urizen, may suggest the severe punishment once meted out to Hera by Zeus, when she was hung suspended in the sky, though the image is in fact taken from the casting out not of Hera but of Ate from Olympus by Zeus:

> . . . *by her bright haire he caught,*
> *Held downe her head, and over her made this infallible vow:*
> *That never to the cope of starres, should reascend that brow,*
> *Being so infortunate to all. Thus, swinging her about,*
> *He cast her from the fierie heaven. . . .*[55]

Compare Blake's account of the casting out of Ahania:

> *Then thunders roll'd around & lightnings darted to & fro;*
> *His visage chang'd to darkness & his strong right hand came forth*
> *To cast Ahania to the Earth: he siez'd her by the hair*
> *And threw her from the steps of ice that froze around his throne* [56]

(Blake, with Chapman's Homer running in his mind, has fallen, consciously or unconsciously, into heptameters.)

The Book of Ahania describes the outcast condition of Earth by a morality that regards the body as evil. Nothing is more dreadful to conceive than a creator who condemns as evil his own creation; and yet, Blake implies, this is the consequence of all those "bibles and sacred codes" that teach that "Evil is alone from the Body." Earth cast out from heaven becomes one of those Newtonian "globes rolling through voidness," a dark shadow circling the sky, more like the dead and sterile moon than the living happy earth:

> *He groan'd anguish'd, & called her Sin,*
> *Kissing her and weeping over her;*
> *Then hid her in darkness, in silence,*
> *Jealous, tho' she was invisible.*
>
> *She fell down a faint shadow wand'ring*
> *In chaos and circling dark Urizen,*
> *As the moon anguish'd circles the earth,*

> *Hopeless! abhorr'd! a death-shadow,*
> *Unseen, unbodied, unknown,*
> *The mother of Pestilence.*[57]

The earth as an immortal divinity is an important Platonic concept; earth, the "moving image of eternity," is called a god by Plato in the *Timaeus*, and his successors pursued the theme of the earth as an immortal god, "eterne in mutability," not undying but perpetually renewed, like the figure of Persephone who dies and lives again. Blake seems to have enriched his thought on the philosophic nature of the earth from his reading of the Hermetica. Like Ahania, the Hermetic earth is "the Fair World, the Feeder and Nurse of Earthly things," [58] "a Body perpetual, than the which there is nothing more ancient, yet always vigorous and young." [59] The world "was once made, and is always, and is ever in generation, and made, and continually makes, or generates things that have quantity and quality. For it is moveable, and every material motion is generation." [60]

Such is Ahania; she is always in generation. In *Earth's Answer* her question arises from her generative nature:

> *Can delight,*
> *Chain'd in night,*
> *The virgins of youth and morning bear?*

In *The Book of Ahania* her complaint is the same: she laments the lost happy time when Urizen's love fell like the showers of Zeus into the lap of earth:

> *"In showers of life on his harvests,*
>
> *"When he gave my happy soul*
> *To the sons of eternal joy,*
> *When he took the daughters of life*
> *Into my chambers of love,*
>
> *"When I found babes of bliss on my beds*
> *And bosoms of milk in my chambers*
> *Fill'd with eternal seed.*
> *O eternal births sung round Ahania*
> *In interchange sweet of their joys!"* [61]

—the fruitfulness of earth as the bride of heaven. The due harmony of heaven and earth is the blissful state of which banished Ahania seeks always to remind Urizen. Of herself she cannot bring forth "eternal births" but only mortal corruption. Everlastingness, according to the *Pymander*, is bestowed upon earth by heaven, which "contains and embraces" her.

> Neither can anything perish, or be destroyed in the World, the World being contained and embraced by Eternity. . . . Eternity, therefore, put into the Matter Immortality and Everlastingness; for the Generation of that depends upon Eternity, even as Eternity doth of God. . . . And the Soul of Eternity is God; and the Soul of the World, Eternity; and of the Earth, Heaven.[62]

Ahania's passivity in relation to Urizen is always stressed. From her "all the lovely sex shall learn obedience"; for is she not the Platonic "image" of eternity?

> *His Shadowy Feminine Semblance here repos'd on a White Couch,*
> *Or hover'd over his starry head; & when he smil'd she brighten'd*
> *Like a bright Cloud in harvest; but when Urizen frown'd she wept*
> *In mists over his carved throne . . .*[63]

Urizen, when he casts her out, condemns her for this very quality, because she is purely passive and receptive in her relation to him:[64]

> *Shall . . .*
> *The passive idle sleep, the enormous night & darkness of Death*
> *Set herself up to give her laws to the active masculine virtue?*
> *Thou little diminutive portion that darst be a counterpart,*
> *Thy passivity, thy laws of obedience & insincerity*
> *Are my abhorrence. . . .*[65]

Urizen follows up this condemnation of the passive feminine principle with a characterization of Ahania in all those images traditionally associated with the world-cave, Porphyry's beautiful "irriguous cavern" of the nymphs:

> *. . . Wherefore hast thou taken that fair form*
>
>   .   .   .
>
> *A sluggish current of dim waters.*[66] *on whose verdant margin*
> *A cavern shaggd with horrid shades. dark cool & deadly. where*
> *I laid my head in the hot noon after the broken clods*
> *Had wearied me. there I laid my plow & there my horses fed.*[67]

Ahania is here the world-cave, a sacred place, beautiful and cool. We remember Porphyry's description of the exterior parts: "pleasant, but its interior and profound parts are obscure, and its very bottom is darkness itself." So Ahania is described as the dark feminine principle, the eternal counterpart of the masculine "light" of Urizen. He looks back to a time of harmony, when the world-cave was a sacred place where the immortals "sleep"; but now he condemns her, calling her "darkness," "deadly," and "horrid."

In thus rejecting "the fair and beautiful world," he has the sanction of many, if not all, of the Platonic philosophers. He is following (while at the same time misunderstanding) the teaching of the first book of the Hermetica, "Nothing good upon Earth, nothing evil in Heaven." [68] Urizen is acting upon the belief that "Things upon Earth do nothing advantage those in Heaven, but all things in Heaven do profit and advantage all things upon Earth." [69] How, then, can Ahania presume to be Urizen's counterpart? All virtue resides in him, he declares, none in her. "The Earth is brutish, the Heaven is reasonable or rational." [70] Urizen does not need Ahania, and casts her out. She retorts by calling him "selfish," because, one may guess, he refuses to give her his love and life, by which alone she lives. Urizen, however, unfamiliar with the philosophy of ancient China, disregarding that of the Smaragdine Table, and pinning his faith to a Platonic half-truth and a long-established tendency of "all Bibles and sacred codes" to impute evil to the body, sees it otherwise:

> *Whatsoever is in Heaven is unalterable.*
> *All upon Earth is alterable.*
> *Nothing in Heaven is servanted; nothing upon Earth free.*
> *Nothing unknown in Heaven; nothing known upon Earth.*
> *The things upon Earth communicate not with those in Heaven.*
> *All things in Heaven are unblameable; all things upon earth are*
> *   subject to reprehension.*[71]

So poor Ahania falls subject to the reprehension of Urizen, who cannot see that he has any need of her. She

> *Fell down, down rushing, ruining, thundering, shuddering,*
> *Into the Caverns of the Grave & places of Human Seed*
> *Where the impressions of Despair & Hope enroot for ever*
> *A world of Darkness. Ahania fell far into Non Entity* [72]

Ahania in nonentity—that is, the place and state of matter—banished from the intelligible world, laments that her productions are a mere generation of death, after the text of the Hermetica, which sees all earth's progeny as changeable, dissolvable, mortal, corruptible; that "which is always made is always corrupted," and earth is "a fit receptacle" only for "corruptible Bodies": [73]

> *Listen to her whose eyes behold the dark body of corruptible death*
> *Looking for Urizen in vain. in vain I seek for morning*
> *The Eternal Man sleeps in the Earth nor feels the vigrous sun.*[74]

If this is all that generated life can give, what difference, Ahania asks, is there between birth and death? Her dialogue with Enion might be—and very likely is—a comment upon the Hermetic test "the Generation of Man is Corruption; the Corruption of Man is the beginning of Generation." [75] The words of Ahania, the generator, are therefore appropriately addressed to Enion, "the wat'ry Grave":

> *Will you erect a lasting habitation in the mouldring Church yard?*
> *Or a pillar & palace of Eternity in the jaws of the hungry grave*
> *Will you seek pleasure from the festering wound or marry for a Wife*
> *The ancient Leprosy that the King & Priest may still feast on your*
> *   decay*
> *And the grave mock & laugh at the plowd field saying*
> *I am the nourisher thou the destroyer in my bosom is milk & wine*
> *And a fountain from my breasts to me come all multitudes*
> *To my breath they obey they worship me I am goddess & queen* [76]

Such is the earth, banished by heaven whose seed, sown in her fields, should be the harvest of eternity.

The image of the relationship of Urizen and Ahania as the sower and the sown (this in itself should be proof enough that Ahania is earth) looks also, and chiefly, to the *Pymander*. "That which is sown is not always begotten; but that which is begotten always is sown." [77] Urizen himself recalls his work as husbandman when he casts out Ahania (he speaks of her "clods" and his "plow"); and in *The Book of Ahania* she reminds him that he is the husband and husbandman of earth:

> *Then thou with thy lap full of seed,*
> *With thy hand full of generous fire*
> *Walked forth from the clouds of morning,*

> *On the virgins of springing joy,*
> *On the human soul to cast*
> *The seed of eternal science.*[78]

—the once familiar figure of the farmer with the seed corn, flinging it broadcast on the plowed earth.

Repentant, Urizen resumes his vocation as earth's husband and husbandman, and again "Eternity is in love with the productions of time." [79] Ahania returns to him, falls at his feet, dead with excess of joy, and is buried in a "cave."

> *. . . She fell down dead at the feet of Urizen*
> *Outstretchd a Smiling corse they buried her in a silent cave* [80]

This, one might say, is a strange beginning to a happy ending; but the descent of the goddess into the "cave" is the beginning of the process of sowing and harvesting. Blake is echoing Plotinus' account of the fallen soul, "She is reported to be buried and concealed in a cave." [81] The goddess must enter this cave, as Persephone in her death-marriage to Hades, in order that the souls of the "dead" may be sown there and spring up into harvest. Therefore, the process must begin with the "death" of the goddess into the world of generation. Next, earth must be plowed:

> *Then siezd the sons of Urizen the Plow they polishd it*
> *From rust of ages all its ornament of gold & silver & ivory*
> *Reshone across the field immense where all the nations*
> *Darkend like Mould in the divided fallows where the weed*
> *Triumphs in its own destruction . . .*[82]

This field of earth is Ahania herself, "the furrowed field."

The "noise of rural work resounded thro the heaven of heavens," as Urizen first plows the earth, then sows the seed:

> *Then he began to sow the seed he girded round his loins*
> *With a bright girdle & his skirt filld with immortal souls*
> *Howling & Wailing fly the souls from Urizens strong hand,*
> *For from the hand of Urizen the myriads fall like stars*
> *Into their own appointed places . . .*[83]

The seed that Urizen sows is "the Seed of Men"; (the image of the falling stars comes from Plato's myth of Er, in the tenth book of the *Republic*) and these souls are the "dead from eternity," waiting for earthly generation:

> *The trembling souls of All the Dead stood before Urizen*
> *Weak wailing in the troubled air. . . .*[84]

They are sown in the fields of earth, and earth is the "grave" from which they spring up:

> *The seed is harrowd in while flames heat the black mould & cause*
> *The human harvest to begin Towards the south first sprang*
> *The myriads, & in silent fear they look out from their graves.*[85]

We are reminded that always underlying Blake's myth is the paradox of death-in-life and the living as the "dead," whose true life is a resurrection[86] when the harvest of the earth is gathered into the barns of eternity. The youth and virgin in *Ah! Sun-flower* who "Arise from their graves" are, likewise, prisoned in the body. The Eternals wait for the harvest to ripen:

> *Then Urizen sits down to rest & all his wearied sons*
> *Take their repose on beds they drink they sing they view the flames*
> *Of Orc in joy they view the human harvest springing up*
> *A time they give to sweet repose till all the harvest is ripe.*[87]

Last comes the harvest:

> *Then Urizen arose & took his sickle in his hand*
>
> .   .   .
>
> *And went forth & began to reap & all his joyful sons*
> *Reapd the wide Universe & bound in sheaves a wondrous harvest.*[88]

A plate in *Milton* shows Ahania with a man and woman ripening as the [69] corn of earth.

Ahania's final apotheosis brings us back once more to the seasonal descent and resurrection of Persephone in an image that beautifully combines the natural and the higher meanings of the symbol; Ahania, like Persephone, is to descend and return, "a Self-renewing Vision":

> *The spring the summer to be thine then sleep the wintry days*
> *In silken garments spun by her own hands against her funeral*

—on those looms of the cave where mortal garments are woven:

The winter thou shalt plow & lay thy stores into thy barns
Expecting to recieve Ahania in the spring with joy.[89]

There is no mistaking the old story; and there is an unbroken continuity from the first appearance of the promise that Earth

Shall arise and seek
For her maker meek

to the perfected mystery of Christian theology.

In her apotheosis Ahania emerges as the great goddess Ceres, or Juno, who by bathing renews her virginity; or as the even more highly exalted Christian figure of the Blessed Virgin, whose Assumption is Catholic doctrine.

And Lo like the harvest Moon Ahania cast off her death clothes
She folded them up in care in silence & her brightning limbs

69 "The Human Harvest": *Milton* (1804–1808), p. 50

The central figure is presumably Ahania "the vegetater happy," who in Blake's mythology corresponds to Ceres.

70 Ceres with poppies of sleep and corn of resurrection: engraving by Chambars for Bryant's *Mythology*, vol. 2 (1774), plate IX

See also [95], in which poppies are associated with the ark of "generation."

Bathd in the clear spring of the rock then from her darksom cave
Issud in majesty divine

  · · ·

And bright Ahania took her seat by Urizen in songs & joy.[90]

A plate in Bryant's *Mythology* expresses, in the form of an emblem, [70] the mystery of the earth-goddess; in her hand she holds the seed of poppies, the flower of sleep, and the seed of corn, emblem of resurrection; for the earth is the place of the soul's sleep and waking, death and resurrection; in the words of St. Paul, "It is sown in corruption; it is raised in incorruption . . . it is sown a natural body; it is raised a spiritual body." And as Blake placed at the beginning of *Songs of Experience* an emblem of the death of the soul, and two poems telling of her burial in the cave or grave of earth, so he added a last plate which brings the myth full circle.[91]

Within the illustration:

To Tirzah

Whate'er is Born of Mortal Birth.
Must be consumed with the Earth
To rise from Generation free:
Then what have I to do with thee?

The Sexes sprung from Shame & Pride
Blow'd in the morn; in evening died
But Mercy chang'd Death into Sleep;
The Sexes rose to work & weep.

Thou Mother of my Mortal part.
With cruelty didst mould my Heart
And with false self-decieving tears.
Didst bind my Nostrils Eyes & Ears

Didst close my Tongue in senseless clay
And me to Mortal Life betray:
The Death of Jesus set me free.
Then what have I to do with thee?

It is Raised a Spiritual Body

71 *To Tirzah* (1801) from *Songs of Experience*

The poem *To Tirzah* was added as the last poem of *Songs of Experience* about 1801; by its addition the series ends, as it had begun, within the framework of the ancient myth of the mystery of corn, the sowing of souls in the grave of Experience. St. Paul in his address to the Corinthians had long ago taken the Eleusinian Mysteries as the foundation of his exposition of the Christian teaching of the Resurrection: "that which thou sowest is not quickened, except it die: And that which thou sowest, thou sowest not that body that shall be, but bare grain, it may chance of wheat, or of some other grain. . . . So also is the resurrection of the dead. It is sown in corruption, it is raised in incorruption: it is sown in dishonour; it is raised in glory: it is sown in weakness; it is raised in power: it is sown a natural body; it is raised a spiritual body. . . . And so it is written, The first man Adam was made a living soul; the last Adam was made a quickening spirit." [92] Thus is the Greek mystery of the corn reinterpreted by the Christian apostle: "Behold, I show you a mystery . . ."; and Blake likewise returned to baptize, as it were, the ancient myth. An apostolic figure is perhaps baptizing a dying man from the vessel he holds; and on his garment are engraved the words, "It is Raised a Spiritual Body," the Christian promise of resurrection. The poem is addressed to the female generative principle, Tirzah:

> *Whate'er is Born of Mortal Birth* [71]
> *Must be consumed with the Earth*
> *To rise from Generation free:*
> *Then what have I to do with thee?*

The power of the female weavers of mortal garments over the generated soul that has "died" into life is removed by Jesus. The Fall and death of Adam and Eve is implicitly equated with the Platonic "sleep" of the soul, the "descent" or "lapse" into mortality:

> *The Sexes sprung from Shame & Pride,*
> *Blow'd in the morn; in evening died;*
> *But Mercy chang'd Death into Sleep;*
> *The Sexes rose to work & weep.*

It is the "Mother of my Mortal part," the female, who "betrays" the generated soul into mortal life; and Blake's last word on the theme of Experience and generation is the Christian affirmation of the triumph of the immortal over the mortal:

> *The Death of Jesus set me free:*
> *Then what have I to do with thee?*

72 Coin from Bryant's *Mythology*, vol. 3 (1776), odd plate

CHAPTER 6

Oothoon in Leutha's Vale

The myth of Oothoon in the *Visions of the Daughters of Albion* makes a third with those of Thel and Lyca; for here, too, Blake has told the story of the soul's descent into generation. Oothoon is the noblest of the three: Thel fears to descend; Lyca falls asleep; but Oothoon brings into the cave the memories and values of eternity. Because she possesses this knowledge she knows that physical forms are embodiments of spiritual essences, and a great part of the poem takes the form of an eloquent debate between the materialistic and idealistic views of the nature of life. (This theme is discussed below, II, 124–126.) She also knows the spiritual nature of love, and eloquently defends Platonic love, "free" love, whose laws are based upon the nature of the soul as the Platonists conceived it. The *Visions* takes up Earth's theme:

> *Selfish! Vain!*
> *Eternal bane!*
> *That free Love with bondage bound.*[1]

Love, as Plato conceived it and as Shelley, Blake, and Mary Wollstonecraft understood it, is of the soul. This love is so far from the promiscuity and license of the profane modern world as to be its direct opposite. Those who defend the "holiness of the heart's affections" against mere legality are not concerned with emancipation of the lower instincts. "What is Immortality but the things relating to the Spirit which Lives Eternally? . . . What are the Pains of Hell but Ignorance, Bodily Lust Idleness & devastation of the things of the Spirit?"[2] But no less is the truth of the soul incompatible with these marriages in which love has no part. Blake knew and perhaps loved Mary Wollstonecraft; and in *Visions of the Daughters of Albion* he has eloquently defended the noble view of love that her life so tragically exemplified. The poem entitled *Mary* is almost certainly addressed to her:

"An Angel is here from the heavenly Climes,
Or again does return the Golden times;
Her eyes outshine every brilliant ray,
She opens her lips—'tis the Month of May."

Mary moves in soft beauty and conscious delight
To augment with sweet smiles all the joys of the Night,
Nor once blushes to own to the rest of the Fair
That sweet Love & Beauty are worthy our care.

In the Morning the Villagers rose with delight
And repeated with pleasure the joys of the night,
And Mary arose among Friends to be free,
But no Friend from henceforward thou, Mary, shalt see.

Some said she was proud, some call'd her a whore,
And some, when she passed by, shut to the door;
A damp cold came o'er her, her blushes all fled;
Her lillies & roses are blighted & shed.[3]

The innate nobility of the soul is called pride, and condemned as unchristian:

To be weak as a Lamb & smooth as a dove,
And not to raise Envy, is call'd Christian Love;

but Mary remains faithful to her inner truth at the cost of her life (as Mary Wollstonecraft did in fact pay for her generous idealism by an early death, after much suffering).

With Faces of Scorn & with Eyes of disdain
Like foul Fiends inhabiting Mary's mild Brain;
She remembers no Face like the Human Divine.
All Faces have Envy, sweet Mary, but thine;

And thine is a Face of sweet Love in despair,
And thine is a Face of mild sorrow & care,
And thine is a Face of wild terror & fear
That shall never be quiet till laid on its bier.

Blake calls her a spirit from the "heavenly Climes," and when he used such phrases he meant what he said. Mary he saw as noble because in the "cave" she attempted to live, as Shelley did with no better success, by the values of

eternity. Blake honored and pitied her; and years later must have remembered her when he wrote: "Many Persons, such as Paine & Voltaire, with
some of the Ancient Greeks, say: 'we will not converse concerning Good &
Evil; we will live in Paradise and Liberty.' You may do so in Spirit, but not
in the Mortal Body as you pretend, till after the Last Judgment . . ." [4]

Mary had attempted, and failed, to rise superior to the limiting
conditions of the cave. *Mary* contains in embryo the theme of the *Visions of
the Daughters of Albion*. Oothoon is Mary; [5] and she continues, in her
prison, to proclaim the morality of the soul. Swinburne wrote that "had it not
seemed inexplicable it must have seemed unbearable." Oothoon's morality
may no longer shock a profane age, but it is extremely doubtful whether it is
better understood now than in the nineteenth century. Its denunciation of
materialism, now as then, will find few supporters.

Mary herself was influenced by Rousseau; and her life was an attempt
to put into practice the philosophy of *Eloisa*. Rousseau's was a natural
morality, but how much nobler and more generous, after all, than the moral
posturings of Richardson's unloving Clarissa and the rest of those monsters
of "virtue" dear to the eighteenth-century novelists. Rousseau affirmed a
natural innocence, which does not, perhaps, sufficiently distinguish, as Blake
did, between the natural and the spiritual man, but which does defend the
living soul against a dead and external morality. Eloisa exclaims: "Nature, O
gentle nature, resume thy rights! I abjure the savage virtues which conspire
to thy destruction. Can the inclinations which thou hast inspired be more
seductive than a specious reason which has so often misled me? . . . No,
no, I am sensible of my crime, but cannot abhor it. Duty, honour, virtue, all
these considerations have lost their influence, but yet I am not a monster: I
am frail, but not unnatural." [6] And her lover replies: "Your remorse – your
remorse! – does it become you to feel remorse? – you whom I loved – you,
whom I shall never cease to adore – Can guilt ever approach your spotless
heart?" [7]

But Blake, by linking the morality of "free" love to the Platonic view
of the soul, places the argument of Oothoon upon a firmer foundation.

Only in this version of the soul's descent does Blake make use of the
episode of the maiden gathering flowers, so beautifully described in Claudian's poem (freely quoted by Taylor in his *Dissertation*) and echoed by
Milton:

> *. . . Proserpin gathring flours*
> *Her Self a fairer Floure by gloomie Dis*
> *Was gather'd, which cost Ceres all that pain*
> *To seek her through the world. . . .*[8]

Blake's Oothoon is, like Persephone, a soul verging upon generation, and attracted to moisture, as symbolized by the "dewy" flower of the "vales of Leutha," which in this poem have replaced Thel's "river of Adona." She

> *. . . wander'd in woe,*
> *Along the vales of Leutha seeking flowers to comfort her;*
>
> *And thus she spoke to the bright Marygold of Leutha's vale:*
> *"Art thou a flower? art thou a nymph? I see thee now a flower,*
> *Now a nymph! I dare not pluck thee from thy dewy bed!"* [9]

The Marygold is a nymph, a naiad of generation; but she also evokes echoes of Shakespeare's "Aubade" from *Cymbeline:*

> *Hark, hark, the lark at Heaven's gate sings*
> *And Phoebus 'gins arise*
> *His Steeds to water at those springs*
> *On chaliced flowers that lies.*
> *And winking Mary-buds begin*
> *To ope their golden eyes.*

Blake had already echoed these lines in *Thel*, where the Cloud asks the virgin:

> *. . . know'st thou not our steeds drink of the golden springs*
> *Where Luvah doth renew his horses? . . .* [10]

The "golden springs" lie "on chaliced flowers," and in the story of Oothoon the chaliced flower itself appears, Shakespeare's Mary-bud, whose chalice for Blake is the cup, honeyed and Lethean, drunk by the soul lured into generation by sexual pleasure. In the eternal cycle of descent and return, the sexual chalice should be a source of renewal and refreshment to the "horses of Luvah" in their perpetual cycle of life and death. Through generation the spirit's vehicle—its "horses"—is renewed by new births, new bodies. The philosophy of Oothoon's Marygold is that of Thel's mutable Lilly and dewdrop: natural forms fade but ever renew themselves. The invitation is the same as that offered to Thel by the matron Clay and the rest—to enter without fear into the round of generation:

The Golden nymph replied: "Pluck thou my flower, Oothoon the
mild!
Another flower shall spring, because the soul of sweet delight
Can never pass away." . . .[11]

The narcissus of Greek myth was both "golden" and "hundred-headed"—this signifying, as Leutha tells Oothoon, that "another flower shall spring," that the generative powers are inexhaustible.

It is not said explicitly of Persephone that she sought her own rape; yet this is implied in the symbolism of her gathering of the hundred-headed golden narcissus; for the narcissus is the watery plant into which the boy Narcissus is metamorphosed, through falling in love with his reflection in water—that is to say, with his physical, natural body. Thus that Persephone was attracted toward generation is implied in her story. This theme Blake found expounded at length in Thomas Taylor's *Dissertation*:

> For by Narcissus falling in love with his shadow appearing in the limpid stream we may behold a beautiful representation of a soul vehemently gazing on the flowing condition of a material body, and in consequence of this, becoming enamoured with a corporeal life, which is nothing more than the delusive image of the true man, or rational and immortal soul. Hence, by an immoderate attachment to this unsubstantial mockery and gliding semblance of the real soul, such an one becomes, at length, wholly changed, as far as is possible to his nature, into a plantal condition of being, into a beautiful but transient flower, that is, into corporeal life.[12]

Taylor applies the argument to the myth of Persephone: "Proserpine, therefore, or the soul, at the very instant of her descent into matter, is, with the utmost propriety, represented as eagerly engaged in plucking this fatal flower."

The plucking of the flower proves as fatal to Oothoon as it did to Persephone; for no sooner is the act performed than, like Persephone, she is raped by a power of the underworld, Bromion, and carried, according to the symbolic sequence described by Taylor (see p. 132), over a length of sea to [76] a cave, where she is confined as Bromion's unwilling slave. The enslavement is that of marriage, when this is an externally imposed legal bondage.

This event takes place in "Leutha's vale," a scene that recalls *Thel*'s "river of Adona." A vale is, as always in Blake, a material or bodily state;

73 "As when a dream of Thiralatha flies the midnight hour": added plate for *America* (1793)
Compare the bowed figure with Lyca under the tree of sleep, in [63].

and Oothoon's descent into physical sexuality is a betrayal of the soul into the power of lower forces. Leutha is sexuality; and her alluring beauty is at best only a shadow or reflection. A fragment probably intended for *America* [13] speaks of "the Vale of Leutha" as a place where the image of eternal beauty is seen but cannot be held:

> *As when a dream of Thiralatha flies the midnight hour:*   [73]
> *In vain the dreamer grasps the joyful images, they fly*
> *Seen in obscured traces in the Vale of Leutha.*

Leutha, in name, is, like Oothoon, Ossianic. The Vale of Lutha is the home of Malvina, to whom the aged Ossian addressed his songs; Blake used the name perhaps because Lutha means "swift stream." Lutha – or Leutha – is a fontal naiad of generation. The "watery" marigold is Narcissus' "hundred-headed" flower which eternally renews itself. She is herself called the "Soft soul of flowers." On the title page of the *Visions* the grey form of Urizen – "Starry Jealousy" – pursues the soul, Oothoon, as she ventures over the waves of hyle. In *Europe*, written a year after the *Visions*, Leutha is seen

74 Satan, Sin, and Death: illustration (c. 1808) for *Paradise Lost*

The dogs which inhabit the womb of Sin suggest the "dogs of Leutha."

luring souls down into generation by her deception: she is here called a bird—the same "wild bird" to whose song Lyca listens, now emerging into Blake's mythology as a person:

> "*Where is my lureing bird of Eden? Leutha, silent love!*
> *Leutha, the many colour'd bow delights upon thy wings:*
> *Soft soul of flowers, Leutha!*
> *Sweet smiling pestilence! I see thy blushing light;*
> *Thy daughters, many changing,*
> *Revolve like sweet perfumes ascending, O Leutha, silken queen!*" [14]

Are we to read this judgment back into the story of Oothoon and to suppose that the Marygold was a deceiver? It seems that we are, for Oothoon's experience after gathering the flower was not such as she had been led to anticipate. The conditions of love in Leutha's Vale do not correspond with the soul's love in eternity, as Oothoon continues to remember it.

The relationship of Oothoon and Leutha in *Milton* is the prototype of the later relationship of Jerusalem and Vala in *Jerusalem*. In the passage quoted she appears in her rainbow colors, a figure much like Vala, even to her moth wings. Oothoon is to Leutha as soul is to body. In eternity they would (if one may guess from their resemblance to the later figures) be as one; on earth they are often in opposition:

> . . . *Oothoon & Leutha hover'd over his* [Orc's] *Couch*
> *Of fire, in interchange of Beauty & Perfection in the darkness*
> *Opening interiorly into Jerusalem & Babylon* . . .[15]

Babylon is Vala, and the two nymphs are forms of the spiritual and physical aspects of love.

In *Milton* Leutha reappears as Milton's Sin, daughter of Satan and mother of Death; but she is penitent.

> *And Leutha stood glowing with varying colours, immortal, heart-*
> *piercing*
> *And lovely, & her moth-like elegance shone over the Assembly* [16]

Leutha's identification with Milton's Sin is further confirmed by her association with dogs. These are only mentioned in her later appearances, and perhaps belong only to her degraded aspect. Leutha's dogs accompany Los, keeper of the gates of generation, as he watches the souls born into, and dying from, this world; these souls are the rising and setting stars:

> . . . *Los all night watches*
> *The stars rising & setting the meteors & terrors of night.*
> *With him went down the Dogs of Leutha* . . .[17]

Barking dogs inhabit the womb of Milton's Sin: [74]

> *The one seem'd Woman to the waste, and fair,*
> *But ended foul in many a scaly fould*
> *Voluminous and vast, a Serpent arm'd*
> *With mortal sting: about her middle round*
> *A cry of Hell Hounds never ceasing bark'd*
> *With wide* Cerberean *mouths full loud, and rung*
> *A hideous Peal: yet, when they list, would creep,*
> *If ought disturb'd their noyse, into her woomb,*
> *And kennel there, yet there still bark'd and howl'd*
> *Within unseen. . . .*

Milton himself suggests other sources:

> *. . . Farr less abhorrd then these*
> *Vex'd Scylla. . . .*
> *Nor uglier follow the Night-Hag. . . .*[18]

The dogs that bark within the womb of the water-demon Scylla are interpreted by Taylor [19] as matter itself. He quotes a hymn of Synesius to the deity, which gives the key at once to Scylla's dogs, those of Milton's Sin, and Leutha's:

> *Blessed, thrice blessed! who with winged speed,*
> *From Hyle's dread voracious barking flies,*
> *And, leaving Earth's obscurity behind,*
> *By a light leap, directs his steps to thee.*

According to Taylor, dogs are "material demons." [20] Into this ambiguous and treacherous kingdom, then, is the soul lured by Leutha. Blake has depicted in his "Judgment of Paris" a dog sleeping at his master's feet, the name Παρις written on his collar—an emblem of Paris' still unawakened carnal lust. If the bird is the higher, the dog is the lower aspect of sexual [22] desire.

The Neoplatonic structure of the poem is wedded to an Ossianic story whose landscape no less than its narrative links it with the symbolism of the Persephone myth—Macpherson's *Oithona*. Oithona comes from the Gaelic *oi*, a virgin, and *thon, thona*, a wave; she is a "virgin of the wave." [21] So [75] Blake has represented Oothoon,[22] in a great green wave, her ankle fettered to the "wat'ry" envelope of hyle, her generated body; she is a "virgin of the wave."

Taylor's translation of the *Cratylus* was published in 1793. Plato there explains that the sea-god Poseidon (foot-fettered) is so named "from the nature of the sea restraining his course when he walks and not permitting him to proceed farther . . . as if it became a bond to his feet." The theme of the hampering of the feet of those who must cross the dangerous sea of material life runs through the illustrations of *Visions of the Daughters of Albion*. On the title page Oothoon walks the waters, the soul setting out upon her course joyfully unaware of danger, as the demiurge Urizen follows her

75 Oothoon fettered in a wave: *Visions of the Daughters of Albion* (1793), plate 6, detail

Compare fettered foot of Oothoon with fettered feet of Bromion [76], of Urizen [14], and of the evil angel [120].

in a cloud. On a later page the soul in the watery envelope of her physical body is shown with fettered foot. Taylor in a note comments on Plato: since the foot "is a very proper symbol of progression and progression of life, there is a remarkable beauty and propriety in representing this god as having a *fettered foot*. . . . He likewise presides over caves, earthquakes and hollow places." On the plate which shows Oothoon held prisoner it is Bromion himself (who like Poseidon is the ruler of the material world) who is shown with fettered feet, and the place is an "irriguous [76] cave" . . . "Souls living in generation are said to be under the dominion of this god," Taylor writes, "and hence the reason why Ulysses is represented by Homer as continually pursued by the anger of Neptune."

Sometimes Urizen, who is also, like Bromion, fettered by the materialist mentality, is represented with fettered feet. With such precision Blake employs the symbolic vocabulary of a mythology whose permanence is, after all, that of Western civilization itself. Was he even—when in a letter he wrote of himself that "our footsteps slide in clay"—still thinking of Plato's image of this world as the place where the soul walks with hampered feet?

Oithona, like Persephone, has been ravished and imprisoned, by a lord of Orkney, who in her lover's absence has carried her off to a cave on a desert island. Her lover, Gaul, returns and seeks out Oithona, learns her story, and avenges her by slaying her ravisher; but the maiden chooses rather to die than to live dishonored.

But if Oithona's story is enacted in the natural setting of Macpherson's western Highlands, the sea-girt cave is, symbolically, that of the myth of Persephone and of Earth: "Prison'd on wat'ry shore" in the house of Poseidon. To Blake it must have seemed that the symbolism of Macpherson's landscape suited his theme of the imprisoned soul. The loss of physical virginity does not in itself defile the soul; and the grief of Theotormon over Oothoon's loss of "purity" is no less of the "cave" than Bromion's carnality. Between them, the pure soul suffers. Bromion exults in her downfall; Theotormon laments it:

> *Thus every morning wails Oothoon; but Theotormon sits*
> *Upon the margin'd ocean conversing with shadows dire.*[23]

By the sea of time and space he sits, and the "shadows dire" with whom he converses are those described by Plotinus, merely physical beings: "Hence as Narcissus, by catching at the shadow, merged himself in the stream and disappeared, so he who is captivated by beautiful bodies, and does not depart from their embrace, is precipitated, not with his body, but with his soul, into a darkness profound and horrid to intellect, through which, becoming blind both here and in Hades, *he converses with nothing but shadows.*" [24]

Oothoon's pleading is addressed to Theotormon; but since his converse is with shadows—natural bodies—he cannot see that the soul is in its essence immortal, pure, and incapable of lasting defilement. Nothing could be less spiritual than the morality which sees the loss of physical virginity as an irreparable defilement. This is the morality of Macpherson's Oithona (indistinguishable, in this respect, from her contemporary Clarissa), who laments the loss of that fragile transient thing: "Why did I not pass away in secret, like the flower of the rock, that lifts its fair head unseen, and strows its withered leaves on the blast." Not so, says Blake's Marygold:

> *Another flower shall spring, because the soul of sweet delight*
> *Can never pass away. . . .*[25]

Macpherson's morality (like Richardson's) is that of materialism, Blake's, that of the soul. Theotormon mistakes the shadow for the substance, like Satan, who is a "dunce" because he cannot tell the garment from the man:

> *Every Harlot was a Virgin once,*
> *Nor can'st thou ever change Kate into Nan.*[26]

It is the teaching of Plotinus that the soul is in its inmost nature incapable of defilement. Taylor's translation of Plotinus' *Concerning the Beautiful* contains all that Blake needed for the foundation of Oothoon's pleading of her essential innocence:

> But may we not say, that this baseness approaches the soul as an adventitious evil . . . [the soul] no longer perceiving the objects of mental vision, nor permitted any more to dwell with itself, because ever hurried away to things obscure, external, and low? Hence, becoming impure, and being on all sides snatched in the unceasing whirl of sensible forms, it is covered with corporeal stains, and wholly given to matter . . . just as the pristine beauty of the most lovely form would be destroyed by its total immersion in mire and clay. . . . If such a one then desires to recover his former beauty, it is necessary to cleanse the infected parts, and thus by a thorough purgation to assume his original form . . .[27]

Oothoon tells Theotormon that her defilement is only like

> *The new wash'd lamb ting'd with the village smoke, & the bright swan*
> *By the red earth of our immortal river. I bathe my wings,*
> *And I am white and pure to hover round Theotormon's breast.*[28]

This is Plotinus' philosophy. The swan—Plato's emblem of the soul—has but dipped its wings in the "red earth" of the natural body, which is the ever-flowing river of generated life. The soul bathes its wings and is pure. Oothoon can say

> *. . . Arise, my Theotormon, I am pure,*
> *Because the night is gone that clos'd me in its deadly black.*[29]

But for him the night is not gone, and he knows only "The starry floor / The wat'ry shore."

Theotormon's morality is the ethics of Protestantism, which Blake condemns in the poem *Mary*. In *The Song of Los* there is an allusion that leaves no doubt of this identification of Theotormon's reign with a perversion of Christianity:

> *Then Oothoon hover'd over Judah & Jerusalem,*
> *And Jesus heard her voice (a man of sorrows) he reciev'd*
> *A Gospel from wretched Theotormon.*[30]

The gospel according to Theotormon is not canonical; but it has been much followed. All the postures of remorse, self-immolation, and self-accusation are derived from this gospel. It shows Jesus not as one who punishes (like the God of the Old Testament) but as a god who weeps for sins perpetually. The Divine Humanity forgives; but Jesus, according to Theotormon, is simply a figure who is made to suffer, whose blameless personality is, as it were, affronted by every human sin. This misguided ethic of a merely external moral purity, and a "repentance" that changes nothing, is a form of materialist thought, for it never rises beyond the values of the natural world to consider, as does Plotinus, the soul's native purity, from which sins may be washed away, as he says, like clay from gold. Whereas the true Jesus purifies by spiritual forgiveness, the only result of this gospel of "goodness" considered in merely natural terms is continual sorrow and self-torment among the religious, and continual eruptions of violent evil in the form of Bromion, who makes a mock of Theotormon's high principles.

Samuel Palmer recalled for Gilchrist Blake's great love of St. Teresa, whom he delighted to quote to his disciples. In *Milton* he names her, together with Fénelon, Hervey, Whitefield, and Madame Guyon, among the "gentle souls who guide the great wine-press of love." It was for her understanding of the soul's love of God that he admired and loved her; and Oothoon seems to use one of St. Teresa's images; for she too understood that sin is extraneous to the soul, like a cloud over its clearness. She writes of the soul's relation with the divine lover and beloved: "it seemed to me that (my soul) was like some clear and pure looking-glass . . . and in the very center thereof Christ our Lord was represented to me, just as I am wont to see him. It seemed to me that I saw him clearly, in all the parts and portions of my soul, as in a looking glass . . . It was given me hereby to understand, that the soul's being in mortal sin, is like covering this glass with a great cloud." [31] This truth is obscured by the "Gospel of Theotormon," so disastrously widespread in the form of the "natural religion" that Blake continually deplores:

> "*I call with holy voice! Kings of the sounding air,*
> *Rend away this defiled bosom that I may reflect*
> *The image of Theotormon on my pure transparent breast.*"
> *The Eagles at her call descend & rend their bleeding prey:*
> *Theotormon severely smiles; her soul reflects the smile,*
> *As the clear spring, mudded with feet of beasts, grows pure &*
> *smiles.*[32]

76 Bromion and Oothoon chained at the mouth of a cave: *Visions of the Daughters of Albion* (1793), frontispiece

Blake has made the looking-glass water, and the cloud that obscures it the mud in the stream, perhaps for the sake of consistency with the Neoplatonic imagery of water, the Narcissus myth of the mirroring pool, and the rest; but the thought is St. Teresa's. The Man of Sorrows, Theotormon, is pleased with self-immolation, but he is incapable of absolving the soul. Blake knew very well that to aspire to natural sinlessness is mere vanity; he reminded Crabb Robinson that God charges the angels with folly. However, Puritan morality is a heresy that seems to have vanished from the world without greatly improving the world's understanding of the nature of spiritual love as understood by St. Teresa or, for that matter, by Mary Wollstonecraft or Shelley.

CHAPTER 7

Blake's Cupid and Psyche

Thel, Lyca, Oothoon, are in varying degrees like Persephone, at once the individual soul who "descends" into generation, and the soul of nature, the spirit of earth. This double role is plainest in Lyca; but Thel also is a nature-goddess, "mistress of the vales of Har," and has her charge over "flocks" of living creatures. Oothoon, less obviously a nature-goddess, and in her protest more purely human than the others, is even more plainly related to Persephone, and her indictment of the morality of the cave is an extended version of the complaint of Earth in *Earth's Answer*. In the person of Vala, Blake again combines the two roles of world-soul and human soul. Vala has affinities with all her predecessors.

Margoliouth in his notes on the text of *Vala* [1] remarks on the resemblance to *The Book of Thel* of the long passage in Night IX which tells the myth of the purified Vala, now called "the sinless soul." This episode is a vision of "lower paradise," earth as it may be experienced in the state of innocence: "Though this whole passage has been compared to *The Book of Thel*, Vala's wish is the exact opposite of that of Thel who wanted to 'sleep the sleep of death.' . . . If this passage is not exactly a recantation of *Thel*, it is at any rate a Vision of a 'lower Paradise' which Thel failed to find."

The flow of the verse, the mood, the imagery, all transport us back into Thel's world of growth and decay:

> *Alas am I but as a flower then will I sit me down*
> *Then will I weep then Ill complain & sigh for immortality*
> *And chide my maker thee O Sun that raisedst me to fall*
>
> *So saying she sat down & wept beneath the apple trees*
>
> *O be thou blotted out thou Sun that raisedst me to trouble*

> *That gavest me a heart to crave & raisedst me thy phantom*
> *To feel thy heat & see thy light & wander here alone*
> *Hopeless if I am like the grass & so shall pass away* [2]

But Vala enters "the land unknown" Thel so much feared, and by that same northern gate from which her predecessor recoiled. "Dark Urthona" is the name now given to the "terrific porter":

> *Luvah & Vala descended & enterd the Gates of Dark Urthona*
> *And walkd from the hands of Urizen in the shadows of Valas*
> *Garden*
> *Where the impressions of Despair & Hope for ever vegetate*
> *In flowers in fruits in fishes birds & beasts & clouds & waters*
> *The Land of doubts & shadows sweet delusions unformd hopes*
> *They saw no more the terrible confusion of the wracking universe*
> *They heard not saw not felt not all the terrible confusion.* [3]

The answer Thel failed to find is that the soul is not transient in the world, but the world transient in the soul. The pathos of the soul, which seems so fleeting in its passage through the fields and gardens of earth, disappears when we recognize that those fields and gardens exist only in the soul and in relation to the soul.

Vala hears the voice of an invisible god who calls to her:

> *Rise sluggish Soul why sitst thou here why dost thou sit & weep*
> *Yon Sun shall wax old & decay but thou shalt ever flourish*
> *The fruit shall ripen & fall down & the flowers consume away*
> *But thou shalt still survive arise O dry thy dewy tears.* [4]

She answers:

> *Hah! shall I still survive whence came that sweet & comforting*
> *voice*
> *And whence that voice of sorrow O sun thou art nothing now to me*
> *Go on thy course rejoicing & let us both rejoice together*
> *I walk among his flocks & hear the bleating of his lambs*
> *O that I could behold his face & follow his pure feet*
> *I walk by the footsteps of his flocks come hither tender flocks*
> *Can you converse with a pure soul that seeketh for her maker* [5]

This echo of the mood of the twenty-third psalm is new; Thel was aware of no divine "maker" guiding her, hence her sense of solitude and fear. But

77 "The Conjugal Union of Cupid and Psyche":
engraving by Blake for Cumberland's *Thoughts
on Outline* (1796)
Note the butterfly emblem of the soul.

Vala's story is, throughout the poem that bears her name, the story of the
soul's relationship with her divine lover, called her "maker" and her "creator." For the first time the story of the soul takes the form of a love story.

Blake was able to find the new metaphysical statement he wanted in
yet another classical myth, the story of Cupid and Psyche. We know from
his notes on *A Vision of the Last Judgment* that Blake had read and admired
Apuleius; he instances this work in illustration of his belief that "The Greek
Fables originated in Spiritual Mystery & Real Visions, which are lost &
clouded in Fable & Allegory": [6] "Apuleius's Golden Ass & Ovid's Metamorphosis & others of the like kind are Fable; yet they contain Vision in a
sublime degree, being derived from real Vision in More ancient Writings." [7]
We shall later see what more ancient writing Blake believed to be the
original of the story of Cupid and Psyche.

Thomas Taylor published his translation of *Cupid and Psyche* in
1795, but the entire *Metamorphoses* only in 1822. We may guess that when
Blake wrote *Vala* he knew Taylor's translation and his interpretation of the
myth; but we may also conclude from his use of the title *The Golden Ass*
that he had read the whole work in Adlington's often reprinted sixteenth-
century translation, probably in about 1793, when he was working on the
[77] engraving of five plates illustrating the story for Cumberland's *Thoughts on*

Outline. This book was not published until 1796, but Blake's plates are dated 1794.

Like the Eleusinian Mysteries, the story of Psyche was fashionable about that time. Erasmus Darwin in his notes on the Portland vase [8] writes that the myth of Cupid and Psyche probably formed a part of these Mysteries. Naturalist as he was, he wrote upon the emblem of the butterfly, first an earthborn caterpillar that seems to "die" into the pupa, to be then resurrected as a winged insect. The butterfly, he says, was the original [78] emblem of Psyche, or the soul, but later was changed to "a lovely female child with the beautiful wings of that insect." This theme is also illustrated in Bryant's *Mythology*. In *Infant Joy* Blake draws the butterfly wings of the little fairy in the same style as in Cumberland's plates.

Like all Blake's major deities Vala undergoes change and development; she gathers tributaries. In *Jerusalem* the earlier Vala has split into two figures, the goddess Nature with her veil (still called Vala), and Jerusalem, the soul; but in *Vala* Jerusalem barely appears: she has not yet become a separate person; and Vala herself is called the soul. On the title page of *Jerusalem* she is represented with glorious butterfly-wings, adorned with sun, moon, and earth; she is still the Greek Psyche, the butterfly. The early Vala is the prototype no less of the later Jerusalem (the soul) than of the later Vala (the goddess Nature). Vala throughout the poem which bears her name is called "the soul," and in her regenerate state "the sinless soul."

On page 13 (verso) of the *Vala* manuscript there is a very strange series of drawings,[9] which contains, so it seems, Blake's first meditation on the figure of Vala, for they occur very near the beginning of the original poem. The first drawing shows a female butterfly-winged "Infant a Span long," a Psyche figure. In the series of drawings that follow we can trace, [79] virtually, the plot of the poem, so far as it concerns Vala herself; for it shows her progressive deterioration. The second drawing shows her still human

78 Emblems of the psyche: Bryant's *Mythology*, vol. 2 (1774), plate x
Note the poppy, funeral urn, and skull as emblems of death, and butterfly emblem of the risen soul.

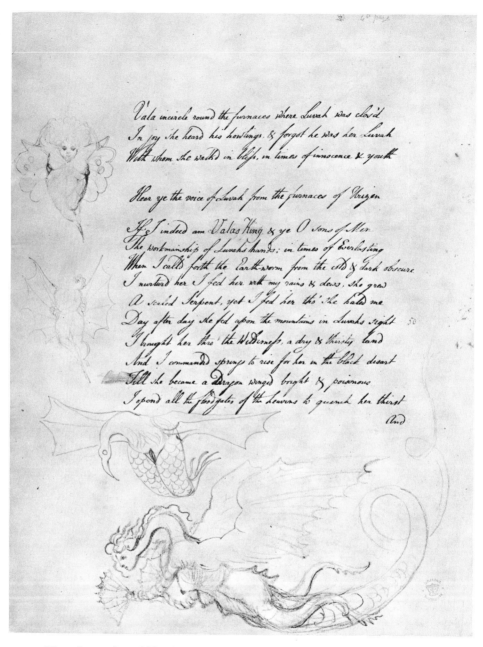

Vala incircle round the furnaces where Luvah was clos'd
In joy she heard his howlings, & forgot he was her Luvah
With whom she walkd in bliss, in times of innocence & youth

Hear ye the voice of Luvah from the furnaces of Urizen

If I indeed am Valas King & ye O sons of Men
The workmanship of Luvahs hands: in times of Everlasting
When I calld forth the Earth-worm from the cold & dark obscure
I nurturd her I fed her with my rains & dews, she grew
A scaled Serpent, yet I fed her tho' she hated me
Day after day she fed upon the mountains in Luvahs sight   50
I brought her thro' the Wilderness, a dry & thirsty land
And I commanded springs to rise for her in the black desart
Till she became a dragon winged bright & poisonous
I opend all the floodgates of the heavens to quench her thirst

And

79 Transformation of Earth: *Vala* MS (1795–1804?), p. 26 Bentley
Compare lines 8–13 above (*F.Z.* II; K. 282, 84–89) and the marginal figures
representing Vala's metamorphoses with the account of the metamorphosis of
Ceres into dragon form.

but bat-winged; next she becomes a dragon-like monster with naked serpent head and scaly thighs; and at last, full grown, she is woman-faced and six-breasted, with a huge serpent's tail, webbed forefeet and indeterminate hindfeet, a dragon-ridged back, and leathery wings. This chimera-like creature could be intended to represent a monster of the four elements; but it is possible that there is another explanation and that the drawings represent the transmutation of the goddess Ceres. If this is so, we have Blake returning yet again to the figure of Earth.

A note by Taylor to the Orphic Hymn to Corybas may throw light on these strange drawings. The lines are:

> *By thee transmuted Ceres' body pure*
> *Becomes a dragon's savage and obscure.*[10]

Taylor interprets "changing the holy body of Ceres into the form of a savage and obscure dragon" as follows: "As in the above lines the intellectual earth is represented under the form of a dragon with a beautiful countenance; the sensible earth, which is but the image of the intellectual, may . . . be called an obscure dragon, since obscurity is an apt symbol of a material nature." If Blake's marginal drawings are his reflection on this theme, we see that he is, in *Vala*, returning yet again to the theme of Earth-Persephone, and that the transmutation of Vala into an "obscure dragon," Nature (whose countenance, in the drawings, is certainly beautiful) is a continuation of the myth that had held him for so long.

In Luvah's first speech, so strangely illustrated by the drawings of the degeneration of Vala, we already find evidence that Blake was using the theme of Cupid and Psyche, for Luvah makes reference to an incident in the story of the separation of the lovers: while the sinful Psyche, who has lost Cupid through her disobedience, is seeking for him all over the earth in sorrow and tribulation, Cupid is locked up by his mother Venus, so that he cannot go in search of her, "closed fast in the moste surest chamber of the house, partly because he should not hurte him selfe with wanton dalliance, and partly because he should not speake with his love, so these two lovers weare dievided one from an other." [11]

Luvah first appears in the story in just this situation; he "was cast into the Furnaces of affliction & sealed," [12] and he speaks in the person of Cupid when he describes, from this sorrowful situation, the earthly paradise that he built for Vala:

> *I loved her I gave her all my soul & my delight*
> *I hid her in soft gardens & in secret bowers of Summer*
> *Weaving mazes of delight along the sunny Paradise*

And he next describes his incarceration:

> *And they have taken her away & hid her from my sight*
> *They have surrounded me with walls of iron & brass. . . .*[13]

Vala, in her first appearance, is the counterpart of her mourning lover; she appears, seeking, like Psyche, for the lover she has lost:

> *. . . I behold the Fallen Man*
> *Seeking to comfort Vala, she will not be comforted*
> *She rises from his throne and seeks the shadows of her garden*
> *Weeping for Luvah lost . . .*
>
> .   .   .
>
> *I see, invisible descend into the Gardens of Vala*
> *Luvah walking on the winds, I see the invisible knife*
> *I see the shower of blood . . .*[14]

We begin to see how Blake has conceived and recreated the story of the lovers: Vala cannot see Luvah, not because he is not there but because she cannot, in her fallen state, recognize him. Psyche lost her lover through wishing to see him with earthly eyes; and so Blake's Vala cannot see Luvah when she, too, wishes to see him carnally. In the old legend Psyche's earthly sisters give her a knife with which to kill her lover, who they tell her is a demon; the knife, too, comes into Blake's story, and even the "shower of blood"—not, in fact, shed in the old myth but which Blake makes a realized event in Vala's cruelty. But Vala, like Psyche, also grieves, as she, too, toils at tasks imposed as a punishment for breaking faith:

> *Thus she lamented day & night, compelld to labour & sorrow*
> *Luvah in vain her lamentations heard; in vain his love*
> *Brought him in various forms before her still she knew him not*
>
> .   .   .
>
> *Still hating still professing love, still labouring in the smoke* [15]

The most explicit use of the story of Cupid and Psyche appears in the long episode in Night IX.

Psyche, the youngest and most beautiful daughter of a king and queen, has incurred the anger of Venus; and she is doomed by an oracle to be wedded, as it seems, to a demon. She is carried to the summit of a mountain, and there left as dead. But she presently "descends" into a beautiful valley, where she finds a house prepared for her. There she is attended by invisible servants, and visited by a lover, whom she is not permitted to see. Taylor, in his notes to his translation of the story,[16] explains at length that the "descent" of Psyche from the mountain to the valley is, once again, the story of the descent of the soul into generation, seen as a death by those in eternity (Psyche's parents) but in reality no death at all. Vala, like her prototype (and like Blake's own Lyca), is carried in "sleep" into the "valley" of generated life, and, like Psyche, wakes to find herself "the mistress of this garden." She finds a beautiful house near a river in which she presently bathes. Blake's landscape, like Apuleius', is all of symbolic correspondences.

Above all, Blake was delighted by Apuleius' description of the house built for Psyche by Cupid, her divine lover, "some Demigod, or God him selfe":

And when she had refreshed her selfe sufficiently with sleepe, she rose with a more quiet and pacified minde, and fortuned to espie a pleasaunt woodde environned with great and mighty trees: she espied likewise a runninge river as cleere as Cristall: In the middest of the woodde, welnie at the fall of the river was a Princely edifice, wrought and builded, not by the arte or hande of man, but by the mighty power of God: and you would judge at the first entrie therein, that it weare some pleasaunt and worthy mansion for the powers of heaven. For the embowinges above weare of Cytern, and Yvery, propped and undermined with pillors of Golde, the walles covered and seeled with Silver, divers sortes of beastes were graven and carved, that seemed to encounter with such as entred in: al thinges weare so curiously and finely wrought, that it seemed either to be the worke of some demigod, or God him selfe, the pavement was all of pretious stone, devided and cut one from an other, whereon was carved divers kindes of pictures, in such sorte that blessed and thrise blessed weare they whiche might goe upon such a pavement: Every parte and angle of the house was so well adorned, that by reason of the pretious stones and inestimable treasure there, it glittered and shone in such sorte, that the chambers, porches, and dores gave light as it had bene the Sunne.[17]

Vala's house, likewise in a valley by a river, is built for her by Luvah, and in it we find Apuleius' pillars of gold and walls of ivory; and Apuleius' Greco-Roman mosaic pavement, which in Adlington becomes "all of precious stones," in Blake becomes "a pavement as of pearl" (neither Adlington nor Blake had seen one). This house is the body, into which the soul descends in her "sleep" or "death" of generation:

And soft sleep fell upon her eyelids in the silent noon of day

Then Luvah passed by & saw the sinless Soul
And said Let a pleasant house arise to be the dwelling place
Of this immortal spirit growing in lower Paradise

He spoke & pillars were builded & walls as white as ivory
The grass she slept upon was pavd with pavement as of pearl
Beneath her rose a downy bed & a cieling coverd all
Vala awoke. When in the pleasant gates of sleep I enterd
I saw my Luvah like a spirit stand in the bright air
Round him stood spirits like me who reard me a bright house
And here I see The house remain in my most pleasant world
My Luvah smild I kneeled down he laid his hand on my head
And when he laid his hand upon me from the gates of sleep I came
Into this bodily house to tend my flocks in my pleasant garden [18]

Psyche, rising from sleep, bathes before she ascends her marriage bed; and in the same way Vala descends into the river before her consciousness can become attuned to the world of matter. Blake's newly-created Eve is depicted at the fall of a river. So in Plato's myth of Er the incarnating souls must pass through Lethe before they can enter upon this life. Vala "stop'd to drink of the clear spring," and, like Thel's sisters who "lead round their sunny flocks,"

She called to her flocks saying Follow me O my flocks

They followd her to the silent vally beneath the spreading trees
And on the rivers margin she ungirded her golden girdle
She stood in the river & viewd herself within the watry glass
And her bright hair was wet with the waters she rose up from the
                                                            river
And as she rose her Eyes were opend to the world of waters [19]

Blake, now using all these symbols with masterly ease, describes the "vision" of the soul that enters the waters of matter and yet retains her spiritual consciousness. Thel identified herself with the "Image in the wat'ry glass"; she describes herself "Like a reflection in a glass; like shadows in the water"; but regenerate Vala *"view'd* herself within the wat'ry glass" without identification with the image; she understood that the body is the reflection or shadow of the soul, cast in the flux of material existence; yet her consciousness is changed by her immersion in the waters: "She saw Tharmas sitting upon the rocks beside the wavy sea"—and she is now aware of the conditions of her "lower paradise," as Lyca in the lion's cave encounters animal forms.

Like Psyche, Vala is attended in her bodily house by invisible serv-ants, who bring her food and drink, and sometimes delight her with music. These are spirits of the celestial world, invisible to the generated soul, who yet is not unaware of them; as Caliban upon his island heard their music in his sleep: "We whose voyces you heare bee your servants, and ready to min-ister unto you according to your desire." Blake interprets Psyche's servants as spiritual agents, the true causes of all appearances; for "every natural effect has a spiritual cause":

> *She heard sweet voices in the winds & in the voices of birds*
> *That rose from waters for the waters were as the voice of Luvah*
> *Not seen to her like waters or like this dark world of death*
> *Tho all those fair perfections which men know only by name*
> *In beautiful substantial forms appeard & served her*
> *As food or drink or ornament or in delightful works*
> *To build her bowers for the Elements brought forth abundantly*
> *The living soul in glorious forms & every one came forth*
> *Walking before her Shadowy face & bowing at her feet* [20]

Doubtless Blake was interpreting the voices according to Taylor, who says of them: "Of this mundane, yet celestial, condition of being, the incorporeal voices which attend upon Psyche are likewise symbolical: for outward discourse is the last image of intellectual energy, according to which the soul alone operates in the intelligible world. As voices, therefore, they signify an establishment subordinate to that which is intelligible, but so far as denu-dated of body, they also signify a condition of being superior to a terrene allotment." [21] In plain terms, they speak to the soul, but "not to the sensual ear."

However, it is not only, or principally, Psyche's servants who are invisible to her; it is also the god himself, who visits her only by "night." When Psyche, disobeying his warnings, takes a lamp in order to look at him as he sleeps, she sees "his tender plume feathers, dispersed upon his shoulders like shining flowrs, & trembling hither and thither." Love is, above all, the winged god, for his nature is aspiring—as Plato beautifully writes in the *Phaedrus* of the sprouting of wing feathers upon the shoulders of those who are in love. All Blake's spirits seem well able to fly without the encumbrance of wings; but Luvah is especially, and typically, in flight, for he is the god of the air (the spirit), and his appearances are, in his unfallen state, in that element, often floating on a bright cloud, like the lover of Thel's dewdrop.[22] Vala therefore hears the voice of Luvah speaking to her from the air, but he is invisible to her, as Love is to Psyche:

> *Invisible Luvah in bright clouds hoverd over Valas head*
> *And thus their ancient golden age renewd for Luvah spoke*
>
> .   .   .
>
> *Come forth O Vala from the grass & from the silent dew*
> *Rise from the dews of death for the Eternal Man is Risen*
>
> .   .   .
>
> *She answerd thus Whose voice is this in the voice of the*
>   *nourishing air*
> *In the spirit of the morning awaking the Soul from its grassy bed*
> *Where dost thou dwell for it is thee I seek & but for thee*
> *I must have slept Eternally . . .*
>
> .   .   .
>
> *O thou creating voice that callest & who shall answer thee*
> *Where dost thou flee O fair one where dost thou seek thy happy*
>   *place* [23]

This blissful but partial perception of the god is the condition of the innocent soul in nature; and Blake is paraphrasing Apuleius' happy ending—Cupid's awakening of the sleeping Psyche. Cupid at last finds Psyche in "an infernall and deadly sleep"—the words are like Blake—after her descent into Hades at the command of Venus: "But Cupide beinge now healed of his wounde and maladie, not able to endure the absence of Psyches, gotte him secreetly out at a windowe of the chamber where he was enclosed, and (receavinge his winges) toke his flight towardes his lovinge wife, whome when he had founde hee wiped away the sleepe from her face, and put it againe into the boxe, and awaked her with the tippe of one of his arrowes." [24] Vala's sleep in "the dews of death," where, had not love awakened her, she "must have slept Eternally," and her subsequent apotheosis at "the Golden Feast" follows the old legend; for the soul is in its nature immortal, and her native place is in eternity: "To yonder brightness there I haste, for sure I came from thence." [25] So Blake implies the Platonic doctrine of the soul's descent and return.

The fragment of dialogue in the last passage quoted from *Vala* strikes an echo from another love story: "Tell me, O thou whom my soul loveth, where thou feedest, where thou makest thy flock to rest at noon: for why should I be as one that turneth aside by the flocks of thy companions?" [26] It is from this "More ancient Writing" that Blake has introduced the pastoral imagery which surrounds Vala, who

> . . . *laid her head on the downy fleece*   [80]
> *Of a curld Ram who stretchd himself in sleep beside his mistress*
> *And soft sleep fell upon her eyelids in the silent noon of day* [27]

Blake, with his perception of the essence of myths, saw that the story of Solomon and the fair Shulamite describes the same spiritual event as the classical legend, the soul's love for her "maker" and God's love for the soul. The Song of Solomon is the Hebrew version, composed into a poem of great beauty, of the soul's quest for her love, of which *Cinderella*, *The Black Bull of Norroway*, and *East of the Sun and West of the Moon* are among our own northern variants. The traditional Christian interpretation of this poem—based upon a similar pre-Christian tradition—is, as a mystical work, veiled in the symbolic language of a love story. The Hebrew version of the myth gives Blake his warrant for describing the lover of Vala as her maker [81] and her creator. The figure of Luvah hovers between the two versions, appearing at times as Eros and at other times as the higher figure of love—not, indeed, with any real contradiction of meaning, but with a certain difference of emphasis or even of style, which very often indicates for us the aspect of the vision that is uppermost in Blake's mind for the moment.

But the two stories are so similar that it is not always possible to say upon which Blake is drawing. The story of the lovers in the Hebrew poem is in all important respects the same as that of Cupid and Psyche. At first, the lovers are united; then (for no stated reason) the woman is abandoned and

In thunders ends the voice. Then Albions Angel wrathful burnt
Beside the Stone of Night; and like the Eternal Lions howl
In famine & war. replyd. Art thou not Orc. who serpent formd
Stands at the gate of Enitharmon to devour her children;
Blasphemous Demon. Antichrist. hater of Dignities:
Lover of wild rebellion. and transgresser of Gods Law;
Why dost thou come to Angels eyes in this terrific form?

80 Luvah and Vala asleep with ram, tree, and birds: *America* (1793), plate 7
Tree, birds, and prostrate figure closely resemble similar figures in [64] and [65].

81 Soul embraced by divine lover: *Jerusalem* (1804–1820), plate 99

must seek for her beloved through the city, in sorrow; and the speech of the
Shulamite might be Psyche herself speaking after Cupid's flight from her
marriage bed:

> *By night on my bed I sought him whom my soul loveth:*
> *I sought him, but I found him not.*
> *I will rise now, and go about the city in the streets, and*
> *in the broad ways I will seek him whom my soul loveth:*
> *I sought him, but I found him not.*
> *The watchmen that go about the city found me: to whom I said,*
> *Saw ye him whom my soul loveth?* [28]

So the Shulamite, like Psyche and like "Vala the sweet wanderer," becomes
an exile seeking her lover. The parallel with Psyche's story is even closer in
another passage in which, though still no reason is given, it seems that the
lover has departed in displeasure or from some hidden necessity: "I opened
to my beloved; but my beloved had withdrawn himself, and was gone: my
soul failed when he spake: I sought him, but I could not find him; I called
him, but he gave me no answer." [29] There is even a suggestion here that, like
Cupid,[30] the lover has become invisible; and she answers him, like Psyche, as
one who cannot see him: "O my dove, that art in the clefts of the rock, in the
secret places of the stairs, let me see thy countenance, let me hear thy voice;
for sweet is thy voice, and thy countenance is comely." [31] Blake's Vala
addresses Luvah as "O thou creating voice that callest." [32] But the identity of
Luvah is yet more unmistakable in the phrase that describes him as hidden
"in clefts of the rock":

> *Where is the voice of God that calld me from the silent dew*
> *Where is the Lord of Vala dost thou hide in clefts of the rock*
> *Why shouldst thou hide thyself from Vala from the soul that*
> *wanders desolate* [33]

It is "the voice of God" who is "the Lord of Vala"; for the lover, in all three
stories alike, is but a symbol of the Divine Beloved. The Shulamite is, like
Vala, the keeper of a garden: "My beloved is gone down into his garden, to
the beds of spices, to feed in the gardens, and to gather lilies." [34] It is from
this work that Vala is called "the lily of the Valley" or "lily of the desart"; for
the Shulamite says: "I am the rose of Sharon, and the lily of the valleys. As
the lily among thorns,[35] so is my love among the daughters." [36] Vala's later
identity with Tirzah may come from the same source; for Tirzah is the type

of feminine beauty: "Thou art beautiful, O my love, as Tirzah, comely as Jerusalem, terrible as an army with banners." [37]

Blake's building of the "bodily house" combines the two legends; for in the Song of Solomon the house is built round the beloved, prototype of the "Turris eburnea, domus aurea" of the Litany of the Blessed Virgin Mary, and the house is the body:

> *We have a little sister, and she hath no breasts: what shall*
> *we do for our sister in the day when she shall be spoken for?*
> *If she be a wall, we will build upon her a palace of silver:*
> *and if she be a door, we will inclose her with boards of cedar.*
> *I am a wall, and my breasts like towers: then was I in his*
> *eyes as one that found favour.*[38]

Psyche's house, with its "embowinges above of Cytern and Yvery, propped and undermined with pillors of golde, the walles covered and seeled with Silver," is almost identical in its symbolic attributes with Solomon's chariot in the Hebrew poem. A chariot or vehicle is no less apt as a symbol of the body than is a house; and Solomon's chariot, like Cupid's palace, is built for the beloved—"For the daughters of Jerusalem": "King Solomon made himself a chariot of the wood of Lebanon. He made the pillars thereof of silver, the bottom thereof of gold, the covering of it of purple, the midst thereof being paved with love, for the daughters of Jerusalem." [39] Thus Blake's house of Vala beautifully combines the two versions of the myth.[40]

If we follow back the clues, we find the symbolism of the house of Psyche appearing in a much earlier poem, *I Saw a Chapel All of Gold*.[41] In this poem a monstrous serpent defiles the "bodily house," here called a chapel, but identifiable as Psyche's house by the white pillars of the door and—especially—the jeweled pavement:

> *I saw a chapel all of gold*   [82]
> *That none did dare to enter in,*
> *And many weeping stood without,*
> *Weeping, mourning, worshipping.*
>
> *I saw a serpent rise between*
> *The white pillars of the door,*
> *And he forc'd & forc'd & forc'd,*
> *Down the golden hinges tore.*

82 "A chapel all of gold": detail from *Vala* MS (1795–1804?), p. 44 Bentley

The symbolic representation of the female genitals as a shrine or chapel may be taken as a representation of Enitharmon's threefold golden gates of birth. Blake is following the tradition which calls the Blessed Virgin the "Domus aurea" (House of gold) in the Litany addressed to her. Cf. the "Door of Death" [42].

And along the pavement sweet,
Set with pearls & rubies bright,
All his slimy length he drew,
Till upon the altar white

Vomiting his poison out
On the bread & on the wine.
So I turn'd into a sty
And laid me down among the swine.

In the phrase "all of gold" Blake has summed up the richness of the treasure house that glittered and shone like the sun; the white pillars and the golden hinges derive from the "embowinges of Cytern and Yvery, propped and undermined with pillors of golde." This poem must have been written soon after Blake's first reading of *The Golden Ass*, while he was working on Cumberland's plates. But here we have another symbol—the serpent.

The serpent who defiles this bodily house of Christian "virtue," of the woman who keeps her lovers outside, "Weeping, mourning, worshipping," has also his origin in Apuleius' legend. Luvah, in *Vala*, is, in his degraded form, a serpent, "wreath'd round the accursed tree"; and Vala, blind to Luvah's presence, calls him "the Tempter," for sexual love is so seen with the eyes of worldly unspirituality. In the world of Innocence erotic love is the most beautiful of the gods; in the world of Experience he is seen as the defiling serpent. A drawing in the margin of the *Vala* manuscript shows Blake's meditation upon the double aspect of Eros: upon the back of a loathsome serpent rides the beautiful winged boy with his bow and arrows.

Here also Blake is drawing upon Apuleius. The story of Cupid and Psyche turns upon precisely this ambiguous nature of love—or, rather, the ambiguity of the world's differing conceptions of the god. Apollo's oracle, which foretells Psyche's marriage, describes the god in ambiguous terms, throwing her parents into despair, for they conclude that their daughter is to be married to a destroying serpent:

> *Let Psyches corps be cladd in mourninge weede,*
> *And sette on rocke of yonder hill aloft*
> *Her husbande is no wight of humaine seede*
> *But Serpent dyre and fierce as may be thought*
> *Who flies with winges above in starry skies,*
> *And doth subdew eche thing with firy flight*
> *The Goddes them selves and powers that seeme so wise*
> *With mighty Jove be subject to his might*
> *The rivers blacke, and deadly floodes of paine*
> *And darkenes eke as thrall to him remaine.*[42]

This most powerful of all the gods is in truth Love; but the oracle implies another aspect, the defiler and destroyer. When Psyche descends into her blissful valley of generation, her two wicked sisters lose no time in attempting to persuade her that her nocturnal invisible lover is this demon-destroyer. They have reason to know that he is a serpent:

[83]

83 Serpent with Eros(?) and bow and arrows—the double aspect of love: *Vala* MS (1795–1804?), p. 4 Bentley

For we are credibly informed, neither can we but utter it unto thee, that there is a great Serpent full of deadly poyson, with a ravenous and gapinge throate, that lieth with thee every night. Remember the Oracle of Apollo, who pronounced that thou shouldest be married to a dyre and fierce Serpent, and many of the inhabitants here by. . . . affirme that they sawe him yesternight returnynge from pasture and swimminge over the river, whereby they do undoubtedly say that he will not pamper thee longe with delicate meates, but when the time of deliverie shall approche, he will devoure both thee and thy childe. . . . And if it be so, that thy solitary life, thy conversation with voyces, this servile and dangerous pleasure, and the love of the Serpent, doo more delight thee, say not but that we have playde the partes of naturall sisters in warninge thee.[43]

We need not suppose that "the inhabitants here by" and the "naturall sisters" are aware of the falsehood of what they affirm; for so Eros does appear in the eyes of Experience. The sisters of Psyche are not merely lying to her, but giving her the world's version of the nature of erotic love. In *I Saw a Chapel All of Gold* we have their version of Psyche's story enacted as they believe it to be—the defilement of the bodily house by the serpent of sexuality. Blake knew, as the ancient Greeks who composed Apollo's oracle knew, that the power of Eros is supreme. The refusal to know this truth does not exclude the god; it only degrades his form. The serpent forces the door of the chapel of false chastity, and vomits poison upon its altar.[44]

This is not a good poem, and Blake never included it among his *Songs*. Its interest lies, rather, in its relation to another and much better poem, which he wrote soon afterward, describing the same "vision" of the degradation of love.[45] Knowing as we do that Blake had so lately been thinking of the Cupid and Psyche legend and the oracle of the serpent, may we not divine in *The Sick Rose* a re-creation of this theme? Here the dire serpent who flies in darkness, in "starry skies," the invisible lover of the soul, becomes "the invisible worm," as darkly conceived in the world of Experience. There are plenty of cankerworms in English poetry, but no other invisible, nocturnal, flying worm:

O Rose, thou art sick!   [47, 48]
The invisible worm
That flies in the night,
In the howling storm,

> *Has found out thy bed*
> *Of crimson joy:*
> *And his dark secret love*
> *Does thy life destroy.*[46]

Blake's imagination has so transformed his material that, were it not for the poem written immediately before, and his return to the Cupid and Psyche theme in *Vala*, we could scarcely recognize in Blake's invisible worm the legendary winged serpent, Eros. Yet *The Sick Rose* does, quite plainly, take up the theme of *A Chapel All of Gold*, as Wicksteed long ago pointed out: [47] the death-bringing serpent-worm and the degraded vision of "dark secret love," which irresistibly defiles and destroys the chapel. We may conclude that Blake engraved *The Sick Rose* as a better version of the theme first attempted in the earlier poem.

The legend of Cupid and Psyche, then, hovers in the background of *The Sick Rose*. Psyche's marriage is celebrated as if it were a death; and this is a symbol of many meanings. The descent of the soul into generation may be so conceived (as Demeter mourns the death of Persephone): we have already seen Blake turning this theme about in his imagination. More specifically, there is a whole range of symbolism linking marriage and death, from the rape of Persephone to the vulgarity of Matthew Prior's *A True Maid*, which may even bear on Blake's poem:

> *No, no, for my virginity*
> *When I lose that, says ROSE, I'll dye:*
> *Behind the Elmes last Night, cry'd Dick,*
> *ROSE, were you not extremely Sick?* [48]

Enough has been said, in the chapter on Porphyry's nymphs of the cave, on this rich association of symbols that link the death of the soul with the generation of the body through the marriage of the nymphs. The same meaning may be found in the lamentations of Psyche's parents, who bid farewell to their daughter as to the dead: "But now the time approched of [84] Psyches marriage, preparation was made, blacke torches were lighted, the pleasaunt songes were turned into pitifull cries, the melody of Hymeneus was ended with deadly howlinge, the maiden that should be married did wipe her eies with her veile . . . And when the solemnitie was ended, they went to bringe this sorrowfull spouse, not to her marriage, but to her finall ende and buriall." [49]

84 Marriage of Cupid and Psyche: engraving (from antique medallion) by Bartolozzi for Bryant's *Mythology*, vol. 2 (1774), at p. 393

Eros is a naked figure, Psyche entirely veiled, from head to feet. Note her butterfly wings.

This, like the marriage of Persephone and Hades, her "descent" into the womb-tomb of the world, seems like a death to the immortal "parents" of the soul; and Blake's powerful image of the "Marriage hearse" [50] summarizes in two words this profound paradox of the marriages of Psyche and of Persephone—the descent into generation (and death from eternity) through sexual desire. It may not be fanciful to recognize in the darkness and "howling" of that marriage feast the atmosphere of *The Sick Rose*, the night and "the howling storm" [51] in which the maiden is married to the serpent. The parents who "hid themselves in darkness," the black torches and lamentations, convey the very atmosphere Blake conveys in three words. *The Sick Rose* languishes in the spiritual night-world of Experience; the night in which love flies as "the invisible worm" is the same "Frowning, frowning Night" that Lyca summons, about to descend into her death-marriage in the cave.

Luvah, with his double nature, manifests in turn all the attributes of Apuleius' ambiguous god, the beautiful, aerial, winged god, the invisible divine voice, and the serpent. The long passage on Luvah and Vala in Night IX of *Vala* is the antithesis, seen with the eyes of Innocence, of the degraded vision of *I Saw a Chapel All of Gold* and *The Sick Rose*, and of "dark secret love," written by Blake as such and from the same story. Here the love theme is enacted in the "noon of day"—a state of spiritual enlightenment contrasting with the "night" and "storm" of the landscape of *The Sick Rose*, or the nocturnal landscape of fallen Earth as she awaits "the break of day."

All the same, we must beware of too static a view of any of these symbols. *The Sick Rose* is the germ not only of the Luvah-Vala myth but also of the birth of Luvah as Orc from Enitharmon, which in *The First Book of Urizen* is described in words that echo *The Sick Rose*. The worm in the rose is here the generated embryo in the womb:

> . . . *Enitharmon, sick,*
> *Felt a Worm within her womb.*
>
> *Yet helpless it lay like a Worm*
> *In the trembling womb*
> *To be moulded into existence.*
>
> *All day the worm lay on her bosom;*
> *All night within her womb*
> *The worm lay till it grew to a serpent,*
> *With dolorous hissings & poisons*
> *Round Enitharmon's loins folding.*
>
> *Coil'd within Enitharmon's womb*
> *The serpent grew, casting its scales,*
> *With sharp pangs the hissings began*
> *To change to a grating cry:*
> *Many sorrows and dismal throes,*
> *Many forms of fish, bird & beast*
> *Brought forth an Infant form*
> *Where was a worm before.*[52]

This is the birth of Luvah as Orc—that is, the birth of love into the world of generation, and the consequent degradation of his nature and metamorphosis into serpent form.

Thus the symbol of worm and rose ramifies into more than one theme, yet all are related to generation and the love or marriage that leads to generation in the world-cave. To sort out the symbolic content of the worm symbol in logical terms would be to lose its essence, which is imaginative and mysterious.

Yet what of the rose? The design which accompanies the poem first appears as an illustration of Shakespeare's fifteenth sonnet, and beneath it he has written the words:

> . . . *every thing that growes*
> *Holds in perfection but a little moment.*

The drawing above these lines shows an open flower, from which emerges a little female figure with upraised arms, a little lover reclining at her feet. In *The Book of Thel* these figures reappear, emerging from Adonis' flower of mutability, the *Anemone pulsatilla;* and Blake has used them again in his design of *The Sick Rose.* The little female figure, arms raised in despair, is embraced this time by the worm, which has wrapped itself round her.

The rose and cankerworm symbolic association is so common that we could not point to a particular source had not Blake thus led us, by a chain of association, to Shakespeare's *Sonnets,* which he must have been reading at the time he made the little pencil-drawing in the Notebook. The beloved of the *Sonnets* is repeatedly called the Rose:

> *From fairest creatures we desire increase,*
> *That thereby beauties Rose might never die*

—so the first sonnet introduces the theme of all. Linked with the Rose is the cankerworm: "For Canker vice the sweetest buds doth love." [53] The Canker may be vice or may be death; and Shakespeare returns again and again to the underlying theme of all his sonnets in praise of the mortal beauty of the beloved youth: natural beauty cannot escape the worm; the two are in their very nature wedded. Blake himself did not, as Shakespeare in his sonnet, see "men as plants," [54] and the pathos of beauty forever doomed to decay; but he did see this grieving over mutability as a state of mind belonging to the world of Experience; it is Thel's theme and the theme, also, of *The Sick Rose.* This tragic vision is, to the fully enlightened soul, an illusion, and is seen as such by the awakened Vala who has realized her own immortality.

But we shall not be wrong in reading into the multiple thought of *The Sick Rose* Blake's meditation upon Shakespeare's love poems. [55]

CHAPTER 8

Emblems of Love

So far we have followed the development of Blake's theme of the descent and return of the soul in terms of Neoplatonic myths. Only with Vala as the Shulamite do we find a Hebraeo-Christian source entering into the ever-growing complexity of the pattern. With the early Vala we have also, for the first time, the theme of the soul's marriage with a divine being, in part based upon Eros, but occasionally spoken of in higher terms as the "creator" and "maker" of the soul.

There is in *Jerusalem* a dichotomy of the original figure of Vala, who in *The Four Zoas* is at once the "shadowy" female and "the sinless soul"; now we have Jerusalem, who is a virgin-mother of human souls, the bride of Jesus, and Vala, who is the goddess Nature, the shadowy image of the soul in this world, the "wife" of Albion, mother of bodies.

The later figure of Jerusalem is a fuller development of the early Vala as "the sinless soul" and "Lilly of Havilah"; but the aspect of the soul's nature and experience that is developed in the later myth is not any longer the "descent," which had preoccupied the young Blake, but rather the high mysteries of the soul's union with God. Jerusalem is a far more developed figure than her predecessor, the early Vala; yet there are echoes of the earlier myth in the later.

Like Psyche, Jerusalem, unable to see her divine lover, labors at the tasks set her by the cruel Vala, who here plays the part of Venus, the soul's tyrant-mistress in Apuleius' myth:

> *But Jerusalem faintly saw him; clos'd in the Dungeons of Babylon*
> *Her Form was held by Beulah's Daughters; but all within unseen*
> *She sat at the Mills, her hair unbound, her feet naked*
> *Cut with the flints, her tears run down, her reason grows like*
> *The Wheel of Hand incessant turning day & night without rest,*

85 Vala and Jerusalem: *Jerusalem* (1804–1820), plate 32 (Coll. Kerrison Preston)
Vala is veiled; Jerusalem naked.

Insane she raves upon the winds, hoarse, inarticulate.
All night Vala hears, she triumphs in pride of holiness
To see Jerusalem deface her lineaments with bitter blows [1]

Jerusalem is the exiled soul who laments:

Babel mocks, saying there is no God nor Son of God,
That thou, O Human Imagination, O Divine Body, art all
A delusion; but I know thee, O Lord, when thou arisest upon
My weary eyes, even in this dungeon & this iron mill. [2]

One might almost say that *Jerusalem* is *Vala* rewritten in Christian terms; but there is now a deeper insight. The soul is that in man which never can wholly forget God, continues to remind man of the spiritual reality, and mourns and weeps when the divine vision is denied. The "anima" of Jungian psychology is the same figure, who in dreams reproaches forgetful man, and who continues to know truths he has forgotten and of which he does not wish to be reminded. She mediates between man and God.

Jerusalem is the daughter or sister of Albion, to whom she says "thou art my Father & my Brother"; but she is never described as his wife. She is the bride of the Lamb, and as such, the mother of the souls of men:

Her Little-ones ran on the fields,
The Lamb of God among them seen,
And fair Jerusalem his Bride,
Among the little meadows green.

. . .

She walks upon our meadows green,
The Lamb of God walks by her side,
And every English Child is seen
Children of Jesus & his Bride. [3]

Vala is the "wife" of Albion and the mother of "generated" bodies, Jerusalem the mother of souls who are not "generated":

I redounded from Albion's bosom in my virgin loveliness:
The Lamb of God reciev'd me in his arms, he smil'd upon us:
He made me his Bride & Wife: he gave thee to Albion.
Then was a time of love. O why is it passed away! [4]

She is a collective figure, a "building of human souls," born of Time and [85, 86]
Space:

> . . . *a vast family, wondrous in beauty & love,*
> *And they appear'd a Universal female form created*
> *From those who were dead in Ulro, from the spectres of the dead.*
>
> *And Enitharmon named the Female, Jerusalem the holy.*
> *Wond'ring, she saw the Lamb of God within Jerusalem's Veil;*
> *The Divine Vision seen within the inmost deep recess*
> *Of fair Jerusalem's bosom in a gently beaming fire.*[5]

Jerusalem's children are the twice-born, those born in the eternal principle,
as children of God: "For Vala produc'd the Bodies, Jerusalem gave the
Souls." [6] Jerusalem's children are the fruits of the soul's heavenly marriage
with the Lamb; and yet they are also Albion's children:

> . . . *As the Soul is to the Body, so Jerusalem's Sons*
> *Are to the Sons of Albion . . .*[7]

and she appears, "Lamenting for her children, for the sons & daughters of
Albion." [8]

Boehme's Virgin Sophia may be one of the elements that entered into
the creation of the figure of Jerusalem.[9] His Virgin is, likewise, at once the
bride of God and the beloved of man. These two aspects are distinct, the
Virgin looking upward, as it were, to God as her creator, but standing in a
"Principle"—to use Boehme's term—higher than man. Boehme's thought is
pre-eminently metaphysical; his Virgin is much more than an aspect of the

86 "Vala produc'd the Bodies, Jerusalem gave the Souls": *Jerusalem*
(1804–1820), plate 18, detail

human soul. The Wisdom is a "Looking-Glass" wherein God the Father, as the Creator, beholds his own image with love and desire: "the Virgin-like Looking-Glass, which there is a *Mother* without Generating, without willing. . . . the Looking-Glass remains eternally a *Virgin*, without generating."

The Wisdom is called a Virgin because she does not "generate," but "manifests." This Virgin is the recipient of the love of the Creator, as Boehme sublimely imagines:

> Also God has had no similitude, wherein he could discover his own Being or Substance, but only the *wisdom* that has been his longing delight, and has stood in his will with his Being or Substance, as a great *wonder*. . . . For it has been the habitation of the spirit of God . . . a virgin, and a *cause* of the divine substantiality . . . Not that, from its own Ability and Production, it manifests or reveals God; but the divine Center [10] out of God's heart, or being and substance, manifests itself *in it*.[11]

The same Virgin of Wisdom, who is the substantial image of God, as well as his bride who "manifests" his wonders, is, in paradise, the object of man's love. There she appears before him as the heavenly mistress or bride. The Wisdom who stands still like a mirror before the face of God is, to man, a revelation and image of the higher Principle. She both is and makes manifest the world of paradise:

> the fair and chaste Virgin of the divine Wisdom always discovers herself according to the Number of the Infinity, out of the many thousand Thousands without End and Number. And in this Discovering there go forth out of the eternal Element, Colours, Arts, and Virtues, and the Sprouts of the Lily of God; at which the Deity continually rejoices itself in the Virgin of the Wisdom; and that Joy goes forth out of the eternal Essences, and is called Paradise, in regard of the Sharpness of the Generating of the pleasant Fruit of the Lily *in infinitum;* where then the Essences of the Lily spring up in Wonders, in many thousand Thousands without Number, of which you have a Similitude in the springing or blossoming Earth.[12]

In this beautiful figure we have again, as in the myth of Persephone, the spirit of earth and the soul mysteriously identified. In paradise all manifestation of the "thousand thousands without number" is in the Wisdom, or Glass—that is, within the soul itself; but in man's fallen state, earth—the "Similitude" of paradise—takes on a separate existence. This present world stands in the relation of shadow to the substance of paradise, reflecting the reality for those who have eyes to see, but concealing it from those who have not; such is Boehme's teaching. In the same way Vala is not (that is, in her latest form in *Jerusalem*) substantially real at all, but is only a shadow or reflection of Jerusalem, animating into a cruel and destructive separate existence. In Vala's world "Accident [is] formed / Into Substance & Principle,"[13] but Blake, like Boehme and like Plato, sees the "real substances" as existing in the intelligible world. This *substantiality* of the Wisdom is emphasized in many passages describing the relationship of Jerusalem and Vala:

> *Vala is but thy Shadow, O thou loveliest among women!*
> *A shadow animated by thy tears, O mournful Jerusalem!*
> *Why wilt thou give to her a Body whose life is but a Shade?*
> *Her joy and love, a shade, a shade of sweet repose:*
> *But animated and vegetated she is a devouring worm.*[14]

According to man's spiritual state, so does the distance between these two figures of shadow and substance become greater or less. Sometimes the two are one; Blake recollects his own married happiness in "Lambeth's vales" when he writes of Albion:

> *He found Jerusalem upon the River of his City, soft repos'd*
> *In the arms of Vala, assimilating in one with Vala,*
> *The Lilly of Havilah; and they sang soft thro' Lambeth's vales*
> *In a sweet moony night & silence that they had created*
> *With a blue sky spread over with wings and a mild moon,*
> *Dividing & uniting into many female forms, Jerusalem*
> *Trembling; then in one comingling in eternal tears,*
> *Sighing to melt his Giant beauty on the moony river.*[15]

Vala is ever most beautiful when she is at one with Jerusalem, who reminds her that:

> *When Albion rent thy beautiful net of gold and silver twine,*
> *Thou hadst woven it with art, thou hadst caught me in the bands*
> *Of love, thou refusedst to let me go: Albion beheld thy beauty,*

Beautiful thro' our Love's comeliness, beautiful thro' pity.
The Veil shone with thy brightness in the eyes of Albion
Because it inclos'd pity & love, because we lov'd one-another.[16]

The "veil" of Vala is nature; and such passages recall not only Boehme but
also Plato's definition of the world as an image of eternity and "the most
beautiful of *generated* things." [17] Boehme, like Plotinus and Plato, insists
that this generated world is nevertheless not man's real world: "in this gross
Body, you are not in Paradise. For that outward Body is but a misty,
excrementitious, dusky, opaque Procreation, or Out-Birth in the third Principle, wherein the Soul lies captive, as in a dark Dungeon." [18] This is Blake's
"excrementitious Husk & Covering" [19] or, as he writes in *Milton*, "a false
Body, an Incrustation over my Immortal Spirit." [20] Thus Jerusalem stands
to Vala as soul to body; yet their destiny is inseparable, even in their exile:

The Starry Wheels revolv'd heavily over the Furnaces,
Drawing Jerusalem in anguish of maternal love
Eastward, a pillar of a cloud with Vala upon the mountains

.   .   .

. . . Jerusalem & Vala weeping in the Cloud
Wander away into the Chaotic Void, lamenting with her Shadow
Among the Daughters of Albion, among the Starry Wheels,
Lamenting for her children, for the sons & daughters of Albion.[21]

Before the Fall—so Boehme writes—there was no barrier between the
present world and paradise, as in Blake's myth there was complete harmony
between Vala and Jerusalem. The natural world, the "Garden of Eden,"
stood within the Principle of paradise: "neither was it any other Garden,
than such as we now have, wherein earthly Fruits (Good and Evil) grow; as
is before our Eyes. But the Paradise is somewhat else; and yet no other
Place, but another Principle, where God and the Angels dwell, and wherein
there is Perfection, where there is mere Love, Joy, and Knowledge. . . .
Which Paradise neither Death nor the Devils touch, neither do they know
it: And yet it has no Wall of Earth or Stones about it." [22]

This paradise and its virgin are man's native home and true love;
and it is still possible, Boehme writes (and Blake follows him in this), to re-
enter paradise. Boehme, writing of that longing in all mankind "which
desires to receive from that Place where it has not sown, and would reap in
that country where the Body dwells not," promises that there "the precious

Virgin of the Wisdom of God meets us, in the middlemost Seat in the Center of the Light of Life." [23] This is "the Gate of the Lily," through which fallen man re-enters the paradisiacal world: "For the Bride says, *Come, and whosoever thirsteth, let him come*, and whatsoever comes, drinks of the Fountain of the Knowledge of the eternal Life in the Smell and Virtue of the Lily of God in Paradise." [24]

This re-entry into paradise is that second birth of which the Gospel speaks, for each Principle is separated from the other by a "gate" or "birth" (the two are synonymous in Boehme). The lily, therefore, is the flower that grows not in earthly soil but in paradise:

> But the Noble Lily Twig or Branch *grows in Patience and Meekness*, and *takes* its essence, power, and smell out of the soil of God, as also out of Christ's Incarnation; for Christ's Spirit is its Essence; God's Substance is its Body. Not out of any *strange* or heterogeneous property, but out of its own included and shut-up in Death, and in Christ's sprouting Essence grows the virgin-like *Lily* Twig or Branch: It seeks not *nor desires* the fairness or excellence of this world, but of the Angelical world. For it also grows, not in this world in the Third Principle, but in the Second Principle in the *Paradisical* World. [25]

(The "Root of the Lily" is the universal Sophia; the "Lily Twig" or "Lily Branch" is, in Boehme's usage, the individual man's experience of the universal principle.) Jerusalem is described as a "lovely root" in the garden of God, in a way that leaves little doubt that Blake conceived her in terms of Boehme's Root of the Lily. The divine Vision reminds her that Spain and Greece had been hers,

> . . . *& the Counties of Albion,*
> *They spread forth like a lovely root into the Garden of God,*
> *They were as Adam before me, united into One Man.* [26]

In *The Four Zoas* Vala herself is "the Lilly of Havilah." The lily virgin of paradise, whom Boehme contrasts with the "rose" of the natural Eve, is as Blake's Jerusalem to his Vala, and perhaps as his "modest rose" who "puts forth a thorn" to his "lily white" of *The Lilly*, which we may then say is the first formulation of a view of love that was to find ever-increasingly clear expression in his later works—the view that "Humanity knows not of Sex," [27] and that

> *. . . Sexes must vanish & cease*
> *To be when Albion arises from his dread repose . . .*[28]

There is no way of eluding the fact that Blake, praised by Swinburne for his supposed advocacy of "evil," and dear to the twenties as a spiritual first cousin of D. H. Lawrence, gave sex a very modest place in the order of things. Blake told Crabb Robinson that he considered Swedenborg's "sexual religion" dangerous.[29] Following Boehme, he attributes sex only to the "garments." "Love," in a sexual sense, is in its nature incompatible with the level of being at which the soul is in union with the paradisiacal virgin. Vala is the inventor of "love":

> *. . . Vala would never have sought & loved Albion*
> *If she had not sought to destroy Jerusalem; such is that false*
> *And Generating Love, a pretence of love to destroy love,*
> *Cruel hipocrisy. . . .*[30]

In other words, the love of the body destroys that of the soul. Vala is the great protagonist of sexual "love which never yet / Immingled God & Man."[31] Albion tells her that "In Eternity they neither marry nor are given in marriage";[32] and perhaps Blake wrote his view so explicitly to disclaim the Swedenborgian teaching. Jerusalem pleads with Vala to remember the lost paradisiacal state in which there are no sexes:

> *Tell me, O Vala, thy purposes; tell me wherefore thy shuttles*
> *Drop with the gore of the slain, why Euphrates is red with blood,*
> *Wherefore in dreadful majesty & beauty outside appears*
> *Thy Masculine from thy Feminine, hardening against the heavens*
> *To devour the Human! Why dost thou weep upon the wind among*
> *These cruel Druid Temples? O Vala! Humanity is far above*
> *Sexual organization & the Visions of the Night of Beulah*
> *Where Sexes wander in dreams of bliss among the Emanations,*
> *Where the Masculine & Feminine are nurs'd into Youth & Maiden*
> *By the tears & smiles of Beulah's Daughters till the time of*
> > *Sleep is past.*
> *Wherefore then do you realize these nets of beauty & delusion*
> *In open day . . .*[33]

"Love," indeed, could not exist at all but for this apparent separateness of individuals brought about by Vala; nor can natural "love" bring about any real union. Vala says:

> *Wherefore did I, loving, create love, which never yet*
> *Immingled God & Man, when thou & I hid the Divine Vision*
> *In cloud of secret gloom. . . .*
>
> .   .   .
>
> *For the Divine appearance is Brotherhood, but I am Love* [34]

"The Imaginative Human Form is but a breathing of Vala," she falsely says; and so it seems in the natural world. But her victims complain:

> *Once Man was occupied in intellectual pleasures & Energies,*
> *But now my Soul is harrow'd with grief & fear & love & desire,*
> *And now I hate & now I love, & Intellect is no more.*
> *There is no time for any thing but the torments of love & desire.*[35]

In the spiritual world natural "love" becomes unnecessary because the same life is in all.

Albion in the fallen state is

> *. . . bound in the bonds*
> *Of spiritual Hate, from which springs Sexual Love as iron chains* [36]

When Jesus is born on earth, he wears "No Human form, but Sexual": the two are contrasted, not identified, in Blake's symbolic terminology, as they are by Boehme, whose unfallen Adam contains his feminine counterpart in himself. "Consider sexual organization," Blake says, "& hide thee in the dust." The lowest of Blake's four worlds—Ulro—corresponds to Boehme's "out-birth" and to Plato's cave; and it is only in this fallen world that "the Sexes rose to work and weep," for

> *Such is the nature of the Ulro, that whatever enters*
> *Becomes Sexual & is Created and Vegetated and Born.*
> *From Hyde Park spread their vegetating roots beneath Albion,*
> *In dreadful pain the Spectrous Uncircumcised Vegetation*
> *Forming a Sexual Machine . . .*[37]

Blake, moreover, held this view from a very early period. In 1794, in *The Book of Urizen*, we already find him writing:

> *All Eternity shudder'd at sight*
> *Of the first female now separate,*
> *Pale as a cloud of snow*
> *Waving before the face of Los.*

Wonder, awe, fear, astonishment
Petrify the eternal myriads
At the first female form now separate.

> .   .   .

But Los saw the Female & pitied;
He embrac'd her; she wept, she refus'd;
In perverse and cruel delight
She fled from his arms, yet he follow'd.

Eternity shudder'd when they saw
Man begetting his likeness
On his own divided image.[38]

In this kind of thought Blake is very close to Boehme, who held that the division of the sexes comes about only in the third Principle, in Adam's "deep sleep." Eve belongs only to this world: "Yet as concerning *Eve*, we must acknowledge that she was created to this corruptible Life, for she is the Woman of this World." [39]

[39]   She is not a separate entity but a part of Adam, his feminine aspect and generative matrix, externalized.[40] She was, Boehme says, "never a virgin" but, as he ingeniously puts it, "half a virgin," for the original Virgin was the undivided wholeness of the paradisiacal Adam. Eve never was, nor could be, a being complete in her own perfection, as the Wisdom is virgin; nor indeed can her male counterpart; and Blake follows Boehme closely when he writes:

> *The Feminine separates from the Masculine & both from Man,*
> *Ceasing to be His Emanations, Life to Themselves assuming* [41]

Blake's latest statement on the sexual order is in *Jerusalem;* and there he writes in terms that are derived from Boehme and, at the same time, answer him. Sexual division, which was "meant for the destruction of Jerusalem" because the Lamb is born in a physical body, is made to serve the purposes of redemption:

> *Pity must join together those whom wrath has torn in sunder,*
> *And the Religion of Generation, which was meant for the destruction*
> *Of Jerusalem, become her covering till the time of the End.*
> *O holy Generation, Image of regeneration!*
> *O point of mutual forgiveness between Enemies!*

> *Birthplace of the Lamb of God incomprehensible!*
> *The Dead despise & scorn thee & cast thee out as accursed,*
> *Seeing the Lamb of God in thy gardens & thy palaces*
> *Where they desire to place the Abomination of Desolation.*[42]

It is noteworthy that Yeats came to the conclusion that Blake condemned sexual love. This might not carry so much weight if it were the view expressed in 1893 in the Ellis and Yeats commentary; it might then be dismissed as an expression of Yeats's "early puritanism"; but in fact it is a later reflection, written in the margin of Denis Saurat's *Blake and Modern Thought*, published in 1929. Saurat's views are those of his decade: "Thus," he says, "Blake reverses the usual conception. Sexual love is legitimate when it goes to *all* women." [43] Yeats comments upon this Gallic paradox, very justly: "It would be more true to say he condemned sexual love because it could not go to all." Yeats also annotated in the same work Blake's line "In lovely copulation, bliss on bliss. . . ." as "Not 'generating love,' or only that because we are in 'the prison house.'" He further stressed in another annotation the need to remember that Blake is talking of conditions in "the prison house" in his statements on sex. These comments are the product not only of a far deeper understanding of Blake than Saurat possessed but of a far better knowledge of the text.

How could Blake, who so realistically indicts and condemns the morality that "calls that chastity which desires and acts not," at the same time assign to sex so humble a position? In fact, there is no contradiction at all: sex belongs to the natural "garments" and *therefore* any attempt to locate chastity in the natural world he calls "hypocrisy." That the soul has no sex is clearly implied in *The Gates of Paradise:* man, falling into the phase of the soul's "sleep," enters the cave of generation:

> *Some find a Female Garment there,*
> *And some a Male, woven with care,*
> *Lest the Sexual Garments sweet*
> *Should grow a devouring Winding sheet.*[44]

It is important to insist upon the humble place that Blake assigns to sexuality and to "love"; for the freedom he claimed for the soul was not based, like the depraved carnality of the present times, upon the importunities of "bodily lust." It is in the name of the soul that he demands freedom. The love of the soul is the "brotherhood" of Eden, the union of all souls in Jesus the Imagination. Blake's sexual doctrine proves after all to be more akin to traditional orthodoxy than it is to the ethics of the modern profane world.

Does *The Lilly* bear the same relation to the later figure of Jerusalem that *The Sick Rose* bears to the early Vala? This suggestion will seem less absurd to those who have read and studied the writings of Boehme than to those who have not. The little poem itself, had it not been written by Blake, would not seem to rise above the level of emblematic commonplace. But knowing Blake's avowed dislike of "natural selfish chastity," we are surely justified in asking what exactly he did find to praise in "the Lilly white" who delights in a love contrasted with that of the rose. We know of Blake's early and passionate admiration for Boehme; and *The Three Principles of the Divine Essence*, included in the first volume of Law's Boehme, contains an eloquent evocation of the "Sophia," whom Boehme calls the "Lily-root of Paradise." It is not merely that a reader of Boehme might be aware of this splendid myth of the lily: no reader of Boehme could possibly overlook it. Boehme's Lily is the Virgin Sophia, man's true love in Paradise, before the creation of Eve, the natural, sexual woman, Adam's "rose-garden." *The Lilly* stands third on a single page with *My Pretty Rose-Tree* and *Ah! Sun-flower*. There is no other page in the *Songs* that contains more than one poem, and we are bound to conclude that Blake intended the three to be read together; for in that order they contain a complete philosophy of love.

The Lilly in its first draft certainly does not suggest Boehme's "Lily-root of Paradise," the lily being introduced in a perfunctory way as the conventional emblem of virginity (as contrasted with "the lustful rose") to provide the basis of one of the four paradoxes which make up the poem. In the first draft (which at this stage has no title),

> *The lustful rose puts forth a thorn,*
> *The coward sheep a threat'ning horn,*
> *While the lily white shall in love delight*
> *And the lion increase freedom & peace.*[45]

"Love" is unkind, cowardice is aggressive, chastity longs for love, and a standing army prevents war—proverbs of experience. The line about the lion was at one stage changed to "The priest loves war & the soldier peace." Blake was evidently not satisfied with the poem; he left it for some time, and only after the completion of that most paradoxical of all poems, *The Tyger*, did he recast it into a different poem altogether. We no longer have four paradoxes; instead we have two paradoxical symbols—rose and sheep—contrasted with the nonparadoxical lily. The contrast is now between the duality of rose and sheep, in the world of good and evil, and the lily, which is above good and evil and contains within its nature no shade of ambiguity:

> *The modest Rose puts forth a thorn,*
> *The humble Sheep a threat'ning horn;*
> *While the Lilly white shall in Love delight,*
> *Nor a thorn, nor a threat, stain her beauty bright.*[46]

The whole temper of the poem is altered by the alteration of "lustful" and "coward" to "modest" and "humble"; and the lily is now given first place and the title of the poem. But the symbol itself has changed its nature. It is an emblem no longer of sexual chastity but of a love above the conflict of opposites to which belongs the rose of sexuality.

My Pretty Rose-Tree is the first poem Blake wrote in his Notebook.[47] It has been described as a poem about a transient marriage estrangement. The poet is attracted toward another woman, whom he renounces for the sake of his wife, only to find that his wife turns away from him in jealousy:

> *A flower was offer'd to me*
> *Such a flower as may never bore;*
> *But I said, "I've a pretty rose tree,"*
> *And I passed the sweet flower o'er.*
>
> *Then I went to my pretty rose tree*
> *To tend it by day & by night*
> *But my rose turn'd away with Jealousy*
> *And her thorns were my only delight.*

But if he turned from his wife, this was only a symbolic reflection of the real situation, which was, rather, a dissatisfaction with "natural" love and a longing for some other object of desire—call it the Muse, the poet's supernatural mistress, the inspirer, glimpsed, possibly, in some other woman, Mary Wollstonecraft perhaps. Love (as apart from mere domestic contentment) in its very nature is bent upon some goal beyond any that is realizable in terms of nature, and there is no doubt of the sincerity of Blake's protest against marriage:

> *Why should I be bound to thee,*
> *O my lovely mirtle tree?*
> *Love, free love, cannot be bound*
> *To any tree that grows on ground.*[48]

Not *ought* not but *can* not; for the goal of love lies beyond "*any* tree that grows on ground"—that is, any natural, "vegetated" being—elsewhere altogether. But even while he is protesting, Blake makes no complaint against his "lovely mirtle tree" and his "pretty rose tree," who is herself shown as sharing in sympathy with the poet's sufferings:

> *Oft my mirtle sigh'd in vain*
> *To behold my heavy chain.*
> *Like to dung upon the ground*
> *Underneath my mirtle bound.*

So runs one canceled variant of *The Mirtle Tree.* In *The Four Zoas* the daemon of love, Luvah, is thrown "for dung on the ground." [49] But sexual love, as the fertilizing agent of natural generation (dung), even of myrtles and roses, could never satisfy Blake. What the imagination longs for is something different altogether, "such a flower as may never bore."

   This flower, I suggest, is Boehme's Lily of Paradise, the divine Wisdom, and not another woman.

Ah! Sun-flower is a poem on the theme of love as prayer or—to use Blake's better word—"aspiration." The lovers in the poem—the youth pined away with desire, and the pale virgin—are longing not so much for one another as, through their love, for "that sweet golden clime," some state beyond the power of mortal love to fulfill but toward which their mutual love reaches out. This is the view of love expressed by Plato in the *Phaedrus*—love as a mediating spirit, which leads, through the attraction of earthly beauty, to the heavenly original. It is in fact a Platonic poem, both in thought and in imagery. We do not know when, in relation to the others, it was written, for it is not taken from the Notebook; but it falls into the series of Blake's Neoplatonic poems. The virgin in her shroud and the youth and virgin in their "graves"—that is, their mortal bodies—are generated souls in the condition the Platonists call a death from eternity. Their love longs to be freed from its bodily limitations.

So much is the general Neoplatonic sense of the poem. But there is also a specific source that confirms the view that this is a poem about prayer. In his introduction to the first edition of his *Hymns of Orpheus* [50] Taylor devotes several pages to the Neoplatonic teaching on prayer. Prayer, he says, does not cause any animadversion in the gods, "or, properly speaking, draw down their beneficence," but is, rather, the means of elevating the "soul to these divinities, and disposing it for the reception of their supernal illumination. For the divine irradiation, which takes place in prayer, shines and energizes spontaneously, restoring unity to the soul, and causing our energy to become one with divine energy. For such, according to these philosophers, is the efficacy of prayer, that it unites all inferior with all superior beings. Since, as the great Theodorus says, all things pray except the first." [51]

Ah! Sun-flower expresses this aspiration of all dependent beings toward the First, the uncreated One, who is alone self-sufficient. Its very grammar is an aspiration, an extended "ah," for the poem has neither verb nor predicate but only a series of dependent clauses opening out of the invocation:

> *Ah, Sun-flower, weary of time,*
> *Who countest the steps of the Sun,*
> *Seeking after that sweet golden clime*
> *Where the traveller's journey is done:*
>
> *Where the Youth pined away with desire,*
> *And the pale Virgin shrouded in snow*
> *Arise from their graves, and aspire*
> *Where my Sun-flower wishes to go.* [52]

The sunflower aspires to the sun as all souls aspire to eternity. Plato makes Diotima the Priestess [53] describe love as the child of want and plenty, and in the *Phaedrus* draws his great picture of the love of lovers as only a point of departure for love of the eternal—as it is for Blake's youth and virgin, who here aspire to the "sweet golden clime."

Both Paracelsus and Agrippa give long lists of herbs, animals, and minerals which possess affinities with sun, moon, or some one or another of the planetary rulers. Thomas Vaughan wrote that "there is not a Compound [87]

87 Vala on a sunflower: *Jerusalem* (1804–1820), plate 53, upper half

Note the sun, moon, and stars in her wings, as on the title page of *Jerusalem* [frontispiece]. Cf. Satan [101] and emblem of Isis [II, 172].

in all Nature but hath in it a little Sun, and a little Moon" [54]—the Sol and Luna of the alchemists, which are rather principles than bodies. In Boehme's writings these affinities are still given the alchemical appellation of "signatures." Blake never doubted this sympathy of similitude, a necessary consequence of the belief that "primary natures distribute their gifts to such as are secondary, by an abundant illumination, and effects are established in the causes from which they proceed." [55]

Blake's sunflower, then, is not vainly longing for the sun. It is a solar flower not only by reason of the external resemblance of its golden disk to the sun with its rays, but because it has within itself the solar nature, the true alchemical Sol, though imprisoned in the lowest (the vegetated) order of being. Therefore it responds at all times to its source and ruler, the heavenly sun. Similarly, the divine in man aspires to the divine source. The sunflower is the example chosen by Proclus to illustrate the principle of the sympathy subsisting between primary and secondary natures. This sympathy Proclus compared to love, basing his simile upon Plato's teaching that love is an aspiration toward the divine. Blake's poem is evidently inspired by this passage (quoted by Taylor in continuation of the extract given above):

> In the same manner as lovers gradually advance from that beauty which is apparent in sensible forms, to that which is divine; so the ancient priests, when they considered that there was a certain alliance and sympathy in natural things to each other, and of things manifest

to occult powers, and by this means discovered that all things subsist in all, they fabricated a sacred science, from this mutual sympathy and similarity. Thus they recognized things supreme, in such as are subordinate, and the subordinate in the supreme: in the celestial regions terrene properties subsisting in a causal and celestial manner: and in earth celestial properties, but according to a terrene condition. *For how shall we account for those plants called heliotropes, that is attendants on the sun, moving in correspondence with the revolution of its orb; but selenitropes, or attendants on the moon, turning in exact conformity with her motion?* it is because all things pray, and compose hymns to the leaders of their respective orders; but some intellectually, and others rationally; some in a natural, and others after a sensible manner. *Hence the sunflower, as far as it is able, moves in a circular dance towards the sun: so that if any one could hear the pulsation made by its circuit in the air, he would perceive something composed by a sound of this kind, in honour of its king,* such as a plant is capable of framing.[56]

This beautiful passage, with that concrete visual quality to which Blake always responded when reading any abstract work, gave him at once the philosophy and the images of the poem. The flower is praying, or aspiring, to the sun, confined as it is to its "terrene" condition. Love, thus realized, is no longer "dung upon the ground," fertilizing only the process of generation; it is a spiritual pilgrimage.

It is likely that in Proclus' heliotrope and selenitrope we have the originals of the youth and the virgin of Blake's poem—the youth obedient to the sun, the virgin to the moon, ruler of women. This pair are the earliest foreshadowing of Los, regent of the sun, and his emanation Enitharmon, ruler of the "moony" night, who, like the "pale Virgin shrouded in snow," is described as "Pale as a cloud of snow." [57] Los on his first appearance, in *Europe,* is called "Possessor of the moon," and must therefore be the sun, whom the moon obeys. These two characters are often identified, in a personal way, with Blake himself and with his wife; and we also feel that *Ah! Sun-flower* is a personal utterance—"*my* Sun-flower" being Blake himself.

Blake must have known, from Ovid's *Metamorphoses,* the story of Clyte, in love with Apollo but abandoned by him, who turned always toward the sun, following his course across the heavens until she was changed into a sunflower. But Blake's flower is specifically masculine – "my Sun-flower" – as he later felt himself to be possessed by the solar Los. If Blake's sunflower comes from Proclus rather than the more familiar story of Ovid, this masculine quality is explained. The masculine soul (or heliotrope) is subject to the sun, the feminine (the selenitrope) to the moon.[58]

Los is also the regent of time; and the sunflower, too, is closely associated with the time process. Los rules the sun itself:

> *. . . the unwearied Sun by Los created*
> *To measure Time and Space to mortal Men every morning.*[59]

The sunflower counting the steps of the sun is, like Los, measuring time. This image may have been suggested to Blake by the Orphic Hymn to the Sun, for here specific mention is made of the sun's dance:

> *Lord of the Seasons, beaming light from far,*
> *Sonorous, dancing in thy four-yok'd car.*[60]

Proclus writes, in his *Hymn to Apollo*, "From thy bland dance repelling deadly ill." [61] Are Blake's "steps of the sun" the steps of this dance across the heavens that forms so beautiful an attribute of the Greek Apollo?

The sunflower is "weary of time." Here again the weariness is no mere mood of the flower or the poet but a necessary condition of the situation described. The soul is compelled to move through time, but aspires to the higher condition, which is timeless. Proclus explains this also: intellect, soul, nature, and matter depend each on the other, "for the microcosmic man comprehends within himself partially all that the world contains totally." Soul, "which, on account of possessing its energy in transition and a mutation of life, requires the circulations of time to the perfection of its nature, and depends on intellect as a more ancient and consequently superior cause. But that which moves and is at the same time moved is nature, or that corporeal life which is distributed about body . . . which is naturally passive, imbecil and inert." [62] (Here Taylor is paraphrasing Plotinus.) Thus soul (held in body) aspires to the higher condition (that of intellect) which is extratemporal.

In this poem Blake adds a new element to his theme of the soul's descent and return: the journey of the Lost Traveller, of the wandering Emmet, of the Traveller who hastens in the evening. The condition of the lapsed soul here appears as, specifically, a lapse into the time-state, which in itself constitutes the journey, or dream.

88 Dürer's engraving of Apollo (1504?)
The reversed name of the god seen in the glass is within the traditional language of symbols according to which reflections and shadows signify earthly embodiments of heavenly originals. Blake in the name Los (Sol reversed as in a mirror-image) signifies the earthly vehicle of the solar principle.

The alchemical Sol likewise is a masculine principle. It is notable that the name "Los" is "Sol" spelled backward. It names the solar principle of the alchemists, present in the whole of creation. Is it fanciful to see the name Los as Sol seen in reflection, or mirrored, in the water, or looking glass, of physical nature? [63]   [88]

This idea might have been suggested to Blake by Dürer's engraving of Apollo, where the god holds a mirror that reflects, among bright flames, the name "Apolo" written in mirror-image. Doubtless Dürer also wished to signify that the visible natural sun is a reflection of the god in the "vegetable glass."

The name expresses the alchemical "as above, so below." The alchemical Sol is not so much the sun as the solar fire-principle itself, diffused throughout nature. Vaughan writes of the alchemical Sol and Luna

89 Los exploring the recesses of the grave: *Jerusalem* (1804–1820), frontispiece

See also [28].

as two principles eternally wedded: "*the Magicians Sun* and *Moon* are *two universall Peerse Male* and *Female*, a *King* and *Queen Regents*, always *young*, and never *old*. These *two* are *Adaequate* to the *whole world*, and *coextended* thorough the *universe*. The *one* is not without the *other*, God having *united* them in his work of *Creation* in a *solemn, Sacramentall union.*" [64]

Paracelsus writes: "This Terrene or earthly Sun is kindled and bred by the Fire of the superior; even so is kindled the Centre of our matter, from the Centre of our World or *Athanor;* which is Fire, bearing a similitude and resemblance with the natural Sun." [65]

Vaughan also writes of this alchemical Sol hidden in matter. Light, he says, is like a lamp in a dark house: [66]

It burns and is not seen, for it shines in a dark place. Every naturall Body is a kind of Black Lanthorne, it carries this Candle within it, but the Light appears not, it is Ecclips'd with the Grossnesse of the matter. The Effects of this Light are apparent in all things; but the Light it self is denied, or else not followed. The great world hath the Sun for his Life and Candle; according to the Absence or presence of this Fire, all things in the world flourish or wither.[67]

This spiritual sun is the "light of light"—*lumen de lumine.*

There is a suggestion of this alchemical allegory in the figure of Los exploring the recesses of the grave, dark lantern in hand, upon which Blake bestowed so much care in the frontispiece of *Jerusalem*. The "globe of life-blood" is also the sun of human life—"the red globule is the unwearied Sun by Los created"—for it is by one's own Sol that every living being explores the cave of generated existence. Berkeley's *Siris* is the same solar principle that Blake intends by the spiritual sun; indeed, the conception is common to all the branches of the alchemical tradition. Boehme says: Sol is "the Heart, viz, the Center to which all Forms tend and press. Thus the outward Sun presses into the Sun in the Herb; and the inward Sun presses into the outward." [68] The two suns are one of Swedenborg's finer realizations: "the Sun of the natural World is perfectly dead, but the Sun of the spiritual World is alive." The natural sun is created by the spiritual sun through influx: "The spiritual sun by its heat vivifies spiritual beings, and renews spiritual things, whereas the sun of the natural world does indeed produce

[89]

[90]

90 Urizen exploring with the globe of life-blood as a lamp: *Urizen* (1794), plate 22, detail

the same effects upon natural man and natural things, not from itself but by the influx of spiritual heat" [69] —and spiritual heat is pure love, that is, life itself. Boehme's thought is similar:

> For as the Deity is the Virtue and Light of Paradise in the second Principle, so the Sun is the Virtue and Light of this material world in the third Principle. And as the Deity shines in the Darkness in the first Principle, so the Sun shines in the Darkness in the third Principle. And as the Deity is the eternal Virtue and the Spirit of the eternal Life, so the Sun is the Spirit and the Virtue in the corruptible Life. [70]

A verse-letter to Thomas Butts [71] presents Blake's own vision of the double sun, with Los as its spiritual living power, in terms closely reminiscent of Swedenborg:

> *Then Los appear'd in all his power:*
> *In the Sun he appear'd, descending before*
> *My face in fierce flames; in my double sight*
> *'Twas outward a Sun: inward Los in his might.*

Blake challenges the physical, visible sun:

> *"This Earth breeds not our happiness.*
> *Another Sun feeds our life's streams,*
> *We are not warmed with thy beams;*
> *Thou measurest not the Time to me,*
> *Nor yet the Space that I do see;*
> *My Mind is not with thy light array'd.*
> *Thy terrors shall not make me afraid."*
>
> *When I had my Defiance given,*
> *The Sun stood trembling in heaven*

Blake's far-darting god is the sun within the soul; Los has his being in consciousness, not in nature:

> *Los flam'd in my path, & the Sun was hot*
> *With the bows of my Mind & the Arrows of Thought—*
> *My bowstring fierce with Ardour breathes,*
> *My arrows glow in their golden sheaves.*

91 Los speaking to the poet: *Milton* (1804–1808), plate 43

Perhaps it is this same spiritual experience that is described in *Milton:*

[91]

> . . . *what time I bound my sandals*
> *On to walk forward thro' Eternity, Los descended to me:*
> *And Los behind me stood, a terrible flaming Sun, just close*
> *Behind my back. I turned round in terror, and behold!*
> *Los stood in that fierce glowing fire, & he also stoop'd down*
> *And bound my sandals on in Udan-Adan; trembling I stood*
> *Exceedingly with fear & terror, standing in the Vale*
> *Of Lambeth; but he kissed me and wish'd me health,*
> *And I became One Man with him arising in my strength.*
> *'Twas too late now to recede. Los had enter'd into my soul:*
> *His terrors now possess'd me whole! I arose in fury & strength.*[72]

Apollo's attribute most famed in antiquity was his power of oracular inspiration, and it is the god of Delphi himself whom Blake knew as Los.

92 "The Bowman": pencil drawing (1805?)

[92] There is a pencil drawing entitled "The Bowman" [73] that represents, visually, the same spiritual event. The glorious powerful figure of the Bowman, with his flaming hair, is inspired by a spiritual sun which descends behind him; from his open mouth a cry of inspiration seems to sound the creative Word itself into the attentive mind of his vehicular form. The well-known verses about the bow of burning gold and chariot of fire have their meaning in the mythology of Los as the spiritual sun, with the bow, arrows, chariot, and prophetic utterance of Apollo, but with the interior existence of the spiritual light "which lighteth every man that cometh into the world."

Again we find Blake's most visionary, most living figure of Los, his attributes and his operations, deeply rooted in a traditional metaphysical theme. Blake's imagination was at all times ready to be kindled by such themes, often in themselves abstract and recondite; and from such germinal ideas we can follow the growth and ramifications of his myths. For Blake no idea seemed fully to exist until it found expression in being, and being in action. For him there were no abstractions; even abstraction itself he saw (and personified in the figure of Urizen) as a mode of being. His own philosophic realizations at all times took the form of an experience of living essence, to the bewilderment of such friends as Crabb Robinson, to whom he said: "I have conversed with the Spiritual Sun. I saw him on Primrose-hill. He said 'Do you take me for the Greek Apollo?' 'No' I said, 'that (pointing to the sky) is the Greek Apollo. He is Satan.' " [74] But the mythological form of Blake's thought should at no time mislead us into imagining that its intellectual foundations are not strongly laid. Thus Blake, in the myth of Los [93] creating the sun of nature, re-creates Swedenborg's doctrine of "influx." Spiritual light and fire descend from the spiritual world to be molded by Los into the orb of the natural sun:

> *And first from those infinite fires,*
> *The light that flow'd down on the winds*
> *He siez'd, beating incessant, condensing*
> *The subtil particles in an Orb.*
>
> *Roaring indignant, the bright sparks*
> *Endur'd the vast Hammer; but unwearied*
> *Los beat on the Anvil, till glorious*
> *An immense Orb of fire he fram'd.*
>
> *Oft he quench'd it beneath in the Deeps,*
> *Then survey'd the all bright mass, Again*
> *Siezing fires from the terrific Orbs,*

93 Los and the sun: *The Book of Los* (1795)

He heated the round Globe, then beat,
While, roaring, his Furnaces endur'd
The chain'd Orb in their infinite wombs.

Nine ages completed their circles
When Los heated the glowing mass, casting
It down into the Deeps: the Deeps fled
Away in redounding smoke: the Sun
Stood self-balanc'd. . . .

      ·   ·   ·

But no light! for the Deep fled away
On all sides, and left an unform'd
Dark vacuity . . .[75]

When Blake says that the visible sun gives "no light," he means, of course, no spiritual or intellectual light. The light of nature is, in this sense, darkness; or as Swedenborg says, "the Sun of the natural World is pure Fire from which all Life is abstracted; but the Sun of the spiritual World is Fire in which there is Divine Life." [76]

Blake's animistic genius was not content with an inanimate sun even in the natural world. For him nothing can exist without life; and in a later passage even the natural sun is transformed into a splendid lion—living, albeit with a life inferior to its spiritual cause:

. . . they took the Sun that glow'd oer Los
And, with immense machines down rolling, the terrific orb
Compell'd. The Sun, redd'ning like a fierce lion in his chains,
Descended to the sound of instruments that drown'd the noise
Of the hoarse wheels & the terrific howlings of wild beasts
That drag'd the wheels of the Sun's chariot; & they put the Sun
Into the temple of Urizen to give light to the Abyss [77]

The sun, chained in the service of Urizen's mechanistic universe, howls its protest like a live creature, unwillingly compelled to such enslavement. Blake's Tyger is another fiery beast, created in the furnaces of the demiurge by the theft of "fire," the solar spiritual principle.[78]

CHAPTER 9

Gates of Birth and Death

Certain themes—perhaps they must be called archetypal—may be seen as acting (on the analogy of a magnetic field) as symbolic fields which draw into their sphere of energy appropriate material. It would be altogether wrong to suppose that in building his myths Blake's symbols ramify, as in Bryant's *Mythology*, through accidental associations and without any organizing principle. There is not one fragment of Blake's myth that is not held together by the adamant of some powerful imaginative idea. But while it often happens, especially in his early Prophetic Books, that the material, however relevant, has not been sufficiently dissolved and dissipated for the process of re-creation to take place, yet Blake certainly fulfilled Coleridge's qualifying sentence: "where this process is rendered impossible" (Coleridge too wrote from experience of the difficulties) "yet still at all events it [the imagination] struggles to idealize and to unify." Struggle Blake certainly did. And his unsuccessful attempts often throw a great deal of light upon his system of thought and symbols by leading us to its origin and foundations. If the pursuit of these sources does little to explain or justify Blake as poet, it does uncover the scope of his knowledge and the vital energy of his thinking, and compels us to recognize and to respect the organization of his poetic thought, down to the most seemingly trifling symbolic detail. His imaginative learning and his view of poetry as the supreme expression of knowledge (since it embraces intellect and feeling, metaphysical intuition and concrete image) are, moreover, in the great central tradition of the major poets, from Vergil to Dante, Goethe to Coleridge and Shelley, Spenser to Yeats. If his way of assembling his material seems strange to many at the present time, it would not have seemed so to any of these or to Blake's supreme poetic master, Milton. The Neoplatonic cycle of the soul's descent and return is the unifying structure of all; and the figures of Los and Enitharmon take their

94 Winged ark guided by females: *Jerusalem* (1804–1820), plate 44, detail

This is the traditional emblem of woman as the *Foederis Arca* (ark of the covenant) in which life travels over the sea of generated existence.

place within this structure. Thus the alchemical Sol and Luna are related to Porphyry's cave by way of the gates ruled by the sun and the moon.

The northern gate of birth, which in Porphyry's myth is the place where the weaving nymphs have erected their looms, has its parallel in those golden looms of Enitharmon, first described in Night VIII of *Vala*. Here the daughters of Beulah weave earthly garments:

> . . . *Then Enitharmon erected Looms in Luban's Gate*
> *And call'd the Looms Cathedron; in these Looms she wove the*
> *Spectres*
> *Bodies of Vegetation, singing lulling Cadences to drive away*
> *Despair from the poor wondering spectres; and Los loved them*
> *With a parental love . . .*[1]

Cathedron is built in the northern gate:

> *And in the North Gate, in the West of the North, toward Beulah,*
> *Cathedron's Looms are builded, and Los's Furnaces in the South.*
> *A wondrous golden Building immense with ornaments sublime*
> *Is bright Cathedron's golden Hall, its Courts, Towers & Pinnacles.*[2]

Through the northern gate of Cancer, governed by the moon, the souls enter generation. Blake calls this lunar gate "Luban's Gate," according to his custom of translating classical into biblical symbols. Luban derives from a piece of information Blake found in Bryant's *Mythology*.[3] Laban, Luban, Labar, and Lubar are all denominations of the Arkite moon. The Ark itself Blake depicts as a moon-boat, an idea he also seems to have derived from Bryant, in whose book a moon-ark appears as a tailpiece. Also, Luban is Ararat, or *Mons Lunaris*. From this mountain all peoples dispersed over the world.

Several very strange features of Enitharmon's generative activities can be understood only if we search the literature of this mythology of the lunar gate. Enitharmon sends the generating specters to earth by the strange

[94, 95]

agency of breathing them down to earth on the wind. It cannot be said that by this image Blake gains either clarity or formal beauty: but it is repeated so frequently that it is clear he attached significance to it. He has been carried away by his passion for eclecticism, or, perhaps, wished to establish beyond question his traditional antecedents. Unfortunately, few have recognized in his new dress the ancient symbols, and the "winds" of Enitharmon are among those mythological attributes which have most bewildered and confused his readers. Too often Blake's allusiveness defeats its own ends. Thus the specters

> *. . . descend thro' the Gate of Pity*
> *The broken heart Gate of Enitharmon. She sighs them forth upon*
> > *the wind*
>
> *Of Golgonooza. Los stood at the Gate recieving them . . .*[4]

and again:

> *. . . she sigh'd forth on the wind the spectres*
> *And wove them bodies, calling them her belov'd sons and daughters* [5]

Blake may have found this theme of the airy nature of the moon in a passage of Aristides' *De Musica*, quoted by Taylor in a note on Plotinus' *On the Descent of Souls*. Aristides describes the "places about the moon" as airy and windy; for the moon "possesses a communion of air, and a repercussive spirit." Or the winds of Enitharmon may come from the ancient belief that the north wind produced conception. Vergil in the *Georgics* describes how

95 Moon-ark and dove of peace: plate engraved by Blake for Bryant's *Mythology*, vol. 3 (1776), p. 60

The work has been identified as Blake's by A. G. B. Russell and Ruthven Todd.

F I N I S.

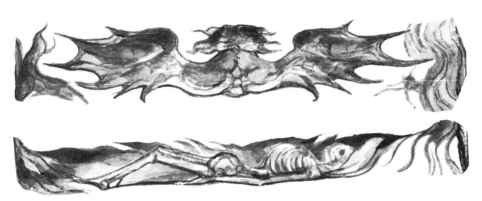

96 Bat-winged female genitals—"The gates of the grave"—and (below) out-stretched skeleton: *Jerusalem* (1804–1820), plate 58, details
Bat-wings, in Blake's symbolism, belong to Satan and his kingdom (Nature). Compare the threefold gates of birth [82].

mares become pregnant by breathing in the north wind; and Porphyry also mentions this property of Boreas: "the north wind is adapted to souls falling into generation. . . . For the north wind, indeed, from its superior cold-ness, congeals [as it were, the animal life] and detains it in the frigidity of terrene generation. But the south wind being hot, dissolves this life, and sends it upward to the heat of a divine nature . . . Since . . . souls proceed into generation through the northern gate, hence this wind is said to be amatory." [6] Enitharmon's winds [7] are likewise amatory:

> . . . with sighs of love,
> Sweet Enitharmon mild, Entranc'd breath'd forth upon the wind
> The spectrous dead. Weeping, the Spectres view'd the immortal
>
> > works
>
> Of Los, Assimilating to those forms, Embodied & Lovely
> In youth & beauty, in the arms of Enitharmon mild reposing. [8]

The gate of birth is, in its least esoteric sense, the female genitals; [96] and this "gate," hideous and bat-winged, is represented on plate 58 of *Jerusalem;* it is "the gates of the grave" by which "mortal worms" enter generation, Platonic death-in-life. A skeleton is outstretched beneath the [97] "gate." On plate 24 of *Jerusalem* the moon-ark, carrying the female "gate," floats on the sea of hyle, an emblem not, in this case, so much of the "gates of the grave" as of the *Foederis Arca* (ark of the covenant), one of the symbolic epithets of the Blessed Virgin, whose womb is blessed because it gives birth to the Divine Child.

A whole range of symbolism associated with Enitharmon's gate is based upon the episode in *Paradise Lost* of the unbarring of the Gates of Hell to Satan by his daughter Sin, who alone has the key. Milton's Sin is sexuality; she unlocks the door into this world and is the mother of Death, who makes his prey all who pass through it. Enitharmon's gate is first mentioned in *Vala*, V:

> *Enitharmon on the road of Dranthon felt the inmost gate*
> *Of her bright heart burst open & again close with a deadly pain.*
> *Within her heart Vala began to reanimate in bursting sobs;*
> *And when the Gate was open she beheld that dreary deep*
> *Where bright Ahania wept. . . .*[9]

Enitharmon has had a momentary glimpse of the horror of "Non-Entity." Ahania, the earth-goddess banished by Urizen from the world of divine light, wanders in the "Non-Entity" of material existence. Enitharmon's "gate" opens from the eternal to the temporal world; and the souls as they pass that gate behold for the first time, like Thel, the "secrets of the land unknown." To Porphyry, Blake has now added Milton's account of the same symbolic situation; for the Gates of Hell open into chaos and night:

> *Before their eyes in sudden view appear*
> *The secrets of the hoarie deep, a dark*
> *Illimitable Ocean without bound.*[10]

When Vala is born, the gates are broken open, not to be closed again:

> *She burst the Gates of Enitharmon's heart with direful Crash,*
> *Nor could they ever be clos'd again; the golden hinges were broken,*
> *And the gates broke in sunder & their ornaments defac'd*
> *Beneath the tree of Mystery, for the immortal shadow shuddering*
> *Brought forth this wonder horrible: a Cloud; she grew & grew*
> *Till many of the Dead burst from the bottoms of their tombs* [11]

97 The moon-ark floating on the waters: *Jerusalem* (1804–1820), plate 24, detail (Rosenwald Coll.)

Here the moon is itself the vehicle of the female genitals.

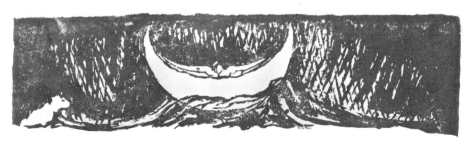

The model for this passage is Milton's account of the opening by Sin of the Adamantine Gates. When these have been opened, the infernal Pit communicates with the new-created world, and like Enitharmon's gates, they can never be closed.

> . . . from her side the fatal Key,
> Sad instrument of all our woe, she took;
> And towards the Gate rouling her bestial train,
> Forthwith the huge Portcullis high up drew,
> Which but her self not all the Stygian powers
> Could once have mov'd; then in the key-hole turns
> Th' intricate wards, and evry Bolt and Bar
> Of massie Iron or sollid Rock with ease
> Unfast'ns: on a sudden op'n flie
> With impetuous recoile and jarring sound
> Th' infernal dores, and on their hinges grate
> Harsh thunder, that the lowest bottom shook
> Of Erebus. She op'nd, but to shut
> Excel'd her power; the Gates wide op'n stood.[12]

Here we have Blake's "direful Crash" and broken hinges and the gate that can never be closed. The gates once open, "many of the dead" descended through them; and here, too, Blake is keeping within the pattern of Milton's myth; for Satan promises Death, the offspring of Sin, that, once the gates are opened, "all things shall be your prey." The Spirits of Hell, following upon Satan's track,

> Pav'd after him a broad and beat'n way
> Over the dark Abyss. . . .
> . . . by which the Spirits perverse
> With easie intercourse pass to and fro.[13]

Similarly, Enitharmon's broken gates become a "broad and beaten way" for the "dead." This reading is the more likely, since these specters are here called "Satans":

> The myriads of the dead burst thro' the bottoms of their tombs,
> Descending on the shadowy female's clouds in Spectrous terror,
> Beyond the Limit of Translucence on the Lake of Udan Adan.
> These they nam'd Satans, & in the Aggregate they nam'd them
> Satan.[14]

Indeed, this perfunctory plural seems to have been introduced as a bridge to the singular "Satan," who then becomes identifiable as Milton's Satan entering by the path opened by Sin and Death.

A passage at the end of "Night the First" is added, it seems, as a logical afterthought to the original appearance of the gates as broken open:

> . . . *the bright female terror*
> *Refus'd to open the bright gates; she clos'd and barr'd them fast*
> *Lest Los should enter into Beulah thro' her beautiful gates.*[15]

The threefold nature of the gates is also an added detail in the same passage:

> . . . *the Inner gates of Enitharmon's bosom,*
> *And of her fine wrought brain, & of her bowels within her loins.*
> *These gates within, Glorious & bright, open into Beulah*

The threefold gates, too, are in Milton:

> . . . *thrice threefold the Gates; three folds were Brass,*
> *Three Iron, three of Adamantine Rock,*
> *Impenetrable, impal'd with circling fire,*
> *Yet unconsum'd . . .*[16]

As Blake moved from a Neoplatonic to a more Christian view of the descent of souls, the terrible "gates of the grave" seemed to him rather the golden "Gate of Pity"; sexual generation is not wholly an evil but a work of "mercy and love divine," because it enables the specters to enter the "space" of this world, "Canaan," into which Jesus is born to save the "dead." Blake's longest additions to the original text of *Vala* all concern the labors of Los and Enitharmon as parents of the specters and guardians of the space, Canaan, created for their redemption.

To Blake, as to all Christians, the deepest mystery of the gate of birth is the Incarnation of Jesus. As the Blessed Virgin in her litany is addressed as *foederis arca, janua coeli,* so in Blake's myth Enitharmon is comforted by the promise that through her "broken" gate the Divine Child will be born.

> *Tremble not so, my Enitharmon, at the awful gates*
> *Of thy poor broken Heart. . . .*
> *. . . but look! behold! take comfort!*

> *Turn inwardly thine Eyes & there behold the Lamb of God*
> *Clothed in Luvah's robes of blood descending to redeem.*[17]

Blake came to see Birth into "Canaan" chiefly as a good, since it offers the souls an opportunity for regeneration:

> *. . . the Religion of Generation, which was meant for the*
> *destruction*
> *Of Jerusalem, become her covering till the time of the End.*
> *O holy Generation, Image of regeneration!* [18]

In his illustration to Dante's Hell Gate,[19] Blake has inset, in contrast to the figures of suffering and evil in the foreground, a tender figure of a woman in a cave surrounded with a vine arbor. She is working at a spinning wheel and distaff. Souls "descend" from her looms into the "hell" of this world, beneath the "bottoms of the graves." She is the Virgin Mary, weaver of the body of the Divine Humanity, and her function here is Enitharmon's "clothing" of those about to be born. In an illustration to *Paradise Regained* the Blessed Virgin is shown with a distaff, emblem of her maternity. The same tenderness, the same sense of the holiness of their task, characterizes all Blake's later accounts of the labors of the Daughters of Beulah, who bring the specters into the space of Canaan:

> *He who is an Infant and whose Cradle is a Manger*
> *Knoweth the Infant sorrow, whence it came and where it goeth*
> *And who weave it a Cradle of the grass that withereth away.*
> *This World is all a Cradle for the erred wandering Phantom,*
> *Rock'd by Year, Month, Day & Hour; and every two Moments*
> *Between dwells a Daughter of Beulah to feed the Human Vegetable.*
> *Entune, Daughters of Albion, your hymning Chorus mildly,*
> *Cord of affection thrilling extatic on the iron Reel*
> *To the golden Loom of Love, to the moth-labour'd Woof,*
> *A Garment and Cradle weaving for the infantine Terror,*
> *For fear, at entering the gate into our World of cruel*
> *Lamentation, it flee back & hide in Non-Entity's dark wild* [20]

Boehme constantly uses the word "Gate" in the sense of birth; and for him also the gate is threefold, according to the *Three Principles of the Divine Essence*, upon which he so sublimely writes. There is a "birth" into each of the three, the "outbirth" into this physical world being the third and lowest; into this world the divine essence descends. A passage of great beauty describes the generation of the Son from the Father in a Gate of especial holiness: "Thus . . . is the Place or Space in the *Center*, or Midst of the angelical Gates, a more pleasant, more gracious, amiable, and blessed Place to the Father, wherein his Son and Heart is generated in the most richly and fully loving Manner, and wherein the Holy Ghost goes from the Father and the Son, in the most richly and fully loving Manner." [21] This may throw light on Blake's "Cathedron," the "throne" situated in the gate of generation; and something of Boehme is surely reflected in the lines:

> *And Jehovah stood in the Gates of the Victim, & he appeared*
> *A weeping Infant in the Gates of Birth in the Midst of Heaven.*[22]

Blake's Jehovah appears as

> *. . . a little weeping Infant pale reflected*
> *Multitudinous in the Looking Glass of Enitharmon, on all sides* [23]

The "Looking Glass" is Boehme's "vegetable glass of nature"; and by the word "multitudinous," Blake means that every birth reflects the central mystery. Thus the myth of Porphyry provides the structure for Blake's interpretation of the Christian mystery of the Incarnation.

Of the process of generation as more usually conceived in a scientific age Blake was perfectly well aware. He distinguishes it, however, by the term "vegetation," not "generation." The Bhagavad-Gita gives as one of the marks of ignorance the belief that life originates in sexual generation. Blake pictures sexual generation under the image of a vast proliferating colony of polyps, drifting in the sea—an image to which science cannot object. The polypus is first described in *The Book of Los*, II and III.[24] Los falls from eternity into the ocean of hyle, and becomes entangled in this monstrous organism. Los falls, like Milton's Satan, until he is carried

> *Sidelong on the purple air, wafting*
> *The weak breeze in efforts o'erwearied.*

He reaches the sublunary world, and then "vegetates" in the waters of matter: [25]

> *The Lungs heave incessant, dull, and heavy;*
> *For as yet were all other parts formless,*

> *Shiv'ring, clinging around like a cloud,*
> *Dim & glutinous as the white Polypus*
> *Driv'n by waves & englob'd on the tide.*
>
> *And the unformed part crav'd repose;*
> *Sleep began; the Lungs heave on the wave;*
> *Weary, overweigh'd, sinking beneath*
> *In a stifling black fluid, he woke.*
>
> *He arose on the waters; but soon*
> *Heavy falling, his organs like roots*
> *Shooting out from the seed, shot beneath,*
> *And a vast world of waters around him*
> *In furious torrents began.*
>
> *Then he sunk, & around his spent Lungs*
> *Began intricate pipes that drew in*
> *The spawn of the waters, Outbranching*
> *An immense Fibrous Form, stretching out*
> *Thro' the bottoms of immensity raging.*

This nightmare-like account of the stifling ensnaring of the soul in a physical organism as it descends into generation seems to be the product of Blake's vivid imaginative realization of passages he found in Erasmus Darwin.

The polypus is an organism Darwin several times mentions; and the embryology of the crocodile [26] has struck many readers besides Blake:

> *So from his shell on Delta's shower-less isle*
> *Burst into life the Monster of the Nile;*
> *First in translucent lymph with cobweb-threads*
> *The Brain's fine floating tissue swells, and spreads*
> *Nerve after nerve the glistening spine descends,*
> *The red Heart dances, the Aorta bends;*
> *Through each new gland the purple current glides,*
> *New veins meandering drink the refluent tides*

The concept of "vegetated" bodies is likewise Darwinian, an odd foreshadowing of the biological science of the poet's grandson, who extended quantitative science into the sphere of life. Darwin is at pains to compare the anatomy and physiology of the plant with that of the animal organism:

The parts which we may expect to find in the anatome of vegetables correspondent to those in the animal economy are, 1) A system of absorbent vessels to imbibe the moisture of the earth similar to the lacteal vessels, as in the roots of plants; and another system of absorbents similar to the lymphatics of animal bodies, opening its mouths on the internal cells and external surfaces of vegetables; and a third system of absorbent vessels correspondent with those of the placentation of the animal foetus. 2) A pulmonary system correspondent to the lungs or gills of quadrupeds and fish, by which the fluid absorbed by the lacteals and lymphatics may be exposed to the influence of the air.[27]

Darwin goes on to list pulmonary, arterial, and glandular systems. (Have we in this and similar passages the source of Enitharmon's "Fibres of blood, milk and tears"?) This vegetable life, almost animal, is, Blake must have felt, horrible, like the polypus, an animal life almost vegetable. Blake saw in this soulless vegetation the same error at work that produced Newton's soulless physics. It is not the real cause or source of life. Descending into generation is called "passing the Polypus"; and the descending souls

> *Could not behold Golgonooza without passing the Polypus,*
> *A wondrous journey not passable by Immortal feet, & none*
> *But the Divine Saviour can pass it without annihilation.*
> *For Golgonooza cannot be seen till having pass'd the Polypus*
> *It is viewed on all sides round by a Four-fold Vision,*
> *Or till you become Mortal & Vegetable in Sexuality,*
> *Then you behold its mighty Spires & Domes of ivory & gold.*[28]

Blake speaks of "passing" the polypus, not as being generated by it. The merely vegetable multiplication of the human species is the proliferation of this great many-headed horror (sometimes Blake uses the tree as synonymous with the polypus), and has nothing whatever to do with the origin of the souls who "descend." It is the *Adamah*, or natural body, "not the Soul or Imagination": [29]

> *No Human Form but only a Fibrous Vegetation,*   [II, 191]
> *A Polypus of soft affections without Thought or Vision* [30]
>
> *. . . every Man born is joined*
> *Within into One mighty Polypus . . .*[31]

It is a form of "death"—that is, of spiritual death:

> *. . . the sea of Time & Space*
> *Beat round the Rock in mighty waves, & as a Polypus*
> *That vegetates beneath the Sea, the limbs of Man vegetated*
> *In monstrous forms of Death, a Human polypus of Death.*[32]

It is the work of "Five Females & the nameless Shadowy Mother," and again Blake is echoing Porphyry, in a passage that captures the very spirit of the Arlington Court tempera and those "cruel" females who bind the souls into life through carnal lust, "Love of Parent, Storgous Appetite, Craving." On Phorcys' phallic coil of flax is wound the "sinewy thread" of "living fibres" from which the polypus is woven:

> *. . . a vast Polypus*
> *Of living fibres down into the Sea of Time & Space growing*
> *A self-devouring monstrous Human Death Twenty seven fold.*
> *Within it sit Five Females & the nameless Shadowy Mother,*
> *Spinning it from their bowels with songs of amorous delight*
> *And melting cadences that lure the Sleepers of Beulah down*
> *The River Storge (which is Arnon) into the Dead Sea.*[33]

Los's stifling descent into a body is echoed in the several accounts given by Los-Urthona of the birth of Los and Enitharmon into the world-cave. The symbolism of *The Cave of the Nymphs* is blended with the Darwinian embryology of *The Book of Los*, and the frightening image of Los swept irresistibly into generation:

> *. . . found myself & her* [Enitharmon] *together issuing down*
> *the tide*
> *Which now our rivers were become, delving thro' caverns huge*
> *Of goary blood, struggling . . .*[34]

A similar account is given by Urthona to Enitharmon.[35]

Porphyry's cave has two gates: the gate of birth, ruled by the moon and the female weavers, and the gate of death, by which the souls return to the "sweet golden clime" of the sun; and so has Blake's Golgonooza:

> *There are Two Gates thro' which all Souls descend, One Southward*
> *From Dover Cliff to Lizard Point, the other toward the North,*

Caithness & rocky Durness, Pentland & John Groat's House.

The Souls descending to the Body wail on the right hand
Of Los, & those deliver'd from the Body on the left hand.
For Los against the east his force continually bends [36]

At Los's gate of death there are no weaving nymphs; it is a gate not terrible   [42]
but beautiful:

There is in Albion a Gate of Precious stones and gold
Seen only by Emanations, by vegetations viewless:
Bending across the road of Oxford Street, it from Hyde Park
To Tyburn's deathful shades admits the wandering souls
Of multitudes who die from Earth: this Gate cannot be found
By Satan's Watch-fiends, tho' they search numbering every grain
Of sand on Earth every night, they never find this Gate.
It is the Gate of Los. Withoutside is the Mill, intricate, dreadful
And fill'd with cruel tortures . . . [37]

Satan cannot find the gate or overtake those who escape from generated life and its cruel laws. The criminals condemned in "Tyburn's deathful
shades" elude the punisher when they pass the secret golden gate of Los.
Satan has no part in "the immortal man that cannot die." The grave is
"heaven's golden gate"; but all in man that belongs to Satan "shall never
pass the Polar Bar." [38] Blake's belief that "Every death is an improvement of
the State of the Departed" [39] has overtones of Neoplatonism; for it is this life
that is the death of the soul. When at the end of his life Blake illustrated
Dante, he made it clear that he regarded Dante's hells as states of the soul
not in another but in this world, where "Satan is named by the Divine
Name." Over the Gate of Hell Blake has shown "the angry God of this
world," who is in truth Satan, the cloven-footed travesty of God shown in
the Job engraving Number 11. Albert S. Roe, in his admirable introductory
essay to *Blake's Illustrations to the Divine Comedy*,[40] has understood that
Blake's hell is "this present world of suffering," and that he has interpreted Dante according to this belief.

Yet it is not necessary to undergo physical death in order to enter
immortal life, for the Gate of Paradise is everywhere; it opens into "another
principle." There are passages in Boehme which so describe a gate that
cannot be found:

The Mind has from the Beginning of the World had so very much to do about this Gate, and has continually so searched therein, that I cannot reckon the wearisome Heap of Writers. But in the Time of the Lily this Gate shall flourish as a Bay-Tree; for its Branches will get Sap from the Virgin, and therefore be greener than Grass, and whiter than the Roses.   .   .   . and it will reach into the Paradise of God . . . The Way to it is very near; whosoever finds that [Way] dares not to reveal it, neither can he, for there is no Language that can express it; And although any seek long after it, if the Tincture will not, he cannot find it; nevertheless it meets them that seek after it right, in its own Way.[41]

But here we run into confusion, for the Gate of Los is at first called the Gate of Urthona, the "eternal" form of Los. It seems that Blake early conceived a mythology in which gods of double aspect were to enact their cosmic drama. Antiquity abounds in such multiplicity; Bryant's *Mythology* gives many representations of *Janus Bifrons;* and Blake himself painted Triple Hecate. He seems in the end to have found this scheme impossible in practice (as his readers have done), the more so as there is a double duplication of the figure of Urthona. Both Urthona and the "Spectre of Urthona" (who is sometimes Los but sometimes another figure) are profoundly obscure and imperfectly realized figures. Nevertheless, in tracing the origins of Urthona we may see Blake attempting to weld into a coherent whole several related trains of symbol.

Repeatedly in *Vala* we are told that Urthona rules the northern gate:

> . . . *in Eternal times the Seat of Urizen is in the South,*
> *Urthona in the North, Luvah in East, Tharmas in West.*[42]

Terrors haunt his seat:

> *North stood Urthona's steadfast throne, a World of Solid darkness*
> *Shut up in stifling obstruction, rooted in dumb despair.*[43]

When presently Urthona and Los are identified, the two are Janus-like, Urthona in eternity, Los looking toward generation:

> *In the Fourth region of Humanity, Urthona nam'd,*
> *Mortality begins to roll the billows of Eternal Death*
> *Before the Gate of Los. Urthona is here named Los.*[44]

Urthona appears in the Prophetic Books before Los; and in his earliest

[43]
[II, 125]

conception he seems to be, quite simply, Death, or Hades, ruler of the underworld; and the underworld he rules is, in accordance with Blake's Neoplatonic enthusiasm at that time, this world. Souls "die" into "the grave," and there are no tender weaving nymphs clothing the specters of "Urthona's dens." He is first named in *A Song of Liberty*, where the Starry King (Urizen) and his counselors are described, "Falling, rushing, ruining! buried in the ruins, on Urthona's dens." [45] We may trace the dens back to the Hades of Lyca's lion king, for Urthona possesses a pillared palace in the "caverns" and "dens" of the underworld. Orc calls Urthona's kingdom "the regions of dark death," and says:

> . . . *anon a serpent folding*
> *Around the pillars of Urthona . . .*
> *. . . feeble my spirit folds,*
> *For chain'd beneath I rend these caverns . . .* [46]

Urthona is "dark death"; he is Hades with his caverned palace.

Why then is he called Urthona? For one reason because "U-thorno" is the Ossianic Hades. It is a mountain in Norway sacred to the god Loda, or Odin. Odin, like Urthona, dwells in northern darkness, and keeps a house of ghosts: "U-thorno, that risest in waters! on whose sides are the meteors of night! I behold the dark moon descending behind thy echoing woods. On thy top dwells the misty Loda, the house of the spirits of men." [47] This passage, with its landscape of north, moon, waters, and forest, is, considered symbolically, a perfect "correspondence" of the gate of "descent." Lyca calls upon moon and darkness under a tree; and the waters of the nymphs are also there. It is not surprising that Blake, in his enthusiasm for Ossian, seized upon it. There are times when to remember how children read fairy tales will help us more toward understanding the mental processes of this mythological poet than a great burden of learning. Imagine, then, Blake reading his Ossian with unlearned delight, as a modern reader might read Tolkien, and in this frame of mind let us accompany him, with the hero Fingal, to the Mountain of the Dead: "The flame was dim and distant; the moon hid her red face in the east. A blast came from the mountain, and bore, on its wings, the Spirit of Loda. He came to his place in his terrors, and he shook his dusky spear.—His eyes appear like flames in his dark face; and his voice is like distant thunder." [48] Urizen's ascent of "the Peaked rock of Urthona," there to encounter that specter, with his eyes glowing like two furnaces and his voice like thunder, is evidently based upon this once famous description of

Fingal's encounter with the god Loda, a passage worth quoting, for it is the very essence of the Gothic style: "He lifted high his shadowy spear; and bent forward his terrible height. But the king, advancing, drew his sword; the blade of dark-brown Luno. The gleaming path of the steel winds through the gloomy ghost. The form fell shapeless into air, like a column of smoke . . . The Spirit of Loda shrieked, as, rolled into himself, he rose on the wind." [49] Blake reflects this Ossianic disintegration of the ghost into cloud:

> *The Spectre of Urthona . . . writh'd*
> *His cloudy form in jealous fear, & muttering thunders hoarse*
> *And casting round thick glooms . . .* [49a]

Yet Loda is also Janus-faced, showing another aspect in the world of eternity: "my dwelling is calm, above the clouds, the fields of my rest are pleasant." [50] Thus Blake found in the Norse no less than in the classical mythology symbols which express the doctrine "Who knows whether to live be not to die and to die to live?"

Since this world is the kingdom of the dead, the "earth owner" (if this pun is implied in the name) is Pluto, because (so says Proclus, quoted by Taylor in a note on the Orphic Hymn to Pluto) "he governs by his providence the earth, and all she contains." [51]

Pluto is called "Terrestrial Jove," and as guardian of the earth he is keeper of the earth's keys (and hence of its gates) and ruler of the "spectres" who are "living their death" on earth. In the Orphic Hymns, Pluto is addressed by many of the epithets Blake gives to Urthona:

> *Terrestrial Jove, thy sacred ear incline,*
>
> . . .
>
> *Earth's keys to thee, illustrious king belong,*
> *Its secret gates unlocking, deep and strong.*
>
> . . .
>
> *To thee, great king, all sovreign earth's assign'd,*
> *The seat of Gods, and basis of mankind.*
> *Thy throne is fix'd in Hade's dismal plains,*
> *Distant, unknown to rest, where darkness reigns;*
> *Where, destitute of breath, pale spectres dwell,*
> *In endless, dire, inexorable hell.* [52]

It is even possible that Blake adopted the word "spectres," invariably used to describe dwellers in this present world, from this Hymn.

Platonic likewise is the conception of the specters as living in a shadow world, as this earth is an image or reflection or shadow of eternity; for the specters are only shadows of the "Eternal Men." As Plotinus writes: "in the particular acts of human life, it is not the interior soul and the true man, but the exterior shadow of the man alone, which laments and weeps, performing his part on the earth as in a more ample and extended scene, in which many shadows of souls and phantom scenes appear." [53] Urthona's world is a shadow world:

> *Luvah & Vala descended & enter'd the Gates of Dark Urthona,*
> *And walk'd from the hands of Urizen in the shadows of Vala's Garden*
> *Where the impressions of Despair & Hope for ever vegetate.*[54]

There also we find the "shadows" of Los and Enitharmon:

> *. . . their bodies lost, they stood*
> *Trembling & weak, a faint embrace, a fierce desire, as when*
> *Two shadows mingle on a wall; they wail & shadowy tears*
> *Fell down, & shadowy forms of joy mix'd with despair & grief—*
> *Their bodies buried in the ruins of the Universe—*
> *Mingled with the confusion. Who shall call them from the Grave?* [55]

So, too, Enitharmon's dream of human history is a shadow play dreamed in "the night of Dark Urthona":

> *Shadows of men in fleeting bands upon the winds*
> *Divide the heavens of Europe . . .*[56]

And again, "War ceas'd, & all the troops like shadows fled to their abodes." [57]

Here we catch another echo, never for long absent in Blake, of the voice of Milton. The fleeting shadows echo the *Hymn on the Morning of Christ's Nativity:*

> *The flocking shadows pale*
> *Troop to th' infernal Jail,*
>   *Each fetter'd Ghost slips to his several grave* [58]

Nor would it have been possible for Blake to compose a figure of death that did not include traces of Milton's Death, a figure he so splendidly illustrated. Thus Urizen's journey, as described in *Vala*, Night VI, is evidently based upon Satan's journey from hell in *Paradise Lost*, Book II. (In *Jerusalem*

Urizen's wanderings do not any longer bear so clearly the traces of this origin.) Urthona, in the earlier version, is called a shadow and a specter, and Urizen comes upon him in a guise that recalls the worst elements of both Milton and Macpherson without the excellences of either:

> . . . *he went down the Vale of Urthona*
> *Between the enormous iron walls built by the Spectre dark.*
> *Dark grew his globe redd'ning with mists, & full before his path,*
> *Striding across the narrow vale, the Shadow of Urthona*
> *A spectre Vast appear'd, whose feet & legs with iron scaled,*
> *Stamp'd the hard rocks expectant of the unknown wanderer*
> *Whom he had seen wandering his nether world when distant far,*
> *And watch'd his swift approach; collected, dark, the Spectre stood.*[59]

The early Urthona was conceived as Death or Hades, and Blake, according to his usual practice, drew the figure from his favorite mythological masters, in a spirit of enthusiastic, if sometimes indiscriminate, eclecticism.

98 Ark on a medal from Apamia: Bryant's
Mythology, vol. 3 (1776), odd plate

CHAPTER 10

Specters and Watchers

Last of all, in following Blake's development of the Platonic themes of which the Cave of the Nymphs is a symbol, we have the souls themselves, who "descend" through the gate of birth into this world. These Blake calls the specters; they are the people of Hades who take the descending path, entering this world "beneath the bottoms of the graves"—a phrase which suggests in a concrete way the location of Porphyry's and Plato's cave, and also that alchemical nether-world Thel saw beneath her "grave plot." ". . . only through the Gates of Death they can enter to Enitharmon." [1] Porphyry's "urns of workmanship divine" are retained in the "funeral urns of Beulah"; and the "funeral veils" are likewise mortal bodies:

> *In Eden, Females sleep the winter in soft silken veils*
> *Woven by their own hands to hide them in the darksom grave.* [2]

Perhaps Taylor's greatest service to the romantic poets (and others since, from Coleridge, Keats, and Shelley to Yeats and A.E.) was in teaching the use of symbolic discourse as the language of metaphysical thought. Plotinus passes with ease from myth to philosophy and from philosophy to myth, as did Plato himself when he soared into the regions of

> *The immortal mind, that hath forsook*
> *Her mansion in this fleshly nook.* [3]

In fact, in Blake's account of the specters we find Plato and Plotinus as his two chief sources. *On the Descent of the Soul* was one of the five books of the *Enneads* translated by Taylor, and Plotinus' doctrine gave Blake the essence of his own.

Souls "descend," Plotinus taught, by reason of some imperfection; in eternity the souls "are all pure, and, as it is said, winged and perfect, ever performing their proper employment: it remains therefore that debility must belong to souls fallen into body; since such as these are neither pure nor have atoned for the evil contracted by corporeal involution. . . . If then we rightly apprehend the cause of the soul's lapse into body, we shall have found what is the debility of the soul." [4]

Thel desires the pure life of eternity; Lyca's desire for "sleep" is the debility of the impure. The soul, if it is not entirely pure of all passionate attachment, is again and again drawn down into generation.[5] Plotinus taught that the reincarnating souls are those who do not know their way back to eternity. It is not certain beyond question that Blake's specters are repeatedly reincarnated, but the presumption that they are is very strong.[6] The transmigrating souls are drawn into life by passion, desire, and terror. Since generation is a mark of imperfection in those who generate (with the exception only of those who willingly descend in order to redeem this world, as Blake supposes of his poet Milton), we need not be surprised to find only sorrowful and evil specters flocking to the gates of birth; they haunt the Lake of Space-Time (Udan-Adan) and the "forests" of nature (Entuthon Benithon), the borders of nonentity:

> *The Lake of Udan-Adan in the Forests of Entuthon Benython,*
> *Where Souls incessant wail, being piteous Passions & Desires*
> *With neither lineament nor form, but like to wat'ry clouds*
> *The Passions & Desires descend upon the hungry winds,*
> *For such alone Sleepers remain, meer passion and appetite.*[7]

Blake clearly insists that only souls possessed by "passion & appetite" remain "Sleepers," or transmigrate, as Plotinus says, "from sleep to sleep, from dream to dream."

It is possible that in his mythology of Enitharmon's "moony" world Blake was drawing directly upon a seminal work through which an ancient mythological theme found its way into the innumerable later beliefs and superstitions that relate the moon to the cycle of generation. It is likely that this myth is a fragment of the ancient Mysteries of the two Goddesses, which Mysteries were indeed an initiation into the states after death, as death itself was, conversely, regarded as an initiation into the Mysteries. Plutarch's *Of the Face, Appearing within the Orb of the Moon* can be found in the translation "by several Hands" of his *Morals*, which reached its fourth edition in 1704 and must therefore have been fairly well known. The passage in question, appearing at the end of this work (pp. 272–74), sets forth the ancient doctrine of the Kore and her concern with the souls after death.

There are, according to tradition, three bodies. Intellect (or, as the translator gives it, understanding) is a light body given by the sun; the moon clothes this body with a second vehicle, the soul, which in its turn descends to earth to be clothed in a hylic or watery body. At death this process is reversed: the physical body is first shed, and the soul then ascends to the moon, into which the second body is in time dissolved as into its own element, just as the physical body is dissolved into earth. The pure cast off these souls like husks or garments, and the freed spirit of light ascends to the Elysian Fields, its native country.

> And of these Souls . . . the Moon is the Element, because Souls re-
> solve into her, as the Bodies of the Deceased do into Earth. Those
> indeed, who have been virtuous and honest, living a quiet and philo-
> sophical Life, without embroiling themselves in troublesome Affairs,
> are quickly resolv'd, because being left by the Understanding, and no
> longer using corporeal Passions, they incontinently vanish away . . .

It may be this world into which, according to Blake, the specters enter "beneath the bottoms of the graves" and "through the Gates of Death"; Enitharmon is the moon, mother of souls, as earth is the mother of bodies.

The souls of the impure, after wandering for a time—as Blake says, "being piteous Passions & Desires With neither lineament nor form"—return to earthly generation and are given "counterparts," physical bodies. Plutarch continues:

> . . . the Souls of the Ambitious, and such as have been busi'd in Nego-
> tiations of the Amorous, and who have been Addicted to Corporeal
> Pleasures, as also of the Angry and Revengeful, calling to mind the
> things they did in their Lives, as Dreams in their Sleep, walk wan-
> dring about here and there, like that of *Endymion;* because their In-
> constancy, and their being over subject to Passions, transports them
> and draws them out of the Moon to another Generation, not letting
> them rest, but alluring them, and calling them away.

According to Plutarch the sun and moon unite to give new lives to the souls lost and wandering "destitute of all Reason and suffering themselves to be carri'd away by the proud Violence of all Passions"; and, just as Los and

Enitharmon, they are the parents and fabricators of the bodies of the generating specters:

> after a long Tract of Time, the Moon receives those Souls, and recomposes them; and the Sun inspiring again, and sowing Understanding in their vital Faculty, makes them new Souls; and the Earth a third time gives them a Body. For she gives nothing (after Death) of all that she takes to Generation: and the Sun takes nothing, but resembles and receives again the Understanding which he gave. But the Moon gives and receives, joyns and disjoyns, unites and separates, according to divers Faculties and Powers.

As it stands, Blake's mythology of the moon remains obscure; and we are tempted to wonder what more we might have learned from the lost *Book of Moonlight*. I have elsewhere suggested that the teaching of the Bhagavad-Gita may have colored Blake's visions of the Great Battle,[8] whose dead return again and again to generation. The three causes of reincarnation given in the sixteenth book of the Gita are lust, wrath, and avarice. Blake's generating specters are similarly characterized. They are "meer passion & appetite"; they are also "Cruel and ravening with Enmity & Hatred & War."[9] That Blake literally believed that degenerate souls pass into the bodies of animals is no more likely than that Plato did so;[10] but there is an echo of this aspect of the Pythagorean and Hindu teaching of metempsychosis in the suggestion that men may become animal incarnations in a symbolical sense, by persistence in wrath, lust, and appetite:

> . . . *only thro' the Gates of Death they can enter to Enitharmon.*
> *Raging they take the human visage & the human form,*
>
> .　　.　　.
>
> *Troop by troop the beastial droves rend one another, sounding loud*
> *The instruments of sound; & troop by troop, in human forms, they*
> urge
>
> *The dire confusion till the battle faints; those that remain*
> *Return in pangs & horrible convulsions to their beastial state;*
> *For the monsters of the Elements, Lions or Tygers or Wolves,*
> *Sound loud the howling music Inspir'd by Los & Enitharmon,*
> sounding loud; terrific men

They seem to one another, laughing terrible among the banners.
And when, the revolution of their day of battles over,
Relapsing in dire torment they return to forms of woe,
To moping visages returning, inanimate tho' furious,
No more erect, tho' strong, drawn out in length they ravin
For senseless gratification, & their visages thrust forth,
Flatten above & beneath & stretch out into beastial length.[11]

This passage may possibly echo a passage in the Gita: "Those who thus hate Me, who are cruel, the dregs of mankind, I condemn them to a continuous, miserable and godless rebirth. So reborn, they spend life after life, enveloped in delusion. And they never reach Me, O Prince! but degenerate into still lower forms of life." [12]

The specters, then, are evil; but they are also pitiable, "little weeping Spectres," "poor Spectres" possessed by "Spectrous terror"; they are objects of tender compassion to Los and Enitharmon and their fellow laborers:

They contend with the weak Spectres, they fabricate soothing forms.
The Spectre refuses, he seeks cruelty: they create the crested Cock.
Terrified the Spectre screams & rushes in fear into their Net
Of kindness & compassion, & is born a weeping terror.
Or they create the Lion & Tyger in compassionate thunderings:
Howling the Spectres flee: they take refuge in Human lineaments.[13]

It is hard to know what was in Blake's mind in this image of the People of Dreams frightened into generation by the crowing of the cock, image of resurrection — perhaps the folk belief that the dead must return to their graves at cockcrow, whether Hamlet's kingly ghost or the three sons of the Wife of Usher's Well.

> *. . . up and crew the red, red cock*
> *And up and crew the grey.*

Another, and perhaps more likely, source is the cock of Odin, described in a passage quoted by Macpherson in his *Introduction to the History of Great Britain and Ireland:* "A cock, with a crest of gold, crows every morning in the presence of the Gods. He awakes the heroes to battle before Odin the father of armies. They rush, armed and clothed, to the field, and slay one another with mutual wounds. These deaths, however, are only temporary.

The power of Odin revives the slain." [14] If this fine image lies behind Blake's "crested cock," the myth of the specters is again brought into the context of reincarnation.

In 1804 Thomas Taylor's Plato was published; and at some time in that year Blake appears to have read the *Republic*, for he adapts to his mythology of the specters, as this is developed in *Milton*, the fable of Er, who witnessed, on the other side of death, the approach of the reincarnating souls about to enter this world. It would have been strange if a fable so apt to his own myth should have escaped Blake's eclectic net; for Plato's fable contains many familiar elements: the spinning women, the planetary circles of destiny, the river Lethe. The souls who are about to enter upon generation come first to the three spinners—Clotho, Atropos, and Lachesis:

> then a certain prophet first of all ranges them in order, and afterwards taking the lots, and the models of lives, from the knees of Lachesis . . . he says: The speech of the virgin Lachesis, the daughter of Necessity: Souls of a day! The beginning of another period of men of mortal race. The daemon shall not receive you as his lot, but you shall choose the daemon: He who draws the first, let him first make choice of a life, to which he must of necessity adhere. . . . when he had said these things, he threw on all of them the lots, and each took up the one which fell beside him, and he was allowed to take no other. And when he had taken it, he knew what number he had drawn. After this he placed on the ground before them the models of lives, many more than those we see at present. And they were all-various. . . . After therefore all the souls had chosen their lives according as they drew their lots, they all went in order to Lachesis, and she gave to every one the daemon he chose, and sent him along with him to be the guardian of his life, and the accomplisher of what he had chosen. [15]

After Plato's souls have chosen their lives, they proceed on their journey toward generation: "They all of them marched into the plain of Lethe amidst dreadful heat and scorching." Plato's narrator further told that

> when night came on, they encamped beside the river Amelete, whose water no vessel contains. Of this water all of them must necessarily drink a certain measure, and such of them as are not preserved by

prudence drink more than the measure, and he who drinks always forgets every thing. But after they were laid asleep, and it became midnight, there was thunder, and an earthquake, and they were thence on a sudden carried upwards, some one way, and some another, approaching to generation like stars [16]

—the image so beautifully used by Wordsworth, of the rising star that "elsewhere had its setting." "By *Lethe*," Taylor notes, "we must understand the whole of visible nature, or, in other words, the realms of generation, which contain . . . oblivion." This is "the light-hating world" with its "winding streams, under which many are drawn." Blake's specters make the same journey, from the spinners with reel and spindle to the river, and from the river to a period of forgetfulness, "the sleep of Ulro":

> *The Daughters of Enitharmon weave the ovarium & the integument*
> *In soft silk, drawn from their own bowels in lascivious delight,*
> *With songs of sweetest cadence to the turning spindle & reel,*
> *Lulling the weeping spectres of the dead, Clothing their limbs*
> *With gifts & gold of Eden. Astonish'd, stupefied with delight,*
> *The terrors put on their sweet clothing on the banks of Arnon,*
> *Whence they plunge into the river of space for a period, till*
> *The dread Sleep of Ulro is past. . . .*[17]

May we not describe the little sleeper in the water, in the foreground of the Arlington Court tempera, as "stupefied with delight"?

Why Arnon and not Amelete? This again is a translation of a classical myth into a biblical equivalent. For a follower of Swedenborg, who as a boy had worked on Bryant's mythology, transpositions of this kind presented no problem. The specters are born into Enitharmon's merciful "space," Canaan, the time-world. The river that borders Canaan is Arnon. The crossing of Arnon is several times mentioned in the history of the Jewish conquest of Canaan, particularly in Deuteronomy 2:24, where Moses orders the tribes to cross the river into their promised land: "Raise ye up, take your journey, and pass over the river Arnon: behold, I have given into thine hand Sihon the Amorite, King of Heshbon, and his land: begin to possess it." We need only translate:

> *The terrors put on their sweet clothing on the banks of Arnon,*
> *Whence they plunge into the river of space for a period . . .*

into the Platonic equivalent symbols to see that Blake is merely retelling
Plato's myth of Er. Perhaps wrongly, he was at this time engaged in
covering his tracks and disowning his immense debt to Greek thought, as
the manifesto in the preface to *Milton* makes clear.

As a further complication, Arnon is sometimes called Storge; the
"Five Females"

> *. . . lure the Sleepers of Beulah down*
> *The River Storge (which is Arnon) into the Dead Sea.*[18]

The identity of Arnon with Storge is explicable once we have seen that
Arnon is Amelete; for we know that the souls are lured down into generation
through sexual desire. "Divine natures become through pleasure bound and
drawn down into generation," says Porphyry.[19] He also describes the souls
that desire to enter generation as "depraved," and in a note Taylor writes of
the "greedy" and "insatiable" nature of the desires of those who "fly to
moisture." Sexual desire draws the souls to the banks of the river, or as Blake
says, "Love of Parent, Storgous Appetite, Craving,"[20] a meaning in itself
wholly incompatible with the crossing of the Arnon by the Israelites, but
entirely consistent with the Platonic view of the depravity of generating
souls. That the Arnon flows into the "Dead Sea" would seem to Blake a
beautiful example of Divine Analogy. To the exhausted reader it may
suggest rather the worst aspects of the influence of Swedenborg, whose
presence can also be detected in Blake's use of the uncouth word "Storge" in
this odd sense. "Little children are . . . the subjects of an influx from the
inmost heaven . . . which influx pervades their interiour, and operates in
them . . . thereby exciting in their parents that natural affection, which we
call by the name of Storge."[21]

Plotinus distinguishes between two parts of the soul, that which "descends"
and that which "abides in the intelligible world," and which may perhaps
be identified with Plato's daemon, as well as with more recent attempts to
define the same reality in other terms, such as Jung's distinction between a higher and a lower self—the collective unconscious and the
ego. The distinction, at all events, is a matter of empirical fact, as Blake
would have insisted no less strongly than did Jung. Both would have
understood Plotinus' definition: "the whole of our soul also does not
enter into body, but something belonging to it always abides in the intel-

ligible, and something different from this in the sensible world; and that which abides in the sensible world, if it conquers, or rather if it is vanquished and disturbed, does not permit us to perceive that which the supreme part of the soul contemplates." [22] This idea Blake expressed in figurative form in the story of Lyca (the generating soul) and her mother (intellect), who is drawn down into Hades after her "daughter"; but in his account of the specters this theme is given fuller and clearer expression. There is a daemon, or higher self, in every man, which remains, as Blake would say, "in eternity." A passage in *Jerusalem* describes these Eternal Men attempting to be heard by their specters and to control and guide them, as Plato says of the daemons that they are the "guardians" of mortal life. While the "Spectres of the Dead cry out from the deeps beneath," where they are imprisoned in the "dreams of Ulro," the "immortal man that cannot die" seeks, like Demeter for Persephone, to reach the soul in the Hades of mortal existence:

> *Their Human majestic Forms sit up upon their Couches*
> *Of death; they curb their Spectres as with iron curbs:*
> *They enquire after Jerusalem in the regions of the dead*
> *With the voices of dead men, low, scarcely articulate,*
> *And with tears cold on their cheeks they weary repose.* [23]

This, in Blakean terms, well describes the relation of the unconscious, or higher self, to waking life and consciousness. The passage continues:

> *O when shall the morning of the grave appear, and when*
> *Shall our salvation come? we sleep upon our watch,*
> *We cannot awake, and our Spectres rage in the forests.*
> *O God of Albion, where art thou? pity the watchers!*
>
> *Thus mourn they . . .* [24]

The mourning "watchers" who remain in eternity are, as it were, the reluctant spectators of the shadowy drama of their mortal lives:

> *For every one open'd within into Eternity at will,*
> *But they refus'd, because their outward forms were in the Abyss.* [25]

Blake makes superb use of this concept of the higher and lower consciousness in *Milton*, whose central theme is poetic inspiration. The poet, "the inspired man," also called "the awakener," the type of generated soul who is not entirely forgetful of eternity, is described in the person of Milton, who for Blake was the supreme poet of imaginative inspiration.

> . . . his Mortal part
> Sat frozen in the rock of Horeb, . . .
> . . . but within that portion
> His real Human walk'd above in power and majesty,
> Tho' darken'd, and the Seven Angels of the Presence attended him.[26]

And at greater length:

> As when a man dreams he reflects not that his body sleeps,
> Else he would wake, so seem'd he entering his Shadow: but
> With him the Spirits of the Seven Angels of the Presence
> Entering, they gave him still perceptions of his Sleeping Body
> Which now arose and walk'd with them in Eden, as an Eighth
> Image Divine tho' darken'd and tho' walking as one walks
> In sleep, and the Seven comforted and supported him.[27]

(The sleeping "body" is the spiritual form; this idea is not only Platonic in origin, for Blake was also familiar with Swedenborg's continual insistence that the true body of man is spiritual, and the physical form what Blake himself calls it, only a garment.)

> Like as a Polypus that vegetates beneath the deep,
> They saw his Shadow vegetated underneath the Couch
> Of death: for when he enter'd into his Shadow, Himself,
> His real and immortal Self, was, as appear'd to those
> Who dwell in immortality, as One sleeping on a couch
> Of gold, and those in immortality gave forth their Emanations
> Like Females of sweet beauty to guard round him & to feed
> His lips with food of Eden in his cold and dim repose:
> But to himself he seem'd a wanderer lost in dreary night.[28]

The eternal world is not, Blake seems to say, unconscious of us as we are of it. Blake did indeed depict, in the drowsy god in the sun-chariot and in the god of Job at the onset of Satan's temptations, the situation in which the eternal world becomes, as modern psychologists say, "unconscious"; but in an absolute sense, the world of eternity is consciousness itself, and mortal consciousness merely relative. The relation between the two worlds Blake seeks to convey in the passage quoted: the poet's consciousness is nourished by "eternals" even while he is himself unaware of their presence and, in his human personality, like the rest of mankind, a Lost Traveller. The difference between the inspired man and others is merely one of degree: his "perceptions of the Sleeping Body" are stronger and clearer than in other men. The poet is one who, because he remembers, can remind; "seeing" in vision the eternal forms, he is able to embody and hold before the "sleepers" images which have in their turn the power to stir and awaken recollection. To Blake the whole meaning and purpose of the arts is this Platonic *anamnesis*.[29] The "worlds" are levels of consciousness, and the function of poetry the transformation of consciousness. The poetic gift is a double one, the power to perceive and the power to embody; but the latter, though it may be called a technical gift, cannot exist apart from the former.

> I do not condemn Pope or Dryden because they did not understand Imagination, but because they did not understand Verse. . . . That is not either Colouring, Graving or Verse which is Unappropriate to the Subject.[30]

> I was once looking over the Prints from Rafael & Michael Angelo in the Library of the Royal Academy. Moser came to me & said: "You should not Study these old Hard, Stiff & Dry, Unfinish'd Works of Art—Stay a little & I will shew you what you should Study." He then went & took down Le Brun's & Rubens's Galleries. How I did secretly Rage! I also spoke my Mind . . . I said to Moser, "These things that you call Finish'd are not Even Begun: how can they then be Finish'd? The Man who does not know The Beginning can never know the End of Art."[31]

All works not copied from the paradigm Blake called "false art," of the kind he told Moser was "not even begun." Such works, copied not from the originals in eternity but from natural appearances, he called "a pretence of art to destroy art"; these have no power to awaken the soul, but rather deepen its sleep. Naturalistic art should be known as "distinct and inferior," because the operation upon the soul of intelligible forms is different not in degree but in kind.

A traditional work of art has a recognized status; it is an embodiment of intelligible form, of the "Divine Reason." The mark of such art is nobility and beauty. The poet, in such works, speaks not to the rational understanding but to our innate higher knowledge: "Allegory address'd to the Intellectual powers, while it is altogether hidden from the Corporeal Understanding, is My Definition of the Most Sublime Poetry; it is also somewhat in the same manner defin'd by Plato." [32]

Plato describes anamnesis in many ways and in many contexts. In the *Meno* he writes:

> The soul then being immortal, having been often born, having beheld the things which are here, the things which are in Hades, and all things, there is nothing of which she has not gained the knowledge. No wonder, therefore, that she is able to recollect, with regard to virtue as well as to other things, what formerly she knew. For all things in nature being linked together in relationship, and the soul having heretofore known all things, nothing hinders but that any man, who has recalled to mind, or, according to the common phrase, who has learnt, one thing only, should of himself recover all his ancient knowledge, and find out again all the rest of things. . . . For inquiry and learning is reminiscence all. [33]

Blake uses a similar language: "I look back into the regions of Reminiscence & behold our ancient days before this Earth appear'd in its vegetated mortality to my mortal vegetated Eyes." And: "I am more famed in Heaven for my works than I could well concieve. In my Brain are studies & Chambers fill'd with books & pictures of old, which I wrote & painted in ages of Eternity before my mortal life; & those works are the delight & Study of Archangels." [34]

Following his practice of Christianizing his mythology, Blake in *Milton* writes of the Daughters of Beulah, who play a part in bringing to the [II, 161] specters remembrance of real being, and who are the inspirers of the poet. They are the Daughters of Inspiration, who stand between the temporal and the eternal worlds or states:

> *And between every two Moments stands a Daughter of Beulah*
> *To feed the Sleepers on their Couches with maternal care.* [35]

These are the "females of sweet beauty" who feed the poet's lips with "food of Eden." It is appropriate that in a poem whose central figure is Milton, Blake should have derived the theme of these inspirers from Milton himself. Into the margin of his Reynolds' *Discourses* Blake copied a passage of Milton which, we must presume, held great significance for him: "A work of Genius is a Work 'Not to be obtain'd by the Invocation of Memory & her Syren Daughters, but by Devout prayer to that Eternal Spirit, who can enrich with all utterance & knowledge & sends out his Seraphim with the hallowed fire of his Altar to touch & purify the lips of whom he pleases.' " [36]

Blake's Daughters of Beulah, who touch the lips of the poet Milton in his mortal dream, are akin to these seraphim who come as messengers from the Eternal Spirit; and although he elsewhere blames the Greeks because their Muses are the "Daughters of Memory" (time memory, that is), they are recognizably also Plato's Muses, who bring "food," "honey and milk out of the springs and fountains" from their "gardens and flowery vales . . . from fountains flowing there with honey, gathering the sweetness of their songs, they bring it to us, like the bees, and . . . withal flying." Their food is the same honey-dew and milk of paradise Coleridge's poet had drunk. The Muses are the mediators between the eternal world and the mortal, the higher and the lower consciousness; they may be "invoked," but over them the mind of the ratio has no control, for they stand in a higher principle, in the intelligible world itself.

Blake's strange association of Noah and his sons with the arts and inspiration is likewise to be understood as a translation of a Platonic into a biblical symbol. We cannot but deplore this practice, which Blake no doubt acquired from Swedenborg and his interminable and arid "correspondences"; it is regrettable because Blake's so to say transliterations obscure his tracks and, with the clues which lead us to the sources of his thought, his meaning also; the symbols, in losing their context, lose their meaning. However, the logic is beyond question: Noah and his sons were the only men who knew and remembered the world before the Flood. Since the Flood is the deluge of matter, which swept away a former mode of consciousness, the symbol is the equivalent not only of Plato's own myth of the drowning of Atlantis but also of the amnesia of the souls who drink the waters of Lethe as they proceed toward generation. Noah and his sons are those who remember, and are therefore likened to poets, painters, and musicians, who are also rememberers.[37]

Blake's first acquaintance with the Platonic theory of art must have come through one of Thomas Taylor's earliest publications, Plotinus' *Concerning the Beautiful.* According to Plotinus, sensible things are beautiful through their participation in form; and the forms we recognize reflected in matter (as Vala the soul saw herself reflected in the watery glass) are innate in the soul, or intellect. We recognize beauty by a process of comparison, as it were, of objects with these innate forms which are the basis of all our judgments, "as a rule is used to compare straightness." The contrary of the beautiful is the formless; beauty is an order and harmony imposed on chaos and the "Non-Entity" of matter, bringing its multiplicity into unity. Thus Blake speaks of the specters as "deformed" and "repugnant to the forms of life," [38] and describes, following Plotinus, the delight of the specters in the recognition of "forms sublime," which remind them of the lineaments of the soul. Like Plotinus he regarded evil as a deformity and accretion, clay or mire [39] that reveals, when washed away, the true lineaments of the soul, which are always beautiful. Blake's Milton, therefore, through poetic anamnesis, brings into sensible embodiment forms whose function is to purify the soul through spiritual self-knowledge. What is to be removed is "the Spectre,"

> . . . a false Body, an Incrustation over my Immortal
> Spirit, a Selfhood which must be put off & annihilated alway.
> To cleanse the Face of my Spirit by Self-examination,
> To bathe in the Waters of Life, to wash off the Not Human.[40]

Thus the "not human" is all in man which is not sublime and beautiful or of the soul. It is a sad reflection that for many modern writers the terms seem to be reversed.

We have seen in a previous chapter how early Blake was using this concept of the radical beauty and innocence of the souls. Intellectual beauty, for Blake as for Plotinus (and as for all poets and artists in the Platonic tradition), is the mark and signature of intelligible form: "The Beauty proper for sublime art is lineaments, or forms and features that are capable of being the receptacles of intellect." [41] Blake's insistence on the clear and determinate outline and bounding form never changed; and it is no mere preference or taste that determined for him this way of seeing. He adopted in its entirety the Platonic view of form, inseparable from other aspects of that philosophy, expressed to perfection in the work of the Florentines, whom of all Italian schools Blake preferred, and who were themselves a flowering of the same view of art, under the influence of Ficino's edition of the works of Plato and his writings on Platonism.

Plotinus takes as an example of form a building that we call beautiful because form infuses into the heap of stones from which it is made an indivisible unity; the form resides not in the bulk of matter but in the artist's idea. Blake uses a similar argument to illustrate Plotinus' very statement, the seeming paradox that form belongs to soul and intellect and not to material bodies:

> The connoisseurs and artists who have made objections to Mr B.'s mode of representing spirits with real bodies, would do well to consider that the Venus, the Minerva, the Jupiter, the Apollo, which they admire in Greek statues are all of them representations of spiritual existences, of Gods immortal, to the mortal perishing organ of sight; and yet they are embodied and organized in solid marble.[42]

It is not by coincidence that he illustrated this argument by a Greek example. Blake perceived that naturalism leads not to clearer form but to loss of form; and loss of form is loss of beauty. Blake's "blotting and blurring demons," which beset the artist who copies from nature, are a manifestation, in art, of Plotinus' doctrine of matter as formless nonentity. "Men think they can Copy Nature as Correctly as I copy Imagination; this they will find Impossible, & all the Copiers or Pretended Copiers of Nature, from Rembrandt to Reynolds, Prove that Nature becomes to its Victim nothing but Blots & Blurs. Why are Copiers of Nature Incorrect, while Copiers of Imagination are Correct? this is manifest to all." [43]

Plato in the *Timaeus* argues that the world itself is generated according to a paradigm:

> In the first place, therefore, as it appears to me, it is necessary to define what that is which is always *real being*, but is without generation; and what that is *which is generated indeed*, or *consists in a state of becoming to be*, but which never *really is* [i.e. the world] . . . For it is every way impossible that any thing should be generated without a cause. When, therefore, an artificer, in the fabrication of any work, looks to that which always subsists according to *same*, and, employing a paradigm of this kind, expresses the idea and power in his work, it is then necessary that the whole of his production should be beautiful. But when he beholds that which is in generation, and uses a generated paradigm, it is alike necessary that his work should be far from beautiful.[44]

The theme of the artist and the paradigm Blake first began to develop in a late addition to *The Four Zoas:* here Los becomes the artist, because he sees that the specters of the dead can be given life only by participation in intelligible form, the life of the soul:

> . . . *Stern desire*
> *I feel to fabricate embodied semblances in which the dead*
> *May live before us in our palaces & in our gardens of labour.*[45]

These semblances will enable the specters to "become what they behold," and to recover, little by little, their lost immortal lineaments. These lineaments are the form of the *Logos*, or as Blake says,

> . . . *the Divine-*
> *Humanity who is the Only General and Universal Form,*
> *To which all Lineaments tend & seek with love & sympathy.*[46]

His consort and vehicle Enitharmon expands the thought of Los: to generate mortal men is not enough; those who merely pass through this world, are born and die, never come any nearer to the return to their native place and state; they blindly transmigrate "from sleep to sleep, and from dream to dream." [47] She says:

> . . . *I can sigh forth on the winds of Golgonooza piteous forms*
> *That vanish again into my bosom; but if thou, my Los,*
> *Wilt in sweet moderated fury fabricate forms sublime*
> *Such as the piteous spectres may assimilate themselves into,*
> *They shall be ransoms for our Souls that we may live.*[48]

The specters are "dead" through the loss of the vision of eternity; but Urthona calls Los "the Spectre of the living" because the poetic imagination or intuitive faculty alone retains, in Albion's fallen state, conscious communication with the world of the soul and its living forms. Therefore, at the Last Judgment, Los is praised "Because he kept the Divine Vision in time of trouble." [49]

For this reason he is able to fabricate "forms sublime," and through his agent the poet, "the awakener," to work for the redemption of Albion from his deadly sleep. Blake is of course thinking specifically of England, where it is indeed the poets who have kept alive the knowledge of the soul. This is the inspiring idea and the theme of *Milton*.

Plato and Plotinus speak of the soul's innate forms as residing in the intelligible world; for Blake the Logos is "Jesus the Imagination," and every creation of inspired art is a depiction of some aspect of this universal Divine

Humanity. Even in the earliest accounts, while Blake was still close to his Platonic originals, these forms are called "divinely human"; and in *Jerusalem* the appearance of Jesus among the Furnaces of Los, first envisaged in *The Four Zoas*, is even more clearly expressed. Los's labors are first encountered in *The Four Zoas* in terms of painting rather than poetry; Blake the craftsman here speaks:

> . . . *Los, his hands divine inspir'd, began* [50]
> *To modulate his fires; studious the loud roaring flames*
> *He vanquish'd with the strength of Art, bending their iron points*
> *And drawing them forth delighted upon the winds of Golgonooza*
>
> . . .
>
> *And first he drew a line upon the walls of shining heaven,*
> *And Enitharmon tinctur'd it with beams of blushing love.* [51]
> *It remain'd permanent, a lovely form, inspir'd, divinely human.*
> *Dividing into just proportions, Los unwearied labour'd*
> *The immortal lines upon the heavens, till with sighs of love,*
> *Sweet Enitharmon mild, Entranc'd breath'd forth upon the wind*
> *The spectrous dead. Weeping, the Spectres view'd the immortal works*
> *Of Los, Assimilating to those forms . . .* [52]

Art, according to this philosophy, is not a mirror held up to nature (or that worse monstrosity, Flaubert's "mirror dawdling down a lane," a definition Yeats held to be responsible for the corruption of poetry and the judgment of poetry so prevalent at this time). Human nature, on the contrary, should follow art and discover itself through art, which mediates between the two worlds or states of consciousness. Only so can spectral man rise above the level of animality and barbarism to which, left to "nature" and naturalistic art, he tends to revert, since these can only show him what he already is and not what he might become; the "mirror" has no transforming power. Poetry, according to Blake's view (which is that of tradition), is not a mere passive reflection but an agent in the evolution of consciousness.

The poet works from the paradigm. Palmer long afterward remembered that Blake had been fond of quoting a passage in which Shakespeare defines the poet's task:

> *The Poets eye in a fine frenzy rolling*
> *Doth glance from heaven to earth, from earth to heaven,*
> *And as imagination bodies forth*

> *The forms of things unknowne, the poets pen*
> *Turnes them to shapes, and gives to aire nothing*
> *A locall habitation, and a name . . .*
> *Such tricks hath strong imagination.*[53]

He used to add that Shakespeare was wrong to speak of "airy nothing," because "the things imagination saw were as much realities as were gross tangible facts." [54]

Los (who is "strong imagination" in person) and his "Sons" perform the task of embodying vision:

> *Some Sons of Los surround the Passions with porches of iron & silver,*
>
>   .   .   .
>
> *Giving to airy nothing a name and a habitation*
> *Delightful, with bounds to the Infinite putting off the Indefinite*
> *Into most holy forms of Thought; such is the power of inspiration*
> *They labour incessant with many tears & afflictions,*
> *Creating the beautiful House for the piteous sufferer.*
>
> *Other Cabinets richly fabricate of gold & ivory*
> *For Doubts & fears unform'd & wretched & melancholy.*[55]

Shakespeare's account of the imagination is appropriately spoken by the "Duke of Athens." But Blake gives the process a yet more Platonic cast; Antamon (the name has a Greek flavor) is the Son of Los who is conceived as Plato's artificer:

> *The little weeping Spectre stands on the threshold of Death*
> *   Eternal. . . .*

and

> *Antamon takes them into his beautiful flexible hands:*
> *As the Sower takes the seed or as the Artist his clay*
> *Or fine wax, to mould artful a model for golden ornaments.*
> *The soft hands of Antamon draw the indelible line,*
> *Form immortal with golden pen, such as the Spectre admiring*
> *Puts on the sweet form: then smiles Antamon bright thro' his*
> *   windows.*[56]

The "golden pen" is surely Shakespeare's "poets pen," which writes of the "golden" age. If this is so, "Form immortal" is a creation of poetry, and the specters learn their humanity by identification with the model created by the poet, an image of the paradigm of the Divine Humanity.

Antamon's "indelible line"—the same that Los drew "on the walls of shining heaven"—was for Blake the primary act of creation. The "bounding line with its infinite inflexions and movements" is the signature of intelligible form, drawn upon the void, the non-ens of the natural world. "Leave out this line, and you leave out life itself." Blake saw in Florentine painting,[57] typically linear, the true imaginative tradition, and in Venetian and Flemish painting a spectral naturalism, the work of "blotting and blurring demons." Line, or melody, is the imaginative definition of form. This is the pure doctrine of Plato and Plotinus. Blake's blotting and blurring demons have, as we see, completed the work begun by the Venetian school and continued by the French Impressionists. Loss of form is the mark of contemporary social realism, as it is of the apparently different school of "abstract impressionism." In both alike the intelligible image has faded, the one into photographic naturalism, the other into nonentity; and as Blake foretold, "all is chaos again, and the line of the almighty must be drawn out upon it before man or beast can exist."[58] It is this line of the Almighty that the Ancient of Days traces upon the abyss with his golden compasses; for "Nature has no [II, 144] Outline, but Imagination has. Nature has no Tune, but Imagination has. Nature has no Supernatural & dissolves: Imagination is Eternity."[59]

It might be said that Blake, himself a craftsman and a friend of craftsmen, had no need to go beyond his own workbench for the image of the artificer making his wax model; yet it is Plato's very image; and a passage of Plotinus is even closer to Blake's description of Antamon:

That nature then is not endued with hands and feet, not any instrument either adventitious or allied to herself, but that matter is necessary, in which she operates, and which she reduces into form, is almost obvious to every one; nor is it to be thought that nature produces her work, as it were, by impelling and pressing; for what impulsion or pressure could effect various and omniform colours and figures? since those who form images out of wax, and by beholding a pattern are supposed to operate similar to nature, could not produce colours, unless they procured these external to their work. It is therefore worth while to consider whether, as among operators of such arts, it is necessary something should remain within the soul, according to whose permanency they fabricate with their hands; in like manner there should be something of this kind in nature, which is a certain permanent power, fabricating without the ministry of hands. . . .[60]

Have we here the original of Antamon's modeling? "But does nature operate from contemplation?" Plotinus asks. "From contemplation entirely. But what if after a certain manner she contemplates herself? . . . such as she is, such she fabricates." [61] In the same way, man's works are from the contemplation of innate ideas, the order of the intelligible world reflected in the soul.

99 The god Sarapis, lord of the underworld: medal from Bryant's *Mythology*, vol. 2 (1774), plate XII

Part III

The Zoas of Physical Life

In the chapters that follow we shall consider the mythology of Enion and Tharmas, with certain other poems related to their story. The names are occasionally mentioned in the later works, but the theme was an early one. These figures are the Zoas of sensory life, and their mythology involves a study of a number of related myths—Hermetic, alchemical, and classical—concerned with the descent of the primal light, the principle of intellect, into matter; its "distribution" in matter; and the alchemical *deus absconditus*.

CHAPTER *11*

A Hermetic Myth

Blake's imaginative preoccupation with origins did not end with the descent of the soul. There are myths, both Neoplatonic and alchemical, which belong to what Sallust terms the theological order, and tell of the creation of the world of which man is but a part, and of a fall anterior to the fall of man.

Margoliouth believes that much of *Vala* was written before 1797, when Blake engraved the date upon his title page, and that the opening passages of "Night the First" of *The Four Zoas* (which precede the original beginning of the *Vala* manuscript) have been retained from a still earlier poem or fragment, which he calls Text F.[1] Here we find an obscure and complicated piece of mythology, which tells of three figures: Enion, Tharmas, and the Spectre of Tharmas—the first of Blake's specters, a failure soon abandoned. If this fragment was written earlier than the *Vala* text, it must belong to the early 1790s, the peak of Blake's enthusiasm for the Neoplatonists and the Hermetic writers.

Common to the alchemical and Neoplatonic systems is a body of mythological and metaphysical writing on the descent of intellect, or light—which is, of course, anterior to the descent of the soul—into matter, or darkness. This event takes place, as St. John says, "in the beginning," where "the Light shineth in darkness and the darkness comprehended it not." As this doctrine is understood by the alchemists, matter is activated by a spiritual principle that has "descended" and is captured like a prisoner; and the release of this imprisoned spirit, the *deus absconditus*, is the task of the Great Work. The two principles are symbolized as a male (spirit) and a female (matter).

We shall presently consider other likely sources of Blake's knowledge of this body of thought; but one book he certainly knew, and at an early stage, for it is mentioned in *The Song of Los*.[2] This is the Hermetica, translated in the seventeenth century by John Everard as *The Divine Pymander of Hermes Trismegistus*. The Hermetica summarizes the Neoplatonic (and possibly Egyptian) philosophy of the "origins," and is the source of all subsequent alchemical writings on the descent of light into matter. It is a work that looks both to the past and to the future; and it is among the more important sources of Berkeley's philosophic answers to Newton and Locke. It is evidently Blake's source for the myth of Enion, Tharmas, and the Spectre; and we shall find continual evidence of Blake's familiarity with the *Pymander*.

The myth in question occurs in Book II. First of all things there are two original principles—the light and the "moist nature." The moist nature first appears like a cloud obscuring the light; it then becomes "unspeakably troubled," and from its union with the light issues smoke, as from a fire: "and from [thence] proceedeth a voice unutterable, and very mournful, but inarticulate, inasmuch as it seemed to have come from the light."[3]

The Hermetic view is essentially that of the Platonists: matter is the principle of evil, obscuring "fallen, fallen light." But the alchemists, preoccupied as they were with matter and its mysteries, seem to have moved, little by little, to a more subtle (though not wholly different) view of the dark feminine principle.

The passage from the *Pymander* is also paraphrased by Vaughan in his *Aula Lucis*, a book that has so many affinities with Blake it seems likely he knew it:

> *Trismegistus*, in his *Vision* of the *Creation*, did first see a pleasing, gladsome *Light*, but *interminated*. Afterwards appeared a horrible sad *Darkenesse*, and this moved *downe-wards*, descending from the *Eye* of the *Light*, as if a *Cloud* should come *from* the *Sunne*. This *darkenesse* (saith he) was condens'd into a *certaine water*, but not without a mournfull inexpressible *Voyce* or *Sound*, as the *Vapours* of the *Elements* are resolved by *Thunder*. After this (saith that great *Philosopher*) the *holy word* came *out* of the *Light*, and did *get upon* the *water*, and out of the *water* he made *all Things*.[4]

Paracelsus, from this same Hermetic dark moist cloud, has built up his grand figure of the Great Mystery, the first matter out of which all things proceed. We have already seen how Blake in his matron Clay reflects the Paracelsian vision of the marriage of light and darkness, heaven and earth;

and indeed, the influence of Paracelsus upon Blake's philosophy of nature was continuous. Without losing sight of her dark nature, Paracelsus sees the greatness of her power:

> this common matter of all things is the *Great Mysterie*, which no certaine essence and prefigured or formed Idaea could comprehend, nor could it comply with any property, it being altogether voyd of colour and elementary nature. The scope of this *Great Mysterie* is as large as the Firmament. And this *Great Mysterie was the mother of all the Elements, and the Grandmother of all the Stars, trees and carnall creatures.* As children are born of a mother, so all created things whether sensible or insensible, all things whatsoever, were uniformly brought out of the *Great Mysterie*. So that the *Great Mysterie* is the onely mother of all perishing things.[5]

Paracelsus' fine image of Nature as "smoke" comes by way of the Hermetic prototype: "For when things were first compacted that *great mysterie* was just like smoke, which spreadeth very wide." [6] Blake's Vala, too, is called "Mystery" and "Nature, mother of all." It is also said of her that "a cloud she grew and grew"; and she is called the "Demoness of smoke," [7] an image that recurs in several passages. Jerusalem dissolves,

> *. . . a pillar of cloud with Vala upon the mountains*
> *Howling in pain . . .*
>
>   .   .   .
>
> *A pillar of smoke writhing afar into Non-Entity, redounding*
> *Till the cloud reaches afar outstretch'd among the Starry Wheels.*[8]

The resemblances both to Paracelsus and to the Hermetic original are obvious.

Before Vala, Blake had created "the nameless shadowy female," who must surely have been called "nameless" because she is Paracelsus' Great Mystery, "which no certain essence and prefigured and formed idea could comprehend." Certain it is that she originates in the alchemical myths and definitions relating to the dark feminine mystery; she is cloud and darkness and moisture and sound:

> *For I am faint with travel,*
> *Like the dark cloud disburden'd in the day of dismal thunder.*
>
>   .   .   .

I wrap my turban of thick clouds around my lab'ring head,
And fold the sheety waters as a mantle round my limbs [9]

She goes on to speak of herself as "mother of the stars," and brings forth "a
progeny of fires." This attribute also she seems to derive from Paracelsus
and perhaps from Vaughan, for the idea is common.[10]

The "nameless shadowy female" disappears after *Europe* and *America*, and in her stead we find two figures who seem to stem from her, but who
reflect different aspects of her nature. Vala becomes the goddess Nature,
while Enion is given the "invisible" attributes of the "first matter." Enion is
also called "a voice eternal wailing in the elements"—the voice "unutterable
and very mournful and inarticulate" that speaks from the cloud.

There is a more elaborate alchemical myth which Blake seems to have
known—again, probably from Vaughan. *The Crystal Cabinet*, an unpublished poem in the Pickering Manuscript, contains recondite alchemical
symbolism which Blake may have found in Vaughan's *Aula Lucis*. There is
no means of knowing when this poem was written. The existing fair copy
was made in about 1803, and it is certainly later than the myth of Enion and
Tharmas. But the "shining tent" of *Thel* (1789) suggests that the symbolism may have been known to Blake earlier. The crystal cabinet, the "shining
tent," and possibly the "crystal house" of Enitharmon [11] are the alchemical
"house of light"—matter—under its usual symbol of water:

> *Matter* . . . is the *House of Light*, here hee (i.e. the light) *dwels*
> and *builds* for himself, and to speake *Truth*, hee takes up his
> *lodging* in *sight* of all the *World*. When he first *enters* it, it is a
> glorious *transparent Roome*, a *Chrystall Castle*, and hee lives like a
> *Familiar* in *Diamonds*. Hee hath then the *Libertie* to look out at the
> *Windows*, his *love* is all in his *sight*, I meane that *liquid Venus*,
> which *lures* him *in*, but this continues not very long. Hee is busie as
> all *Lovers* are, labours for a more close *Union*, insinuates and
> conveyes *himself* into the very substance of his *Love*, so that his
> *Heat* and *action* stirre up her *moyst Essences*, by whose *meanes*
> he becomes an *absolute Prisoner*. For at last the *Earth* growes
> *over him* out of the *water*, so that he is quite shut up in darknesse.[12]

Blake's poem tells of the capturing of a spirit by a "Maiden":

> *The Maiden caught me in the Wild,*
> *Where I was dancing merrily;*

> *She put me into her Cabinet*
> *And Lock'd me up with a golden Key.*

(Is the merry dancer a sunbeam?) "Cabinet" is a word that Vaughan constantly uses in just this sense: "to say that the soul formed the body because she is in the body is to say that the jewel made the cabinet because she is in the cabinet"—and Vaughan in his turn is remembering Paracelsus' "coffers in which the senses are generated."

Is the poem a paraphrase of Vaughan's allegory? Many of the images and phrases suggest it: "Now as soone as the *Passive* spirit attracts the *Anima* . . . then the *aethereall water* in a moment attracts the *Passive spirit*, for this is the first visible Receptacle wherein the *superiour Natures* are *Concentrated*. The Soule being thus confined and imprisoned by lawfull *Magick* in this *Liquid Chrystall*, the Light which is in her streams thorough the Water, and then it is *Lux manifeste visibilis ad oculum*." [13]

Vaughan's "lawfull magick" seems to describe the power of Blake's maiden. But the most striking feature of Blake's poem is the threefold nature of the maiden. The cabinet is of gold, pearl, and crystal; and the maiden of the cabinet is threefold. The outer "cabinet" or body opens into

> *Another Maiden like herself,*
> *Translucent, lovely, shining clear,*
> *Threefold each in the other clos'd—*
> *O, what a pleasant trembling fear!*
>
> *O, what a smile! a threefold Smile*
> *Fill'd me, that like a flame I burn'd;*
> *I bent to Kiss the lovely Maid,*
> *And found a Threefold Kiss return'd.*
>
> *I strove to sieze the inmost Form*
> *With ardor fierce & hands of flame*

This triplicity is an alchemical theme. Vaughan elaborates on the feminine principle, who "below" corresponds to the masculine deity "above," and who is likewise a trinity. He describes the natural triplicity, or "three mothers": "For there are Three above and three beneath, Three—as St. John saith—in Heaven and three on earth. The inferior bear witness of the Superior and are their only proper receptacles. They are signatures and created books wherein we may read the Mysteries of the Supernatural Trinity." [14] Thus

the "superior is masculine and eternal, the inferior is feminine and mortal."
This feminine trinity Vaughan equates with the three "mothers" of cabalism: "*Emes*, or *Aleph*, *Mem* and *Shin*, are Air, Water and Fire . . . The
Heavens were made of the Fire, the Earth was made of the Water . . . and
the Ayre proceeded from a middle spirit." [15] Elsewhere [16] he calls these the
elementary earth (water), the celestial earth (air), and the spiritual earth
(fire). Blake's attempt to grasp the threefold maiden reflects a process
commonly described by the alchemists, whose teaching is that the descent
into generation takes place in three stages. The fiery soul must initiate the
process by wrapping itself in the aerial vestment, and clothed in this airy
body, descend into the watery envelope of matter. This process Vaughan
describes in his *Anima Magica Abscondita*.[17] A similar triplicity is described
by Plutarch (see above, p. 251).

Such, then, is the background of Blake's mysterious little poem,
whose simplicity is, as so often, deceptive. The maiden is Vaughan's "liquid
Venus," and the soul of light, who has "liberty to look out of the windows,"
becomes, in Blake, the lover who tells that

> . . . *within it opens into a World*
> *And a little lovely Moony Night.*
>
> *Another England there I saw,*
> *Another London with its Tower*

But in Blake's poem, as in Vaughan's allegory, the "ardor fierce" of the lover
leads not to the end he had hoped for but to an incarceration. In Vaughan the
earth "grows over" the light; in Blake's poem the spirit becomes "a Weeping
Babe":

> *I strove to sieze the inmost Form*
> *With ardor fierce & hands of flame,*
> *But burst the Crystal Cabinet,*
> *And like a Weeping Babe became—*
>
> *A weeping Babe upon the wild,*
> *And Weeping Woman pale reclin'd,*
> *And in the outward air again*
> *I fill'd with woes the passing Wind.*

The spirit, lured to become the lover of the "liquid Venus" in her crystal
house of matter, finds himself snared, taken, and generated.

In *Jerusalem* this threefold ensnarer reappears as Rahab, the sexual and generative aspect of Vala. Just as in the Hermetic myth, she lures spirits into generation through her irresistible powers of downward attraction:

> *. . . a Three-fold Wonder, feminine, most beautiful, Three-fold*
> *Each within other. On her white marble & even Neck, her Heart,*
> *Inorb'd and bonified, with locks of shadowing modesty, shining*
> *Over her beautiful Female features soft flourishing in beauty,*
> *Beams mild, all love and all perfection, that when the lips*
> *Recieve a kiss from Gods or Men, a threefold kiss returns*
> *From the press'd loveliness; so her whole immortal form three-fold,*
> *Three-fold embrace returns, consuming lives of Gods & Men,*
> *In fires of beauty melting them as gold & silver in the furnace.*
> *Her Brain enlabyrinths the whole heaven of her bosom & loins*
> *To put in act what her Heart wills. O who can withstand her power!* [18]

This threefold Venus, whose heart is in her head and whose brain is in her body, is the enchantress, the witch, the feminine principle whose power over "gods and men" is the "cruel" (so Blake continually calls it) feminine power of "binding" the immortal within a mortal body.

By now it should be evident that Blake's acquaintance with the Hermetic tradition was more than superficial. He must, when he wrote the Text F poem, have planned a perhaps ambitious treatment of a theme of which the descent of the soul is but an aspect: a cosmic epic, beginning with anterior causes. Therefore the story must "Begin with Tharmas, Parent pow'r." [19]

We shall now turn again to the Hermetic myth. The *Pymander* tells that after the mingling of the light with the darkness, the archetypal man fell from his original condition of pure spirituality. Man is the son of "the Father of all things," and in his nature is like his divine Father, "all beauteous, having the image of his Father." [20] But after the creation of the world by the mingling of light and moisture, the spiritual man is attracted downward. Several of the illustrations of *The Book of Urizen* show "Eternals" gazing down into the cloudy and turbulent abyss; and these resemble the account of the Eternal Man who in the Hermetica "resolved to pierce and break through the circumference of the Circles"—that is, the planetary circles turned by the seven "governors" or planetary spirits. He stooped, so the myth tells, "peeped through the Harmony," [21] and saw himself reflected in the water. With this beautiful image he fell, like Narcissus, in love: "he smiled for love, as if he had seen the shape or likeness in the Water, or the shadow upon the Earth, of the fairest Human form. And seeing in the water a Shape, a Shape like unto himself, in himself he loved it, and would cohabit with it, and immediately upon the resolution ensued the operation, and brought forth the unreasonable Image or Shape." Like Thel he identifies himself with the image, or body. (Platonic thought is full of such shadows and reflections as metaphors of the material bodies. Plotinus himself uses the myth of Narcissus and also the reflection seen in water; [22] the "things which enter and depart from matter," he says, are nothing but imitations of being and "semblances, flowing about a formless semblance.") [23] The narrative continues: "Nature presently laying hold of what it so much loved, did wholly wrap herself about it, and they were mingled, for they loved one another." This is the original of all alchemical accounts of the liquid Venus; and the result of this ensnaring is man's double nature: "And from this cause Man above all things that live upon earth is double: *Mortal*, because of his body, and *Immortal*, because of the substantial Man. For being immortal, and having power of all things, he yet suffers mortal things, and such as are subject to Fate or Destiny." [24]

We find in Boehme's *Forty Questions concerning the Soul* an account that is astonishingly close to the Hermetic myth, and seems to point to a continuous and living tradition that had reached Boehme, also, through alchemy:

> For the water in the deep arises from the fire, not from the wrath, but from the light; for the light proceeds from the fire, and has a seeking of its own, it seeks a Glass to behold itself in, and it seeks an Habitation, and draws it by its desire into itself, and dwells therein, and that which is drawn in is water, which receives the light; else if the light did not dwell in the water, the deep of the world could not comprehend the light: the water is the satiating of the Desire of the light.
>
> And the water again seeks the Glass, and would have a House to dwell in, and that is flesh; as you see, the water receives the shadow of all bodily substances, so that the body may be seen in the water, and that is, because the seeking of the water has captivated it.[25]

In all these myths the reflected image in the water is, of course, the physical body in which the light of the spirit is captivated.

This, then, is the story told of Tharmas and Enion. Tharmas is the Eternal Man who looks down, sets turning the planetary circles, and sinks into the bodily image reflected in the sea, there to become enwrapped and overgrown with the "filmy woof" of the liquid Venus, Enion:

> *. . . Tharmas groand among his Clouds*
> *Weeping, and bending from his Clouds he stoopd his holy head*
> *And stretching out his holy hand in the vast deep sublime*
> *Turnd round the circle of Destiny with tears & bitter sighs*
> *And said. Return O wanderer when the day of Clouds is oer.*
>
> *So saying he sunk down & flowd among her filmy Woof.*
> *In dismal pain drawn out by her lovd fingers every nerve*
> *She counted, every vein & lacteal threading them among*
> *Her woof of terror . . .*[26]

There is in the *Vala* manuscript a drawing which appears to be of Tharmas turning the starry "circle of Destiny." The "holy" and "innocent" nature of Tharmas here clearly derives from the archetypal man of the Hermetic narrative, made in the image of God. To Enion's woof we will later return, for this, too, is Hermetic.   [100]

The mingling of "nature" with the spiritual man produces what the Hermetic writer calls a "Wonder"—*Thaumas;* for "Nature being mingled with man, brought forth a Wonder most Wonderful." [27] This "Wonder" is the unreasonable image or shape of a spiritual being imaged in matter, an

100 Tharmas turns the "circle of Destiny": *Vala* MS (1795–1804?), p. 82 Bentley

Destiny is ruled by the stars; this is indicated by their depiction upon the circle held by Tharmas. Compare with Freher's cosmological diagrams for Law's Boehme [II, 131, 132; cf. I, 67; II, 192].

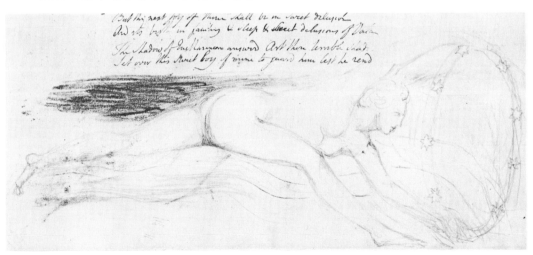

unnatural horror, according to a philosophy which sees matter as evil and the fall of spirit into matter as the original cosmic tragedy. Blake constantly employs the word "wonder" to describe the Spectre of Tharmas; he is a being of "wondrous beauty," "a bright wonder, Nature," and "a wonder abhorr'd by Gods and Men." [28] The Hermetic "Wonder," mating with the nature-spirit, brought forth the generations of seven sublime men, according to the natures of the seven planetary spirits. *Thaumas* is therefore the "parent power" of the theogony of the Hermetica, as is Tharmas in the myth of *The Four Zoas*. In calling him the "Parent pow'r," no doubt Blake originally intended all the Zoas to be his progeny.

Tharmas is light, mind, spirit, the *deus absconditus* of alchemy, whose indwelling animates the matter that imprisons him. From one of the canceled fragments it looks as though Blake at first conceived Tharmas only as "the unreasonable Image or Shape" produced by the mingling of spirit with matter, and "the ancient man" as a distinct mythical person. This would be more strictly in keeping with the myth of the Hermetica, whose "Wonder" (*Thaumas*) is the double-natured image. So in Blake's earliest conception it is "the ancient man" who bowed his bright head, but Tharmas who rises from "beneath the veil"—that is, from under Enion's woof of terror, her watery, or bodily, "garment." A few lines below, "Tharmas with wing'd speed flew to the sandy shore"—this Tharmas being the Spectre. As the poem now stands Tharmas is the original god who "stoop'd his innocent head"; and the Spectre is never called Tharmas, but "the Spectre of Tharmas," while the "ancient man" (later called Albion) is distinct from both. Yet Blake's Albion retains many affinities with the archetypal man of the *Pymander*. Albion, who throughout all the later Prophetic books lies submerged in the ocean, "vegetated" upon his weed-grown rock, is in the same situation as the archetypal man who falls into the water and is ensnared and enwoven in matter.

In the Hermetic allegory there are three actors—the spiritual form of man, the female watery nature, and the "unreasonable Image or Shape," the "double" product of their mingling, who is earthly man, "mortal because of his body, and immortal because of the substantial man." (The "substantial" man is, of course, spiritual, the body being only a shadow or reflection.) In Blake's myth we have Tharmas, Enion, and the Spectre, who also is of double nature. Blake made two attempts to depict this specter as hermaphrodite—that is, of double nature. In the first he is called Tharmas:

> *Male form'd the demon mild athletic force his shoulders spread,*
> *And his bright feet firm as a brazen altar; but the parts*
> *To love devoted, female; all astonish'd stood the hosts*
> *Of heaven, while Tharmas with wing'd speed fled to the sandy shore,*
> *He rested on the desart wild, & on the raging sea*
> *He stood & stretch'd his wings &c.*[29]

The second attempt describes this same "double" monster as Enion:

> *With printless feet scorning the concave of the joyful sky,*
> *Female her form bright as the summer but the parts of love*
> *Male & her brow radiant as day. darted a lovely scorn.*
> *Tharmas beheld from his high rocks &c.*[30]

The "Immortals" looked upon this demon of double nature with horror: "Pitying they viewd the newborn demon. for they could not love." [31] (They "could not love" a monstrous confusion of mortal and immortal natures.) The description of the Spectre that was allowed to stand is no longer hermaphrodite, but remains monstrous:

> *But standing on the Rocks her woven shadow Glowing bright*
> *Reard up a form of gold & stood upon the glittering rock*
> *A shadowy human form winged. & in his depths*
> *The dazzlings as of gems shone clear, rapturous in joy*
> *Glorying in his own eyes Exalted in terrific Pride*
> *Searching for glory wishing that the heavens had eyes to see*
> *And courting that the Earth would ope her Eyelids & behold*
> *Such wondrous beauty repining in the midst of all his glory*
> *That nought but Enion could be found to praise adore & love.*[32]

Only Enion—matter—who is responsible for this unnatural being could "praise adore and love" the animated shadow, to the eyes of Immortals a monstrosity. Enion herself is "Terrified in her own Creation, viewing her woven shadow." [33]

But something of the hermaphrodite quality of the original Spectre haunts later appearances of the theme. We recognize the jeweled glittering "Wonder" in a passage from *Jerusalem*, associated no longer with Enion but with Vala:

> *Then the Spectre drew Vala into his bosom, magnificent, terrific,*
> *Glittering with precious stones & gold, with Garments of blood & fire.*

He wept in deadly wrath of the Spectre, in self-contradicting agony,
Crimson with Wrath & green with Jealousy, dazling with Love
And Jealousy immingled, & the purple of the violet darken'd deep,

　　　　.　　　　.　　　　.

A dark Hermaphrodite they stood frowning upon London's River;
And the Distaff & Spindle in the hands of Vala, with the Flax of
Human Miseries . . .[34]

The self-contradiction of the Spectre is, again, his double nature—mortal and immortal. Vala now weaves the "flax" that first was Enion's, from which she wove her "woof of terror" over the Spectre; and it is still a bodily garment of "miseries" that Vala weaves. The colors of the spectrum so insisted upon in this description—gold, blood red, fiery crimson, green, purple—bring us back to the Hermetic allegory of the union of light and water. Was this also in Blake's mind when he wrote of the mingling of Enion and the Spectre ". . . all his lovely changing colours mix / With her fair crystal clearness. . ."? It would be like him if this were so; we know of his interest in Newton's *Opticks;* and the "vision of light" that he described in a verse-letter to Butts is precise in its reference to the Newtonian "particles bright" of color. Is not Enion here the "crystal" house of light—water—and the "lovely changing colours" the spectrum of the rainbow, light refracted from the "crystal" water? [35]

The genesis of the Spectre is followed (as in the Hermetic myth) by an account of the mating of this monster with Enion; and we now find Blake drawing freely upon another source, Ovid's *Metamorphoses,* Book IV, where the story is told of the water nymph Salmacis and Hermaphroditus. We know that Blake regarded the legends of Ovid as containing symbolic meaning: "Apuleius's Golden Ass & Ovid's Metamorphosis & others of the like kind are Fable; yet they contain Vision in a sublime degree, being derived from real Vision in More ancient Writings." [36]

　　Here we can again with some confidence point to one of the "more ancient Writings" that Blake had in mind (for he never generalized without some sort of basis). The *Pymander* was believed until the seventeenth century to date from before Moses. In fact, it was written long after Ovid; but Blake did not know that, and in any case, he was right in essence: more ancient or not, the Hermetic fable of the fall of the archetypal man is nearer to the only "original" source that matters, the inner meaning of the symbols.

There is no doubt that Blake saw the identity of the two fables of the mingling of man with a female water-nymph to produce a "double" and unnatural hermaphrodite. Ovid's elegant fable tells the story of the lovesick Salmacis and the boy who bathed in her stream. His account, though devoid of any indication that the narrative is symbolic, contains so many details of the Hermetic myth that it is evident that somewhere there is a common source. Ovid was faithful in preserving every detail of traditional narratives, respecting them even when he appears to be unaware of, or indifferent to, their deeper significance. Instructed by the Hermetica, Blake could read Ovid's story as a symbolic narrative.

The story tells of the stream of Salmacis, which enervates and enfeebles all who bathe in its waters. It is hardly necessary at this point to say that bathing in the waters of Lethe (matter) enervates and enfeebles the soul. The meaning of the symbolism of the river-nymph and the stream is clear. A handsome boy comes to the river, and, at first repulsing the importunate nymph, afterward bathes in her waters. She thereupon takes possession of him, like the water-spirit of the *Pymander:*

> *And now she fastens on him as he swims,*
> *And holds him close, and wraps about his Limbs.*
> *The more the Boy resisted, and was coy,*
> *The more she clipt, and kist the strugling Boy.*
> *So when the wrigling Snake is snacht on high*
> *In* Eagle's *Claws, and hisses in the* Sky,
> *Around the Foe his twirling Tail he flings,*
> *The restless Boy still obstinately strove*
> *To free himself, and still refus'd her Love.*
> *Amidst his Limbs she kept her Limbs intwin'd,*
> *"And why, coy Youth, she cries, why thus unkind."*

Until at last

> *. . . they run*
> *Together, and incorporate in One:*
>
> .   .   .
>
> *Both Bodies in a single Body mix,*
> *A single Body with a double Sex.*[37]

Compare this with the contending and mingling of Enion and the Spectre—the love of Enion and the hate of Tharmas:

Thus they contended all the day among the Caves of Tharmas.
Twisting in fearful forms & howling, howling harsh shrieking
Howling harsh shrieking, mingling their bodies join in burning
                                                          anguish.
Mingling his horrible brightness with her tender limbs; then high
                                                        she soar'd
Above the ocean; a bright wonder, that Beulah shudderd at
Half Woman & half Serpent [38]

In the final version Blake changed "half Serpent" to "half Spectre," thereby effacing a clue to the image of eagle and serpent which suggested this fearsome nuptial flight. "Half Woman & half desart" is another reading,[39] this image suggesting her nature as mere matter, the "desart" of atomic "particles," the "sands upon the dead sea shore." "That Beulah shuddered at" becomes, uncompromisingly, "Nature."

It is quite clear that Blake was reading Ovid in the light of the *Pymander*'s "Nature presently laying hold of what it so much loved, did wholly wrap herself about it, and they were mingled, for they loved one another."

Many details of Blake's imagery are taken from Ovid. The boy of Ovid's fable is described as blushing when the nymph approaches him, and the blushes are dwelt upon for several lines. Blake takes them over, and the "rising blushes" of a conventional Augustan decoration take, in Blake, a forceful and terrifying literalness. "In rising Blushes still fresh Beauties rose" becomes:

> *. . . in her lips & cheeks his poisons rose*
> *In blushes like the morning* [40]

The conventional snake and eagle simile becomes in Blake intensely and horrifically animated, and incorporated into the metamorphosis itself; the image is sustained:

> *. . . and his scaly armour softening*
> *A monster lovely in the heavens or wandering on the earth,*
> *With Serpent voice incessant wailing; in incessant thirst*
> *Beauty all blushing with desire mocking her fell despair.*[41]

"Serpent voice" becomes in the final draft "Spectre voice"—again obliterating the traces of Ovid's influence. But in both accounts the stress upon the "voice" of the Spectre is significant. The canceled version reads: [42] "With female voice warbling upon the hills & hollow vales."

This strange image, far from being the product of Blake's wild fancy, is taken over from the story of poor Hermaphroditus, who found, after his mingling with Salmacis, that his voice was altered:

> *The Boy, thus lost in Woman, now survey'd*
> *The River's guilty Stream, and thus he pray'd.*
> *(He pray'd, but wonder'd at his softer Tone,*
> *Surpriz'd to hear a Voice but half his own)*
> *You Parent-Gods, whose Heav'nly Names* [43] *I bear,*
> *Hear your* Hermaphrodite, *and grant my Pray'r;*
> *Oh grant, that whomsoe'er these Streams contain,*
> *If Man he enter'd, he may rise again*
> *Supple, unsinew'd, and but half a Man!*

With the mourning voice we are back once more with the troubled cloud of the Hermetic myth; and this strange detail of the voice in Ovid's fable, introduced with all the seeming naturalness of his exquisite artistry, must certainly point to some common source. So significant are even the smallest and, to the uninitiated, seemingly irrelevant details of myths.

The apparent confusion of Blake's narrative—the two minglings, first of Tharmas with the "filmy woof," then of the Spectre with Enion—points us to his source. The Hermetic myth is reminiscent, in its reduplications, of those elaborate chains of successive emanation characteristic of Gnostic writings of the same period. There are three distinct events: the mingling of the primal light with matter; the falling of the archetypal man into the reflection in the water; and the mating of the resulting "Wonder" with Nature to produce the generations of "sublime men." Such complexity is more than Blake's myth could sustain in an age unfamiliar not only with this particular—and very complex—myth but with mythological thought altogether. After this one episode he very wisely dropped the Spectre of Tharmas, retaining only Tharmas the god, "distributed"—as Taylor says—in matter, and Enion, matter itself. The hermaphrodite abruptly disappears, leaving us with Enion the earth mother:

> *Till with fierce pain she brought forth on the rocks her sorrow & woe*
> *Behold two little Infants wept upon the desolate wind.*[44]

These are matter's twin children, time and space, Los and Enitharmon.

There is no mention of a water garment in the Hermetic fable Blake has retold; did Blake add Enion's "woof of terror" without precedent? This would not have been in keeping with his practice. The alchemists conceived the process of entering generation as a vesting of the soul in bodies of air and of water. Porphyry's nymphs are weavers of hylic garments; but in fact, Enion's garment is also Hermetic. There is a description of the mortal body altogether in keeping with the view that a fall into matter is the source of every evil, and the cause of death to the soul. The horrible nature of Enion's woof reflects this account of "the web of Ignorance; the foundation of all Mischief; the bond of Corruption; the dark Coverture; the living Death; the sensible Carcass; the Sepulchre, carried about with us . . . Such is the hurtful Apparel, wherewith thou art clothed, which draws and pulls thee downward by its own self, lest looking upward and seeing the beauty of Truth, and the Good that is reposed therein, thou shouldst hate the wickedness of this Garment." [45] The garment in which Enion entraps Tharmas is of this kind. It is the body, drawn ". . . From her bosom weaving soft in sinewy threads / A tabernacle of delight . . ." [46] Tharmas is said to "flow" among her garment because of its watery (hylic) nature; [47] and in *The Four Zoas* an added line stresses the deathly aspect of generation in Enion's garment: " . . . he sunk down into the sea, a pale white corse." Tharmas is now "the living death, the sensible Carcasse." Later additions to the *Vala* text all serve to strengthen the Hermetic allusion (see p. 385, n. 15):

> *Wond'ring she saw her woof begin to animate, & not*
> *As Garments woven subservient to her hands, but having a will*
> *Of its own, perverse & wayward . . .*[48]

Another late addition to the text describes the mantles woven by Rahab and Tirzah, the cruel and beautiful ensnarers of the later writings. Here the Hermetic origin of the imagery is clearer still, the very cadences echoed in Blake's words:

> *. . . Rahab & Tirzah far different mantles prepare: webs of torture,*
> *Mantles of despair, girdles of bitter compunction, shoes of indolence,*
> *Veils of ignorance covering from head to feet with a cold web.*
> *We look down into Ulro; we behold the Wonders of the Grave.*[49]

Tirzah, like the maiden of the crystal cabinet, is an ensnarer because of her great beauty, Rahab because of her association with "stalks of flax." There is no mention of these stalks of flax in the earliest version of the "woof of terror"; but in a later addition, Tharmas asks Enion:

Why wilt thou Examine every little fibre of my soul,
Spreading them out before the sun like stalks of flax to dry? [50]

The allusion is to the flax in which Rahab hid the Hebrews who came to spy out the Land of Canaan; [51] she covered them "with stalks of flax, which she had laid in order upon the roof." The addition of the stalks of flax belongs to a period when Blake was attempting to Christianize the poem, and perhaps to the time when he added the theme of Canaan to his system. It is interesting also to note that when Blake shows weavers with a distaff, it is flax and not wool that he depicts on it; the mortal garments are woven of "stalks of flax."

The Christianization of the symbol leads finally to the "robes of blood" worn by Jesus; but there are always details of the original fable that reveal the consistent continuity of the theme; and always the horror of the Hermetic original clings to Blake's descriptions of the garments of mortality:

They unweave the soft threads, then they weave them anew in the
forms
Of dark death & despair, & none from Eternity to Eternity could
Escape,
But thou, O Universal Humanity—who is One Man, blessed for
Ever—
Recievest the Integuments woven. Rahab beholds the Lamb of God.
She smites with her knife of flint. She destroys her own work   [II, 187]
Times upon times, thinking to destroy the Lamb blessed for Ever
He puts off the clothing of blood, he redeems the spectres from their
bonds.[52]

It is not surprising that so impressive an image as the animated garment of the Hermetica should have captured Blake's imagination; and there seems little doubt that here we have one of the clues to the origin of Vala herself. Margoliouth has pointed to the very moment when the name Vala first occurred to Blake. It is written over a canceled illegible word:

Beneath the veil of [name del.] *Vala rose Tharmas from dewy tears.*
The ancient man bow'd his bright head, & Urizen, prince of light,
Astonish'd look'd from his bright portals. Luvah, King of Love
Awaken'd Vala . . .[53]

"The actual genesis of the name may be before our eyes," Margoliouth

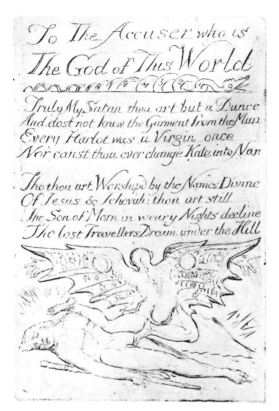

To The Accuser who is
The God of This World

Truly My. Satan thou art but a Dunce
And dost not know the Garment from the Man
Every Harlot was a Virgin once
Nor canst thou ever change Kate into Nan

Tho thou art Worshipd by the Names Divine
Of Jesus & Jehovah: thou art still
The Son of Morn in weary Nights decline
The lost Travellers Dream under the Hill

101 Satan as the soul of the natural frame:
For the Sexes: The Gates of Paradise
(1810?), plate 19

Satan (the specter), like Vala, is depicted with sun, moon, and stars of the natural universe in his wings. [Cf. 1, frontispiece and 1, 87.]

writes, for "the word 'Vala' is written above the line and above a deleted and illegible word . . . whatever the word was Blake took very great care to obliterate it. He had just thought of something much better—the veil itself, personified as Vala." [54] It is tempting to guess that the deleted word was Enion, since she was the original weaver of the filmy woof.

We can also guess why at this point Blake abandoned the Spectre. The figure who first rose from under Enion's veil was Tharmas, the illusion or "Wonder"; and the later Vala possesses all the essential metaphysical attributes of an illusion, shadow, and reflection. There was no place in the myth for both figures, and Vala, the living "veil," is obviously a far better conception. This view would also explain the later association of the Spectre [101] with Vala and her occasional guise as a hermaphrodite (see p. 214, above). There is surely also an echo of the Hermetic fable of the generation of the Eternal Man in *The Gates of Paradise:*

My Eternal Man set in Repose,
The Female from his darkness rose

.   .   .

A dark Hermaphrodite we stood.[55]

The poem goes on to describe the finding of bodily "garments," "a devouring Winding sheet," in the "grave."

Blake's use of the strange figure of the hermaphrodite becomes explicable when we look to the origin of the myth and discover in the unnatural double nature our human condition, which has troubled mankind since the reign of Gilgamesh: the destiny of a being part mortal, part divine.

102 Device from Bryant's *Mythology*, vol. 1 (1774), plate VIII

CHAPTER *12*

Enion

Enion, as matter, signifies all that is "beneath" in the nether abyss of the alchemists. She is the successor of matron Clay, the first matter out of which all things are generated and to which they return. She is hylic, and her imagery is of water, mist, and dew; she is "a showery form," "a tear wiped away," and there are passages describing her that suggest Thel's landscape of watery evanescence:

Image of grief, thy fading lineaments make my eyelids fail.

. . .

Looking upon thee, Image of faint waters, I recoil
From my fierce rage into thy semblance. Enion, return.
Why does thy piteous face Evanish like a rainy cloud
Melting, a shower of falling tears, nothing but tears! Enion,
Substanceless, voiceless, weeping, vanish'd, nothing but tears! [1]

Tharmas describes his fall from paradise into

. . . *a wat'ry world of woe when Enion stood*
Trembling before me like a shadow, like a mist, like air. [2]

She is a more complex figure than her predecessors, enriched by tributary sources, some of which have already been described. But the strongest element in her composition is not myth but philosophy. Enion brings to life the Neoplatonic definitions of matter. The fable of Salmacis, the "moist nature" of the *Pymander*, and Vaughan's "liquid Venus" serve as a bridge connecting allegory with Platonic metaphysics. The philosophic definitions of Plotinus are but a fuller statement of the doctrine of the Hermetica. Indeed, in all these works myth shades into philosophy, and philosophy into myth; for myth is the natural, the inseparable dress of the metaphysical.

103 Enion, blind and age-bent, eluded by the youthful Los and Enitharmon: *Jerusalem* (1804–1820), plate 87, detail
The other figures are probably Urizen and Ahania "in the void."

Blake, whose mythopoeic thought so bewildered his contemporaries, was returning to a traditional and normal mode of expression.

Matter, in the philosophic language of Plotinus, is a "non-entity." By this he does not mean that matter is absolutely nonexistent, but that it possesses no inherent qualities. Qualities inhere only in intellect and in soul. But, Plotinus argues,

> Since matter is neither soul nor intellect, nor life, nor form, nor reason, nor bound, but a certain indefiniteness, nor yet capacity, for what can it produce? Since it is foreign from all these, it cannot merit the appellation of being, but is deservedly called *non-entity*. . . . the mere shadow and imagination of bulk, and the desire of subsistence; abiding without station, of itself invisible, and avoiding the desire of him who wishes to perceive its nature.[3]

This, translated into figurative terms, might describe the nature of Enion and of her world and state; her very name suggests *non-ens*.[4] She is a figure perpetually fading and dissolving, "substanceless, voiceless, weeping, vanish'd"; dissolution is the thing she fears, and "desire of subsistence" is the motive of her action; and her elusive avoidance of the desire of Tharmas, who perpetually seeks her, is the cause of his torment and her grief. She is said to exist on "the margin of Non Entity":

[103]
> *On to the margin of Non Entity the bright Female came*
> *There she beheld the* Spectrous *form of Enion in the Void* [5]

She laments:

> *. . . I wander like a cloud into the deep*
> *Where never yet Existence came . . .*[6]

Her great fear—"to fall into the indefinite"—is a plain paraphrase of Plotinus' characterization of matter:

> *She wanders in Eternal fear of falling into the indefinite,*
> *For her bright eyes behold the Abyss. Sometimes a little sleep*
> *Weighs down her eyelids; then she falls; then starting, wakes in fears*
> *Sleepless to wander round, repell'd on the margin of Non Entity.*[7]

Enion, one might say, is pure quantity, as distinct from quality, which she can only reflect from soul, intellect, life, since matter may be said to possess, as such, a merely quantitative existence, and quantity without any qualities can only be imagined as a vanishing point, "on the margin of nonentity," as Blake says.

Enion fears dissolution, for she is not an absolute nothing. Plotinus' "non-entity" is of this equivocal kind:

> By non-entity in this place, I do not mean *nothing*, but that alone which is different from being . . . I understand that kind of non-entity which is no more than the mere image of being, or something even more remote than this from reality; and this is no other than our visible universe.[8]
>
> Hence, when no one perceives it, it is then in a manner present: but cannot be viewed by him who strives intently to behold it. . . . So that it is a phantom, neither abiding nor yet able to fly away. . . . shade as it were of all real being. Hence, too, in each of its vanishing appellations, it eludes our search.[9]

Whatever criticisms modern science might have to bring against Neoplatonic doctrine, it could scarcely criticize this definition of matter, which in its ultimate nature cannot, obviously, be perceived by the senses. Nature (Vala) is a system of sensible appearances; matter (Enion) is the invisible something or nothing beneath nature's veil.

It is only by the mirroring of intellect that matter takes on such equivocal being as Plotinus allows her; and that is why Blake makes Enion plead with Tharmas to bestow upon her, by proximity to himself, some semblance of being and quality:

> *These are the words of Enion, heard from the cold waves of*
> *despair:*

> .   .   .

> "*O Tharmas, do not thou destroy me quite, but let*
> *A little shadow, but a little showery form of Enion*
> *Be near thee, loved Terror; let me still remain, & then do thou*
> *Thy righteous doom upon me; only let me hear thy voice.*
> *Driven by thy rage I wander like a cloud into the deep*
> *Where never yet Existence came; there losing all my life*
> *I back return weaker & weaker; consume me not away*
> *In thy great wrath; tho' I have sinned, tho' I have rebell'd*
> *Make me not like the things forgotten as they had not been.*
> *Make not the thing that loveth thee a tear wiped away.*" [10]

Not an image, not an action, is accidental; all belongs to the philosophic concept of matter that is Blake's source. Enion pleads as one guilty, "Tho' I have sinned. Tho' I have rebell'd"—and this leads us back to the guilt of the Hermetic moist principle, which ensnares intellect, and the underlying bias in the Platonic philosophy as a whole of regarding matter as evil and the cause of evil. To Blake, however, the revolt of matter against mind, quantity against informing quality, had a contemporary relevance and urgency, for what else was the mechanistic scientific philosophy? But Plotinus' account of the lapse of the soul through the "guilt" of matter has more than a general resemblance to the story of Enion and Tharmas; it has given Blake his particular images, almost his plot:

> Matter, indeed, being present, with wanton importunity affects, and desires, as it were, to penetrate into the recesses of the soul; but the whole place is sacred, and nothing there is destitute of soul. Matter,

therefore, opposing herself to soul, is illustrated by its divine light, yet is incapable of receiving that by which it is illustrated; for it cannot sustain the irradiations of soul though present, because, through its depravity, it is incapable of beholding a nature so pure and divine.[11]

Look now at the story of Enion. She begs to be allowed to remain near Tharmas, whom she both loves (since upon him her existence depends) and fears (since she wishes to exist independently), whom she has sought to ensnare, but whose presence she, at the same time, says she cannot sustain:

> *Enion said:* *"Thy fear has made me tremble, thy terrors have*
> *surrounded me.*
> *All Love is lost: Terror succeeds, & Hatred instead of Love.*
>
> .   .   .
>
> *Once thou wast to Me the loveliest son of heaven — But now*
> *Why art thou Terrible? and yet I love thee in thy terror till*
> *I am almost Extinct & soon shall be a shadow in Oblivion,*
> *Unless some way can be found that I may look upon thee & live.*
> *Hide me some shadowy semblance. . . ."* [12]

A strange opening speech if it is intended to illuminate any conceivable human situation; but as a statement by Plotinus' principle of matter, addressed to intellect, upon which matter depends but whose supremacy she wishes to evade and deny, it becomes, what in human terms it could scarcely be, a clear statement of the situation from which the myth takes its departure. A disharmony between spirit and matter has come about through an exaltation of the material principle. The balance is about to be destroyed. Matter both depends for her very existence upon the "irradiations of soul," and opposes herself to his nature; she is "incapable of beholding a nature so pure and divine," and yet unable to exist unless "some way can be found that I may look upon thee and live," since pure quantity can only be said to exist in reflecting, from mind, qualities. Her "wanton importunity" is about to cause the downfall of the intellectual principle; and it presently appears that she has attempted to "penetrate into the recesses of the soul."

> *I have look'd into the secret soul of him I lov'd,*
> *And in the Dark recesses found Sin & cannot return.*[13]

This added passage in *The Four Zoas* was inserted, evidently, to fill in an omitted minute particular of Plotinus' account of the unstable relationship between matter and spirit.

The fall of Tharmas follows; he becomes ensnared in matter's "filmy woof," and she, in attempting to usurp supremacy, destroys both Tharmas and herself. Enion confesses her "depravity": [14]

> *"What have I done," said Enion, "accursed wretch! What deed?*
> *Is this a deed of Love? I know what I have done. I know*
> *Too late now to repent. Love is chang'd to deadly Hate,*
> *A life is blotted out, & I alone remain, possess'd with Fears." [15]*

Spirit is destroyed and matter only remains, "hidden in the darksom Cave," the place of this world. Blake is describing the rise of scientific materialism and the desolation of a material world empty of spirit:

> *She spoke: "What am I? wherefore was I put forth on these rocks*
> *Among the Clouds to tremble in the wind in solitude?*
> *Where is the voice that lately woke the desart? Where the Face*
> *That wept among the clouds, & where the voice that shall reply?*
> *No other living thing is here. The Sea, the Earth, the Heaven,*
> *And Enion, desolate: where art thou, Tharmas? O return." [16]*

Strangely enough, such passages become not only more comprehensible but also more moving, when all supposition of the words being spoken on a human level is abandoned.

Fallen Enion lives "in the darksom Cave"; she is also called blind—"blind & age bent." Her blindness and darkness are characteristic of material existence; for whoever pursues matter (says Plotinus)[17] "is precipitated, not so much in his body, as in his soul, into profound and horrid darkness, and thus blind, like those in the infernal regions, converses only with phantoms." Intellect is light, "abiding in her own essence and at the same time illuminating the obscure nature of matter with a secondary life." But the soul that no longer abides in its own essence is said to live in darkness, because it "beholds nothing but obscurity; it now participates deeply in matter, looking at that which it cannot perceive"—that is, matter, which possesses no intelligible form.

In one passage Blake presents the blindness of Enion as merciful, because it saves her from the realization of her condition:

> *Ah, happy blindness! Enion sees not the terrors of the uncertain,*
> *And thus she wails from the dark deep; the golden heavens tremble.*[18]

As the voice of matter in a universe from which spirit has been blotted out, the lament takes on not only meaning but tragedy and horror. For Blake the history of ideas was not an abstraction but a human experience affecting the whole of life, and not confined to the conceptual faculty—an experience that literally changes the character of the world in which we live. The "dark deep" she inhabits is the nonentity and darkness of matter; her blindness and the darkness of her dwelling are one and the same:

> *. . . Enion, blind & age bent,*
> *Plung'd into the cold billows, living a life in midst of waters;*
> *In terrors she wither'd away to Entuthon Benithon,*
> *A world of deep darkness where all things in horrors are rooted.*[19]

Does Entuthon Benithon derive from ἐντύθεν (thenceforth, afterward) and βένθος (the depths of the sea)? The meaning "thenceforth in the depths of the sea" describes very well the condition of matter when divided from informing spirit and sunk into hylic existence. Here there is surely an echo of Spenser's world of chaos, the source of the material bodies with which the generating souls are clothed:

> *For in the wide wombe of the world there lyes,*
> *In hatefull darkenesse and in deepe horrore,*
> *An huge eternall* Chaos, *which supplyes*
> *The substances of natures fruitfull progenyes.*

> *All things from thence doe their first being fetch,*
> *And borrow matter, whereof they are made,*
> *Which when as forme and feature it does ketch,*
> *Becomes a bodie, and doth then invade*
> *The state of life, out of the griesly shade.*
> *That substance is eterne, and bideth so,*
> *Ne when the life decayes, and forme does fade,*
> *Doth it consume, and into nothing go,*
> *But chaunged is, and often altred to and fro.*[20]

For Spenser, as also for Milton,[21] the characteristic of the material matrix is precisely its want of form and quality, which intellect alone can bestow.

Enion is the dust of the earth of the Old Testament, which God cursed at the Fall, along with Adam: "Cursed is the ground for thy sake; in sorrow shalt thou eat of it all the days of thy life; Thorns also and thistles shall it bring forth to thee . . . In the sweat of thy face shalt thou eat bread, till thou return unto the ground; for out of it wast thou taken: for dust thou art, and unto dust shalt thou return." [22] For she laments:

> *I am made to sow the thistle for wheat, the nettle for a*
> *nourishing dainty.*
> *I have planted a false oath in the earth; it has brought forth*
> *a poison tree.*
> *I have chosen the serpent for a councellor, & the dog* [23]
> *For a schoolmaster to my children* [24]

—the serpent matter. This is the condition of the material world alienated from the spiritual source. Her lamentation and protest proceed to describe the bitterness of experience in the material world, subject to decay and destruction. With the grand speech that begins:

> *What is the price of Experience? do men buy it for a song?*
> *Or wisdom for a dance in the street?*

ends Night II of *The Four Zoas*. It is spoken by "the terrible form of Enion in the Void," and belongs, again, altogether to her nature: matter as conceived by the philosophy of Newton and Locke, which describes the sorrowful consequences of her isolation from spiritual cause.

Enion's last great speech (for there is no finer poetry in all Blake's writings than that assigned to her) is made in her character as the "dark consumer," the grave. Enion can tell "what is done in the caverns of the grave" (matter) into which the souls die from eternity; for she is herself that grave. She is called "the wat'ry Grave" in the same sense as Thel's "dewy grave," for she is Paracelsus' feminine and gross "waters of the valley of darkness." The watery grave is not a metaphor of death by drowning; the body, everflowing, is the watery grave of the incarnate soul. [25] It is self-evident that the grave is a "consumer"; but so, symbolically, is water, and I believe that Blake's description of Enion as the dark consumer includes an allusion to Paracelsus on the four elements: "that which consumeth, is the Element of water." [26] Here Blake presents the material principle not as mechanistic science but as alchemy conceives it, as the matrix in which spirit embodies itself. Like matron Clay the grave nourishes the earthworm, emblem of mortality, in her bosom; and like her the lowliest of things, Enion is beloved by the highest God. Again we are reminded of the union of "that which is above" with "that which is beneath." Her speech addressed to Ahania, the "vegetater happy," recalls the words spoken to Thel by matron Clay:

> *Once I wail'd desolate like thee; my fallow fields in fear*
> *Cried to the Churchyards & the Earthworm came in dismal state.*
> *I found him in my bosom, & I said the time of love*
> *Appears upon the rocks & hills in silent shades; but soon*
> *A voice came in the night, a midnight cry upon the mountains:*
> *"Awake! the bridegroom cometh!" I awoke to sleep no more;*
> *But an Eternal consummation is dark Enion,*
> *The wat'ry Grave. O thou corn field! O thou vegetater happy!*
> *More happy is the dark consumer; hope drowns all my torment.*[27]

This whole passage is full of the vision of alchemy. We remember Philalethes' initiation by Thalia into the mysteries of the *prima materia* in her sanctuary and workshop under the graves. Enion's speech is filled with the exaltation of all that (in the Platonic hierarchy) is lowest, to a mysterious kinship with the highest; and her speech concludes with a promise of the resurrection of the "scatter'd portions" of the immortal body of man—the *deus absconditus* of alchemy, to be liberated by the Great Work. The immortal spirit awaits its resurrection from its mutable watery grave of matter; Enion, who brought about the entanglement and drowning of spirit, now, repentant, sees his approaching resurrection:

> *Listen. I will tell thee what is done in the caverns of the grave.*
>
> .   .   .
>
> *And as the seed waits Eagerly watching for its flower & fruit,*
> *Anxious its little soul looks out into the clear expanse*
> *To see if hungry winds are abroad with their invisible army,*
> *So Man looks out in tree & herb & fish & bird & beast*
> *Collecting up the scatter'd portions of his immortal body*
> *Into the Elemental forms of every thing that grows.*
>
> .   .   .
>
> *In pain he sighs, in pain he labours in his universe,*
> *Sorrowing in birds over the deep, & howling in the wolf*
> *Over the slain, & moaning in the cattle, & in the winds,*

And weeping over Orc & Urizen in clouds & flaming fires,
And in the cries of birth & in the groans of death his voice
Is heard throughout the Universe: wherever a grass grows
Or a leaf buds, The Eternal Man is seen, is heard, is felt,
And all his sorrows, till he reassumes his ancient bliss.[28]

The "scatter'd portions" of the Eternal Man relate not only to the alchemical *deus absconditus* but to the great myths of Dionysus and Osiris. Enion speaks as Isis seeking for the scattered portions of Osiris and as the preserver of Dionysus in his laceration. There is not in literature, ancient or modern, a more profoundly imagined expression of the myth of the god, sacrificed, scattered, and entombed in the material universe, awaiting his resurrection. "Night the Eighth" ends appropriately with the figure of Christ entombed:

And Los & Enitharmon took the Body of the Lamb
Down from the Cross & plac'd it in a sepulcher which Los had hewn
For himself in the Rock of Eternity, trembling & in despair.
Jerusalem wept over the Sepulcher two thousand years.[29]

Christ is entombed, Osiris scattered, Dionysus lacerated; the divine principle in the modern world is dead, so Blake implies, and philosophic materialism is the tomb.

Enion, earth mother and grave, has her most perfect manifestation as the virgin *prima materia* of the alchemists, Vaughan's "liquid crystal." For, Vaughan says, "The Earth. . . . in her owne *nature* is a glorious Chrystallized body, bright as the *Heavens*." [30] Tharmas calls Enion' "my Crystal form that lived in my bosom." [31] The Spectre mingles with "her fair crystal clearness"; she is the "crystal house" in which light takes up its residence. Tharmas begs Los to help him to gather his "daughters" that "my crystal form may come to me." [32] When Enion does at last return, it is as a little girl in Vala's "crystal world," the world of matter restored to its original innocence and purity. The crystal imagery is introduced with special reference to Enion and Tharmas:

And in the morning, when the sun arose in the crystal sky,
Vala awoke & call'd the children from their gentle slumbers:

> *"Awake, O Enion, awake & let thine innocent Eyes*
> *Enlighten all the Crystal house of Vala! awake! awake!*
> *Awake, Tharmas! awake, awake thou child of dewy tears.*[33]

Enion in her crystal form is matter purified.

In the Gardens of Vala, Enion does nevertheless retain her mutable nature; she comes and goes, and Tharmas cannot retain her, although she always returns to reflect his desires:

> *. . . Enion, let Tharmas kiss thy Cheek.*
>
> *Why dost thou turn thyself away from his sweet wat'ry eyes?*[34]

Vala asks:

> *Why weep'st thou, Tharmas, Child of tears, in the bright house of*
> *joy?*
> *Doth Enion avoid the sight of thy blue heavenly Eyes?*[35]

Enion remains Plotinus' "flying mockery," "avoiding the desire of him who wishes to perceive its nature." Blake now uses the word "shadow" and not "spectre":

> *In infant sorrow & joy alternate, Enion & Tharmas play'd*
> *Round Vala in the Gardens of Vala & by her river's margin.*
> *They are the shadows of Tharmas & of Enion in Vala's world.*[36]

At the Last Judgment, matter, united with her spiritual counterpart, takes her place in the eternal order; there is a last echo of the alchemical theme of Thel's matron Clay as the nourisher in the humanizing of the "black mould" and her infant race:

> *. . . Enion spoke, saying*
>
> *"O Dreams of Death! the human form dissolving, companied*
> *By beasts & worms & creeping things, & darkness & despair.*
> *The clouds fall off from my wet brow, the dust from my cold limbs*
> *Into the sea of Tharmas. Soon renew'd, a Golden Moth,*
> *I shall cast off my death clothes & Embrace Tharmas again.*
> *For Lo, the winter melted away upon the distant hills*
> *And all the black mould sings." She speaks to her infant race; her*
> *milk*

Descends down on the sand; the thirsty sand drinks & rejoices

.   .   .

Joy thrill'd thro' all the Furious forms of Tharmas humanizing
         [those forms described "in the caverns of the grave"].
Mild he Embrac'd her whom he sought; he rais'd her thro' the
                                                           heavens,
Sounding his trumpet to awake the dead, on high he soar'd
Over the ruin'd worlds . . .[37]

This soaring of the reunited Tharmas and Enion is in contrast with the
soaring of the sinister Spectre, with Enion in his grasp. The latter was an
act of *hybris*, but the last apotheosis is a true assumption of the material
principle into the spiritual kingdom, as that in which spirit is reflected and
embodied.

104 Woodcut by Blake (1821) for Vergil's first Eclogue

CHAPTER 13

Tharmas and the Mental Traveller

When Blake came to write the poem *Vala* he began (if Margoliouth's reconstruction of the text is to be accepted) not with the passages of Enion, Tharmas, and the Spectre but with the present "Night the Second." [1] Later, in the expanded *Four Zoas*, he evidently decided to restore the early material, feeling that, unsatisfactory as it might be, it had great importance as a point of departure for the myth. Blake's motives for retaining the theme of the fall of spirit into matter as the beginning both of the myth of man and of his own indictment of the positivist age are not at all hard to understand. But in the later passages both Enion and Tharmas have somewhat changed in character and grown immeasurably in imaginative stature.

Tharmas, as he reappears at the end of "Night the Third," attempts to rise from the ocean of hyle and to reassume his lost human shape. He speaks as the *deus absconditus:*

> . . . *one like a shadow of smoke appear'd*
> *And human bones rattling together in the smoke & stamping*
> *The nether Abyss, & gnashing in fierce despair, panting in sobs,*
> *Thick, short, incessant, bursting, sobbing, deep despairing, stamping,*
> *struggling,*
> *Struggling to utter the voice of Man, struggling to take the features*
> *of Man, struggling*
> *To take the limbs of Man, at length emerging from the smoke*
> *Of Urizen dashed in pieces from his precipitant fall,*
> *Tharmas rear'd up his hands & stood on the affrighted Ocean:*
> *The dead rear'd up his Voice & stood on the resounding shore,*
>
> *Crying: "Fury in my limbs! destruction in my bones & marrow!*
> *My skull riven into filaments, my eyes into sea jellies*
> *Floating upon the tide wander bubbling & bubbling,*

Uttering my lamentations & begetting little monsters
Who sit mocking upon the little pebbles of the tide
In all my rivers & on dried shells that the fish
Have quite forsaken." . . .[2]

This is not inconsistent with the earlier account of Tharmas, who sank into the sea and flowed among Enion's filmy woof; but the god who now emerges from the waters, seeking to reassume the lost shape of man, is far more splendid than the petulant monster who emerged from beneath the woven veil of Enion. This is no longer merely the fallen man of the Hermetica or Vaughan's lover of the crystal cabinet. Neither is Blake's ocean god, but for a few accidental attributes—his chariots and horses and trumpets, mentioned only once—like Oceanus or Neptune. The myths of these gods contain no element of *suffering* through immersion in matter, which is of the very nature of Tharmas. The new Tharmas speaks with the tragic voice of the dismembered god of the Orphic Mysteries, Dionysus, whose resurrection was the theme of his initiatory mysteries. Bryant obligingly makes possible the identification of Thaumas with Dionysus, who is, he says, "the same as Thamas or Thamuz."[3]

His dead and scattered bones are taken from a biblical equivalent of the same myth (recognized as such by Blake with his penetrating symbolic insight), Ezekiel's valley of dry bones: "And he said unto me, Son of man, can these bones live? . . . Thus saith the Lord God unto these bones; Behold, I will cause breath to enter into you, and ye shall live: and I will lay sinews upon you, and will bring up flesh upon you, and cover you with skin, and put breath into you, and ye shall live. . . . And as I prophesied there was a noise, and behold a shaking, and the bones came together, bone to his bone."[4]

Tharmas, though sunk in the waters of hyle, can still raise a storm: "For if I will, I urge these waters. If I will, they sleep";[5] but he lives "in immortal torment, never to be deliver'd." He is the suffering god, and his state, under the dominance of the material principle, is that of an "eternal death," the living death of spirit in the grave of matter:

Like a famish'd Eagle, Eyeless, raging in the vast expanse,
Incessant tears are now my food, incessant rage & tears.
Deathless for ever now I wander seeking oblivion
In torrents of despair: in vain; for if I plunge beneath,

Stifling I live: If dash'd in pieces from a rocky height,
I reunite in endless torment; would I had never risen
From death's cold sleep beneath the bottom of the raging Ocean.

   . . .

Immortal in immortal torment, never to be deliver'd! [6]

Tharmas says it is "love" that has brought him to this living death; and we are reminded that the archetypal man has become immersed in matter, through the ensnaring in the "filmy woof" of Enion. Tharmas now speaks as one doomed to a living death. Himself disintegrated and drowned in matter, he threatens the Eternal Man with disintegration:

. . . Tharmas
Is God. The Eternal Man is seal'd, never to be deliver'd.
I roll my floods over his body, my billows & waves pass over him,
The sea encompasses him & monsters of the deep are his companions.
Dreamer of furious oceans, cold sleeper of weeds & shells,
Thy Eternal form shall never renew, my uncertain prevails against
               thee. [7]

It is not surprising to find that Blake has made use of the myth of Dionysus in elaborating the figure of Tharmas. [8] He made such extensive use of the first part of Taylor's *Dissertation* that it would have been strange had we found no trace of his having used the second part, on the Mysteries of Dionysus, his "fall into Division & his Resurrection to Unity." [9] In his story we have yet another version of the ensnaring of spirit in matter, as told in the Hermetica.

The Orphic myth of Bacchus is given by Taylor:

Dionysius [*sic*], or Bacchus, while he was yet a boy, was engaged by the Titans, through the stratagems of Juno, in a variety of sports. . . . and among the rest, he was particularly captivated with beholding his image in a mirror; during his admiration of which, he was miserably torn in pieces by the Titans; who, not content with this cruelty, first boiled his members in water, and afterwards roasted them by the fire. But while they were tasting his flesh thus dressed, Jupiter, excited by the steam, and perceiving the cruelty of the deed, hurled his thunder at the Titans; but committed his members to Apollo, the brother of Bacchus, that they might be properly interred. And this being performed, Dionysius, (whose heart during his laceration was snatched away by Pallas and preserved,) by a new regeneration, again emerged, and being restored to his pristine life and integrity, he afterwards filled up the number of the gods. But in the mean time, from the exhalations formed from the ashes of the burning bodies of the Titans, mankind were produced.[10]

The boiling and roasting of the god symbolizes "the procession and distribution of intellect into matter"—the "boiling," the descent into matter (water), and the "roasting," the natural symbol of the fiery ascent from matter which completes the cycle of descent and return.

Olympiodorus in his commentary on the *Phaedo* explains the myth of the fall into division and the resurrection to unity in these words:

> In order to the soul's descent, it is necessary that she should first establish an animating image of herself in the body; and in the second place, that she should sympathize with the image, according to a similitude of form. . . . In the third place, being situated in a divisible nature, it is necessary that she should be lacerated and scattered together with such a nature, and that she should fall into an ultimate distribution, till, through the energies of a cathartic life, she raises herself from the extreme dispersion, and loosens the bond of sympathy through which she is united with body; and till, at the same time, energizing without the image, she becomes established according to her primary life. And we may behold a resemblance of all this in the fable respecting Bacchus, the exemplar of our intellect. For it is said that Dionysius [*sic*], establishing his image in a mirror, pursued it, and thus became distributed into the universe.[11]

Olympiodorus says in conclusion that the purpose of the Mysteries is to lead us back to the perfection from which, as our source and origin, we are fallen. The passages from *Vala* already quoted describe Tharmas, "lacerated and scattered," in the condition of Bacchus.

The god who is "captivated with beholding his image in a mirror" is the archetypal man; the "animating image . . . situated in a divisible nature" is the "unreasonable image," Blake's Spectre; and the intellect "energizing without the image" is the spiritual man at last released from the power of the Spectre. All these myths of captivation by a mirror or by a reflection in the water have the same meaning; and the symbolism persisted in the alchemical tradition from which Boehme also derived; for the traditional language of symbols, seemingly protean, leads us back again and again to the same themes. We may remember that mermaids long continued to lure sailors to a death by water by the magic of the looking glass they carried in their hands.

There is a magnificent account in Boehme's *Forty Questions* of this same "Glass in the Abyss," which is, as in all the earlier versions, a feminine principle: "Seeing then there is a Glass in the Abyss, in which the source beholds itself; so it is also a Figure and Image of the source, which stands before the source, and does or brings forth nothing, but is a Virgin of the source, wherein the wrathfulness of the Flash discerns itself infinitely without number; and always opens its wonders therein." [12]

In the story of Dionysus it is again a feminine principle, Juno, who causes his fall through the stratagem of the looking glass.

We must now leave Enion and Tharmas in order to examine that strange poem *The Mental Traveller*.[13] Although it was written later than *Vala*, this does not lessen its interest in throwing light upon many obscurities in the mythology of Enion and Tharmas, and in confirming the surmise that Blake was drawing upon the mythology of Dionysus. The poem occurs as a fair copy in the Pickering Manuscript; Keynes gives the approximate date for this as 1803. Yet on the evidence it contains of Blake's familiarity with Plato's *Politicus*, I suggest that the date should probably be 1804, the year in which Thomas Taylor's translation of that dialogue appeared.

It has been said [14] that *The Mental Traveller* contains elements of all Blake's four Zoas. The Babe is the victim of a "woman old," like Tharmas; he "rends his manacles" like Orc; he pursues his feminine counterpart as Los pursues Enitharmon; and he is aged like Urizen. But I believe that the resemblances with the other Zoas are incidental; the parallel with Enion, Tharmas, and Orc fundamental.

The Mental Traveller is a poem upon the cyclic nature of history. This was understood by Yeats, not indeed when in 1893 he published with Edwin Ellis his commentary upon the poem, but in 1925, in the first edition of *A Vision*. Yeats then knew he had understood the poem, for he wrote:

When Edwin J. Ellis and I had finished our big book on the

philosophy of William Blake, I felt that we had no understanding of this poem: we had explained its details, for they occur elsewhere in his verse or his pictures, but not the poem as a whole, not the myth, the perpetual return to the same thing; not that which certainly moved Blake to write it; but when I had understood the double cones, I understood it also. The woman and the man are two competing gyres growing at one another's expense.[15]

This invocation of gyres to explain the man and woman who move alternately from youth to age, from age to youth, may seem to explain the obscure by the more obscure; but this is not so. Although Yeats says that Blake received his myth from "those beings that gave that knowledge, as it is in *The Spiritual Diary*" of Swedenborg, it is quite plain that Yeats had now discovered Blake's source, and with his source his meaning. Yeats was himself to elaborate in *A Vision* the same cyclic myth.

The gyres, Blake's as well as Yeats's, derive ultimately from a myth in Plato's *Politicus*. *The Mental Traveller* is a poem upon the theme of history, conceived as a perpetual cycle, with the alternate dominance of two principles, symbolized by the man and the woman. Yeats nowhere wrote an exegesis of Blake's poem; but the evidence that he had understood it is to be found in his own mythology of the gyres, and especially in his play *The Resurrection*.

History, Plato says, is a perpetual alternation of ages, according as the god Saturn controls or relinquishes the revolutions of the years:

> Hear, then. Divinity himself sometimes conducts this universe in its progression, and convolves it: but at another time he remits the reins of his government, when the periods of the universe have received a convenient measure of time. But the world is again spontaneously led round to things contrary. . . . This progression, however, to things contrary is naturally implanted in it through the following cause. . . .[16]

And Plato proceeds to explain that the reversal of the revolutions of the world takes place automatically, like a coiled spring that has been tightly wound in one direction and unwinds itself spontaneously when it is released. Therefore the world, when it is no longer conducted by the god, "proceeds by itself, and being thus left for a time, performs many myriads of retrograde revolutions."

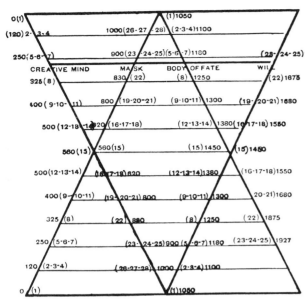

105 Yeats's gyres: diagram from *A Vision* (2nd edn.), p. 266

Headed "The Historical Cones," with this explanation: "The numbers in brackets refer to phases, and the other numbers to dates A.D. The line cutting the cones a little below 250, 900, 1180 and 1927 shows four historical *Faculties* related to the present moment. May 1925."

[105] This is the Great Year of the ancients; and Plato's image of the coiled spring is the original of Yeats's gyres. But why, we must ask, was Yeats so certain that Blake's two figures, with their alternating phases of youth and age, correspond to the Platonic gyres? At those times, Plato says, when the divine ruler leaves the earth to revolve retrograde, man advances, as now, from youth to age; but when the god is in control, man progresses from age to youth. The literalness of Plato's imagery is no less than that of Blake's poem, and is unquestionably the source of its central image:

> That which takes place first of all, when, in whatsoever age a mortal animal is constituted, he is no longer seen advancing to old age, but is again changed to the contrary, and naturally becomes, as it were, younger and more delicate. The white hairs, too, of those more advanced in years then become black, and the cheeks of those that had beards become smooth; and thus each was restored to the past flower of his age. The bodies, likewise, of such as were in the bloom of youth, becoming smoother and smaller every day and night, again returning to the nature of a child, recently born; and at length, their bodies rapidly wasting away, perished.[17]

Thus man becomes, under Saturn's golden rule, "as a little child"—an idea that could not fail to delight Blake, whose symbol of the soul's radical innocence is also the child. In *The Mental Traveller* the image of the boy-child is presented as both an initial and a terminal state. His appearance marks the beginning of a cycle, but, we are also told, his birth is the joyful outcome of a long process of effort and suffering, the contrary of the nature of birth in this present world, where the biblical curse upon Eve—that she shall bring forth her children in sorrow—holds good:

> *For there the Babe is born in joy*
> *That was begotten in dire woe;*
> *Just as we Reap in joy the fruit*
> *Which we in bitter tears did sow.*

Childhood, here, is conceived in Platonic terms as the state of perfection, the end toward which we strive and emblem of the Golden Age. This babe is no sooner born into time than he is sacrificed:

> *And if the Babe is born a Boy*
> *He's given to a Woman Old,*
> *Who nails him down upon a rock,*
> *Catches his shrieks in cups of gold.*

[112]

> *She binds iron thorns around his head,*
> *She pierces both his hands & feet,*
> *She cuts his heart out at his side*
> *To make it feel both cold & heat.*

What has this sacrifice of a boy-child to do with the inception of an historical cycle? Who is Blake's Babe? He is manacled to the rock like Prometheus; he wears Christ's crown of thorns; and his heart is cut out of his side by "a Woman Old," as Dionysus was lacerated at the instigation of Juno.

The introductory verses of Yeats's *Resurrection* are clearly based upon the same episode; he gives the name that Blake withholds, and also relates the laceration of the god to the myth of the Great Year:

> *I saw a staring virgin stand*
> *Where holy Dionysus died,*
> *And tear the heart out of his side,*
> *And lay the heart upon her hand*
> *And bear that beating heart away;*
> *And then did all the Muses sing*
> *Of Magnus Annus at the spring,*
> *As though God's death were but a play.*

Yeats's poem and Blake's mutually explain one another; the tearing out of the heart of Dionysus initiates, in both poems, a new revolution of the Great Year. Yeats and Blake have both seized upon the image of the tearing out of the living heart by a goddess; Blake has stressed the sacrifice of the divine child by the "Woman Old"—Juno; Yeats, the preservation of the heart by the "staring virgin"—Athena. But both poets have been wise in leaving their female figures ambiguous; for the woman in Blake's poem later becomes the preserver and regenerator of the sacrificed male principle; and Yeats's "staring virgin" has some of the sinister attributes of Juno the destroyer when she "tears the heart out of his side." The identity of the "Woman Old" with Enion is established by the verse that follows:

> *Her fingers number every Nerve,*
> *Just as a Miser counts his gold;*
> *She lives upon his shrieks & cries,*
> *And she grows young as he grows old.*

In *Vala* Enion, who weaves the "sinewy threads" of a mortal body for Tharmas, numbers every nerve:

> *In gnawing pain drawn out by her lov'd fingers, every nerve*
> *She counted, every vein & lacteal, threading them among*
> *Her woof of terror. . . .*[18]

In *The Four Zoas* an added passage introduces the image of the lacerated "infant"; Tharmas asks:

> *Why wilt thou Examine every little fibre of my soul,*
> *Spreading them out before the sun like stalks of flax to dry?*
> *The infant joy is beautiful, but its anatomy*
> *Horrible, Ghast & Deadly . . .*[19]

The poem *To Tirzah*, addressing the cruel "mother of my mortal part," also specifies the "heart" which she sacrifices; and the laceration of Albion by Rahab and Tirzah is a later development of the same theme, by which generation is conceived as a cruel sacrifice of spirit at the hands of the feminine principle. The tearing out of the heart is shown on page 69 of *Jerusalem*. Albion himself summons Vala to lacerate him:

> *. . . come, O Vala, with knife & cup, drain my blood*
> *To the last drop, then hide me in thy Scarlet Tabernacle* [20]

106 Albion sacrificed by women with knives and a cup ("to catch his shrieks"?):
Jerusalem (1804–1820), plate 69, detail

The woman on left holds an object which may be the torn-out heart of the victim.
Compare [II, 187], where Albion's heart or viscera are being drawn out by
women; and [I, 71], "To Tirzah."

And a later passage [21] describes the sacrifice of Albion by the Daughters of
Albion, in a passage that combines, again, the sacrifices of Christ and
Dionysus. The "Knife of flint," as Margoliouth has pointed out, suggests
that Blake had also been reading some of the books describing the Aztec
human sacrifices,[22] Bernal Diaz or Clavigero's *History of Mexico:*

> *The Knife of flint passes over the howling Victim: his blood*   [106]
> *Gushes & stains the fair side of the fair Daughters of Albion.*
> *They put aside his curls, they divide his seven locks upon*
> *His forehead, they bind his forehead with thorns of iron,*
> *They put into his hand a reed, they mock, Saying: "Behold*
> *The King of Canaan whose are seven hundred chariots of iron!"*
> *They take off his vesture whole with their Knives of flint,*
> *But they cut asunder his inner garments, searching with*
> *Their cruel fingers for his heart, & there they enter in pomp,*
> *In many tears, & there they erect a temple & an altar.*
> *They pour cold water on his brain in front, to cause*
> *Lids to grow over his eyes in veils of tears, and caverns*
> *To freeze over his nostrils, while they feed his tongue from cups*
> *And dishes of painted clay. . . .*

The "cold water" poured over his eyes to make "veils" suggests the watery
(material or hylic) woof of Enion. Most of the images are already present in
To Tirzah—the tears of the cruel sacrificers, as they bind "nostrils, Eyes &
Ears" with "senseless clay."

But why should Blake and Yeats both have supposed the sacrifice of

107 Dionysus with his alter ego: Greek vase painting

Dionysus to be symbolically associated with the beginning of a cycle of the Great Year? This belongs to the Orphic tradition, known to both poets through, again, Thomas Taylor's *Dissertation*.[23] Dionysus is a god of two aspects, child and man; and he is often shown on Greek vases and the like as a bearded man holding on his knee his own infant alter ego. It is the divine child who is the higher aspect of the god, as he is manifested in the eternal world. This Thomas Taylor explains: "by the puerile state of Bacchus at the period of his laceration, the flourishing condition of an intellectual nature is implied; since, according to the Orphic theology, souls, while under the government of Saturn, who is pure intellect, instead of proceeding, as now, from youth to age, advance in a retrograde progression from age to youth." [24] The child Dionysus is the exemplar of the youth and perfection of the spiritual principle, which, when distributed in the material universe, ages and weakens under the power of the opposite principle, feminine and material.

Blake's man and woman are spirit and matter, or, on another level, body and soul: ". . . when the body with which a soul is connected is beautiful and young, then the soul is oppressed and its vigour diminished; but when this grows old, the soul revives, and increases in strength and vigour." [25] This is a key to the real meaning of Plato's fable: the principle which grows from age to youth is not the body but the soul, or intellect, waxing as body wanes; the allegory concerns the substantial man, not his body. On one level Blake's *Mental Traveller* is an allegory of this alternate dominance of body and soul in the individual or racial life-cycle. Yeats suggests that the two figures signify beauty and wisdom, adding that the symbol can be read on several levels: "With Blake it is not enough to say that one is beauty and one is wisdom, for he conceives this conflict as that of all love—whether between the elements of Parmenides, the 'wanton love' of Aristotle, or between man and woman—which compels each to be slave and tyrant by turn." [26] I do not think Yeats is right in his suggestion of beauty and wisdom, except insofar as beauty may be assigned to body, wisdom to soul; [27] nor do I think that the difference of sex is more than a symbol; for this is not in any other sense a poem about the relation between the sexes. The man and woman are the two figures of the alchemical "marriage" of light and water, spirit and matter, the "parents" of all manifested being, the yin and yang of Chinese philosophy. But from the use that Yeats makes of Blake's poem in constructing his own myth of the gyres, it is evident that he later understood the symbols correctly.

In Plato's myth the world is alternately conducted and abandoned by the god. There is only one agent. When the world is no longer guided by Saturn, "it proceeds by itself, and, being thus left for a time, performs many myriads of retrograde revolutions." [28] Blake symbolizes both phases as active persons, following, in this, those other sources which justify his personification of a female principle of matter, in perpetual antithesis with spirit, the Juno of the myth of Dionysus.

There is every reason, then, for Blake to have made the laceration of the child-god stand at the beginning of the Great Year. There is plenty of traditional precedent, also, for the placing of the Incarnation of Jesus at the beginning of such a cycle. Blake no doubt knew Vergil's famous prophecy, taken throughout the Middle Ages as referring to the birth of Christ:

> *The last great age, foretold by sacred rhymes,*
> *Renews its finish'd course: Saturnian times*
> *Roll round again; and mighty years, begun*

From their first orb, in radiant circles run.
The base degen'rate iron offspring ends:
A golden progeny from heav'n descends.[29]

This is why Yeats also places at the beginning of a play on the theme of
Christ an allusion to the sacrifice of Dionysus and the beginning of the Great
Year. In Yeats's play it is the beating heart of Dionysus that animates the
risen Christ. It is, significantly, a Greek who presses his hand to the side of
the risen Christ, and cries, "The heart of a phantom is beating"—a phantom
being, according to the Platonic philosophy, a material existence, like
Blake's specter or shadow; and Thomas, seeking conviction of the reality of
the Resurrection, "puts his hand where the heart is."

Blake's poem, then, follows tradition in marking the beginning of a
new cycle by the birth and sacrifice of the divine child: the divine enters
history, and as the Babe grows (according to the nature of this world) older,
his power increases, and that of the opposite gyre, the material principle,
weakens. He grows older, she younger, until the moment of the reversal of
the gyres comes with the aged weakness of the man and the birth of the
woman as a new Babe:

Till from the fire on the hearth
A little Female Babe does spring.

From this point, the female Babe ages and the now aged man "grows /
Younger & younger every day," until at the end of the poem the double cycle
is completed, and begins again with the birth of the male Babe.

But this process passes through many phases. The Babe grows in
strength,

Till he becomes a bleeding youth,
And she becomes a Virgin bright;
Then he rends up his Manacles
And binds her down for his delight.

There is a suggestion here of Prometheus, who is to rend up his manacles
when the reign of Zeus is at an end; but in the context of Blake we think
more immediately of Orc, who is the Messiah of Swedenborg's New Age.
We are, by now, meant to have realized that Blake's theme is history;
therefore, when he tells us of a brief period of harmony between spirit and
matter, of the youth and the virgin, we are to think of an age when matter

bears the impress of intellect to perfection, and intellect finds in matter a medium plastic to its will. Such a period of spiritual ascendency tends to produce art; it is formative, and matter is the "delight" of spirit, who "binds" her in forms of beauty. Blake does not specify any historical period. Yeats, in *A Vision*, does attempt to define the phases of the gyres in great elaboration of detail; and Blake's later version of the historic cycle, his twenty-seven Churches,[30] also specifies phases. (This piece of symbolism, together with Blake's own sources, Swedenborg and Boehme, no doubt had its influence upon Yeats's cycle of the twenty-eight phases of the moon.) In *The Mental Traveller* Blake is specific about the process of change but general in his application of it.

A moment of harmony between the two principles leads on inevitably to decadence, and the spiritual impulse weakens in the very process of realization: the youth becomes an old man. This is an idea Blake would also have found in Swedenborg, who describes the "circles" of all things, and especially of "Churches," which, originating in a spiritual impulse, decline in the course of realization, just as human life begins in infancy and passes through youth and manhood to old age and death. (See below, Appendix I, pp. 325 ff.) There follows then a period no longer of creation but of the enjoyment of the accumulated treasures of civilization,

> *Which he by industry had got.*

> *And these are the gems of the Human Soul,*
> *The rubies & pearls of a lovesick eye,*
> *The countless gold of the akeing heart,*
> *The martyr's groan & the lover's sigh.*

The "industry" of the spirit is in the love and suffering of the martyrs and the lovers; and a record of them remains in works of art and poetry, the treasures of mankind. Human kind are the "guests" fed (for man does not live by bread alone) at the "house" of an ancient civilization. In the formative and potent years these treasures are in the making, and in its decline enjoyed and distributed:

> *They are his meat, they are his drink;*
> *He feeds the Beggar & the Poor*
> *And the wayfaring Traveller:*
> *For ever open is his door.*

Yeats (from his later writings we may surmise that it was he and not Ellis)

well understood this part of Blake's poem, when he wrote in the 1893
commentary: "The wealth of his soul consists of the accumulation of his own
smiles and tears. . . . He is male, and mental, and these things make the
joy of others, when he 'teaches in song'—as the overworked phrase has
it—what he 'learned in suffering' ": [31]

> *His grief is their eternal joy;*
> *They make the roofs & walls to ring;*
> *Till from the fire on the hearth*
> *A little Female Babe does spring.*

The creative impulse is now spent; and from its decadence a new age has
begun, the gyre is reversed, and a phase of materialism commences. The
spiritual impulse has exhausted itself:

> *He wanders weeping far away,*
> *Untill some other take him in*

Blake is still pursuing his historical allegory. A spent culture may be
"taken in" to renew its energy in some new and vital civilization, as Greek
culture was "taken in" by Rome, or antiquity by the Renaissance, or the
Jewish religion by the young barbarous civilization of Europe, there to
renew itself in Christendom. Thus the old and spent force may be rejuve-
nated, but "until he can a Maiden win"—that is to say, find a physical
medium in which the fertilizing idea can germinate—it can accomplish
nothing, and must, according to Blake's allegory, wander houseless, like
some school of poetry or philosophy that has no relevance to the later course
of history.

Yeats must have pondered this theme for many years after the writing
of the 1893 commentary; for the closing lines of the epilogue of *The
Resurrection* are a superb restatement of Blake's meaning, and the best
possible commentary upon the earlier poem:

> *Everything that man esteems*
> *Endures a moment or a day.*
> *Love's pleasure drives his love away,*
> *The painter's brush consumes his dreams;*
> *The herald's cry, the soldier's tread*
> *Exhaust his glory and his might:*
> *Whatever flames upon the night*
> *Man's own resinous heart has fed.*

Achievement in realization is, in both poems, an impulse of the spirit, spent; and again in Yeats's poem we have the image of the deathless heart of Dionysus. Yeats's poem may be the finer; but the imaginative foundations had been laid by Blake, and Yeats has but clarified and elaborated the thought and images of *The Mental Traveller*. [32]

We return to Blake's poem at the point of reversal: the god no longer guides the world. At this moment, when aged and weary spirit embraces the infant female of the material principle, Saturn's Golden Age ends, or, in Blake's image (which has the same symbolic meaning), the vision of Eden fades as spirit embraces matter:

> *And to allay his freezing Age*
> *The Poor Man takes her in his arms;*
> *The Cottage fades before his sight,*
> *The Garden & its lovely Charms.*

The fading garden also occurs in the myth of Enion and Tharmas, and forebodes the fall. Tharmas says:

> *. . . O Vala, once I liv'd in a garden of delight;*
> *I waken'd Enion in the morning, & she turn'd away*
> *Among the apple trees; & all the garden of delight*
> *Swam like a dream before my eyes. I went to seek the steps*
> *Of Enion in the gardens, & the shadows compass'd me*
> *And clos'd me in a wat'ry world of woe when Enion stood*
> *Trembling before me like a shadow, like a mist, like air.*[33]

Tharmas describes the alternate fading and renewal of the vision of Paradise as phases of sleeping and waking, day and night, while Enion comes and goes:

> *He said: "O Vala, I am sick, & all this garden of Pleasure*
> *Swims like a dream before my eyes; but the sweet smelling fruit*
> *Revives me to new deaths. I fade, even as a water lilly*
> *In the sun's heat, till in the night on the couch of Enion*
> *I drink new life & feel the breath of sleeping Enion.*
> *But in the morning she arises to avoid my Eyes,*
> *Then my loins fade & in the house I sit me down & weep."* [34]

Tharmas is restored by "the sleeping Enion" by night—a material phase—

and by day wanes from strength to weakness in her absence. The "sweet smelling fruit" is the woman's gift which tempts the male principle to fall into the world of mortality—"Revives me to new deaths"—fittingly symbolized by the hylic image of the water lily, which suggests Tharmas sunk into Enion's water-garment as "a pale white corse."

In *The Mental Traveller* the fading of Eden is more clearly conceived; and Blake, no more impartial than was Plato, who conceived the Iron Age of the world as revolving without the guidance of God, presents the phase of material dominance as the desolation he habitually associated with the philosophy of Locke and Newton:

> *For the Eye altering alters all;*
> *The Senses roll themselves in fear,*
> *And the flat Earth becomes a Ball;*
>
> *The stars, sun, Moon, all shrink away,*
> *A desert vast without a bound,*
> *And nothing left to eat or drink,*
> *And a dark desert all around.*

The "desart" of materialist philosophy takes the place of the poet's "flat Earth," the earth man perceives imaginatively:

> *And on its verge the Sun rises & sets, the Clouds bow*
> *To meet the flat Earth & the Sea in such an order'd Space:*
> *The Starry heavens reach no further, but here bend and set*
> *On all sides, & the two Poles turn on their valves of gold* [35]

In contrast, the Newtonian solar system of "globes" spinning in immeasurable space is an abstraction, not an experience.

> *As to that false appearance which appears to the reasoner*
> *As of a Globe rolling thro' Voidness, it is a delusion of Ulro.* [36]

Blake's desert is the hypothetical world of "atoms" and "particles"—again, abstractions of science, to which he would allow no substantial existence:

> *The Atoms of Democritus*
> *And Newton's Particles of light*
> *Are the sands upon the Red sea shore,*
> *Where Israel's tents do shine so bright.* [37]

This is the desert of Enion and the Spectre, described in the opening passages of *The Four Zoas*.[38]

But it was clear to Blake that history must take its inevitable course. Upon the decline of a spiritual age succeeds a phase of materialism. In this phase intellect is no longer engaged in the "binding" of imaginative form in art; instead, it "pursues" the maiden in "labyrinths." Blake invariably uses the labyrinth in the sense in which he found the word constantly used by Thomas Taylor, who wrote that "to pursue matter, through its infinite divisions, and wander in its dark labyrinths, is the employment of the philosophy in vogue"[39]—that is, the scientific "pursuit" of knowledge:

> *And on the desart wild they both*
> *Wander in terror & dismay.*
>
> *Like the wild Stag she flees away,*
> *Her fear plants many a thicket wild;*
> *While he pursues her night & day,*
> *By various arts of Love beguil'd,*
>
> *By various arts of Love & Hate,*
> *Till the wide desart planted o'er*
> *With Labyrinths of wayward Love*

Enion's "terrors" are those of this fleeing maiden; indeed, Enion's words might be spoken by her:

> *Enion said: "Thy fear has made me tremble, thy terrors have*
>   *surrounded me.*
> *All Love is lost: Terror succeeds, & Hatred instead of Love,*
>
>   .   .   .
>
> *I am almost Extinct & soon shall be a shadow in Oblivion,*
> *Unless some way can be found that I may look upon thee & live.*
> *Hide me some shadowy semblance, secret whisp'ring in my Ear,*
> *In secret of soft wings, in mazes of delusive beauty."*[40]

Tharmas recognizes, in Enion's expressed wish for her "mazes" and her subsequent creation of "a wat'ry globe," the onset of a new cycle; he turns the circle of destiny and can but sorrowfully await the completion of the revolution that will bring Enion back to him: "Return, O wanderer, when the day of Clouds is o'er."[41] The thicket is the forest of nature; and the desert and labyrinth are also symbols associated with Enion. "Enion in the Desart" creates her shadow-world; and Tharmas, like the lover of *The Mental Traveller*, promises to build her a "Labyrinth": "I will build thee a Labyrinth where we may remain for ever alone."⁴² She hides "in mazes of delusive beauty" in order to "beguile" Tharmas by her love and bring about the fall. The labyrinth is the "infinite divisions" of scientific investigation. In this scientific phase intellect is engaged not in imposing form on matter (art) but in investigating and subdividing matter; it does not now reflect itself (as art), but can know only matter (as science). This is surely the meaning of the contrasted activities of "binding" and "pursuit."

The flowering of a period of scientific pursuits brings round, in its turn, its antithesis. Perhaps we ourselves live at such a moment; and the great age of materialist thought, from Descartes to Einstein, has come full circle round to a dematerialization of the concept of matter. The maiden ages and weakens, and the youth moves once more toward his prime, as Saturn's Golden Age returns. So Blake envisaged Newton's globes "rolling thro' Voidness," inevitably leading once more to the imaginative vision:

> *The Sun & Stars are nearer roll'd.*
>
> *The trees bring forth sweet Extacy*
> *To all who in the desert roam;*
> *Till many a City there is Built,*
> *And many a pleasant Shepherd's home.*

Matter becomes in its turn a spent force, whose task of nourishing her opposite principle is now accomplished. The new Babe—Christ or Dionysus—enters history at the moment when, in the completeness of achievement, the materialist dominance is both at its height and at its limit:

> *But when they find the frowning Babe,*
> *Terror strikes thro' the region wide:*
> *They cry "The Babe! the Babe is Born!"*
> *And flee away on Every side.*

Yeats relates that cry to the beginning of the Christian Era, which was for him, as for Blake, the overthrow of rational Rome by the forces of the irrational: "Meanwhile the irrational force that would create confusion and uproar as with the cry 'The Babe, the Babe is born'—the women speaking unknown tongues, the barbers and weavers expounding Divine revelation with all the vulgarity of their servitude." [43] Both Blake and Yeats had read Gibbon, from whose *Decline and Fall of the Roman Empire* the image of the barbers is taken. Much as Blake disliked Gibbon's anti-Christianity, he was certainly indebted to him for his survey of the phases of history.

The processes of human history are divinely directed, Blake finally indicates, and can be neither arrested nor diverted. The divine child will descend when his time comes. Blake employs the symbol of the ark that the Israelites carried in their long wanderings: "man is either the ark of God or a phantom of the earth & of the water; if thou seekest by human policy to guide this ark, remember Uzzah." These words Blake wrote in a marginal comment to Lavater's Aphorisms.[44] It was Uzzah who laid his hand upon the shrine in its progress;[45] and of the divine Babe, Blake writes:

> *For who dare touch the frowning form,*
> *His arm is wither'd to its root*

Uzzah was in fact killed when he laid his hand upon the ark; and but for the prose quotation that refers to his story, the clue would lead us directly to another story, from the Books of Kings. Blake, student as he was of the Bible, was no doubt composing his poem on the providential course of history in the light of the Judeo-Christian view of the divinely directed course of the "six thousand years" of time; and the story of King Jeroboam illustrates in a striking manner man's impotence to divert that predestined progress. The King is about to burn incense on the altar when "a man of God" appears and prophesies the birth of a marvelous child, a type of the Messiah, and certainly one of the models of the "Babe" of Blake's poem:

> O altar, altar, thus saith the Lord; Behold, a child shall be born unto the house of David, Josiah by name; and upon thee shall he offer the priests of the high places that burn incense upon thee, and men's bones shall be burnt upon thee.
>
> And he gave a sign the same day, saying, This is the sign which the Lord hath spoken; Behold, the altar shall be rent, and the ashes that are upon it shall be poured out.
>
> And it came to pass when king Jeroboam heard the saying of the [108] man of God, which had cried against the altar in Beth-el, that he put forth his hand from the altar, saying, Lay hold on him. And his hand, which he put forth against him, dried up, so that he could not pull it in again to him.[46]

108 Jeroboam with withered arm: pen and
water-color wash

The sin of Jeroboam was to attempt to divert the divinely directed
course of events; and the terrible Babe who consumes the priests on their
own altar is much in the mood of Blake's Red Orc, the Messiah of revolution,
as it is also of the terrible epiphany of a "frowning" Babe in the present
poem.

Swedenborg brings the two stories together.[47] The "putting forth of
the hand" in both stories signifies the exercise of power:

> How far hand signified and represented ability, may appear from
> what is written in the Word concerning Uzzah and Jeroboam;
> concerning Uzzah that he "*put forth* [*his hand*] to the ark of God,
> and took hold of it," on which account he died. (2 Sam. vi. 6, 7).
> The ark represented the Lord, consequently all that is holy and
> celestial; Uzzah's *putting forth* to the ark represented self-ability,
> or man's *proprium*, which being profane, the Word *hand* is not
> mentioned, but still it is understood.

Swedenborg then goes on to the story of Jeroboam, of which he writes,
"Here in like manner by *putting forth the hand* is signified self-ability or

proprium, which is profane, in that it was desirous to violate what was holy, by putting forth the hand against the man of God; wherefore the hand was dried up."

There seems little doubt that Blake is following Swedenborg in his interpretation of these symbols.[48] Man's destiny is to carry, through history, the divine spirit within him, as a holy presence within the shrine of his mortality, a presence that guides him on his pilgrimage through the "six thousand years" in which the divine purpose is accomplished. That journey fulfilled, the Last Judgment of the material world is announced in an image from the *Apocalypse*,[49] "even as a fig tree casteth her untimely figs": "And every Tree does shed its fruit."

This is the end of time. But at this point the "Woman Old" again appears to sacrifice the child, and the cycle begins anew:

> *And none can touch that frowning form,*
> *Except it be a Woman Old;*
> *She nails him down upon the Rock,*
> *And all is done as I have told.*

So Blake's poem comes round full circle; its smooth uninterrupted progression, its rapid, unemphatic quatrains, lead us round to the repetition of the inevitable sacrifice of the god with a sort of grave indifference. Yeats writes that to the Muses, "God's death is but a play," yet Blake's poem is playful, and Yeats, writing of the gyres, is deeply moved and dismayed by the ever-turning circle and what seems an impending reversal. The Christian Era—an age of spirit—is ended; and the era unguided by the god is at hand, heralded, as Yeats tells, by tumult and destruction:

> *Turning and turning in the widening gyre*
> *The falcon cannot hear the falconer;*
> *Things fall apart; the centre cannot hold;*
> *Mere anarchy is loosed upon the world,*
> *The blood-dimmed tide is loosed . . .*

the tide of matter, hyle. The Antichrist approaches the place of Incarnation:

> *And what rough beast, its hour come round at last,*
> *Slouches towards Bethlehem to be born?* [50]

To Blake it is not the Antichrist who approaches, but the Judge, who, in his epiphany at the end of time, comes in anger, "frowning." Yeats, like Blake, adopts the tradition according to which animal forms belong to the material world, human to the spiritual. Thus in Blake's poem, at the approach of the divine child, "Lions, Boars, Wolves, all howling flee." [51] Yeats writes of an end of the Golden Age; Blake believed that, as his master Swedenborg had taught, "A new age is begun."

It is in no way surprising that Yeats should have adopted the ancient cyclic view of history; but that Blake should have so far departed from the more usual Christian view is remarkable. The Christian plan of history is more usually conceived as linear – time that has a beginning (the Creation), a middle (the Incarnation), and an end (the Last Judgment). But even when Blake later Christianized his myth of history, following Swedenborg and Boehme, in his successive phases of twenty-seven Churches,[52] from Adam to Luther, he surprisingly enough kept the Platonic cyclic pattern: "And where Luther ends Adam begins again in Eternal Circle." [53] He retained the pattern that had first claimed his interest in the myth of Plato and the Orphic cult of Dionysus.

Both Greek and Hindu cosmic myths envisage the endless succession of such cycles; and Blake may very well have known that the Hindu tradition confirms Plato's fable, for an article by Sir William Jones published in 1790, "On the Chronology of the Hindoos," gives this information:

> There are alternate creations and destructions of worlds through innumerable *manwantaras;* the Being Supremely Desirable performs this again and again. A human year is a day to the Gods, four ages each of twelve thousand divine years is called an Age of the Gods. This is a day of Brahma; this night has also the same duration. The before mentioned age of the Gods, multiplied by seventy-one, forms what is named here below a *Manwantara.*[54]

The same doctrine is taught in the Bhagavad-Gita, and Blake would have read Charles Wilkins' note to the effect that a "day of Brahma is as a thousand revolutions of the Yoogs [4,320,000,000 years] and that his night extendeth for a thousand more. On the coming of that day, all things proceed from invisibility to visibility, so, on the approach of night, they are all dissolved away in that which is called *invisible*. The universe, even, having existed, is again dissolved; and now again, on the approach of day, by divine necessity, it is reproduced." [55]

In *The Reign of Quantity* Guénon writes of the progress of world-cycles from pure spirit (the qualitative) to pure matter (the quantitative).

The progress from a spiritual beginning to a material fulfillment is, from one point of view, a decline. But seen in another way, it is the realization of the original impulse. Then comes the apocatastasis, the reversal and renewal of all things, or according to the Vedantic symbolism, the inbreathing by Brahma of the worlds that his outbreathing had created.

Appendix I

Blake's twenty-seven Churches are twice listed. They run through time from Adam to the end of the "six thousand years" of history, when the cycle begins anew with a return to Paradise (as foretold in the *Marriage*) and the Golden Age. "A new heaven is begun . . . Now is the dominion of Edom, & the return of Adam into Paradise." The version in *Milton* is as follows:

> *And these the names of the Twenty-seven Heavens & their Churches:*
> *Adam, Seth, Enos, Cainan, Mahalaleel, Jared, Enoch,*
> *Methuselah, Lamech, these are Giants mighty, Hermaphroditic;*
> *Noah, Shem, Arphaxad, Cainan the second, Salah, Heber,*
> *Peleg, Reu, Serug, Nahor, Terah, these are the Female-Males,*
> *A Male within a Female hid as in an Ark & Curtains;*
> *Abraham, Moses, Solomon, Paul, Constantine, Charlemaine,*
> *Luther, these seven are the Male-Females, the Dragon Forms,*
> *Religion hid in War, a Dragon red & hidden Harlot.*
>
> *All these are seen in Milton's Shadow, who is the Covering Cherub,*
> *The Spectre of Albion in which the Spectre of Luvah inhabits*
> *In the Newtonian Voids between the Substances of Creation.*[56]

The version given in *Jerusalem* is exactly the same, but contains after "the Dragon forms":

> *The Female hid within a Male; thus Rahab is reveal'd,*
> *Mystery, Babylon the Great, the Abomination of Desolation,*
> *Religion hid in War, a Dragon red & hidden Harlot.*
> *But Jesus, breaking thro' the Central Zones of Death & Hell,*
> *Opens Eternity in Time & Space, triumphant in Mercy*

Thus are the Heavens form'd by Los within the Mundane Shell.
And where Luther ends Adam begins again in Eternal Circle [57]

Thus from the *Milton* version we learn that the Churches form the "Cover-ing Cherub" and that this cherub is "the Spectre of Albion" (and therefore Satan or the selfhood), whose kingdom is in the "Newtonian voids" of the apparent externality of the space-time world. From *Jerusalem* we further learn that the "Heavens" or Churches are "form'd by Los" (as the agent of time). Elsewhere [58] we read that the Churches are built "by the Spectres."

Ellis and Yeats first pointed out that Blake is following Swedenborg's system. The words "Heavens" in this context is Swedenborgian; a Last Judgment, he taught, is passed "in the heavens," or inner worlds, and what then follows on earth, outwardly, is determined by that inner event. *The True Christian Religion*, Chapter 14, tells at length of the founding of the New Church. It opens with an account of the nature of Churches, which is to decline from an original spiritual impulse to mere externality. Thus no "Church" can in its nature last forever. In this respect "Churches" differ from "the religion of Jesus," which, being of the imagination and not of history, is eternal, existing outside and beyond history, true "yesterday, today, and tomorrow":

> There have existed on this earth Several Churches, all of which in Process of Time have come to their Consummation, and then have been succeeded by new Ones, and so on to the present Time; the Consummation of the Church cometh to pass when there remaineth no Divine Truth but what is falsified and rejected, in which Case there cannot remain any genuine Good. . . . Wherefore whensoever truth comes to its Consummation in the Church, Good also cometh to its Consummation at the same Time, and when this is the Case, the Church is at an End, that is, cometh to its Consummation.[59]

Swedenborg goes on to announce the consummation of the present Christian Church and the beginning of "a New Age," announced to him in "the heavens." Blake followed him in seeing the New Age as the "return of Adam to Paradise," a final revelation of truth absolute; and it may be that Swedenborg, as Blake, saw in the New Age not so much a turn of the circle as a stepping out of it, as Jesus "Opens Eternity in Time & Space," an imaginative vision which can break the circle at any point and give access to another level of understanding. This seems at least possible, as he is quite definite about the cyclic nature of the time process: "The Consummation of the Age may receive Illustration from various T[h]ings in the natural World; for whatever existeth on the Face of the Earth, whether it be considered in a general or particular View, cometh to its Full Age and Consummation, but by alternate Changes called the Circles of Things; Times, or Seasons, both in general and in particular, describe such Circles"; and Swedenborg proceeds, at characteristic length, to describe the succession of the four seasons of the year, and of the day, morning, noon, evening, and night: "Every Man also describeth a Circle of Nature; he beginneth Life in Infancy, from which he advanceth to Youth and Manhood, and thence to Old Age, and then dieth. . . . and thus every Thing cometh to its Birth, and thence to its Death, and thence to its Birth again, to the Intent that Creation may be continued." [60] A Church is subject to a similar law, "because it consisteth of the human Race."

Swedenborg describes four Churches that have been since the creation. The first, or "most ancient church," endured from Adam to the Flood; the second, or "ancient church," "came to its Consummation and Destruction by Idolatries." The third, or Israelitish Church, began with the promulgation of the decalogue on Mount Sinai, and endured until the coming of Jesus in the flesh. The fourth Church is the Christian; but this is subdivided into two parts: "from the Time of the Lord till the Council of Nice, and the other from that Council to the present Time." There is a further division into the Greek, the Roman, and the Reformed. "Moreover, within every general Church have existed several particular Ones." [61]

Here certainly we have the general pattern of Blake's system. The first nine Churches (Adam to Lamech) are named from the generations from Adam to the Flood, and correspond to Swedenborg's "most ancient church": "these are Giants mighty, Hermaphroditic." With due hesitation, we may surmise that before the Flood ("the flood of the five senses") was a time of clearer spiritual illumination than succeeding ages. The "Giants" would then be such mighty spiritual beings as Albion—who is, in this sense, called "the Giant Albion—before the Starry Heavens fled from his mighty limbs and left man "a little grovelling Root." These giants were hermaphroditic in their balance between the spirit (male) and the body (female), equally and harmoniously united.

The generations from Noah to Abraham (taken from Genesis 10) are called "Female-Males / A Male within a Female hid as in an Ark & Curtains." These Churches correspond more or less (Blake begins the new phase with Abraham, Swedenborg with Moses) to the "ancient church," which perished through "idolatry." This is implied by the image of the male within a female, a spiritual essence veiled in material outward forms. The mythological phase of human thought decays through the falling into "idolatry"—that is to say, the misunderstanding of a symbolic language taken, in its decline, in a material and literal sense.

Blake departs from Swedenborg altogether in his third series:

> *Abraham, Moses, Solomon, Paul, Constantine, Charlemaine,*
> *Luther, these seven are the Male-Females . . .*

He classes all these as mystery religions, in which Rahab, who is Vala, is worshiped in reality, under the pretense of a spiritual religion: "Religion hid in War, a Dragon red & hidden Harlot." This is true of the Pauline Church (before the Council of Nice), the Greek (Constantine), the Roman (Charlemagne), and the Reformed (Luther). A "Male-Female" is presumably an aggressive and militant materialism (matter being feminine). The nature worship latent in the Mosaic and Christian "Churches" has issued in religious war and persecution, the very mark of Satan's religion. Only now, Blake believed, the reign of the Divine Humanity may be about to begin, as the "Reign of Literature & the Arts Commences."

Yeats attached great significance to Blake's symbolism of the cycles, not only in *The Mental Traveller* but in its more elaborate form, as the twenty-seven Churches. His own twenty-eight phases of the moon, which move in continual rotation upon the two "gyres" of objective and subjective experience (male and female, in Blake's language), are certainly in part based upon Blake's rotation of the twenty-seven; for in Ellis and Yeats's book [62] an entire chapter is devoted to the Covering Cherub. Ellis and Yeats were the first to point out the Swedenborgian parallel, and also the source of the "covering cherub" symbol in Ezekiel:

> Thou hast been in Eden the garden of God; every precious stone was thy covering . . .
>
> Thou art the anointed cherub that covereth; and I have set thee so: thou wast upon the holy mountain of God; thou hast walked up and down in the midst of the stones of fire.
>
> Thou wast perfect in thy ways from the day that thou wast created, till iniquity was found in thee.
>
> By the multitude of thy merchandise they have filled the midst of thee with violence, and thou hast sinned: therefore I will cast

thee as profane out of the mountain of God: and I will destroy thee, O covering cherub, from the midst of the stones of fire.[63]

Jesus, who "walks about among the stones of fire in bliss & woe," [64] is perpetually and in every phase releasing mankind from the covering cherub, whom Blake interprets quite plainly as Satan:

> *Thus was the Covering Cherub reveal'd, majestic image*
> *Of Selfhood, Body put off, the Antichrist accursed,*
> *Cover'd with precious stones: a Human Dragon terrible*
> *And bright stretch'd over Europe & Asia gorgeous.*[65]

Certainly Blake's Covering Cherub derives from the imagery of Ezekiel; but his identification of the Churches with the cherub that guards the tree of life comes by way of Boehme. The "churches of stone" usurp the internal church in the hearts of men, and this is the cherub:

> indeed, the holy *Jared*, viz. Christ's voice, ruled in Christ's Children *internally;* but *externally* the Cherub with the Sword did *only* bear rule; for the outward *Authority*, which these self-elected Priests *manage*, is the *Sword* of the Cherub. . . . they, who have been born of God, have heard the true *Jared*, viz. Christ's Voice, *in them:* But the other have heard only the outward Voice in *Babel*, viz. Disputation and Contention about Christ's Kingdom. For all *War* which the Christians manage is only the *Sword* of the Cherub proceeding from *Babel: True Christians wage no War.*[66]

Hence Blake's association of the "Dragon red" of religious war with the sword of the cherub. Yeats quite correctly points out that the cherub is a mask of created form, "Cherubs being always powers of bodily creation." This no doubt he learned from Agrippa, whose definitions of the angelic powers were equally known to Blake. Those Grinling Gibbons infant cherubs of St. Paul's Cathedral are certainly far from Blake's bloodstained Covering Cherub; but the infant body is a "covering cherub" of the soul.

Boehme describes seven Churches, or phases of the cherub, which span time from the beginning to the end. These he names from the generations starting with the creation–Adam, Seth, Enos, down to Methuselah. With Methuselah comes the fire of the last day and the end of the temporal world. Blake has evidently combined Boehme's allegory with Swedenborg's, in constructing his own version. Boehme teaches that "There are *seven Times* appointed to proceed from the Tree of Life in the Word of

Power; the *first* proceeds from the pure Life of *Adam;* for before the
Creature, the Life was in the Word, whence it was brought *pure* into the
Image; this continued till the *Fall*." [67] The second time begins with Seth and
continues to the Deluge; the third time is that of Enos, a "hidden kingdom"
that continued until Abraham, "to whom the covenant by Christ was
established in the flesh" and was thus no longer "hidden." Blake seems to be
following Boehme here, with his male hidden in a female, "as in an Ark &
Curtains," until the time of Abraham. The fourth time, that of Cainan,
"which is the spiritual form in prayers and spiritual offerings," continued to
manifest itself with Moses, and remained until the coming of Christ in the
flesh.

The time of Mahalaleel is the apostolic age, when the "angelical
image, which did disappear in Adam, was again manifest in the humanity of
Christ." The time of Jared succeeds—the period of the outward dominance
of the "stone churches" but the rule of "Christ's voice" within. The reign of
Enoch,[68] the "prophetical mouth," is destined to succeed—an age when the
mysteries are no longer veiled in allegory. Methuselah's time is the last and
highest age of the world; and the time of Noah then "denounceth the deluge
of anger to come upon Babel." This is the end of time and the coming of
Christ's kingdom. According to Blake, and presumably Swedenborg and
Boehme, this is the restitution of Adam to Paradise. Does this initiate
another cycle, according to the classical and Indian traditional teaching, or
does it represent a stepping beyond the cycles, into an "eternal" instead of a
temporal world?

Appendix II

The symbol of the Covering Cherub, which makes its appearance for the
first time in the *Marriage*, Blake probably derived from Boehme: [69]

> The ancient tradition that the world will be consumed in fire at the
> end of six thousand years is true, as I have heard from Hell.
>
> For the cherub with his flaming sword is hereby commanded to
> leave his guard at tree of life; and when he does, the whole creation
> will be consumed and appear infinite and holy [70]

Boehme's cherub is death, and his sword is judgment: "the *Cherubim which drove Adam and Eve out of Paradise*, viz. the stern or strong, Angel, which signifies the Cutter off of the *Earthly life* from Paradise, where Body and Soul must part asunder." [71] Boehme's interpretation of the Genesis myth of the cherub who bars the way to the tree of life cannot be understood in isolation from his whole system. The concept of the *Principles* is involved, which principles, in the fallen state of devils and man, are divided from one another; the devils cannot leave their fires, nor can mankind enter the principle of the angelic world, by reason of the "Great Gulf" that now stands between. This gulf or cliff is also called a gate; and the cherub at the gate of Paradise stands to bar the way to the angelical world which before the Fall was not divided from man's earthly Paradise. When man and woman were banished from Paradise, God gave to each of them "a bestial Garment to cover their shame"—the physical body; and now none can re-enter Paradise until the cherub has severed with his sword of death this bestial body from man's true body, which is spiritual—Imagination, the real eternal body, as Blake calls it. In *Auguries of Innocence* those who "cannot pass the Polar bar" are those who live in the earthly principle:

> yet the Sword cuts the earthly Body quite away from the holy Element, and then the new Man may enter into Paradise by the Way of Life. And the Sword is nothing else, but the Kingdom or Gate of the Fierceness in the Anger of God, where Man must press in, through the fierce Death, through the Center, into the second Principle, into the Paradise of the holy Element before God; where the fierce Death cuts off the earthly Body from the holy Element.
>
> And the Keeper of the Garden is the Cherubim, the Cutter off of the Source of the Stars, which holds the four Elements for a while. . . . This Keeper is here in the Way, that we cannot come to the Tree of the eternal Life; he is in the Midst, and suffers us not to come into Paradise. The gross Garden of *Eden* (which is our earthly Flesh) is the Hedge before the Garden. [72]

When the cherub leaves his guard, body and soul will again be one—that is, realized as one. The sword is that described in Genesis: "So he drove out the man; and he placed at the east of the garden of Eden Cherubims, and a flaming sword which turned every way, to keep the way of the tree of life." [73]

Blake writes again of this sword in the verse preface to the fourth book of *Jerusalem*. Its operation is described in terms of the symbols he constantly used to express the effect upon man of the false philosophy of Locke and Newton—the sun and moon rolled into "globes" and "orbs" traveling in space, and man shrunk into the little groveling root or "worm of sixty winters"; and the sword that keeps man from entering paradise is also the religion of "sin, of sorrow, & of punishment," which is the inevitable accompaniment of the loss of the imaginative vision:

> *I stood among my valleys of the south*
> *And saw a flame of fire, even as a Wheel*
> *Of fire surrounding all the heavens: it went*
> *From west to east, against the current of*
> *Creation, and devour'd all things in its loud*
> *Fury & thundering course round heaven & earth.*
> *By it the Sun was roll'd into an orb,*
> *By it the Moon faded into a globe*
> *Travelling thro' the night; for, from its dire*
> *And restless fury, Man himself shrunk up*
> *Into a little root a fathom long.*
> *And I asked a Watcher & a Holy-One*
> *Its Name; he answered: "It is the Wheel of Religion."*
> *I wept & said: "Is this the law of Jesus,*
> *This terrible devouring sword turning every way?"*
> *He answer'd: "Jesus died because he strove*
> *Against the current of this Wheel; its Name*
> *Is Caiaphas, the dark Preacher of Death,*
> *Of sin, of sorrow & of punishment"* [74]

Jesus, Boehme teaches, has broken the sword of death: "Now if any Body would come into the Garden, he must press in through the Sword of Death; though indeed Christ has broken the Sword, so that now we can much easier enter in with our Souls, yet there is a Sword before it still; but he that finds the Way right, him it does not cut very much, for it is blunt, and it is bent." [75] Over Jesus the Imagination, "the true Man," the sword of the cherub has no power; it is in fact illusion, maya, and, as Boehme says, it is blunted and broken by Jesus; or as Blake more joyously prophesies, the cherub leaves its guard at the tree of life when illusion is conquered by imagination.

Part IV

The Zoas of Energy

In the section that follows we shall examine another group of related symbols, those centering round the ideas of energy that occupied Blake especially in *The Marriage of Heaven and Hell* and in the figure who plays a prominent part in the early Lambeth books and in *Vala*—the demon Orc. We must now leave for a time the Neoplatonic mythology to consider further Blake's borrowings from alchemy, Boehme, and Swedenborg.

CHAPTER 14

The Demon Red

In *The Marriage of Heaven and Hell* Blake has his mind continually upon the Swedenborgian system, in part as the ground of his own, in part as that from which he wishes to define his own points of difference. Very few of Blake's critics have been fair to Swedenborg, and recognized him for the great figure that (his prosaic mind notwithstanding) he certainly was. When Blake wrote:

> As a new heaven is begun, and it is now thirty-three years since its advent, the Eternal Hell revives. And lo! Swedenborg is the Angel sitting at the tomb: his writings are the linen clothes folded up. Now is the dominion of Edom, & the return of Adam into Paradise; see Isaiah xxxiv & xxxv Chap.[1]

he was not casting doubt on Swedenborg's prophecy of a New Age, but assuming both the prophecy and Swedenborg's authenticity as the Angel; Blake did not reject Swedenborg for the reasons of a modern rationalist. For Blake he was not a madman gone astray in a world of fantasy; on the contrary, he was a man of conventional mind who did not realize the implications of his own teachings. In *Milton* Blake describes Swedenborg as the "strongest of men, the Samson shorn by the Churches."[2] Conventional religious ideas were the bonds that curbed his natural genius. This we may suppose to be Blake's final judgment upon him.

The central claim of Swedenborg's teaching is that a Last Judgment has been passed in the heavens[3] (that is, in the inner, spiritual world) upon all the Churches that had existed until the beginning of the New Age.[4] In 1757 "the New Heaven was formed, and a New Church established in the Heavens, which is understood by the New Jerusalem."[5]

It was a tenet of the Swedenborgians that a Last Judgment has taken place twice before: once at the time of the Flood and again "by the Lord himself when he was in the world." These cycles are an ever-recurring fact of history, for all things decline from spirituality to materiality, in the course of their realization: "every Church at it's Commencement is spiritual, for it takes it's Rise from Charity; but in Process of Time it declines from Charity to Faith, and then from an Internal Church becomes External, and when this is the Case, it is at an End, or no longer a Church." [6]

This decline, and necessary renewal, is implied in the "Argument" that prefaces the *Marriage:*

> *Now the sneaking serpent walks*
> *In mild humility,*
> *And the just man rages in the wilds*
> *Where lions roam.* [7]

The modern pilgrim is driven, in simple honesty, outside the Churches, whose "Heaven" is an exhausted platitude; and there is now more virtue to be found in the wilderness:

> *Then the perilous path was planted,*
> *And a river and a spring*
> *On every cliff and tomb,*
> *And on the bleached bones*
> *Red clay brought forth;*
>
> *Till the villain left the paths of ease,*
> *To walk in perilous paths, and drive*
> *The just man into barren climes.* [8]

So far this is orthodox Swedenborgian doctrine.

These verses are directly related to the chapters of Isaiah to which Blake refers in the next section. Isaiah 34:9–13 describes the divine vengeance that destroyed the land of Idumea (Edom), turning a heaven into a hell:

> And the streams thereof shall be turned into pitch, and the dust thereof into brimstone, and the land thereof shall become burning pitch.
>
> It shall not be quenched night nor day; the smoke thereof shall go up for ever: from generation to generation it shall lie waste; none shall pass through it for ever and ever. . . .

And thorns shall come up in her palace, nettles and brambles in the fortresses thereof: and it shall be a habitation of dragons, and a court for owls.

In Isaiah 35:1–9 is described the reversal of this creation of a hell from a heaven:

The wilderness and the solitary place shall be glad for them; and the desert shall rejoice, and blossom as the rose.

. . . for in the wilderness shall waters break out, and streams in the desert.

And the parched ground shall become a pool, and the thirsty land springs of water: in the habitation of dragons, where each lay, shall be grass with reeds and rushes.

And an highway shall be there, and a way, and it shall be called The way of holiness; the unclean shall not pass over it; but it shall be for those: the wayfaring men, though fools, shall not err therein.

No lion shall be there, nor any ravenous beast shall go up thereon, it shall not be found there; but the redeemed shall walk there.

We may take Blake's "Argument" simply as a gloss upon the orthodox reading of Isaiah. Chapter 34 in the Authorized Version is headed, "The joyful flourishing of Christ's Kingdom." Blake's meaning is that once again the time of reversal has come and the accursed land is to blossom again. So far this is but another variant of the theme of *The Mental Traveller*.

But paradise is, according to the tradition of Boehme and Swedenborg, the body; and Blake's "red clay" that brings forth is at once the land of Edom and the body of Adam, whose name also signifies the red clay:

> *Abstinence sows sand all over*
> *The ruddy limbs & flaming hair,*
> *But Desire Gratified*
> *Plants fruits of life & beauty there.*[9]

Blake was presently to develop this theme in Orc the demon of ruddy limbs and flaming hair; for he, also, is Edom or Esau (who is also so named). It is not merely the land of Edom, but the man Edom, Esau, or Adam, who is to be restored to his lost dominion. "The return of Adam to Paradise" means, therefore, the reintegration of the body, together with the physical universe, into the kingdom of the soul. This we could scarcely discover from the Bible alone, but if we interpret the symbolism of Edom according to Swedenborg, all becomes clear.

Swedenborg reads the story of the stolen birthright in a sense very different from other interpreters of the old legend. He holds that the birthright of Esau was in fact stolen by Jacob, and that the intention of Isaac was to bless Esau: "Whosoever pronounces a blessing, blesses him of whom he thinks, and not him at that time of whom he does not think . . . he who takes it, and thereby makes it his own, is like one who steals somewhat which is to be restored to another: that Isaac, when he pronounced blessing, thought of Esau, and not of Jacob, may appear from all and singular the things which precede." [10]

After a stated time, the blessing is to revert to Esau: "Then essential good, which lay intimately concealed, and thence arranged all and singular the things which appeared to be of truth or which truth had attributed to itself, comes forth and has open dominion." [11] "Now is the dominion of Edom" or, as Blake understood the parable, of the energies of life over the rational mind.

By Edom above all is represented "the Lord's divine human principle as to the natural and corporeal." [12] The reinstating of Edom, therefore, meant for Blake, as it did for Swedenborg, a reinstatement of the bodily man in the Divine Humanity of Jesus.

The dominion of Edom is Swedenborg's "New Heaven," the reign of the Divine Humanity. But also, since it reinstates corporeal humanity, it is said to be "the return of Adam to Paradise." Edom is the "red" land, Esau is "the red," and Adam, the bodily natural man, was made from the "red clay" of Edom. Now what was dead is to live again,

> *And on the bleached bones*
> *Red clay brought forth.*[13]

The tradition that Jesus was to enter his Kingdom by way of Edom is the Church's traditional reading of the text of Isaiah: "Who is this that cometh from Edom red as to his apparel, and his garments as one that treadeth in the wine-press?" The esoteric meaning of the coming of Jesus from Edom is that his divinity enters the world in or through the flesh—the red earth from which Adam was made.[14]

Orc, the energy of life, first appears by name in *America*, but his attributes are identical with those of "the new-born terror" of *A Song of*

Liberty. This babe appears in the designs of the *Marriage.* On the third page, under the text that begins, "As a new heaven is begun . . . Now is the dominion of Edom," there is depicted a woman in labor and a babe leaping from her womb. This is the red hairy Esau, the first-born, who now is to inherit his stolen birthright. Blake's Orc is called "red Orc," and in *America* he is "the hairy youth"; his "hairy shoulders rend the links." Esau was born both red and hairy, "wholly red, as an hairy garment." He is the prototype of Orc, the "frowning babe" whose hour has come.

In the figure of Orc Blake has personified his vision of "hell, or energy"; he is called a "demon," and his name suggests Orcus (hell). Other roots of the name suggest no less. There are two orcs in Ariosto's *Orlando furioso*,[15] and both are destroying monsters. Ariosto's first orc is a sea monster based upon the ravisher of maidens turned to stone by Perseus; the second resembles Homer's Cyclops, but he too keeps in his cave not shipwrecked sailors but maidens: both share with Blake's demon sexual passion. Orcs, according to the Oxford Dictionary, are a kind of whale; and the name was "formerly applied to more than one vaguely identified sea-monster." Blake's Orc, too, is also called "a Whale in the South-sea."[16] In this sense the word was used by Milton:

> *. . . then shall this Mount*
> *Of Paradise by might of Waves be moovd*
> *Out of his place, pushd by the horned floud,*
> *With all his verdure spoil'd, and Trees adrift*
> *Down the great River to the op'ning Gulf,*
> *And there take root an Iland salt and bare,*
> *The haunt of Seales and Orcs, and Sea-mews clang.*[17]

Orc is the only one of Blake's Zoas whose place of birth is specified: he is born upon the mountains of Atlantis. "On those infinite mountains of light, now barr'd out by the atlantic sea, the new born fire stood before the starry king!"[18] The lost Atlantis is yet another version of the myth of the lost paradise. Its "infinite mountains" are the same holy mountain that Milton describes as overwhelmed by the sea of hyle. Orc's birthplace is paradise; and paradise, in the esoteric sense, is the body itself, the world of the senses. Adam's body is "created out of the eternal element which was and is Paradise." Edom is Swedenborg's symbol for that lost paradise, the body, birthplace of the Divine Humanity. Milton's description of the fate of the Mount of Paradise is like the story of Edom, once fertile, but laid under a curse. With all these themes in mind, we may understand the depth of meaning of Blake's symbol of the birth of Orc into the land accursed, which, in the restoration of Christ's Kingdom, is to flower again in its original beauty.

Between the mountains of Atlantis (now submerged, like Milton's mountain, by the ocean of hyle) and the heavenly world there was formerly direct communication:

> *On those vast shady hills between America &· Albion's shore,*
> *Now barr'd out by the Atlantic sea, call'd Atlantean hills,*
> *Because from their bright summits you may pass to the Golden world,*
> *An ancient palace, archetype of mighty Emperies,*
> *Rears its immortal pinnacles, built in the forest of God*
> *By Ariston, the king of beauty, for his stolen bride.*[19]

This is to say that the body communicated, in man's unfallen state, with the eternal world itself, the "sweet golden clime." But this is no longer so, for the body is a place accursed. Instead of living in joy on "infinite mountains of light," Orc is chained "to the iron mountain's top."

Like the Infant Sorrow, he leaps into this "dangerous world" with all its tragic conditions,

> *Helpless, naked, piping loud,*
> *Like a fiend hid in a cloud.*[20]

On page 19 of the Notebook there is a pencil drawing (later used as one of the emblems of *The Gates of Paradise*) of a schoolboy knocking down fairies, like butterflies, with his hat. Under the drawing Blake wrote some lines from *The Faerie Queene*:

[109]
> *Ah lucklesse babe, born under cruel starre,*
> *And in dead parents balefull ashes bred,*
> *Full litle weenest thou, what sorrowes are*
> *Left thee for portion of thy livelihed.*[21]

Spenser's babe is the newborn child of Mordant and Amavia, and the blood of his dead parents cannot be washed from his hands. Red Orc is akin to this red-handed babe, like him "conceived and born in sin," no sooner entered into the world of Experience than its conditions weigh heavily upon him.

109 Schoolboy knocking down fairies: Blake's Note-
book, p. 19
The faint pencil writing below is the passage from
Spenser quoted on p. 340.

The place of Orc's birth is already told in *A Song of Liberty*, but its
manner only later, in *The Book of Urizen*. He is born in fury and sorrow:

> *Delving earth in his resistless way,*
> *Howling, the Child with fierce flames*
> *Issu'd from Enitharmon.*[22]

Los takes his newborn son:

> *In his hands he siez'd the infant,*
> *He bathed him in springs of sorrow,*
> *He gave him to Enitharmon.*[23]

This action of Los is imitated from that of Spenser's Sir Guyon, who
likewise washes the red-handed child in a spring that could well be called a
spring of sorrow, since its waters flow from the eyes of a nymph turned to
stone. This weeping nymph is, of course, but a variant of the myth of the
Cave of the Nymphs, whose waters are the ever-flowing source of mortal
life:

> *Then soft himselfe inclyning on his knee*
> *Downe to that well, did in the water weene*
> .   .   .

His guiltie hands from bloudie gore to cleene,
He washt them oft and oft, yet nought they beene
For all his washing cleaner. Still he strove,
Yet still the litle hands were bloudie seene.

In *The Four Zoas* the birth of Orc is again described, with some details added:

[110]

The groans of Enitharmon shake the skies, the lab'ring Earth,
Till from her heart rending his way, a terrible child sprang forth
In thunder, smoke & sullen flames, & howlings & fury & blood.

Soon as his burning Eyes were open'd on the Abyss,
The horrid trumpets of the deep bellow'd with bitter blasts.
The Enormous Demons woke & howl'd around the new born King,
Crying, "Luvah, King of Love, thou art the King of rage & death." [24]

This is an infernal Nativity, written according to the Bible of hell. The newborn king is trumpeted not by angels of heaven but by demons of the Abyss:

Enitharmon nurs'd her fiery child in the dark deeps
Sitting in darkness . . . [25]

Blake's "deeps" always recall the alchemical "As above, so below"; and the god who is the gentle Luvah above, is Orc below:

. . . Luvah hath burst his way from Enitharmon.
When Thought is clos'd in Caves Then love shall shew its root in
deepest Hell.[26]

One of the roots of the myth of Orc is the Swedenborgian "chimney-sweeper" of the "seminal vessels" of the Grand Man, whence perhaps one of the associations of his name, ὄρχις (testicle). The little spirit who is called "black" but who turns into a form of shining radiance well expresses Blake's vision of the innocence of sexual desire, whose passionate dreams are all of

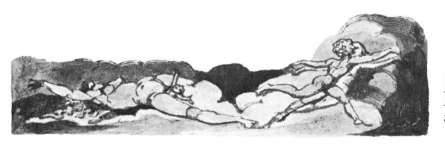

110 Birth of Orc: *The Marriage of Heaven and Hell* (1790–93?), plate 3, bottom detail

the lost paradise. But in the world of Experience, Eros is condemned as a demon even in his infant form:

> *Infancy! fearless, lustful, happy, nestling for delight*
> *In laps of pleasure: Innocence! honest, open, seeking*
> *The vigorous joys of morning light; open to virgin bliss.*
> *Who taught thee modesty, subtil modesty, child of night and sleep?* [27]

In *A Little Boy Lost* [28] the spontaneity of the energy of self-delighting life is condemned. In the allegorical burning of this innocent who is called a "fiend" Blake must have remembered that one little boy was actually burned by Calvin in Geneva for striking his father.

> *The weeping child could not be heard,*
> *The weeping parents wept in vain;*
> *They strip'd him to his little shirt,*
> *And bound him in an iron chain;*
>
> *And burn'd him in a holy place,*
> *Where many had been burn'd before:*
> *The weeping parents wept in vain.*
> *Are such things done on Albion's shore?* [28]

The same story is expanded into the myth of Orc, first told in *The Book of Urizen*, V1. Los becomes jealous of his son's love for his mother Enitharmon. Each day his jealousy forms a tight "girdle" round his bosom; and as each is broken, yet another forms:

> *. . . O sorrow & pain!*
> *A tight'ning girdle grew*
> *Around his bosom. In sobbings*
> *He burst the girdle in twain;*
> *But still another girdle*
> *Oppress'd his bosom. In sobbings*
> *Again he burst it. Again*
> *Another girdle succeeds.*
> *The girdle was form'd by day,*
> *By night was burst in twain.*
>
> *These falling down on the rock*
> *Into an iron Chain*
> *In each other link by link lock'd.*

111 Enitharmon, Orc, and Los: *Urizen* (1794), plate 21

> *They took Orc to the top of a mountain.*
> *O how Enitharmon wept!*
> *They chain'd his young limbs to the rock*
> *With the Chain of Jealousy* [29]

The later version – *The Four Zoas*, Night V – is fuller but substantially the same.

[111]   An illustration to the account given in *The Book of Urizen* shows Orc, a beautiful half-grown boy, embracing Enitharmon, who looks only at Orc, while Los, excluded, is overcome with jealous grief, the chain forming about him. The later account leaves no doubt that Enitharmon, on her side, returns the love of Orc, according to the classical situation:

> *. . . He siez'd the boy in his immortal hands,*
> *While Enitharmon follow'd him, weeping in dismal woe,*
> *Up to the iron mountain's top, & there the jealous chain*
> *Fell from his bosom on the mountain. The spectre dark*

344

The text within the illustration reads:

Preludium

The shadowy daughter of Urthona stood before red Orc.
When fourteen suns had faintly journey'd o'er his dark abode;
His food she brought in iron baskets, his drink in cups of iron;
Crown'd with a helmet & dark hair the nameless female stood;
A quiver with its burning stores, a bow like that of night,
When pestilence is shot from heaven; no other arms she need:
Invulnerable tho' naked, save where clouds roll round her loins,
Their awful folds in the dark air; silent she stood as night;
For never from her iron tongue could voice or sound arise;
But dumb till that dread day when Orc assay'd his fierce embrace.

Dark virgin; said the hairy youth, thy father stern abhorr'd;
Rivet my tenfold chains while still on high my spirit soars;
Sometimes an eagle screaming in the sky, sometimes a lion,
Stalking upon the mountains, & sometimes a whale I lash
The raging fathomless abyss, anon a serpent folding
Around the pillars of Urthona, and round thy dark limbs,
On the Canadian wilds I fold, feeble my spirit folds.
For chain'd beneath I rend these caverns; when thou bringest food
I howl my joy and my red eyes seek to behold thy face;
In vain! these clouds roll to & fro, & hide thee from my sight.

112 Orc fettered by Los and Enitharmon: *America* (1793), plate 2

Compare the figure in "The Mental Traveller" as described on p. 309. The small figure below the roots may be Orc in "deepest hell"; see p. 342, l. 22.

Held the fierce boy. Los nail'd him down, binding around his limbs [112]
The accursed chain. O how bright Enitharmon howl'd & cried
Over her son! Obdurate, Los bound down her loved Joy.

The hammer of Urthona smote the rivets in terror, of brass
Tenfold; the Demon's rage flam'd tenfold forth, rending,
Roaring, redounding, . . .[30]

The manner of the forming of the chain of jealousy suggests Odin's golden ring, which every ninth night produced eight rings of equal weight. Los, like Odin, is the maker of the "mighty chains" of temporal sequence, of hours and months and days. This chain of time is illustrated in *Jerusalem*, page 65, where it is shown descending, with all its oppressive weight, the full length of the margin. Blake deepens the meaning of the symbol, understanding how the chain becomes a heavy burden, more binding as each day renews the sorrows of the last, until the chain that at first binds only the father shackles the son.

The fettering of Orc to the mountain suggests Prometheus manacled to his mountain rock by Hephaestos, the smith-god, who has many attributes in common with Los. But, again, there is an episode in the Eddas that is even nearer to Blake's myth. The gods of Asgard, warned by their oracles that the wolf Fenris would one day prove fatal to them, "determined to make very strong iron fetters for him, and presenting them to the Wolf, desired him to put them on to shew his strength, in endeavouring to break them." The wolf breaks the first set of fetters and a second; then a strong cord was bound upon him, "but the more efforts he made, the closer and straiter he drew the knot . . . Observing him then so fast tied, as to be unable ever to get loose again, they took one end of the string, and having drilled a hole for it, drew it through the middle of a large broad rock, which they sunk very deep into the earth." [31] The gods also pierced the jaw of the wolf with a sword: "The howlings which he then made were horrible; and since that time, the foam flows continually from his mouth, in such abundance that it forms a river, called *Vam*, or The Vices."

Orc's chaining is like that of Fenris; [31a] for the chain that binds him goes down to the rocky center of the earth, and can never after be loosed. Los repents his stern jealousy, "parental love return'd," and he goes with Enitharmon to free their son; but it is too late:

> But when they came to the dark rock & to the spectrous cave,
> Lo, the young limbs had strucken root into the rock, & strong
> Fibres had from the Chain of Jealousy inwove themselves
> In a swift vegetation round the rock & round the Cave
> And over the immortal limbs of the terrible fiery boy.
> In vain they strove now to unchain. . . .
> . . . not Enitharmon's death
> Nor the Consummation of Los could ever melt the chain
> Nor unroot the infernal fibres from their rocky bed,
>
>   .   .   .
>
> . . . for it had taken root
> Into the iron rock & grew a chain beneath the Earth
> Even to the Center, wrapping round the Center; & the limbs
> Of Orc entering with fibres become one with him, a living Chain
> Sustained by the Demon's life. . . . [32]

[113]

A detail from another Norse legend has gone into the forging of Orc's living chain. Loki, spirit of evil, is, like Fenris, bound with cords of restraint,

Thus wept the Angel voice & as he wept the terrible blasts
Of trumpets, blew a loud alarm across the Atlantic deep.
No trumpets answer; no reply of clarions or of fifes,
Silent the Colonies remain and refuse the loud alarm.

On those vast shady hills between America & Albions shore;
Now barr'd out by the Atlantic sea: call'd Atlantean hills:
Because from their bright summits you may pass to the Golden world
An ancient palace, archetype of mighty Emperies,
Rears its immortal pinnacles, built in the forest of God
By Ariston the king of beauty for his stolen bride.

Here on their magic seats the thirteen Angels sat perturb'd
For clouds from the Atlantic hover oer the solemn roof.

113 Orc in the fires of energy:
America (1793), plate 10

made from the intestines of his own son; these cords were afterward changed into chains of iron. Blake, in the myth of Orc, has used this grim metamorphosis; for the chain is first a "bloody cord" [33] formed about Los's bosom, and the human fiber presently turns into the links of a chain of iron. Bound upon Orc, it again changes from iron to flesh and blood. Blake understood that what is at first an inner condition of the father's mind presently becomes an external restraint laid upon the son, and that an external restraint, once imposed, turns again into an inner condition, no longer to be removed, even by those who first imposed it.

"War is energy enslav'd." Thus, chained and manacled, Orc becomes enslaved and is the god of war. The demon is "red" with bloodshed. Blake was neither for war nor against it; he understood what it was: the last resource of the energies of life, under the oppression of law, empire, exploitation, and the tyranny of the ruler of this world under whatever form:

"war is honest energy." Blake did not ask what the living principle ought to do; he knew what it will do. Since life is holy, no judgment can be passed upon that which is beyond human understanding. Human morality cannot pass judgment upon the divine essence. Thus, while we cannot say that Blake favored war, we can certainly say that he was on the side of life; and there are times when life manifests its power as war. Perhaps it would be true to say that Blake was for all war against tyrants, but never for war made by tyrants against life. He was on the side of revolution, not only of some particular revolution but of all revolutions; for that which revolts is life, that against which life revolts is tyranny. A pacifist he was not. His first prophetic poem, *The French Revolution*, is a celebration of war. What seemed evil to him was the injustice that makes revolt inevitable and right, not the spirit of revolt. Yet he well knew what appalling forms Orc may be forced into by the tyrant. Let life be free, then, he would say, and the "demon red" will be the spirit of joy and love, the manifestation of life unhindered and beautiful.

Thus in *Europe* Blake celebrated the French Revolution with Orc as a liberator–a terrible Bacchanalia. The Dionysian Orc is lord of the harvest of war, crowned "with garlands of the ruddy vine" [34] in "the vineyards of red France." The treading of the grapes of wrath is a biblical symbol and associated with Edom. Isaiah prophesies a Messiah who brings not peace but a sword:

> Who is this that cometh from Edom, with dyed garments from Bozrah? . . .
>
> Wherefore art thou red in thine apparel, and thy garments like him that treadeth in the winefat?
>
> I have trodden the winepress alone; and of the people there was none with me: for I will tread them in mine anger, and trample them in my fury; and their blood shall be sprinkled upon my garments, and I will stain all my raiment.
>
> For the day of vengeance is in mine heart, and the year of my redeemed is come.
>
> And I looked, and there was none to help; and I wondered that there was none to uphold: therefore mine own arm brought salvation unto me; and my fury, it upheld me.
>
> And I will tread down the people in mine anger, and make them drunk in my fury, and I will bring down their strength to the earth. [35]

This is the "frowning babe" to whose birth into European history Blake bore prophetic witness; his wrath is holy, for he is the Messiah who brings not peace but a sword.

The creed of the humanist who, believing this life to be all, sees death as the worst of evils was no more for Blake than it was for the prophet who wrote of the harvest of the earth:

> And I looked, and behold a white cloud, and upon the cloud one sat like unto the Son of man, having on his head a golden crown, and in his hand a sharp sickle.
>
> And another angel came out of the temple, crying with a loud voice to him that sat on the cloud, Thrust in thy sickle, and reap: for the time is come for thee to reap; for the harvest of the earth is ripe.
>
> And he that sat on the cloud thrust in his sickle on the earth; and the earth was reaped.[36]

Blake, when in *Vala* IX he wrote his own vision of the Last Judgment, named the angel of the harvest not Orc but Luvah, spirit of love.

> . . . *Luvah sat*
> *Above on the bright heavens in peace; the Spirits of Men beneath*
> *Cried out to be deliver'd, & the spirit of Luvah wept*
> *Over the human harvest . . .*[37]

Urizen is the angel with the sickle,[38] death the reaper:

> *Then Urizen arose & took his sickle in his hand.*
> *There is a brazen sickle, & a scythe of iron hid*
> *Deep in the South, guarded by a few solitary stars.*
> *This sickle Urizen took; the scythe his sons embrac'd*
> *And went forth & began to reap; & all his joyful sons*
> *Reap'd the wide Universe & bound in sheaves a wondrous harvest* [39]

The sickle of death is associated with Porphyry's southern gate, by which souls die from this world.

In *Milton* the wine press is called "the Wine-press of Los," who is "by mortals nam'd Time"; and "Luvah laid the foundation & Urizen finish'd it in howling woe." It is also called "the Printing-Press Of Los." Upon these presses the tragi-heroic story of the unending battle is printed, the long record of war that man calls history. Blake lived (who does not?) in a time of war, and he had read much history—Herodotus, Plutarch, Josephus,

Gibbon, Geoffrey of Monmouth—and all the epics of battle, from Homer to Milton; and he looked upon that vision of unending slaughter as all prophets must: there can be no doubt that Blake contemplating the overthrow of tyrants was on the side of the tygers of wrath.

> *Go down, ye Kings & Councellors & Giant Warriors,*
> *Go down into the depths, go down & hide yourselves beneath,*
> *Go down with horse & Chariots & Trumpets of hoarse war.*
>
> *Lo, how the Pomp of Mystery goes down into the Caves!*
> *Her great men howl & throw the dust, & rend their hoary hair.*
> *Her delicate women & children shriek upon the bitter wind,*
> *Spoil'd of their beauty, their hair rent & their skin shrivel'd up.*
> *Lo, darkness covers the long pomp of banners on the wind,*
> *And black horses & armed men & miserable bound captives.*
> *Where shall the graves recieve them all, & where shall be their*
>
> > > *place?* [40]

So the long war has always gone on and always will until

> *. . . the Vintage is over*
> *And all gather'd in, till the Plow has pass'd over the Nations*
> *And the Harrow & heavy thundering Roller upon the mountains.* [41]

The Great Battle is one of the archetypal themes of all religions, including the Christian, whether as myth—as in the Norse legends of the Twilight of the Gods—or as a metaphysical theme, as in the Bhagavad-Gita. Blake's vision of the great armies going down to the grave recalls Arjuna's vision of Krishna in his terrible aspect as "Time, the destroyer of mankind," with "widely-opened mouths and bright expanded eyes":

> The sons of Dhreetarashtra, now, with all those rulers of the land, Bheeshma, Dron, the son of Soot, and even the fronts of our army, seem to be precipitating themselves hastily into thy mouths, discovering such frightful rows of teeth! whilst some appear to stick between thy teeth with their bodies sorely mangled. As the rapid streams of full flowing rivers roll on to meet the ocean's bed; even so these heroes of the human race rush on towards thy flaming mouths. As troops of insects, with increasing speed, seek their own destruction in the flaming fire, even so these people, with swelling fury, seek their

own destruction. Thou involvest and swallowest them altogether, even unto the last, with thy flaming mouths, whilst the whole world is filled with thy glory, as thy awful beams, O Veeshnoo, shine forth on all sides.[42]

Los, also, as Lord of the wine press, is "Time, the destroyer."

Blake had read Wilkins' *Geeta* [43] before 1795, when he wrote *The Song of Los*. This poem opens with a survey of all the major religions of mankind; Blake would not have written such a commentary had he not read the scriptures of the religions he names: Odin's "code of war," the "loose Bible" of Mohammed, the philosophy of Trismegistus, Pythagoras, Socrates, and Plato, and the Hindu philosophy:

> *. . . Rintrah gave Abstract Philosophy* [44] *to Brama* [45] *in the East.*
> (*Night spoke to the Cloud:*
> "*Lo these Human form'd spirits, in smiling hipocrisy, War*
> *Against one another; so let them War on, slaves to the eternal*
> *Elements.*") [46]

If we but substitute the Lord Krishna for "Night," and the mortal warrior Arjuna for the "Cloud," this is seen to be a paraphrase of the teaching of Krishna to Arjuna.

The epic opens upon the scene of the battlefield, where the opposing armies are drawn up in all their power and glory; and Arjuna, seeing on both sides blood relations, friends, and teachers, declares that he will not fight: "I wish not to fight them; not even for the dominion of the three regions of the universe, much less for this little earth." Krishna replies that the war must go on; why grieve for those for whom no grief is due:

> The wise neither grieve for the dead nor for the living. I myself never *was not*, nor thou, nor all the princes of the earth; nor shall we ever hereafter cease *to be*. As the soul in this mortal frame findeth infancy, youth, and old age; so, in some future frame, will it find the like. . . . These bodies, which envelope the souls which inhabit them, which are eternal, incorruptible, and surpassing all conception, are declared to be finite beings; wherefore, O *Arjoon*, resolve to fight. The man who believeth that it is the soul which killeth, and he who thinketh that the soul may be destroyed, are both alike deceived; for it neither killeth, nor is killed.

The soul, Lord Krishna continues, is without birth and without death: "As a man throweth away old garments, and putteth on new, even so the soul, having quitted its old mortal frames, entereth into others which are new. The weapon divideth it not, the fire burneth it not, the water corrupteth it not, the wind drieth it not away." [47]

Blake argues that it is hypocrisy to make war on the pretext that no one is really killed; but for the rest there is little difference between his own vision of the Great Battle and that of Krishna; the incarnating spirits plunge again and again into the elements, returning to the battlefield:

> *But in the Wine presses is wailing, terror & despair.*
> *Forsaken of their Elements they vanish & are no more,*
> *No more but a desire of Being, a distracted, ravening desire.*
> *Desiring like the hungry worm & like the gaping grave.*
> *They plunge into the Elements; the Elements cast them forth*
> *Or else consume their shadowy semblance. Yet they, obstinate*
> *Tho' pained to distraction, cry, "O let us Exist! for*
> *This dreadful Non Existence is worse than pains of Eternal Birth:*
> *Eternal death who can Endure? let us consume in fires,*
> *In waters stifling, or in air corroding, or in earth shut up.*
> *The Pangs of Eternal birth are better than the Pangs of Eternal*
> *   death."* [48]

The souls who plunge into the elements to be cast forth again and again, and "Tho' pained to distraction, cry, O let us Exist," are the same as the "human formed spirits" of *The Song of Los*, who "war on, slaves to the eternal Elements"; and the passage:

> *. . . Let us consume in fires,*
> *In waters stifling, or in air corroding, or in earth shut up*

seems to echo Lord Krishna's words spoken of the soul: "The weapon divideth it not, the fire burneth it not, the water corrupteth it not, the wind drieth it not away." The specters do not know the immortality that Krishna taught, and in which Blake also, of course, believed.

Blake's "Pangs of Eternal birth" bring the souls back to the battle again and again; but this, they say, is better than the "Eternal death" that would come about from a refusal to go on with the Great Battle; for with all its suffering, it is an affirmation of life, the process by which the souls are harvested. The anguish of the body is as nothing to the "Eternal death" of the apathetic soul who refuses to engage in life. In the Norse mythology he so much admired [49] Blake found the same view of the Great Battle.

Certainly this battle is not easy to see justified except in terms of a perpetual return of souls to incarnation; Plotinus taught the same, and Blake had no doubt read his discourse *On Providence:*

> But the arms which men mutually employ against each other, since they are mortal, and contend in a becoming order, like those who sport by dancing in armour, plainly declare that all the studies of men are mere sports, and that dissolution is by no means to be accounted dreadful and hard. So that those who are suddenly slain in battle only anticipate future death in old age, by passing away more swiftly and returning again. . . . We ought therefore to contemplate the slaughter and destruction of cities, the rapine and prey, like the scenes in a theatre, as nothing more than certain transmutations and alternate changes of figures; and weeping and distress every where as delusive and fictitious. For in the particular acts of human life, it is not the interior soul and the true man, but the exterior shadow of the man alone, which laments and weeps.[50]

Did Blake assume reincarnation? Scholars differ on this point: Northrop Frye and others say that he did not; Yeats thought that he did. Milton O. Percival suggests that Blake held the higher philosophic view that Spirit is the only transmigrant. On the evidence of such passages as the last quoted, I am inclined to Yeats's opinion, the more so as there are, in this passage, echoes of the Gita.

Luvah, god of the wine press, is, after the great harvest, the cupbearer at "the Golden Feast"; and "the wine of delight" (love) and "the bread of sweet thought" (wisdom) are the food of eternity.

From the great vintage the "Odors of life" are distilled:

> *Down, down thro' the immense with outcry, fury & despair,*
> *Into the wine presses of Luvah; howling fell the clusters*
> *Of human families thro' the deep; the wine presses were fill'd;*
> *The blood of life flow'd plentiful. Odors of life arose*
> *All round the heavenly arches, & the Odors rose singing this song:*
>
> *"O terrible wine presses of Luvah! O caverns of the Grave!*

How lovely the delights of those risen again from death!
O trembling joy! excess of joy is like Excess of grief."
So sang the Human Odors round the wine presses of Luvah.[51]

"In pain the human harvest wav'd, in horrible groans of woe." [52] But it is
after this harvest of sorrow that

> *. . . the Eternal Man*
> *Sat at the feast rejoicing, & the wine of Eternity*
> *Was serv'd round by the flames of Luvah all day & all the night.*[53]

The odors bring us back, once again, to that other god of the vintage,
Dionysus. Taylor calls Dionysus "intellect": "by Dionys[i]us, or Bacchus. . . . we must understand the intellect of the mundane soul." [54] This
intellectual essence is "scattered into generation," and by the dismembering
and resurrection of the god, "the procession or distribution of intellect into
matter, and its subsequent conversion from thence, is evidently implied."
This is suggested in the account of the "Odors" that ascend from "the human
grapes," like souls rejoicing as they rise from death. Such strange personification of the "Odors" ("So sang the Human Odors round the wine
presses of Luvah") is explicable and justifiable when we remember that
"from the exhalations formed from the ashes of the burning bodies of the
Titans, mankind were produced," [55] and that distillation is a central symbol
of the cult of the wine-god. Those purified by the Dionysian initiation were
called Bacchuses, as partaking of the nature of the god whose pure essence is
distilled from the grapes. This symbolism of the distribution and resurrection of Intellect (Blake uses this word) is clearly present in Los's summons
to the Great Vintage:

> *Fellow Labourers! The Great Vintage & Harvest is now upon Earth.*
> *The whole extent of the Globe is explored. Every scatter'd Atom*
> *Of Human Intellect now is flocking to the sound of the Trumpet.*
> *All the Wisdom which was hidden in caves & dens from ancient*
> *Time is now sought out from Animal & Vegetable & Mineral.*[56]

It would not be true to say that Luvah is based upon Dionysus, but
because the Great Vintage forms part of the Orc-Luvah cycle, some of the
symbolic attributes of that god are incorporated into the myth, for like
Isaiah's Messiah and the Angel of Revelation, he is Lord of the Vintage.

But the Wine-press of Los is eastward of Golgonooza before the Seat
Of Satan. Luvah laid the foundation & Urizen finish'd it in howling woe.
How red the sons & daughters of Luvah! here they tread the grapes.
Laughing & shouting drunk with odours many fall, oerwearied
Drown'd in the wine is many a youth & maiden: those around
Lay them on skins of Tygers & of the spotted Leopard & the Wild Ass
Till they revive, or bury them in cool grots, making lamentation.
This Wine-press is call'd War on Earth, it is the Printing-Press
Of Los; and here he lays his words in order above the mortal brain
As cogs are form'd in a wheel to turn the cogs of the adverse wheel.
Timbrels & violins sport round the Wine-presses: the little Seed;
The sportive Root, the Earth-worm, the gold Beetle: the wise Emmet;
Dance round the Wine-presses of Luvah: the Centipede is there:
The ground Spider with many eyes: the Mole clothed in velvet
The ambitious Spider in his sullen web: the lucky golden Spinner:
The Earwig arm'd: the tender Maggot emblem of immortality:
The Flea: Louse: Bug: the Tape-Worm: all the Armies of Disease:
Visible or invisible to the slothful vegetating Man.
The slow Slug: the Grasshopper that sings & laughs & drinks:
Winter comes: he folds his slender bones without a murmur.
The cruel Scorpion is there: the Gnat: Wasp: Hornet & the Honey Bee:
The Toad & venomous Newt: the Serpent clothd in gems & gold:
They throw off their gorgeous raiment: they rejoice with loud jubilee
Around the Wine-presses of Luvah, naked & drunk with wine.
There is the Nettle that stings with soft down: and there
The indignant Thistle: whose bitterness is bred in his milk:
Who feeds on contempt of his neighbour: there all the idle Weeds
That creep around the obscure places, shew their various limbs.
Naked in all their beauty dancing round the Wine-presses.

114 Vermin of the wine press: *Milton* (1804–1808), plate 29, detail

Blake in his eclecticism was nothing if not thorough. From the symbolic theme of the wine harvest it was natural that he should pass to Vergil's charming description of a real threshing-floor, from the first *Georgic:*

> Delve of convenient Depth your threshing Floor;
> With temper'd Clay, then fill and face it o're:
> And let the weighty Rowler run the round,
> To smooth the Surface of th'unequal Ground;
> Lest crack'd with Summer Heats the flooring flies,
> Or sinks, and thro' the Crannies Weeds arise.
> For sundry Foes the Rural Realm surround:
> The Field Mouse builds her Garner under ground
> For gather'd Grain the blind laborious Mole,
> In winding Mazes works her hidden Hole.
> In hollow Caverns Vermine make abode,
> The hissing Serpent, and the swelling Toad:
> The Corn devouring Weezel here abides,
> And the wise Ant her wintry Store provides.[57]

This passage gave Blake the groundwork of his beautiful description of the vermin of the wine press that first occurs in *The Four Zoas* [58] and is repeated in *Milton*, with certain alterations and additions, all of them apparently intended to stress the imagery of war and disease.

[114]

And the clouds & fires pale rolld round in the night of Enitharmon
Round Albions cliffs & Londons walls: still Enitharmon slept:
Rolling volumes of grey mist involve Churches, Palaces, Towers:
For Urizen unclaspd his Book; feeding his soul with pity
The youth of England hid in gloom curse the paind heavens; compelld
Into the deadly night to see the form of Albions Angel
Their parents brought them forth & aged ignorance preaches canting:
On a vast rock, perceivd by those senses that are closd from thought:
Bleak, dark, abrupt, it stands & overshadows London city
They saw his bony feet on the rock, the flesh consumd in flames:
They saw the Serpent temple lifted above, shadowing the Island white:
They heard the voice of Albions Angel howling in flames of Orc,
Seeking the trump of the last doom

Above the rest the howl was heard from Westminster louder & louder:
The Guardian of the secret codes forsook his ancient mansion,
Driven out by the flames of Orc; his furrd robes & false locks
Adhered and grew one with his flesh and nerves & veins shot thro' them
With dismal torment sick hanging upon the wind: he fled
Groveling along Great George Street thro' the Park gate; all the soldiers
Fled from his sight: he dragd his torments to the wilderness.

Thus was the howl thro Europe!
For Orc rejoicd to hear the howling shadows
But Palamabron shot his lightnings trenching down his wide back
And Rintrah hung with all his legions in the nether deep

Enitharmon laughd in her sleep to see (O womans triumph)
Every house a den, every man bound; the shadows are filld
With spectres, and the windows wove over with curses of iron:
Over the doors Thou shalt not; & over the chimneys Fear is written:
With bands of iron round their necks fastend into the walls
The citizens: in leaden gyves the inhabitants of suburbs
Walk heavy: soft and bent are the bones of villagers

Between the clouds of Urizen the flames of Orc roll heavy
Around the limbs of Albions Guardian, his flesh consuming
Howlings & hissings, shrieks & groans, & voices of despair
Arise around him in the cloudy
Heavens of Albion, Furious

115 Insects and cobwebs:
Europe (1794), plate 10

All the creatures listed may be seen as emblems of evil, but also, in
Blake's symbolic terms of hell, of energy and delight, as "portions of
eternity," if not, like "the roaring of lions, the howling of wolves, the raging
of the stormy sea, and the destructive sword," too great, then at all events too
strange, for the eye of man:

> *This Wine-press is call'd War on Earth: it is the Printing-Press*
> *Of Los, and here he lays his words in order above the mortal brain,*
> *As cogs are form'd in a wheel to turn the cogs of the adverse wheel.*

Timbrels & violins sport round the Wine-presses; the little Seed,
The sportive Root, the Earth-worm, the gold Beetle, the wise Emmet
Dance round the Wine-presses of Luvah: the Centipede is there,
The ground Spider with many eyes, the Mole clothed in velvet,
The ambitious Spider in his sullen web, the lucky golden Spinner,   [115]
The Earwig arm'd, the tender Maggot, emblem of immortality,
The Flea, Louse, Bug, the Tape-Worm, all the Armies of Disease,
Visible or invisible to the slothful vegetating Man.
The slow Slug, the Grasshopper that sings & laughs & drinks:
Winter comes, he folds his slender bones without a murmur.
The cruel Scorpion is there, the Gnat, Wasp, Hornet & the Honey
                                     Bee,
The Toad & venomous Newt, the Serpent cloth'd in gems & gold.
They throw off their gorgeous raiment: they rejoice with loud jubilee
Around the Wine-presses of Luvah, naked & drunk with wine.

There is the Nettle that stings with soft down, and there
The indignant Thistle whose bitterness is bred in his milk,
Who feeds on contempt of his neighbour: there all the idle Weeds
That creep around the obscure places shew their various limbs
Naked in all their beauty dancing round the Wine-presses.[59]

This is evidently a Bacchanalia. The earlier version forms part of a bacchanalian revelry at the Great Vintage, based perhaps on Blake's favorite work of Ovid, the *Fasti*. Not only have we "Timbrels & violins"; Luvah,

. . . descending to the Vineyards bright.
His sons, arising from the feast with golden baskets, follow,
A fiery train, as when the Sun sings in the ripe vineyards.
Then Luvah stood before the Wine press: all his fiery sons
Brought up the loaded Waggons with shoutings; ramping tygers
                                     play
In the jingling traces; furious lions sound the song of joy
To the golden wheels circling upon the pavement of heaven, & all
The Villages of Luvah ring; the golden tiles of the villages
Reply to violins & tabors, to the pipe, flute, lyre, & cymbal.[60]

There is explicit allusion to two of Bacchus' cult objects a few lines below, the skins of the leopard and the ass:

116 Pitt guiding Behemoth: tempera (1808?)

How red the sons & daughters of Luvah! how they tread the Grapes!
Laughing & shouting, drunk with odors, many fall o'erwearied:
Drown'd in the wine is many a youth & maiden; those around
Lay them on skins of tygers or the spotted Leopard or Wild Ass.[61]

Did Blake continue to hold this view of war, expressed most violently
in the early Lambeth poems, but still implicit in the passages describing the

wine presses in *Milton?* Certainly he ceased to believe that the French Revolution heralded the Last Judgment of the world and the reign of Jesus, as perhaps he had at one time half-believed; the later version of the struggles of Orc and Vala are clear proof of this change of mind upon the righteousness of that particular war. In *Jerusalem,*

> . . . *Fenelon, Guion, Teresa,*
> *Whitefield & Hervey guard that Gate, with all the gentle Souls*
> *Who guide the great Wine-press of Love. . . .*[62]

It is now the quietists and the people of prayer who guide the wine press. He condemned, in his preface to *Milton,* "the silly Greek & Latin slaves of the Sword." Perhaps this is a recantation. And yet his two paintings of the Spiritual Forms of Pitt and Nelson showed that Blake saw the war against Napoleon as righteously waged by the two great powers of land and sea. He still saw war as a divine act. Addison had written of Marlborough,

> *Pleas'd the Almighty's orders to perform*
> *He rides the whirlwind, and directs the storm*

and Blake, stirred by an impulse of whole-hearted patriotism, applies these rousing words to Pitt: "he is that Angel who, pleased to perform the [116] Almighty's orders, rides on the whirlwind, directing the storms of war: He is ordering the Reaper to reap the Vine of the Earth, and the Plowman to plow up the Cities and Towers" [63] — the same images from Revelation that he had used earlier in the Last Judgment passages of *Vala.*

117 Coin from Bryant's *Mythology,* vol. 3 (1776), odd plate

CHAPTER 15

Energy Is the Only Life

In two significant passages Blake mentions together the names of Boehme and Paracelsus: in the *Marriage* itself ("Any man of mechanical talents may, from the writings of Paracelsus or Jacob Behmen, produce ten thousand volumes of equal value with Swedenborg's") and in a verse epistle to Flaxman, in which he recalls his early masters: first Isaiah and Ezra, Shakespeare and Milton, then:

> *Paracelsus & Behmen appear'd to me, terrors appear'd in the*
> > *Heavens above*
> *And in Hell beneath . . .*[1]

The two were linked together in Blake's mind; and (this too we may deduce from the verse quotation given) what so fired Blake's imagination was the root idea common to both, the teaching of the alchemists, "that which is above is like that which is beneath, and that which is beneath is like that which is above"—the concept that is like a thread upon which all the various aphorisms and "fancies" of the *Marriage* are strung. Paracelsus was an alchemist in fact; Boehme uses the alchemical terms as his symbolic vocabulary, although he is speaking of spiritual and not natural phenomena. We have already seen that in *The Book of Thel* Blake was weighing in his mind the two philosophies—the Platonic dualism and the alchemical unity; a unity of all being, which includes even the apparently external physical world, within mind itself. In the *Marriage* these two trains of laborious thought are fused, and Blake's grand and certain realization of the unity of all things flames forth in a work that to this day remains something more than a work of literature: it is a work of transforming power.

In the *Marriage* the debate between the Platonizing Thel and the alchemical matron Clay is settled in favor of the teaching of the Smaragdine Table. It is plainly this doctrine that so moved Blake when "terrors" appeared "in the Heavens above / And in Hell beneath," on his reading Paracelsus and Boehme. The idea of the "marriage" in all likelihood originated in Paracelsus, who describes the relation of the stars above to their earthly sisters beneath, in terms of just such a marriage: "a Concordancy of Celestial Virtues may be found with us in the vally of darknesse (said Hermes). . . . That which is beneath, is like that which is above, and the things beneath are so related to the things above as Man and Wife." [2] And again: "In the first Creation, the things above, and the things below, the upper and lower Heaven or Water, the Superiour Coagulated Nature or Stars, and the inferiour Terrestrial Nature were all commixt in one, and were but one thing. But God Separated the Subtile from the gross, that so of one Water might be made two, the Superiour Water was Subtile, and to be accounted of as a Masculine Sex to the inferiour, more gross, Feminine Water." [3]

The title page of the *Marriage* shows many pairs of spirits in loving embrace, and the female comes from hell's flames, to meet the male, from what appears to be a bank of clouds. The whole scene might be a depiction of the alchemical marriage described by Paracelsus. Agrippa likewise was committed to this nondualistic philosophy. He evidently realized that the doctrine of an eternal hell outside the divine Being was a doctrine incompatible with the omnipotence of God; and he quoted Origen in defence of his belief that there is ultimate salvation for the devils.[4] [118]

This same doctrine of the one root from which spring the contraries is taught by Boehme. For him the contraries are not, as for the practicing alchemists, natural principles simply considered; they are, explicitly, good and evil, heaven and hell.

In the eternal nature there are, Boehme teaches, first the Father, the source, who is eternal fire; from the Father proceeds the Son, who, while eternally generated from the Father, as light from fire, yet is in himself a second Principle, distinct from the fire. The fire is nature, the light wisdom, or mind. Boehme's third Principle is this world.

Blake seems to have known other versions of the same symbol. Indeed, he seems to have had a more than superficial acquaintance with the thought of the alchemists. This was the philosophy he himself adopted with so much zeal as to reject all Bibles and sacred codes that held to a duality rather than to the unity of opposites. Thomas Vaughan alludes to the mystical tradition of the cabala and the generation of the "light Aleph," the Son, from the "dark Aleph," the Father (this Blake may also have known from Fludd),

118 Spirits of heaven and hell: title page of *The Marriage of Heaven and Hell* (1790–93?)

and to St. John's light that "shineth in darkness." He then speaks of the Hermetic myth of the light "which shone forth out of the shadow." [5] The same teaching, he says, is found in Venetus, *De Harmonia Mundi:*

> Yea, Zoroaster witnesseth that all things made out of fire when he saith: all things were produced from a single fire, namely, which *God, the dweller in the fiery essence*—as Plato hath it—did ordain to appear in the substance of heaven and earth, at that time created

rude and formless, that it might assume life and form. Hereupon the Fabricator did straightway give forth the *Sit Lux*, for which a mendacious rendering hath substituted *Fiat Lux*. For the Light is in no wise made but is communicated and admitted to things heretofore obscure.[6]

The fires of the Father, Boehme repeats in countless passages, are the abyss of hell, and the light of the Son is heaven; yet the two are one, springing from a single root: "For the God of the holy World, and the God of the dark World, are *not two* Gods; there is but *one* only God. He himself is the whole Being; he is Evil and Good, Heaven and Hell; Light and Darkness; Eternity and Time; Beginning and End. Where his Love is *hid* in any Thing, there his Anger is *manifest*. In many a Thing Love and Anger are in equal Measure and Weight; as is to be understood in this outward World's Essence." [7]

Boehme's fires are, as Blake also calls hell, "evil, or energy"; and without this energy there is no life possible:

> . . . God is also an *Angry* Zealous or *Jealous God, and a consuming*   [II, 186]
> *Fire;* and in that source standeth the Abyss of *Hell*, the anger and
> malice of all the Devils, as also the Poison of all Creatures: and it is
> found that without poison and eagerness there is no Life: and from
> thence ariseth all contrariety and strife; and it is found, that the
> strongest and most eager, is the most useful and profitable: for it
> *maketh* all things, and is the *only cause* of all mobility and life.[8]

It is from passages like these that Blake derived such thoughts as: "Without Contraries is no progression"; [9] "Energy is the only life, and is from the Body"; and "Attraction and Repulsion, Reason and Energy, Love and Hate, are necessary to human existence." It is likewise on the authority of Boehme that Blake dares to affirm that the Jehovah of the Bible is "no other than he who dwells in flaming fire." Blake had no doubt also read *Siris*, section 267: "They [the Pythagoreans and Platonists] understood that all things were alive and in motion: they supposed a concord and discord, union and disunion, in particles, some attracting, others repelling each other: and that those attractions and repulsions, so various, regular, and useful, could not be accounted for but by an intelligence presiding and directing all particular motions, for the conservation and benefit of the whole." [10] Plotinus' *On Providence* states at length a similar view, that "both good and evil are led through contraries in a beautiful order." Indeed, we find that all the most essential themes of traditional metaphysics recur again and again in the writings that were Blake's studies, so that it is not always possible to say which was his source of knowledge; nor does it matter; for authorship is of no significance when we consider themes common to tradition.

This philosophy of energy as "the only life" that is "from the Body" was certainly no invention of Blake's. Boehme's Father and his seven nature-spirits is nothing less than the energy of nature and of the body:

> For here you must understand, that there are two Wills in one Being, and they cause *two Principles:* One is the Love and the other is the Anger or the Source of Wrath. The *first* Will is not called God, but Nature: the second Will is called A and O, the beginning and the End, from Eternity to Eternity: and in the first Will, Nature could not be manifest, the second Will maketh Nature manifest. . . . and the one would be *nothing* without the other.[11]

The Deity is not separate from nature, Boehme insists: "no, but they are as Body and Soul: Nature is the Body, and the *Heart of God* [i.e. the Son] is the Soul." [12]

Thus we must beware of supposing that when Blake declares that energy is "from the Body" he attaches the same meaning to the words as would a materialist; for "Body is a portion of Soul discern'd by the five Senses, the chief inlets of Soul in this age." The real existing principle is not matter but life. The senses are the "Eye of Imagination." "Forms must be apprehended by Sense or the Eye of Imagination. Man is All Imagination." [13]

[11, 186, top left-hand figure]

In the fires of the Father, says Boehme, the devils dwell: "The Devils and damned souls are only living Spirits in the Essences of the Eternal Original: out of which they are also created. . . . And in that respect, God calleth himself a *Zealous* [or *Jealous*] *Angry God, and a Consuming fire*." [14] It is easy to see how, from his reading of Boehme, Blake came to interpret "Devils" as principles of energy, subsisting in the fire principle, and the fires of hell as the only source of life, with the devils as their active agents.

Between each of Boehme's three Principles—heaven, hell, and the present world—there is "a Great Gulf" fixed. Each spirit is confined with its own Principle, the devils in hell, the angels in heaven. So, according to Boehme, the devils can never enter paradise: "Neither do they know it: And yet it has no Wall of Earth or Stones about it, but there is a Great Gulf [or

Cliff] between Paradise and this World, so that they who will pass from hence thither, cannot; and they who would come from thence to us cannot neither; and the Hell and the Kingdom of Darkness is between them." [15] Blake, with his artist's visualizing imagination, turns that fine image of the cliff which prevents access between the worlds into a picture of a mighty devil hovering on the side of a rock: "on the abyss of the five senses, where a flat sided steep frowns over the present world, I saw a mighty Devil folded in black clouds, hovering on the sides of the rock." [16]

Elsewhere Boehme describes the impassable barrier that divides the Principles of heaven and hell, as a blindness that prevents the devils from seeing the things of heaven or the angels those of hell; even though their worlds should occupy the same place, they are states that cannot meet:

> Each Spirit is cloathed with his own World's Property wherein it dwells. The Beginning of each World's Source is that Limit which divides one World from the View and Observation of the other; for the *Devils* are a Nothing in the heavenly Source, for they have not its Source in them. . . . So likewise the Angels are a Nothing in the Darkness; they are verily in it, but they neither see nor feel it; that which is a *Pain* to the Devils, that same is a *Joy* to the Angels in their Source; and so, what is *pleasing* and delightful to the Devils, that the Angels *cannot endure; there is a great Gulf between them.* . . . Thus we are to understand that the *Evil* and *Good* Angels dwell near one another, and yet there is the greatest immense Distance between them. For the *Heaven is in Hell*, and the *Hell is in Heaven*, and yet the one is not manifest to the other; and although the Devil should go many Millions of Miles, [119, 120] desiring to enter into Heaven, and to see it, yet he would be still in Hell, and not see it. [17]

Blake shows in the frontispiece of the *Marriage* each spirit in its own

119 Angel and devil: *The Marriage of Heaven and Hell* (1790–93?), plate 4, bottom detail

120 Good and evil angels: color printed drawing (1795?)

world's property of fire or light. The design on page 4 shows a "mighty Devil" in his fires, his energies chained by the heel as he vainly attempts to advance toward an angel who stands in the light. The superb figure of the devil can be seen more clearly in the larger color-print made two years later for Thomas Butts and entitled "Good and Evil Angels." It might be an illustration to Boehme's theme; for the devil is here seen to be blind; and his blindness would seem to be of that kind described by Boehme: he cannot perceive the principle of light, in which the angel has his being.[18]

Boehme's Father, then, is fire, nature, and hell: "Nature was kindled in the wrath-fire, which fire is now called the *Wrath of God*, or the Burning Hell." But he is also named with another of the attributes of Blake's hell—"desire."

This word Blake also took from Boehme as one of the attributes of hell: "Now the Fire has a wrathful, harsh, strong, bitter desiring source, which begetteth thirst, a devouring and consuming, and the great bitterness is its right Spirit, an Enrager and Awakener, which has all Essences of the Life in it." [19] And again: "the Fire has in itself, for its source or quality, its own Form, *viz.* the Desiring, out of which, and in which, all Forms of Nature are generated." [20]

The creating "fiat" Boehme calls "the eternal desire" or "hunger"; for "the Desire is the Father's Property. . . . and the Wisdom, is the Son's Property." [21]

On the fifth page of the *Marriage* Blake introduces his antithesis of reason and desire—desire as the attribute of hell: "Those who restrain desire, do so because theirs is weak enough to be restrained; and the restrainer or reason usurps its place & governs the unwilling." Blake goes on to apply this argument to *Paradise Lost*, with Satan as the figure of desire: "the Governor or Reason is call'd Messiah. And the original Archangel, or possessor of the command of the heavenly host, is call'd the Devil or Satan." This is Milton read in the light of Boehme.

Reading the Book of Job in the same light, Blake concludes that "in the Book of Job, Milton's Messiah is call'd Satan." This is a fair deduction, for the God of Job justifies himself not by reason but by revealing to Job that the ways of the Creator cannot be measured or understood. It is Satan who tempts Job to set his reason against God's mystery. So Blake can justly say:

> For this history has been adopted by both parties.
> It indeed appear'd to Reason as if Desire was cast out; but the Devil's account is, that the Messiah fell, & formed a heaven of what he stole from the Abyss.[22]

Boehme so far supports this reading of the myth: that it is from the Father alone that the energies of creation originate, "the Jehovah of the Bible being no other than he who dwells in flaming fire"—so Blake summarizes Boehme's vision. Father and Son dwell in eternal harmony, but a harmony of opposites, of good and evil, darkness and light: "For the Father's Power generates the Son continually from Eternity to Eternity: But if the Father should *cease to generate*, then the Son would be no more; Also if the Son should shine no more in the Father, then the Father would be a dark Valley." [23]

"Energy is Eternal Delight" is still also within the structure of Swedenborgian thought. It is true that Swedenborg conversed (Blake blames him for doing so) chiefly with angels and not with devils, so that his teachings are biased in the direction of conventional values. But on one occasion he listened to the devils, and this is what they told him: "Know that every one, whether he be called good or evil, is on the Enjoyment of his own particular Delight, he that is called good in the Enjoyment of his Delight, and he that is called Evil in the Enjoyment of his . . . everyone is allowed the Enjoyment of his Delight, even the most unclean as they call it." [24]

This Swedenborg expands. Delight, he discovers, "is the universal constituent of heaven, and the universal constituent of hell." An Angel pronounces, "Enquire and learn what Delight is, and thou wilt know what thou wantest"; and to this, spirits of wisdom reply:

> Delight is the All of Life to every one in Heaven, and the All of Life to every one in hell: they who are in Heaven perceive the Delight of what is good and true, but they who are in Hell, the Delight of what is evil and false: for all delight is of Love, and Love is the *Esse* of the Life of Man; wherefore Man is Man according to the Quality of his Love, so he is Man also according to the Quality of his Delight; the Activity of Love is what causeth a Sense of Delight, which Activity in Heaven is attended with Wisdom, and in Hell with Insanity, each whereof in their respective Subjects exciteth Delight; but the Heavens and the Hells are in opposite Delights.

Blake takes for his own the essence of this wisdom of hell: love is the *esse* of a man's life; delight is the energy that inspires all action; and he goes beyond Swedenborg, for he realizes that "the soul of sweet delight can never be defiled." The contraries of good and evil are established by reason; but energy is life itself, arising from beyond all contraries and all reason. "As I was walking among the fires of hell, delighted with the enjoyments of Genius, which to Angels look like torment and insanity . . ." [25] The words "torment" and "insanity" are both habitually used by Swedenborg to describe the hells; but "delight," Blake understood, transcends good and evil. This is the "infernal wisdom" inscribed by a devil in "corroding fires":

> *How do you know but ev'ry Bird that cuts the airy way,*
> *Is an immense world of delight, clos'd by your senses five?* [26]

Every living creature is a "world of delight," for delight is the *esse* of life.

The Infant Joy of the *Songs* says, "Joy is my name," for that is the ultimate nature of the life principle, the *ananda* of Vedanta.

The Devourer is another name given by Boehme to the Abyss of God. From this abyss issues all being, which is again swallowed up in the abyss:

> the *Fire-flagrat* is consuming, it apprehends the conceived *Essence* . . . and consumes it in the Twinkling of an Eye, for here the Eternal Will, which is an *Abyss*, becomes manifest in the Fire: No *Essence* can subsist before it, it devours all into its *Nothing*. And here is the Original of the Eternal Death, or Devouring; and in this Devouring is the highest *Arcanum* or *Secret:* For the true essential lively Spirit and Understanding proceeds out of this Devouring, and makes another Beginning . . . this Beginning which proceeds again out of the Devouring . . . makes three Worlds [27]

—that is, the fire principle, the light principle, and the human world.

So, Boehme goes on to say, the divine Being continually issues from the abyss, "introduces itself into the *Byss* and Essence; *viz.* into an eternal *Generation* and *Devouring*, wherein the manifestation of the *Abyss* consists, and is an eternal *Love play*." [28] Blake seems to be looking toward Boehme when he writes: "Thus one portion of being is the Prolific, the other the Devouring. . . . the Prolific would cease to be Prolific unless the Devourer, as a sea, recieved the excess of his delights."

On plate 16 also, the energies are called Giants: "The Giants who   [121, 122] formed this world into its sensual existence, and now seem to live in it in chains, are in truth the causes of its life & the sources of all activity."

Thomas Taylor's translations of the Orphic Hymns include one addressed to the Titans [29] as the artificers of the world and of man:

> *O Mighty Titans, who from heav'n and earth*
> *Derive your noble and illustrious birth,*
> *Our fathers sires,*[30] *in Tartarus profound*
> *Who dwell, deep merg'd beneath the solid ground:*
> *Fountains and principles, from whom began*
> *Th' afflicted, miserable, race of man:*
> *Who not alone in earth's retreats abide,*
> *But in the ocean and the air reside;*

121 Five giants sunk in the soil: illustration no. 60 (1826) for Dante's *Inferno*

Possibly they represent the five senses.

Since ev'ry species from your nature flows,
Which all prolific, nothing barren knows:
Avert your rage. . . .

Taylor in his *Dissertation* explains the nature of the Titans: they are the forces of the irrational—again, akin to the energy, desire, and delight that Blake had learned from Boehme to regard as the source of all life: "the Titans are the ultimate artificers of things, and the most proximate to their fabrication. But farther, our irrational life is Titannic, under which the rational life is torn to pieces. And hence, when we disperse the Dionysus, or intellect contained in the secret recesses of our nature . . . then we become Titans."

Prometheus Chain'd, with its championing of the Titan's cause against the usurper Zeus, must likewise have awakened in Blake all his hatred of tyrants and the "cunning of weak and tame minds which have power to resist energy."[31] Prometheus foretells the overthrow of Zeus and his own ultimate triumph and liberation—a prophecy strangely in harmony with the Swedenborgian New Age and the "dominion of Edom." The last great lines of the play echo all that Blake himself felt on behalf of the enchained energies of life:

. . . th' impetuous storm
Rolls all its terrible fury on my head.
Seest thou this, awefull Themis; and thou, Aether,
Thro' whose pure azure floats the general stream
Of liquid light, see you what wrongs I suffer! [32]

So Swedenborg's prophecy of the New Age meets that of Prometheus, and Blake's *Marriage* is in its genesis, as it is in its substance, akin to Shelley's *Prometheus Unbound*.

122 Engraving by Blake (1817) of Titans, after Flaxman's design for *Hesiod*

The text is concluded in Volume II.

Notes: Chapters 1–15

with Abbreviations and Bibliographical Note

Abbreviations and Bibliographical Note

QUOTATIONS from Blake's writings, except for certain of those from *The Four Zoas*, are taken from *The Complete Writings of William Blake*, ed. Geoffrey Keynes (London: Nonesuch Press, and New York: Random House, 1957). References are indicated by number of plate (in the case of an engraved poem), book, or part (when the poem is so divided), and the letter "K," followed by Keynes's page and line numbers. When *The Four Zoas* is quoted or cited in the edition of H. M. Margoliouth (*Blake's Vala*, London: Oxford University Press, 1956), the title *Vala* is used, followed by the recto or verso numbering; line and page references to Keynes are also given for these citations. For Blake's Notebook (the Rossetti Manuscript) references are to the manuscript pages as given by Keynes.

For the convenience of scholars I have used the same abbreviations for the titles of Blake's works as Northrop Frye's in *Fearful Symmetry* (Princeton University Press, 1947):

A.R.O.	*All Religions Are One*		M.H.H.	*The Marriage of Heaven and Hell*
B.A.	*The Book of Ahania*		N.N.R.	*There is No Natural Religion*
B.L.	*The Book of Los*			
B.T.	*The Book of Thel*		P.A.	*Public Address* (Notebook)
B.U.	*The Book of Urizen*			
D.C.	*A Descriptive Catalogue*		P.S.	*Poetical Sketches*
E.G.	*The Everlasting Gospel*		S.E.	*Songs of Experience*
F.R.	*The French Revolution*		S.I.	*Songs of Innocence*
F.Z.	*The Four Zoas*		S.L.	*The Song of Los*
G.P.	*The Gates of Paradise*		S.Lib.	*A Song of Liberty*
I.M.	*An Island in the Moon*		V.D.A.	*Visions of the Daughters of Albion*
J.	*Jerusalem*			
M.	*Milton*		V.L.J.	*A Vision of the Last Judgment* (Notebook)

[*continued*]

The following abbreviations for works other than Blake's have been used (full particulars of which are given in the Bibliography, below, Vol. II, pp. 323 ff.):

A.C.	Swedenborg, *Arcana Coelestia*	*O.H.*	Taylor, *The Mystical Initiations, or, Hymns of Orpheus*
D.E.	Taylor, *A Dissertation on the Eleusinian and Bacchic Mysteries*	*P.C.B.*	Taylor [Plotinus], *Concerning the Beautiful*
D.L.W.	Swedenborg, *The Wisdom of Angels concerning Divine Love and Divine Wisdom*	*P.F.B.*	Taylor, *Five Books of Plotinus*
		P.L.	Milton, *Paradise Lost*
E.P.T.	Taylor, *An Essay on the Restoration of the Platonic Theology*	*P.R.*	Milton, *Paradise Regained*
F.Q.	Spenser, *The Faerie Queene*	*Pym.*	[Hermes], *Divine Pymander of Hermes Mercurius Trismegistus*
H.H.	Swedenborg, *A Treatise concerning Heaven and Hell*	*T.C.R.*	Swedenborg, *True Christian Religion*

References to the writings of Jacob Boehme are to *The Works of Jacob Behmen*, ed. Ward and Langcake (4 vols., London, 1764–81), known as "Law's Boehme." For the writings of Thomas Vaughan, references are given both to the original editions and to the A. E. Waite edition (London, 1919).

Notes

Introduction

1. Edith J. Morley, ed., *Blake, Coleridge, Wordsworth, Lamb, etc.*, p. 19. "Blake and Coleridge when in company, seemed like congenial beings of another sphere, breathing for a while on our earth; which may easily be perceived, from the similarity of thought pervading their works." (London University Magazine, 1830.)
2. Cf. *The Consecrated Urn*, p. 135.
3. Milton, *Il Penseroso*, lines 85–92.
4. *A Preface to Paradise Lost*, p. 56.
5. *The Christian and Oriental or True Philosophy of Art*, p. 17.
6. Notebook 68–69; K. 605.
7. *A Vision* (2nd edn.), pp. 23–24.
8. *Gnosis*, p. 110.
9. See Edgar Wind, *Pagan Mysteries in the Renaissance*.
10. William Butler Yeats, *Autobiographies* (2nd edn.), p. 490.

1. The Swedenborgian Songs

1. *T.C.R.*, Vol. II, § 623, pp. 237–39.
2. *D.C.;* K. 581.
3. *H.H.*, § 89, p. 53.
4. Coleridge's definition of a symbol will make this clear. His symbol in no way differs from a Swedenborgian "correspondence," translated into literary terms:

   > Now an Allegory is but a translation of abstract notions into a picture-language which is itself nothing but an abstraction from objects of the senses; the principal being more worthless even than its phantom proxy, both alike unsubstantial, and the former shapeless to boot. On the other hand a Symbol is characterized by a translucence of the Special in the Individual or of the General in the Especial or of the Universal in the General. Above all by the translucence of the Eternal through and in the Temporal. It always partakes of the Reality which it renders intelligible; and while it enunciates the whole, abides itself as a living part in that Unity, of which it is the representative.
   > [*The Statesman's Manual*, pp. 36–37. In Kathleen Coburn, ed., *Inquiring Spirit*, pp. 103–104.]

5. *T.C.R.*, Vol. I, § 200, pp. 275–76.
6. *A.C.*, Index, and Vol. I, § 273, p. 105.
7. Notebook 115; K. 162.
8. The relevant passage is in *Mysterium Magnum*, III, Chap. 33, § 27, p. 178:

> For the *Rainbow* has the *Colour* of all the three Principles, *viz.* The Colour of the *first* Principle is *red* and *darkish-brown*, which denotes the dark and Fire-world, that is, the first Principle, the Kingdom of God's Anger. The Colour of the *second* Principle is *white* and *yellow:* this is the majestatical Colour, signifying, as a Type of the holy World, God's Love. The *Colour* of the *third* Principle is *green* and *blue;* blue from the Chaos, and green from the Water or Salt-petre; where, in the Flagrat or Crack of the Fire, the *Sulphur* and *Mercury* seperate themselves, and produce distinct, various and several Colours, which denote to us the inward spiritual Worlds.

9. *Annotations to D.L.W.* 12; K. 90.
10. Wicksteed interprets the two postures as representing the spiritual and the material sides of man. This is, I believe, a near approximation; the alternatives are wisdom and love. The difference in interpretation is slight but nevertheless important. This interpretation of right and left is traditional—the two pillars of justice (or severity) and mercy of the cabalistic tree, and these in turn derived from Jachin and Boaz, the pillars of Solomon's Temple. Blake knew of these pillars, and refers to them in his description of *A Vision of the Last Judgment*, "Jesus seated between the Two Pillars, Jachin & Boaz" (*V.L.J.* 76; K. 606). The context suggests their symbolic meaning.
11. Notebook 114; K. 164.
12. *Aurora*, Chap. 26, § 92; *Works*, I, 264.
13. *J.* 22; K. 622.
14. *D.L.W.*, § 292, pp. 266–67.
15. *Infant Sorrow, S.E.;* K. 217. The image was evidently one that had great power in Blake's imagination, for he chose to illustrate the same archetypal figure from *Macbeth*, in one of his finest paintings:

> *And pity like a naked new born babe*
> *Striding the blast. . . .*

There is surely in the "fiend hid in a cloud" also a reminiscence of that other, more sinister babe who summons Hecate:

> *My little Spirit see*
> *Sits in a Foggy cloud, and stayes for me.*

16. *S.I.;* K. 125.
17. *Mysteries of Creation*, Bk. III, text 3–4, p. 58.
18. *D.C.* IV; K. 576.
19. *T.C.R.*, Vol. II, § 787, p. 419.
20. *D.L.W.*, § 11, p. 12.
21. *Annotations to D.L.W.* 12; K. 90.
22. *D.L.W.*, § 157, p. 128.

23. Ibid., § 129, p. 105. Cf. the orientation of churches to the east.
24. Ibid., § 120, p. 99.
25. Notebook 105; K. 179.
26. *D.L.W.*, § 5, p. 5.
27. *Auguries of Innocence;* K. 434, 129–32.
28. *S.I.;* K. 120.
29. *S.I.;* K. 121.
29a. I, 24 ff.
30. *Blake's Innocence and Experience*, p. 39.
31. *The Last Judgment*, §§ 3–6, pp. 3–5.
32. *D.C.;* K. 577.
33. The exact date of *An Island in the Moon* is not known. Foster Damon suggested 1788, because it seems to lead on naturally to *Songs of Innocence*. Keynes formerly dated it approximately 1787, but in his 1957 edition moves the date back to 1784–85, on such evidence as the women's fashions mentioned by Blake that were "in" during those years. I question this earlier date because it seems to me that Blake was already familiar with Neoplatonic symbolism, which can most easily be explained by supposing he had read Taylor's translation of Plotinus' *Concerning the Beautiful* (1787). Both Damon and Keynes, however, allow that Sipsop the Pythagorean is (whatever the date of the *Island*) Taylor himself; so that my objection is not conclusive. Blake knew Taylor, and may have learned much from him in conversation.
34. P. 24; *Ennead* I.6.5.
35. See our I, pp. 84–85, 108, 153.
36. *H.H.*, § 78, p. 47.
37. *T.C.R.*, Vol. I, § 33, p. 48.
38. Ibid., Vol. II, § 470, p. 93.
39. *F.Z.* VIIa; K. 329, 359–60.
40. *F.Z.* IX; K. 374, 641–42.
41. *J.* 91; K. 738, 30–31.
42. *P.C.B.*, pp. 11–12 n.; *Ennead* VI.3.7.
43. Ibid., pp. 36–37; *Ennead* I.6.8.
44. *S.I.;* K. 117.
45. *H.H.*, § 514, p. 353.
46. *Aurora*, Chap. 11, §§ 58–60; *Works*, I, 97.
47. *S.I.;* K. 117.
48. *P.C.B.*, p. 25; *Ennead* I.6.5.
49. *Dissertation*, pp. 6–8. Cf. "I should not wonder if Euripides spoke the truth when he says, 'Who knows whether to live is not to die, and to die, is not to live?' And we, perhaps, are in reality dead. For I have heard from one of the wise, that we are now dead; and that the body is our sepulchre." (Plato, *Gorgias* 492E; *Works*, tr. Taylor, IV, 410. All translations from Plato in the present book are by Taylor.)
50. *The Land of Dreams;* K. 427.
51. See our I, pp. 129 ff.
52. *Aeneid* VI.673–75; *Works*, tr. Dryden, p. 389.
53. Ibid. 998–1001; p. 392
54. *London;* K. 216.

55. *M.* 40; K. 533, 37–41, 1.
56. *Concerning the Earths in Our Solar System,* § 79, pp. 87–88.
57. *F.Z.* viia; K. 321, 59–66.
58. *S.E.;* K. 211.
59. *D.L.W.,* § 47, p. 39.
60. Cf. also Milton, *P.L.* 1.254–55: "The Mind is its own place and in itself / Can make a Heav'n of Hell, a Hell of Heav'n."
61. *T.C.R.,* Vol. ii, § 785, p. 417. See continuation of this passage, our ii, p. 127.
62. *B.T.* 4; K. 129, 7–12.
63. *T.C.R.,* Vol. i, § 385, p. 456.
64. *Three Principles of the Divine Essence,* Chap. 20, § 28; *Works,* i, 201.
65. Watts, *Divine Songs* (1728 edn.), p. 43.
66. Ibid., p. 9.
67. *The Divine Image, S.I.;* K. 117.
68. *Divine Songs* (1728 edn.), p. 44.
69. *S.E.;* K. 215.
70. *Divine Songs* (1728 edn.), p. 45.
71. Ibid. (1790 edn.), pp. 82–83.
72. *S.I.;* K. 111.
73. *S.I.;* K. 124.

2.   Tiriel

1. *Works of William Blake,* ii, 81.
2. *Blake: Prophet against Empire,* p. 122.
3. Bk. ii, p. 243.
4. The Sphinx of Oedipus and the Sphinx of Egypt perhaps form another link that explains and justifies this Greco-Egyptian scene.
5. Tr. Potter. Blake possessed a copy of the second (1779) edition of Potter's Aeschylus.
6. *Tiriel* 1; K. 100, 43–44.
7. *Tiriel* 1; K. 100, 45–46.
8. Tr. Potter, p. 213, lines 432–36.
9. *Tiriel* 1; K. 100, 37–39.
10. Tr. Potter, pp. 160–64, lines 1329–38, 1435–38.
11. Tr. Francklin, p. 376.
12. Tr. Potter, p. 166, lines 1481–84.
13. Tr. Francklin, p. 367.
14. *Tiriel* 3; K. 102, 17–21.
15. *Tiriel* 2; K. 100, 1–4.
16. Tr. Francklin, p. 297.
17. *Tiriel* 2; K. 102, 48–53.
18. Tr. Francklin, p. 303.
19. Ibid., pp. 385–86.
20. Ibid., pp. 386–87.
21. *Tiriel* 5; K. 106, 1–7.
22. Ossian, *Carric-Thura; Works,* i, 277.

23. Tr. Potter, p. 394.
24. *King Lear* I.iv.
25. *Tiriel* 7; K. 108–109, 9, 11.
26. *Tiriel* 3; K. 102, 17.
27. *King Lear* III.ii.
28. *Tiriel* 5; K. 106, 8.
29. *King Lear* II.iv.
30. *Tiriel* 1; K. 99, 23. Clytemnestra (*Choephoroe*) uses the serpent image, applied to thankless children.
31. *The Structure of Complex Words*, p. 134.
32. *King Lear* v.iii.
33. Ellis and Yeats say, I know not upon what authority, that these are the cabalistic names of Adam and Eve (*Blake's Works*, I, 282).
34. *Tiriel* 2; K. 100, 6–7.
35. *Tiriel* 3; K. 102–103, 13–15, 22–23.
36. *Auguries of Innocence;* K. 431, 5–6. Blake is paraphrasing an English proverb that he must have known in one of its many forms (all employing the meter he himself uses in *Auguries of Innocence*), which makes the injury of a robin a forbidden act. See Edward Armstrong, *The Folklore of Birds*, p. 167.
37. *S.I.;* K. 124.
38. *S.L.* 6; K. 246, 4–12. The more familiar passage in *Paradise Lost* (x.504 ff.) describing the shrinking of the fallen angels into serpent forms does not seem to have been Blake's model, for the metamorphosis of the two ancestral figures belongs only to Ovid; the error of Cadmus, besides, is materialism, and two lines may give the clue to Blake's interest in the myth:

> *Mean time, the wretched* Cadmus *mourns, nor knows*
> *That they who mortal fell, immortal rose.*

There follows his metamorphosis into serpent form, outcome of his own despair, the result of his ignorance of the immortality of the soul:

> *That Serpent sure was hallow'd,* Cadmus *cry'd,*
> *Which once my Spear transfix'd with foolish Pride;*
> *When the big Teeth, a Seed before unknown,*
> *By me along the wond'ring Glebe were sown,*
> *And sprouting Armies by themselves o'erthrown.*
> *If thence the Wrath of Heav'n on me is bent,*
> *May Heav'n conclude it with one sad Event;*
> *To an extended Serpent change the Man,*
> *And while he spoke, the wish'd-for Change began.*
> *His Skin with Sea-green Spots was vary'd round,*
> *And on his Belly prone he prest the Ground.*
> *He glitter'd soon with many a golden Scale,*
> *And his shrunk Legs clos'd in a spiry Tail.*
> *Arms yet remain'd, remaining Arms he spread*
> *To his lov'd Wife, and human Tears yet shed.*
> . . . .

> *Both, Serpents now, with Fold involv'd in Fold,*
> *To the next Covert amicably roul'd.*
> *There curl'd they lie, or wave along the Green,*
> *Feerless see Men, by Men are fearless seen,*
> *Still mild, and conscious, what they once have been.*
> [*Metamorphoses*, Bk. IV; ed. Garth, tr. Eusden, pp. 128 ff.]

Blake uses the phrase "reptile coverts" in *America* 15; K. 202, 20.

39. Again, according to Bryant (*Mythology*, II, 148), Cadmus founded the Academy at Athens. May this explain the association of Blake's Har with education and with Mnetha (Athena)? Blake's wild identifications of figures as remote as Har and Cadmus seem restrained beside Bryant's.

40. *Europe* 10; K. 241, 10–11.

41. *Abury*, pp. 80–81.

42. *Mythology*, II, 474–75.

43. *Tiriel* 2; K. 101, 39.

44. *Tiriel* 2; K. 101, 40–41.

45. *Tiriel* 2; K. 101, 43.

46. This seems the more likely as the name *Heuxos*, one of the sons of Tiriel, is derived from the same work; the *Hycsi* (Hyksos) were the dynasty of shepherd-kings of Egypt. Manethon is also quoted in Bryant's *Mythology*.

47. *Annotations to Watson* 15–16; K. 392.

48. Fitzwilliam Museum, Cambridge.

49. *Abury*.

50. Har, Jafnhar, and Thridi are all homonyms for the god Odin. But Blake may not have known this, for it is nowhere mentioned in Mallet.

51. Mallet, *Northern Antiquities*, II, 3.

52. Ibid., pp. 7–8.

53. Self-annihilation, in Blake's sense, is not a form of suicide but a dying to, or transcending of, the self or ego. It is the theme of the poem *Milton*.

54. Mallet, *Northern Antiquities*, II, 86.

55. 1780 edn., pp. 307–308.

56. *Tiriel* 6–7; K. 108, 40–46, 1.

57. *Tiriel* 1; K. 99, 13.

58. There are other traces of Ossian in *Tiriel*. Lotho is probably from "Lotha's roaring stream." The name *Matha*, in the phrase used by Tiriel of his fallen house, "as false as Matha and as dark as Orcus," is likewise Ossianic.

59. *Introduction to the History of Great Britain and Ireland*, p. 305.

60. It is interesting to find that Blake's interpretation of the "youngest daughter" theme is exactly that given by Freud (in "The Theme of the Three Caskets") to Cordelia in *King Lear*. In Lear's relations with his three daughters Freud sees man's three inevitable relations with women; and when mother and wife will no longer love the aged man, it is woman as the grave who alone will receive him —that is, the third of the three Fates, Atropos, the inexorable. It is with bitter reluctance that Lear is compelled to learn that the two elder sisters will give him nothing, and that he must turn to the third, the silent daughter. In the last scene, when we read "Enter Lear with Cordelia dead in his arms," Freud sees that Cordelia is not merely dead: "Cordelia is Death. If we reverse the situation it becomes intelligible and familiar to us. She is the Death-goddess who . . .

carries away the dead hero . . . Eternal wisdom, clothed in the primaeval myth, bids the old man renounce love, choose death and make friends with the necessity of dying." Cordelia is the kindest daughter, in spite of all appearances to the contrary; and Lear's reconciliation with her at last is what leaves us, at the end of the play, with the same sense of all being resolved that we experience from the last scenes of *Oedipus at Colonus*, when the goddess of death receives the aged wanderer to her bosom. Cordelia in her death is beautiful and dear to Lear; but Tiriel curses his youngest daughter most bitterly of all his children, and she who might have been a gentle guide becomes fury-like and serpent-haired.

61. Bk. III, p. 475. Large extracts from Agrippa were published by Francis Barrett in *The Magus*, but not until 1801. Blake evidently knew Agrippa earlier.

62. *Tiriel* 1; K. 100, 34–35.

63. *Tiriel* 1; K. 100, 36–42.

64. *Tiriel* 7; K. 108, 9.

65. Gen. 3:14–19.

66. *The Laocoön;* K. 776.

67. Pl. 11, also perhaps Pls. 1 and 4.

68. *Tiriel* 7; K. 108–109, 1–15.

69. *G.P.;* K. 771, 39–42.

70. *Three Books*, Bk. III, p. 475.

71. Ibid., pp. 473 ff.

72. *Tiriel* 4; K. 104, 20–27.

73. *Fearful Symmetry*, pp. 242–44.

74. Vol. I, § 45, p. 66. Both Ochim and Ijim are named among the Sons of Los (*F.Z.* VIII; K. 350, 360), "Har, Ochim, Ijim, Adam, Reuben," etc.

75. *T.C.R.*, Vol. II, § 661, p. 276.

76. *Tiriel* 4; K. 103, 6.

77. *Tiriel* 4; K. 104, 17–18.

78. *Tiriel* 4; K. 105, 48.

79. *Tiriel* 4; K. 105, 69–71.

80. *Three Books*, Bk. III, pp. 479–80.

81. *Tiriel* 4; K. 104, 40.

82. *Three Books*, Bk. III, p. 480.

83. This highly sophisticated account of the post-mortem state as illusory and dream-like is, it seems, a source of Blake's own thought upon the illusory nature of the "states"—of all mental states, good or evil, other than those of eternity. Blake may have read the vivid account of the hells and heavens of Buddhist mythology in an article in *Asiatick Researches*, VII (1801), 32–56, by Captain Mahony, on "*Singhala*, or *Ceylon*, and the Doctrines of Bhooddha." But the contributors to *Asiatick Researches* seldom reveal the intellectual insight and boldness of Agrippa; and the knowledge that the heavens and hells are a fantasy of the "people of dreams" seems certainly to come from Agrippa and not from the un-comprehending, though scholarly, accounts of Eastern religion, for the first time appearing in Sir William Jones's *Asiatick Researches*. Agrippa's statement may be compared with W. Y. Evans-Wentz's account in *The Tibetan Book of the Dead*, pp. 34–35, in which the fantastic nature of the visions of departed souls is again and again insisted upon:

> The after-death state is very much like a dream state, and its dreams are the

> children of the mentality of the dreamer. . . . what the percipient on the *Bardo* plane sees is due entirely to his own mental-content, there are no visions of gods or of demons, of heavens or of hells, other than those born of the hallucinatory *karmic* thought-forms constituting his personality, which is an impermanent product arising from the thirst for existence . . . the *Bible* of the Christians, like the Koran of the Moslems, never seems to consider that the spiritual experiences in the form of hallucinatory visions by prophet or devotee, reported therein, may, in the last analysis, not be real. But the *Bardo Thödol* is so sweeping in its assertions that it leaves its reader with the clear-cut impression that every vision, without any exception whatsoever, in which spiritual beings, gods or demons, or paradises or places of torment and purgation play any part . . . is purely illusionary.

Blake would have understood this perfectly; but in fact he received the same teaching from Cornelius Agrippa.

84. Vergil, fourth *Georgic*.
85. *Three Books*, Bk. III, p. 480.
86. *Tiriel* 4; K. 104, 43.
87. *Tiriel* 4; K. 105, 50–62.
88. Probably in Vernon's translation; this passage was not translated by Dryden. A pencil sketch of Daphne changed into a laurel, an early entry in Blake's Notebook (p. 27), indicates his familiarity with Ovid.
89. *P.L.* IV.799–803.
90. *Tiriel* 8; K. 110, 36–37.
91. *J.* 98; K. 746, 31–33.
92. Letter to George Cumberland, April 12, 1827; K. 878.

3.   *The Sea of Time and Space*

1. See our I, pp. 396–97, n. 34.
2. Mona Wilson, *The Life of William Blake*, p. 359.
3. Dec. 6, 1795; K. 790.
4. Coleridge later retracted his admiration for Taylor, avowedly on grounds of style, but really, perhaps, in conformity with his own increasingly specific Christian tendencies.
5. He was nevertheless invited to Oxford, where he was treated with every kindness.
6. *D.E.*, pp. iii–iv.
7. Notes to *P.C.B.*, p. 47.
8. *M.* 1; K. 480.
9. Letter to Dr. Trusler, Aug. 16, 1799; K. 792.
10. *M.* 1; K. 480.
11. So many of Blake's most frequent symbols are here that some critics have thought this painting too personal to be an illustration of any allegory but Blake's own. Such an interpretation is given by Sir Geoffrey Keynes in his notes to the painting in the Arts Council catalogue of the exhibition of Blake's tempera paintings, arranged in 1951 by the William Blake Trust, and also in a publication of the Princeton University Press entitled *Studies in Art and Literature*, for Belle da Costa Greene (Dorothy Miner, ed., 1954). Much that is true and valuable can be

discovered by this method. Another distinguished authority who has held a similar view is Mr. Kerrison Preston, who has kindly allowed me to read an unpublished essay on the Arlington Court painting, which in many respects differs from Sir Geoffrey Keynes's exposition, but is no less true to Blake's symbolic system as a whole. Mr. Preston is prepared to grant that Blake is illustrating Porphyry, but suggests that the pencil drawing in the Pierpont Morgan Library (published in *Pencil Drawings by William Blake*, 2nd ser.) was made at a time when Blake was more closely following Porphyry's symbols than he was when the finished painting was elaborated. The date of the pencil drawing is not certainly known, and Mr. Preston suggests the possibility that it may have been made much earlier than the finished work. I feel it right to give this view of a distinguished Blake scholar, although I cannot accept it. There seems to be more, rather than less, detail that is specifically related to the classical sources in the later work. In the drawing Odysseus is in the act of throwing, but the sea-girdle is not shown. The figures of the horses are not there, nor is there more than the barest indication of the group about the sun. The Fates are recognizable in the foreground, but not Phorcys; and in the later version the characterization of Odysseus is more studied. In fact, it is not possible to examine the face of Blake's central figure without feeling that he has exactly captured the character of Homer's "wary-wise," intelligent, eloquent, and, above all, guileful Greek.

Since I wrote this, Mr. G. Wingfield Digby has also published an account of the Arlington Court painting in his *Symbol and Image in William Blake*. His exegesis demonstrates the sureness with which Blake's painting conveys its essential meaning to any scholar naturally responsive to symbolic statement or familiar with the symbolic terms of the perennial philosophy in any of its branches. Much is valid in Mr. Digby's exegesis; I cannot agree, however, that Blake invented this elaborate composition piecemeal.

12. Perhaps deliberately or perhaps (as Mr. H. M. Margoliouth suggested to me in conversation) because he was painting from memory and the two landings had become fused in his recollection.

13. Vs.400–401; tr. Cowper, p. 121.

14. Vs.412–21; ibid. Blake possessed a copy of Chapman's *Homer*, but Chapman's translation makes no mention of the gesture of throwing "with averted face," so clearly depicted by Blake. Pope emphasizes this detail, even repeating it in the account of Odysseus' obeying of Leucothea's instructions. My reason for believing that Blake was using Cowper's translation rather than Pope's (apart from Blake's recorded dislike of Pope's *Homer*—"Hayley upon his Toilet seeing the sope, / Cries, 'Homer is very much improv'd by Pope' ") is that another detail made use of by Blake is not to be found in Pope, although it is retained by both Chapman and Cowper. This is the simile of the ship compared to four stallions. Pope does not specify the number.

Blake had read all three translations, and perhaps even a little in Greek.

15. Vs.553–57; ibid., p. 128. The garment that Odysseus has thrown back into the sea is evidently a sea-garment or material body, for which he has no further use and must return, for it was only lent. The theme of the sea-garment is one that he used in "Night the First" of *The Four Zoas*, and while there are other sources (the Hermetica, notably), there are traces in this episode, attributed to Enion and Tharmas, "demon of the waters," of allusion to Leucothea's sea-girdle. It is

Blake's Enion who weaves such a garment for the Spectre (i.e. material manifestation) of Tharmas. There are links between Blake's Enion and Ino or Leucothea. In the passage quoted the weaver is Enion; but in *The Mental Traveller* there is "a Woman Old," whose "fingers number every Nerve" of a baby boy. This nurse is "Eno, aged mother," in fact Ino, who, when a mortal, was the nurse of Dionysus. The story of the boy child of *The Mental Traveller* is recognizably drawn from Taylor's account of the Mysteries of Dionysus, and thus we find that Blake's eclectic mind had early established a link between the Homeric account of Ino and her sea-girdle, and Ino as nurse of Bacchus. Enion's "filmy woof" Blake understands as the mortal body; and it is that same filmy woof which in the painting we see dissolving into cloud (see our I, p. 74).

16. XIII.96–99; ibid., p. 299. These four horses doubtless had for Blake a symbolic significance not intended by Homer. The fourfold vehicle is a symbol to which he had given much thought; his own four Zoas—Ezekiel's four living creatures—are central to his symbolic system. Are those above the energies of the spiritual humanity, and the dark horses of the sea their "vehicular forms" or manifestation in the physical world? Where Homer gives but an image, Blake may read into it a symbolic meaning reached by other ways.
17. *The Little Black Boy;* K. 125.
18. Taylor, *E.P.T.*, p. 278.
19. Used in a letter to Butts, Jan. 10, 1802; K. 812.
20. Taylor, note to *P.C.B.*, pp. 37–38.
21. *O.H.* (1824 edn.), p. 192.
22. In *E.P.T.*, pp. 233–34.
23. Proclus, *Hymn to the Sun;* in Taylor, *Sallust*, p. 124.
24. See Yeats's paraphrase of this passage: *The Delphic Oracle upon Plotinus*, in *Collected Poems*, pp. 306–7.
25. *On the Cave of the Nymphs*, § 3; in Taylor, *Select Works of Porphyry*, pp. 174–75.
26. Ibid., § 4; *Works*, p. 177.
27. There can be no doubt that Coleridge, familiar as he was with the Neoplatonists, had this symbolism in mind when he wrote of his river, descending from a paradisiacal world, through caverns, to "a sunless sea."
28. And also in the Hymn to the Furies, who seem to bear a mysterious kinship to the Fates. See *O.H.* (1792 edn.) LVIII, p. 190, and LXVIII, p. 200. Cf. our II, p. 89.
29. See our I, pp. 189–90.
30. *Cave of the Nymphs*, § 2; *Works*, p. 175.
31. Cf. in *The Little Boy Lost*, "The child was wet with dew"; K. 121.
32. *Cave of the Nymphs*, § 5; *Works*, p. 179.
33. Ibid., § 6; *Works*, p. 179.
34. Quoted by Taylor in note to *Cave of the Nymphs*, § 13; *Works*, p. 195.
35. Ibid., p. 196. See also Plato, *Gorgias*, in *Works*, IV, 410 and n.
36. Shelley's moon, who presides over the stars as a swarm of silvery bees, is in strict accordance with tradition (*The Cloud*). So is Yeats's "honey of generation" (*Among School Children*). Honey involves a whole range of symbols associated with the lure of generation, many of which are to be found in Porphyry's *De Antro Nympharum*. Mallet's *Northern Antiquities* (II, 53) describes the dew of

which the bees make their honey, shed from the world-tree Yggdrasil; Coleridge's symbol of "honey-dew" combines both the "moisture" and the sweetness that lures the souls.

37. *Cave of the Nymphs*, § 6; *Works*, p. 190.
38. *G.P.*; K. 771, 19–24.
39. *J.* 67; K. 704, 3–12.
40. *J.* 90; K. 736, 19–22, 27.
41. Note to *Cave of the Nymphs*, § 17; *Works*, p. 198. The phallic nature of the distaff of Phorcys has been pointed out by Keynes. A comparable image is to be seen in *J.* 25, where women wind a ball of yarn from the navel of the giant Albion. When Los is materialized in the sea of matter,

> . . . *his organs like roots*
> *Shooting out from the seed, shot beneath,*
> *And a vast world of waters around him.*
> *In furious torments began.*
>
> [*B.L.* III; K. 259, 64–67]

This is the ever-branching "Polypus" of natural generation, those veins

> *Which now my rivers were become, rolling in tubelike forms*
> *Shut up within themselves descending down. I sunk along*
> *The goary tide even to the place of seed, & there dividing*
> *I was divided in darkness and oblivion. . . .*
>
> [*F.Z.* VII; K. 327, 285–88]

Plato in the *Timaeus* names Phorcys among the ennead of gods who fabricate generation, and Taylor quotes Proclus' commentary: "as the Jupiter in this ennead causes the unapparent divisions and separation of forms made by Saturn to become apparent, and as Rhea calls them forth into motion and generation; so Phorcys inserts them into matter, produces sensible natures, and adorns the visible essence." This is also quoted by Taylor in a note to § 17.

42. Tharmas is described as a "shepherd," an occupation that seems strangely inconsistent with his marine kingdom. Was he, like the "old man of the sea," the shepherd not of sheep but of the seals? This is pure speculation. Phorcys is, in this sense, described as a shepherd.
43. *M.* 29; K. 517–18, 55–63. The Erythrean, or "red," sea is, of course, the blood of life.
44. II, 217 ff.
45. *Cave of the Nymphs*, § 10; *Works*, p. 186.
46. Ibid., § 11; *Works*, pp. 186 ff.
47. Cornelius Agrippa also writes of these, quoting Orpheus as his authority: "The gates of Pluto cannot be unlocked: within is a people of dreams" (Bk. III, p. 480).
48. Cf. Keats's figure of Saturn in *Hyperion*.
49. This was pointed out to me by Sir Anthony Blunt.
50. K. 770, 1–2.
51. *G.P.*; K. 771, 39–42.
52. *Ah! Sun-flower*, *S.E.*; K. 215.

4. *Thel*

·1. The images recall Eccles. 12:5–6: "The mourners go about the streets; or ever the silver cord be loosed, or the golden bowl be broken, or the pitcher be broken at the fountain." Rod and bowl might also be sexual symbols. Wisdom, in cabalistic symbolism, is associated with a silver pillar.

2. *B.T.* 6; K. 130, 1–3. Northrop Frye makes this attribution. Spenser describes two gates, in his Garden of Adonis, by which the souls enter and return, but does not relate them to the north and south. The Happy Valley of Dr. Johnson's *Rasselas* has northern and southern gates, but to these no symbolic meaning attached.

3. *F.Q.* III.vi.31.

4. Dedication of the illustrations to Blair's *Grave*, 1808; K. 442.

5. *F.Q.* III.vi.31.

6. Ibid. 32.

7. The Platonic cycle of death and rebirth is implicit in Blake's opening line, "The daughters of Mne Seraphim led round their sunny flocks." Spenser follows Plato himself (*Republic* x.615A) in giving a thousand years as the time of this cycle:

> *Some thousand yeares so doen they there remaine;*
> *And then of him are clad with other hew,*
> *Or sent into the chaungefull world againe,*
> *Till thither they returne, where first they grew:*
> *So like a wheele around they runne from old to new.*
>
> [*F.Q.* III.vi.33]

8. *F.Q.* III.vi.34.

9. *B.T.* 1; K. 127, 6–7.

10. *F.Q.* III.vi.40.

11. *B.T.* 5; K. 130, 7.

12. *Three Books of Occult Philosophy.* Miss Piloo Nanavutty ("Some Eastern Influences on William Blake's Prophetic Books"—unpublished) points out that "Bne Seraphim" appeared in the *Conjurer's Magazine*, edited by Barrett, who later published *The Magus*, with many extracts from Agrippa. The *Conjurer's Magazine* was not published until 1791, but Miss Nanavutty suggests that Blake or some of his friends (Fuseli was a contributor, and the miniaturist Cosway was said to have studied magic) may for a time have been associated with "some society for the study of these very mysterious occult arts." One might then guess that through Barrett himself, or at a remove, Blake came to read Cornelius Agrippa. Miss Nanavutty does not, of course, suggest that "Bne Seraphim" was taken from the magazine article. There is, besides, abundant evidence that Blake had read Agrippa at some time before he wrote *Tiriel*. His association with Barrett and his circle, if such there was, must therefore have been before 1789.

13. *O.H.* (1792 edn.), p. 113, lines 50–51.

14. *P.L.* I.447–51. Northrop Frye traced this allusion.

15. The *Anemone pulsatilla* grows wild in Cambridgeshire, where the legend

clings to it in the form of a folk belief that this plant grows wherever "a Dane's blood" (Adonis' blood?) was shed. The name *pasqueflower* associates the anemone with the dying God of Christianity.

16. *B.T.* 1; K. 127, 23–25.
17. *F.Q.* III.vi.38.
18. Ibid. 33.
19. P. 21.
20. See our I, p. 203.
21. See also *The Little Boy Lost*, who was "wet with dew," above, p. 18.
22. *E.P.T.*, p. 233.
23. *P.C.B.*, pp. 11–12 n.; Ennead III.6.7.
24. *B.T.* 1; K. 127, 8–11.
25. *F.Q.* III.vi.47.
26. Ibid. 38.
27. *B.T.* 2; K. 128, 5–12.
28. *B.T.* 5; K. 130, 12–13.
29. *B.T.* 6; K. 130, 21–22.
30. *P.C.B.*, pp. 36–37; *Ennead* I.6.8. The quotation is from the *Iliad* II.140. Thel's flight to "the vales of Har" is one of the most mysterious elements of the poem. Har's country, as we know it from *Tiriel*, is an earthly paradise that proves to be a fool's paradise also, for Har and Heva are earth-bound. Is Thel, in her flight from incarnation, placing herself, after all, not in eternity but in the spiritual state of materialism? In *Vala* IX we find Vala solving Thel's riddle by the discovery that body exists in soul and not soul in body (see below, our I, pp. 180–81). Since Thel has failed to realize this, she might be said to be the victim of materialism, taking the land of sorrows in the "grave" for a substantial reality, whereas in fact it is a world of shadows only, herself the immortal substance. If Blake meant this, it must be said that he does not make his meaning clear; the emphasis that falls on "the vales of Har" from the fact that these are the last words of the poem leaves us puzzling over the question of where, precisely, Thel's flight does take her. Does she fly, hoping to reach "our father's delightful land"—eternity—only to find that her cowardice takes her to Har's country and the materialist fallacy which inevitably leads to the serpent metamorphosis?
31. Northrop Frye has observed this, but the expanded parallel seems worth giving.
32. *Rasselas*, ed. Chapman, p. 8. Did this name in part suggest "the vales of Har" to which Thel fled?
33. Ibid., p. 28.
34. Ibid., pp. 12–13.
35. *B.T.* 1; K. 127, 1–2.
36. *Rasselas*, pp. 13–15. There is perhaps another echo from *Rasselas* in Thel's reluctance to enter the land of the dead. Rasselas, his sister, and her maid are visiting a pyramid, which Dr. Johnson understood to be a place of burial:

> they prepared to enter its interiour apartments . . . when the favourite of the princess, looking into the cavity, stepped back and trembled. "Pekuah, said the Princess, of what art thou afraid?" "Of the narrow entrance, answered the lady, and of the dreadful gloom. I dare not enter a place which

must surely be inhabited by unquiet souls. The original possessors of these dreadful vaults will start up before us, and, perhaps, shut us in for ever.

[P. 141]

Thel is similarly reluctant; she enters only to withdraw in terror:

> *Thel enter'd in & saw the secrets of the land unknown.*
> *She saw the couches of the dead . . .*
>
> [B.T. 6; K. 130, 2–3]

The graves are indeed inhabited by unquiet souls:

> *She wander'd in the land of clouds thro' valleys dark, list'ning*
> *Dolours & lamentations; waiting oft beside a dewy grave*
> *She stood in silence, list'ning to the voices of the ground*
>
> [B.T. 6; K. 130, 6–8]

She withdraws in terror. Blake has captured, in Thel's fear of entering the "grave" of this world, the horror of the grave that possessed Pekuah—the mood of the late eighteenth-century Gothic romances, of Blair's *Grave* and Young's *Night Thoughts.*

37. Spenser's innermost sanctuary of Adonis is similarly described.

38. *Lumen de Lumine*, p. 3; *Works*, p. 245. (The A. E. Waite edition is not entirely satisfactory—the passages of Greek and Latin are anglicized in the text by the editor—but it is convenient for purposes of reference.) The copy of *The Book of Thel* in the Fitzwilliam Museum, which according to Keynes may be the earliest, shows Thel dressed all in green. It seems a possible guess that Blake was still thinking of her in terms of Vaughan's green-clad Thalia. The similar figure of Hyanthe in Vaughan's *Coelum Terrae* (pp. 93–94; *Works*, pp. 202–203) is perhaps also merged into the charming figure of Thel:

> *I saw Hyanthe and her throne.*
> *In fresh, green Damascs she was drest*
> *And o're a Saphir Globe did rest . . .*

Hyanthe is a weeping figure like Thel:

> *Sleepie shee look'd to my first sight,*
> *As if shee had Watch'd all the Night,*
> *And underneath, her hand was spread,*
> *The White Supporter of her head.*
> *But at my Second, studied View*
> *I could perceive a silent Dew*
> *Steal down her Cheeks; lest it should Stayne*
> *Those Cheeks where onely Smiles should reigne.*
> *The Tears stream'd down for haste, and all*
> *In Chaines of liquid Pearle did fall.*

She is called "Pretty, white Foole," because she is the white, pure *prima materia* of the alchemists; for similar reasons, perhaps, Thel is described as drying her tears on her "white veil." (She is often dressed in white, in later copies.) Certainly she is a figure much in the mood of the seventeenth century and of Vaughan in particular.

39. *Lumen de Lumine*, pp. 7–8; *Works*, p. 247.
40. Ibid., p. 7; *Works*, p. 247.
41. *Coelum Terrae*, p. 83; *Works*, p. 195: "This fine substance is the Child of the Elements and it is a most pure, sweet Virgin; for nothing as yet hath been generated out of her: . . . Shee is no Animal, no Vegetable, no Mineral, neither is shee extracted out of Animals, Vegetables or Minerals, but shee is prae-existent to them all, for shee is the Mother of them. . . . Shee yeelds to nothing but Love, for her End is Generation." She is the philosophers' stone itself, but described by Vaughan in terms of *water*. The alchemical masters, he says, call it "white Gum and Water of their Sea, water of Life, most pure, and most blessed water, and yet they minde not water of the Clouds, or Rain-water, nor water of the Wel, nor Dew: but a certain thick, permanent, saltish water, a water that is drie, and wetts not the hand"—and more of the same.
42. *Lumen de Lumine*, p. 12; *Works*, p. 250.
43. *B.T.* 6; K. 130, 2–4.
43a. *The Life of William Blake*, p. 34.
44. Proclus is a notable exception to this generalization.
45. *Annotations to Lavater* 630; K. 87.
46. As given by Roger Bacon in *The Mirror of Alchimy*, tr. Thomas Creede, p. 16. The passage continues:

> His father is the sun, his mother is the moone, the wind bore it in hir belly. The earth is his nurse. The father of all the telesme of this world is here. His force and power is perfect, if it be turned into earth. Thou shalt seperate the earth from the fire, the thinne from the thicke, and that gently with great discretion. It ascendeth from the Earth into Heaven: and againe it descend-eth into the earth, and receiveth the power of the superiours and inferiours: so shalt thou have the glorie of the whole worlde. All obscuritie therefore shall flie away from thee. This is the mightie power of all power, for it shal overcome every subtile thing, and pearce through every solide thing. So was the worlde created. Here shall be marvailous adaptations, whereof this is the meane.

It is by no means certain that Blake knew the whole text of the Smaragdine Table, as given by Roger Bacon; it is the first sentence that is continually quoted by all alchemical writers, but this alone contains the essence of the philosophy. However, Roger Bacon was one of the spirit-heads drawn by Blake, which suggests that he knew something of him.
47. *Magia Adamica*, p. 70; *Works*, p. 183.
48. Also in the Hermetica: "of contraposition, that is, setting one against another, and contrariety, all things must consist" (*Pym.* IV.35; p. 24). This is, of course, the Heraclitean tradition of the composition of all things from Ares and Eros, concord and discord.
49. *V.D.A.* 5–6; K. 193, 39–41, 1.
50. *B.T.* 6; K. 130, 11–20.
51. *V.L.J.;* K. 605, 68–69.
52. *J.* 91; K. 738, 33–42.
53. See also our I, p. 28.
54. *B.T.* 4–5; K. 129, 11–12, 1–4.

55. *Annotations to Lavater* 630; K. 87.

56. *G.P.;* K. 770, 16.

57. *J.* 12; K. 631, 15.

58. *Pym.* XI.117–26; p. 80.

59. Paracelsus, *Mysteries of Creation*, Bk. II, text 5, p. 32.

60. *Anthroposophia Theomagica*, p. 12; *Works*, p. 19.

61. Vaughan, *Coelum Terrae*, pp. 88–89; *Works*, p. 199. The process that Vaughan describes with so much charm he derives from the more fundamental thought of Paracelsus:

> Here consider, that in the beginning there was but one thing, without any inclination and form, from which afterwards all things came forth. That rise or originall was no other but as a temperate colour, suppose purple, having no inclination in it to any other colour, but plainly to be seen in its just temperature. Yet in it are all colours. The red, green, azure, yellow, white, black colour cannot be separated from it. . . . After the same manner every thing had its essence in the great mystery, which afterward the supream workmaster separated.
>
> [*Mysteries of Creation*, Bk. III, text 5, pp. 59–60]

This is the "one thing," the *prima materia*, whose miracles are performed as described in the Smaragdine Table, the bride of the Macroprosopos.

62. *Magia Adamica*, pp. 68–69; *Works*, p. 182.

63. *Coelum Terrae*, pp. 86–87; *Works*, p. 197.

64. *Magia Adamica*, "To the Reader" (not paged); *Works*, p. 129.

65. Further confirmation that Blake knew Vaughan's works may perhaps be found in *America*, pl. 4 [53], where Urizen is shown pursued by a basilisk or cockatrice, accurately depicted (with head, wings, and feet of a cock terminating in a serpent with a barbed tail), and in a clumsy style not characteristic of Blake's draftsmanship, but closely resembling the creatures shown in Vaughan's *Lumen de Lumine* [50]. The figure of Matter encircled by the cockatrice in this plate is an emblem of the passage quoted.

66. *The Couch of Death;* K. 36.

67. Ossian, *Songs of Selma; Works*, I, 291–92. I have broken the prose paragraph into lines, to simplify comparison.

68. *B.T.* 2; K. 128, 11–15.

69. *B.T.* 3; K. 128, 5–6.

70. *Carric-Thura; Works*, I, 274–75.

5. The Myth of the Kore

1. In Wolf Mankowitz, *The Portland Vase and the Wedgwood Copies*, p. 66 n.

2. *Blake Studies*, pp. 68–69.

3. *F.Z.* VIIb; K. 340, 291–94.

4. According to Keynes, the title page of *Milton* was engraved first.

5. There is no date on the title page of this work, which bears the (possibly fictitious) imprint of Amsterdam. There is no record of its publication in the Dutch lists. The year assigned is 1790, but this date is by no means certain. *The*

Little Girl Lost and *Found* may have been written as late as 1790; or Taylor's *Dissertation* may have been published earlier. There remains the possibility that Blake saw Taylor's work in manuscript or in proof before the date of publication.

6. Erasmus Darwin, *The Botanic Garden*, p. 54.

7. *The Little Girl Lost;* K. 112.

8. Minucius Felix; *D.E.*, pp. 94–95.

9. *D.E.*, pp. 61–62.

10. Ibid., pp. 95–96. Intellect in the Platonic sense, the universal Logos (Blake's Jesus the Imagination), the universal humanity from which the individual human being depends. This relationship of individual to universal humanity is discussed in Chapter 26 (vol. II). In terms of Jungian psychology one might liken Demeter to the self, not subject to temporal events, and Persephone to the ego.

11. What is the origin of the name Lyca? Possibly λευκός (white) appropriate to a virgin soul. A more interesting suggestion I owe to Mr. John Heath Stubbs. A famous figure in the eighteenth century was "Peter the Wild Boy," a child said to have been reared in Germany by wolves, and who was brought to England in 1726, there to remain until his death in 1785. Swift, Defoe, Arbuthnot, and Monboddo are among the many eminent authors who wrote about him. The revival of interest in the wild Peter after his death must have reached Blake's circle; and the idea of a child safely reared by wolves may have seemed to him sufficiently poetic to serve as a point of departure for a poem for children on the subject. The name Lyca means, on the face of it, "she-wolf." The wolves have given place to the nobler lions—all but the "wolvish howl" in the last verse, which remains, perhaps, as a clue to one of the sources of the poem.

12. *F.Z.* IX; K. 373, 617–19.

13. *Aeneid* VI.282–84; *Works*, tr. Dryden, p. 374, lines 394–97. Cf. also: "Once a dream did weave a shade / O'er my Angel-guarded bed."

14. *A Dream, S.I.;* K. 111.

15. *A Cradle Song, S.I.;* K. 120.

16. Darwin identifies the two trees on the reverse side of the Portland vase with the dual tree of knowledge.

17. Browning observed "the brushwood sheaf on the elm-tree bole" in his *Home Thoughts from Abroad*.

18. Taylor, *Select Works of Porphyry*, p. 182. Cf. Yeats's *Among School Children:*

> *What youthful mother, a shape upon her lap*
> *Honey of generation had betrayed,*
> *And that must sleep, shriek, struggle to escape*
> *As recollection or the drug decide*

Recollection is anamnesis, the drug, the Lethean drink.

19. See Keynes, ed., *William Blake's Illustrations to the Bible*, No. 5.

20. Who does nevertheless incur it by gathering the flower of the hundred-headed golden Narcissus, whose symbolism is discussed in the next chapter. Blake's Oothoon is raped by Bromion after gathering a golden flower, the "Marygold" (*V.D.A.* 1; K. 189, 5).

21. *D.E.*, p. 72. The traditional midnight celebration of the first Christmas Mass no doubt perpetuates this ancient belief about the time of Incarnation.

22. Macrobius. In Taylor, *E.P.T.*, p. 287.

23. Ibid.
24. *The Divine Legation of Moses* (4th rev. and enl. edn.), Vol. i, Pt. i, Bk. ii, § 4, p. 157 n. Taylor refers to this work in the opening sentence of his *Dissertation*, so that there is good reason to suppose that Blake knew Warburton. Darwin also quotes him.
25. *G.P.*; K. 771, 21–22.
26. *D.E.*, p. 102.
27. *D.E.*, pp. 129–30.
28. *On the Descent of the Soul; P.F.B.*, pp. 254–55; *Ennead* iv.8.1.
29. *The Little Girl Found;* K. 113.
30. *D.E.*, p. 126.
31. *Metamorphoses*, Bk. v.
32. *Republic* x.615D–16B; in Taylor, *Works of Plato*, i, 471.
33. Jung and Kerényi, *Essays on a Science of Mythology*.
34. *D.E.*, pp. 88–91. The account continues:

> Fables are theological which employ nothing corporeal, but speculate the very essences of the gods; such as the fable which asserts that Saturn devoured his children: for it insinuates nothing more than the nature of an intellectual god; since every intellect returns into itself. But we speculate fables physically when we speak concerning the energies of the gods about the world; as when considering Saturn the same as time, and calling the parts of time the children of the universe, we assert that the children are devoured by their parent. But we employ fables in an animastic mode, when we contemplate the energies of soul; because the intellections of our souls, though by a discursive energy they run into other things, yet abide in their parents. Lastly, fables are material, such as the Egyptians ignorantly employ, considering and calling corporeal natures divinities: such as Isis, earth, Osiris, humidity, Typhon, heat: or, again, denominating Saturn water, Adonis, fruits, and Bacchus, wine. And, indeed, to assert that these are dedicated to the gods, in the same manner as herbs, stones, and animals, is the part of wise men; but to call them gods is alone the province of fools and mad men; unless we speak in the same manner as when, from established custom, we call the orb of the sun and its rays the sun itself. . . . But of these species of fables, such as are theological belong to philosophers; the physical and animastic to poets; but the mixt to initiatory rites (τελεταῖς) since the intention of all mystic ceremonies is to conjoin us with the world and the gods.

Sallust's remarkable statement about the sun is altogether in the spirit of Blake (and indeed of Swedenborg), and must certainly have won his assent, possibly helping to form his own splendid imagery of the living spiritual sun that "informs" the lifeless material sun. Blake's painting "The Judgment of Paris" (above, p. 71) seems to be taken from the example given by Sallust of the "mixt" fable that concludes the above extract:

> But we may perceive the mixed kind of fables, as well in many other particulars, when they relate that Discord, at a banquet of the gods, threw a golden apple, and that a dispute about it arising among the goddesses, they were sent by Jupiter to take the judgment of Paris, who, charmed with the beauty of

Venus, gave her the apple in preference to the rest. For in this fable the banquet denotes the supermundane powers of the gods; and on this account they
subsist in conjunction with each other; but the golden apple denotes the
world, which, on account of its composition from contrary natures, is not im-
properly said to be thrown by Discord, or strife. But again, since different
gifts are imparted to the world by different gods, they appear to contest with
each other for the apple. And a soul living according to sense (for this
is Paris) not perceiving other powers in the universe, asserts that the apple is
alone the beauty of Venus.

The emphasis in Blake's composition of the figure of Discord is striking; and in
his characterization of Paris he seems to follow Sallust very closely in portraying
Paris as the sense-dulled soul. His downward drowsy look conveys this, and his
whole aspect conveys that his choice is made not from perception but from want
of perception: he seems not to be aware of the other goddesses. For added
emphasis on this meaning, there is a sleeping dog at his feet (dogs according to
Taylor are "material demons"), with the name of his master written on his
collar, ΠΑΡΙϚ. There is no written pre-Alexandrian authority for the Apple
of Discord, and Eris is not usually represented in compositions on this story.
Ovid tells of the apple, but Blake's treatment of the theme strongly suggests
that he knew Sallust.

35. *D.E.*, p. 47. That Bacon, surely the most unimaginative mind ever to comment
on myths, should have been credited, even fancifully, with the writing of the
works of Shakespeare, the most mythopoeic of all poets, must be the measure of
the modern mentality's incomprehension of the entire nature of mythological
thought. Bacon gives what Sallust calls a physical interpretation of the myths,
and what he writes of Pluto and Proserpina is not without interest here. His
interpretation accords with his scientific interests:

> This spirit is fained to be rapted by the Earth, because nothing can with-hold
> it when it hath time and leasure to escape. It is therefore caught and stayed
> by a sudden contraction, no other wise then if a man should goe about to mix
> ayre with water, which can be done by no meanes, but by a speedy and rapid
> agitation, as may be seene in froth, wherein the ayre is rapted by the water.
> Neither is it inelegantly added that *Proserpina* was rapte as shee was gather-
> ing *Narcissus* Flowers in the valleyes, because Narcissus hath his name from
> slownesse or stupiditie; for indeed then is this Spirit most prepared and fitted
> to be snatcht by terrestriall matter, when it beginnes to be coagulated, and
> becomes as it were slowe.
> [*The Wisedome of the Ancients*, tr. A. Gorges, pp. 159–60]

36. Robert Graves has, however, reverted to a physical (euhemerist) interpretation
of myths.

37. A comparison between Wordsworth's presumably intuitive myth-making in this
poem with Blake's deliberate working within a traditional framework is interesting; neither poet suffers by the comparison.

38. See our I, p. 178.

39. Notebook III; K. 168.

40. *S.E.;* K. 210–11.

41. *V.D.A.*
42. This essay appears as a long footnote to *An Essay on the Restoration of the Platonic Theology*, II, 294 ff.; and also in shorter form in a note on Plotinus' *Concerning the Beautiful.*
43. *D.E.*, p. 3. See also Plotinus, *On the Descent of the Soul; P.F.B.*, p. 253; *Ennead* IV.8.1.
44. *P.F.B.*, p. 268; *Ennead* IV.8.4.
45. *Ibid.*, p. 280; *Ennead* IV.8.7.
46. The *Songs of Experience* were advertised in October 1793, but no copy is known to have existed at that time; since the title page is dated 1794, it is highly probable that the *Introduction* was written in that year and not in 1793, replacing, perhaps, some other intended poem. On the other hand, it is equally possible that he saw Taylor's essay before publication.
47. See also our II, p. 92.
48. *S.E.;* K. 210.
49. *P.F.B.*, pp. 104–105; *Ennead* 1.8.14.
50. *Ibid.*, pp. 99–100; *Ennead* 1.8.13.
51. *P.C.B.*, p. 36; *Ennead* 1.6.8.
52. *Ibid.*, p. 46 n.
53. K. 211.
54. *B.A.* 5; K. 255, 39–47.
55. *Iliad* XIX.122–26; tr. Chapman, I, 210. Blake possessed a copy of Chapman's *Homer.*
56. *Vala* 22ᴿ, 1–5 (*F.Z.* III; K. 294, 109–12).
57. *B.A.* 2; K. 250, 34–43.
58. *Pym.* X.58; p. 63.
59. *Ibid.* 53; p. 63.
60. *Ibid.* IV.37–38; p. 24.
61. *B.A.* 5; K. 254–55, 14–23.
62. *Pym.* X.31–35; p. 61.
63. *F.Z.* II; K. 284–85, 181–84.
64. We are reminded of the Chinese yang, the active principle of heaven, and yin, the passive feminine principle of earth, from whose interplay all things are created.
65. *Vala* 22ᴿ, 7–11 (*F.Z.* III; K. 295, 114–19).
66. Sluggish because although πάντα ῥεῖ, the flowing away of forms is relatively slow?
67. *Vala* 22ᴿ, 11–15 (*F.Z.* III; K. 295, 119–24).
68. *Pym.* 1.44; p. 4.
69. *Ibid.* 72; p. 5.
70. *Ibid.* 74; p. 5.
71. *Ibid.* 53–58; p. 4.
72. *F.Z.* III; K. 295, 141–44.
73. *Pym.* 1.73; p. 5.
74. *Vala* 54ᵛ, 19–21 (*F.Z.* VIII; K. 354, 505–507).
75. *Pym.* 1.65; p. 5.
76. *Vala* 54ᵛ, 9–16 (*F.Z.* VIII; K. 353–54, 495–502).
77. *Pym.* 1.60; p. 4.

78. *B.A.* 5; K. 255, 29–34.
79. *M.H.H.* 7; K. 151, 10.
80. *Vala* 61^R, 37–38 (*F.Z.* IX; K. 362, 198–99).
81. See quotation above, our I, p. 153.
82. *Vala* 62^V, 6–10 (*F.Z.* IX; K. 364, 291–95).
83. *Vala* 63^R, 3–7 (*F.Z.* IX; K. 365, 321–25).
84. *Vala* 62^V, 32–33 (*F.Z.* IX; K. 365, 317–18).
85. *Vala* 63^R, 17–19 (*F.Z.* IX; K. 366, 337–39).
86. Cf. St. Paul, I Cor. 15.
87. *Vala* 63^R, 20–23 (*F.Z.* IX; K. 366, 340–43).
88. *Vala* 66^V, 2–7 (*F.Z.* IX; K. 372, 579–84).
89. *Vala* 61^V, 8–11 (*F.Z.* IX; K. 362, 212–15).
90. *Vala* 63^R, 24–33 (*F.Z.* IX; K. 366, 344–53). Did Blake know the myth of the annual bath by which Hera renews her virginity?
91. There is a canceled plate that was actually used in one of two copies of *Songs of Experience* before Blake substituted the poem *To Tirzah*, which shows a majestic androgynous figure upborne by six winged cherubs. The figure's hands are pressed together in a traditional attitude of prayer found in numberless paintings of the Christian Virgin. Is this the assumption of Earth? That the figure is androgynous makes this seem by no means certain. Keynes suggests, with likelihood, that it is man who is so raised—the two sexes, which were torn apart when Eve became externalized, once more restored to him. Yet the position of the plate at the end of the series of poems that opens with Earth's lamentation lends some possibility to the view that this is the "return" of Earth. The plate is reproduced in Wicksteed's *Blake's Innocence and Experience*.
92. I Cor. 15:36–45.

6.   *Oothoon in Leutha's Vale*

1. K. 211.
2. *J.* 77; K. 717.
3. K. 428.
4. *V.L.J.* 92–95; K. 615–16.
5. This attribution was first made by Middleton Murry in his introduction to the Dent facsimile edition of the *Visions of the Daughters of Albion*, 1932. Max Plowman held the same view.
6. *Eloisa*, Vol. II, Letter CVIII, p. 198.
7. Ibid., Letter CIX, pp. 200–201.
8. *P.L.* IV.269–73.
9. *V.D.A.* 1; K. 189, 3–7.
10. *B.T.* 3; K. 128, 7–8.
11. *V.D.A.* 1; K. 189, 8–10.
12. Pp. 105–106.
13. K. 206.
14. *Europe* 14; K. 244, 9–14.
15. *M.* 18; K. 500, 39–41.
16. *M.* 11; K. 492, 32–33.

17.   *J.* 83; K. 729, 80–82.

18.   *P.L.* II. 650–61.

19.   Porphyry (*On the Cave of the Nymphs*, § 11; *Works*, p. 189) writes that "the star Sothis, which the Greeks call the Dog, is near to Cancer"—that is, to the northern gate of generation. Is Sothis the original of Blake's "Sotha," who "in the North" gave to Odin "a Code of War" (*S.L.* 3; K. 246, 30)?

20.   Cerberus, according to Taylor's *Dissertation*, is a material demon; and there is a curious monster, described in *Jerusalem* (70; K. 708, 2–16), with three heads, which prove to be those of the three philosophers of materialism:

> *. . . a mighty threat'ning Form:*
>
> *His bosom wide & shoulders huge, overspreading wondrous,*
> *Bear Three strong sinewy Necks & Three awful & terrible Heads,*
> *Three Brains, in contradictory council brooding incessantly,*
> *Neither daring to put in act its councils, fearing each-other,*
> *Therefore rejecting Ideas as nothing & holding all Wisdom*
> *To consist in the agreements & disagreements of Ideas*

These are "Three Forms named Bacon & Newton & Locke." The origin of the monster is Cerberus, but Cerberus interpreted in such a way as to make the attribution of the three heads to the intellects of Bacon, Newton, and Locke particularly apt. Taylor certainly gave Blake the lead in the following passage:

> by Cerberus we must understand the discriminative part of the soul, of which a dog, on account of its sagacity, is an emblem; and the three heads signify the triple distinction of this part, into the intellective, cogitative, and opinionative powers.—With respect to the three kinds of persons described as situated on the borders of the infernal realms, the poet [Vergil] doubtless intended by this enumeration to represent to us the three most remarkable characters, who, though not apparently deserving of punishment, are yet each of them similarly merged in matter, and consequently require a similar degree of purification. [*D.E.*, pp. 30–31]

Blake also places these three characters on the borders of hell:

> *. . . the key-bones & the chest dividing in pain*
> *Disclose a hideous orifice; thence issuing, the Giant-brood*
> *Arise, as the smoke of the furnace, shaking the rocks from sea to sea,*
> *And there they combine into Three Forms named Bacon & Newton & Locke*
> [*J.* 70; K. 708, 12–15]

21.   In the notes of Ossian Blake found a glossary of many such roots: Utha (water), Atha (a shallow river, used perhaps in Thiralatha), and the name Nathos, one of the sons of Usnoth. Theotormon probably derives from the root Torman (thunder).

22.   *V.D.A.* 6; K. 193–94.

23.   *V.D.A.* 8; K. 195, 11–12.

24.   *Ennead* I.6.8. In Taylor, *D.E.*, pp. 12–13. Italics mine.

25.   *V.D.A.* 1; K. 189, 9–10.

26.   *G.P.;* K. 771.

27. *P.C.B.*, pp. 23–24; *Ennead* 1.6.5.
28. *V.D.A.* 3; K. 191, 18–20.
29. *V.D.A.* 2; K. 191, 28–29.
30. *S.L.* 3; K. 246, 22–24.
31. *The Life of the Holy Mother St. Teresa*, p. 170. Another image that Blake has clearly taken from St. Teresa is the figure of the "monk of Charlemain," in the poem prefixed to *J.* 3 (K. 683):

> *His body bent, his arms & knees*
> *Like to the roots of ancient trees.*

This is St. Teresa's description of St. Peter of Alcántara, the hermit who was her master: "As to the extending of his body at length in his cell, it was not possible to him; for his cell, as it is known, was not above four foot and a half in length. When I came to know him, he was very old, and his weakness so extreme that he seemed not to be composed, but as of the roots of trees" (pp. 82–83).

32. *V.D.A.* 2; K. 190, 14–19.

7. *Blake's Cupid and Psyche*

1. *Blake's Vala*, note to 64ᴿ, p. 150.
2. *Vala* 64ᴿ, 16–23 (*F.Z.* IX; K. 368, 410–17).
3. *Vala* 63ᵛ, 18–24 (*F.Z.* IX; K. 367, 375–81).
4. *Vala* 64ᴿ, 24–27 (*F.Z.* IX; K. 368, 418–21).
5. *Vala* 64ᴿ, 28–34 (*F.Z.* IX; K. 368, 422–28).
6. *V.L.J.;* K. 605, 71–72.
7. *V.L.J.;* K. 607, 79.
8. *Botanic Garden*, Pt. I, pp. 56–57.
9. Margoliouth, *Vala*, p. 4. The drawings are reproduced in Ellis and Yeats, *Works of Blake*, III.
10. *O.H.* (1792 edn.) XXXVIII, p. 170.
11. Tr. Adlington, Qivᵛ.
12. *Vala* 13ᴿ, 10 (*F.Z.* II; K. 282, 72).
13. *Vala* 14ᴿ, 4–9 (*F.Z.* II; K. 282, 94–99).
14. *Vala* 6ᴿ, 5–12 (*F.Z.* I; K. 272, 284–87, 299–301).
15. *Vala* 16ᴿ, 15–17; 16ᵛ, 2 (*F.Z.* II; K. 286, 231–35). The smoke is Paracelsus' simile for the great mystery, nature.
16. *Fable of Cupid and Psyche*, p. vi.
17. Tr. Adlington, Lviiiʳ.
18. *Vala* 64ᵛ, 27–37; 65ᴿ, 1–3 (*F.Z.* IX; K. 369, 457–70).
19. *Vala* 65ᴿ, 11–16 (*F.Z.* IX; K. 369, 478–83).
20. *Vala* 47ᵛ, 24–32 (*F.Z.* IX; VII, K. 340, 271–79).
21. *Fable of Cupid and Psyche*, p. vii. This is Taylor's prose style at its worst, but I take him to mean that the consciousness of the generated but innocent soul is a little lower than that of spirits of the intelligible world, yet higher than that of souls fallen into complete amnesia. Psyche's link with the gods, so long as she re-

mains innocent, is not severed, for she can still communicate with spirits of an intermediate order—the daimons or mundane gods.

22. "Whatever is fixt, is from the Element of earth. That which nourisheth, is from the Element of aire. And that which consumeth, is of the Element of water. To grow is the property onely of fire" (Paracelsus, *Mysteries of Creation*, Bk. II, text 6, p. 33). An unlikely word is nearly always, in Blake, not a clumsiness but a clue. The "consuming" action of water is described by Enion, as the "wat'ry grave," the "dark consumer."

23. *Vala* 63ᵛ, 26–35; 64ᴿ, 6–8 (*F.Z.* IX; K. 367, 385–401).

24. Tr. Adlington, Riiʳ.

25. *F.Z.* IX; K. 367, 402.

26. Song of Sol. 1:7.

27. *Vala* 64ᵛ, 25–28 (*F.Z.* IX; K. 369, 455–57).

28. Song of Sol. 3:1–3.

29. Ibid. 5:6.

30. There are other parallels. The sufferings of the Shulamite are the toils of love in exile. In the Greek legend it is Venus who "leaped upon the face of poor Psyche, and (tearing her apparell) tooke her by the haire, and dashed her head upon the ground." In the biblical story: "The watchmen that went about the city found me, they smote me, they wounded me; the keepers of the walls took away my veil from me" (5:7). There is much in both stories that he did not use but that may have confirmed Blake in his identification of the two myths; for example, the crowning of King Solomon by his mother "in the day of his espousals."

31. Song of Sol. 2:14.

32. *Vala* 64ᴿ, 6 (*F.Z.* IX; K. 367, 400).

33. *Vala* 65ᴿ, 29–31 (*F.Z.* IX; K. 370, 500–2).

34. Song of Sol. 6:2.

35. Psyche among her sisters might be compared to "the lily among thorns."

36. Song of Sol. 2:1–2.

37. Ibid. 6:4.

38. Ibid. 8:8–10.

39. Ibid. 3:9–10.

40. Is it fanciful to surmise that the story of Vala is likewise in part drawn from a more homely version of this same myth? Like Cinderella, Vala has wonderful garments—her glittering veil and her magic shoes; and like Cinderella also, she toils in servitude, her beauty bemired with clay and ashes. If Blake perceived the identity of the story of Cupid and Psyche with the Song of Solomon, may he not also have recognized in Cinderella "the lapsed Soul," bemired like Persephone with the dust of Hades? I know of no more likely source of Vala's *shoes:*

> *Lift up thy blue eyes, Vala, & put on thy sapphire shoes. . . .*
> *Gird on thy flaming Zone, descend into the Sepulchre,*
> *Scatter the blood from thy golden brow, the tears from thy silver locks,*
> *Shake off the water from thy wings & the dust from thy white garments*
> [*Vala* VIIb, 47ᴿ, 1–5; K. 337, 191–95]

There are versions of the Cinderella story in which the famous glass slippers are *blue* (Harold Bayley, *The Lost Language of Symbolism*, I, 212). Blake, who lived before the story had become standardized, may have known this version. Sapphire is mentioned in the Song of Solomon, but not sapphire shoes. This familiar fairy-tale image, followed by a call to wash "the dust from thy white garments," to lift up "blue eyes," and to gird on a "flaming zone," certainly suggests the traditional princess of the fairy tale, with her dress "of splendour passing description" and her magic slippers. Was Vala—when she "fell, a heap of Ashes / Beneath the furnaces, a woful heap in living death" (*F.Z.* II, 14ᵛ, 4–5; K. 283, 115–16)—enacting an episode from Cinderella's variant of the universal story of the lapse of the soul into the mire and clay of Hades?

The labors of Cinderella and Psyche's toils in the house of Venus, as well as the sufferings of the Children of Israel in the land of Pharaoh, are suggested by another passage from *Vala*, which describes the toils of the soul in exile:

> *The King of Light beheld her mourning among the Brick kilns, compell'd*
> *To labour night & day among the fires; her lamenting voice*
> *Is heard when silent night returns & the labourers take their rest.*
> *"O Lord, wilt thou not look upon our sore afflictions*
> *Among these flames incessant labouring? our hard masters laugh*
> *At all our sorrow. We are made to turn the wheel for water,*
> *To carry the heavy basket on our scorched shoulders, to sift*
> *The sand & ashes, & to mix the clay with tears & repentance.*
> *The times are now return'd upon us; we have given ourselves*
> *To scorn, and now are scorned by the slaves of our enemies.*
> *Our beauty is cover'd over with clay & ashes, & our backs*
> *Furrow'd with whips, & our flesh bruised with the heavy basket.*
> *Forgive us, O thou piteous one whom we have offended! forgive*
> *The weak remaining shadow of Vala that returns in sorrow to thee."*
>
> .   .   .
>
> *Thus she lamented day & night . . .*
>
> [*F.Z.* II; K. 285–86, 215–31]

The *anima mundi* of the alchemists, like Psyche and Cinderella, labors at menial tasks in the material world; and is there an overtone, likewise, of this philosophy in Blake's account of Vala's toils among the clay and ashes? As, for example, this, from Thomas Vaughan's *Anima Magica Abscondita*, p. 10 (*Works*, p. 78): "This *Anima* [of the world] is retaind in the Matter . . . and missing a Vent, doth *Organizzare Molem*. She labours what she can to resume her former Liberty, frames for her selfe a Habitation here in the Center; puts her *Prison* into some good order." Or in *Anthroposophia Theomagica*, p. 4 (*Works*, p. 12):

> *So view my* fetterd Soule, *that must*
> *Struggle with this her* Load *of* Dust
> *Meet her* Addresse, *and add one* Ray
> *To this* mew'd Parcell *of thy* Day
> *She would though here* imprison'd, *see,*
> *Through all her* Dirt *thy* Throne *and* Thee.

41.   Notebook 115; K. 163.
42.   Tr. Adlington, Niiʳ.

43.   Ibid., Oiv^{r–v}

44.   Blake's allusion here to bread and wine has not solely Christian associations; for Psyche in her beautiful house was served with "all sorts of divine meates and wines." These—"the bread of sweet thought and the wine of delight"—are the true divine body, the Imagination. For Blake (as for Apuleius) things of the imagination are the heavenly food; and it is this food of thought that is desecrated and poisoned by the degradation of love.

45.   Is there, in another unpublished poem, which immediately precedes *I Saw a Chapel All of Gold* in the Notebook (4; K. 162), another allusion to the story of Psyche?

> *I laid me down upon a bank*
> *Where love lay sleeping.*
> *I heard among the rushes dank*
> *Weeping, Weeping.*

Psyche, after the departure of Cupid, tries to drown herself in a river; but the river "threw her upon the bank amongst the herbs," where she is found by Pan, who comforts her.

46.   *S.E.;* K. 213.

47.   *Blake's Innocence and Experience*, p. 157.

48.   This poem was brought to my notice by Mr. Martin Bell.

49.   Tr. Adlington, Nii^{r–v}.

50.   *London;* K. 216.

51.   The storm is one of the Neoplatonic symbols for material existence.

52.   *B.U.* 19; K. 232, 19–36.

53.   Sonnet 70.

54.   Sonnet 15.

55.   There is some confusion of the sexes of the rose and the worm in the early drafts of the poem. There is nothing in the first draft to indicate the sex of either, for the "And his . . . ," which alone defines the sexes, is not there:

> *O, dark secret love*
> *Doth life destroy.*
> [Notebook 107; K. 175]

Blake then changed these two lines to the form in which we have them:

> *And his dark secret love*
> *Does thy life destroy*

He then altered "his" to "her." Was he thinking of the male sex of the beloved of Shakespeare's sonnets, called the Rose? Or of the feminine worm of Job, which he illustrated in *The Gates of Paradise?* "I have said to the Worm: Thou art my mother & my sister" (16; K. 770).

Whatever the causes of his hesitation, he soon reverted to the male worm and female rose—conformable, besides, with another Shakespeare passage,

> *. . . she never told her love*
> *But let concealment, like a worm i' the bud*
> *Feed on her damask cheek . . .*
> [*Twelfth Night* II. iv]

The worm here is concealment—a rendering that fits well with Blake's known views on unsatisfied desire: "Sooner murder an infant in its cradle than nurse unacted desires" (*M.H.H.* 10; K. 152, 7).

This meaning would bring us back to the desecration of the chapel of gold by the serpent of eroticism. We shall be nearest the truth in seeing *The Sick Rose* as the point of convergence of all these themes.

8. *Emblems of Love*

1. *J.* 60; K. 693, 39–46.
2. *J.* 60; K. 693, 56–60.
3. *J.* 27; K. 649–50, 5–8, 17–20.
4. *J.* 20; K. 643, 38–41.
5. *F.Z.* viii; K. 345–46, 187–93.
6. *J.* 18; K. 640, 7.
7. *J.* 71; K. 709, 4–5.
8. *J.* 5; K. 624, 65.
9. *Treatise of the Incarnation*, Pt. ii, Chap. 2, §§ 5–7; *Works*, ii, 92.
10. This is Boehme's term for God the Son.
11. *Treatise of the Incarnation*, Pt. i, Chap. 1, §§ 61 ff.; *Works*, ii, 17.
12. *Three Principles*, Chap. 14, § 88; *Works*, i, 121. See Chap. 23, note 4, for a discussion of the cabalistic "Eden" and the "Wisdom" symbol. As the "Wisdom" is to the "Shekhinah," Hokhmah to Malkuth, "Eden" to "the Garden of Eden," so is Boehme's "lily" of wisdom to "Eve" (man's rose-garden) and Blake's Jerusalem to his (later) Vala.
13. *M.* 29; K. 517, 35–36.
14. *J.* 11–12; K. 631, 24–25, 1–3.
15. *J.* 19; K. 642, 40–47.
16. *J.* 20; K. 643, 30–35.
17. *Timaeus* 29A; *Works*, ii, 475.
18. *Three Principles*, Chap. 7, § 23; *Works*, i, 46.
19. *J.* 98; K. 745, 18–19.
20. *M.* 40; K. 533, 35–36.
21. *J.* 5; K. 624, 46–65.
22. *Three Principles*, Chap. 9, § § 6–7; *Works*, i, 57.
23. Ibid., Chap. 16, § 3; *Works*, i, 156.
24. Ibid., Chap. 14, § 83; *Works*, i, 120. The words italicized are from Rev. 22:17.
25. *Treatise of the Incarnation*, Pt. i, Chap. 13, §§ 44–46; *Works*, ii, 80.
26. *J.* 60; K. 692, 14–16.
27. *J.* 30; K. 656, 33.
28. *J.* 92; K. 739, 13–14.
29. "Parts of his scheme are dangerous. His sexual religion is dangerous" (Morley, *Blake, Coleridge etc.*, p. 6).
30. *J.* 17; K. 639, 24–27.
31. *J.* 33; K. 660, 45–46.
32. *J.* 34; K. 660, 15.
33. *J.* 79; K. 721, 68–79.

34.   *J.* 33; K. 660, 45–47, 52.
35.   *J.* 68; K. 707, 65–68.
36.   *J.* 54; K. 685, 11–12.
37.   *J.* 44; K. 674, 21–25.
38.   *B.U.* 18–19; K. 231–32, 9–15, 1–16.
39.   *Three Principles*, Chap. 17, § 10; *Works*, I, 147.
40.   Blake's borrowings from Boehme comprise some of the most crabbed puzzles in
his own far from lucid works. The term "limit" is one of these. The two human
"limits" of opacity and contraction (Satan and Adam) Blake has developed
from two sources: the Christian cabalism of Fludd (see our II, p. 78) gives
the concepts of opacity and contraction; but the term "limit" is one that he has
clearly taken from Boehme, who uses it in the special sense in which it has
been adopted by Blake. The reason for taking up the subject of the limit at this
point is its special relationship to the concept of woman. God the Son sets a
limit to the fall of man into opacity and contraction; in mercy he forms, out
of the limit of contraction, woman—that is to say, from Adam in his fallen
condition—but for which Adam's fall, like that of Satan, would be absolute:

> *There is a limit of Opakeness and a limit of Contraction*
> *In every Individual Man, and the limit of Opakeness*
> *Is named Satan, and the limit of Contraction is named Adam.*
> *But when Man sleeps in Beulah, the Saviour in Mercy takes*
> *Contraction's Limit, and of the Limit he forms Woman, That*
> *Himself may in process of time be born Man to redeem.*
> [*J.* 2; K. 670, 29–34]

Such is Blake's gloss of the story of Adam's rib and the sleep of man in Eden;
and it is but a condensed paraphrase of Boehme's doctrine, obscure without the
key, but with it clear enough.

The "Limit," as Boehme writes of it, is the same as the Jewish Covenant,
God's pledge to redeem fallen man in the fullness of time, through the promised
Messiah. Man's fall is not to be final and for all time, for a limit is set to it,
specifically (as Blake says also) by the Saviour, God the Son, the merciful
second Person of the Holy Trinity, who eternally tempers and assuages the
anger of the Father.

Boehme writes of this limit:

> And this Covenant of his Incarnation which was to come, he put into the
> Light of Life; to which Covenant the Jewish Sacrifices pointed as to a
> Mark or *Limit*, to which God had promised himself with his Love; for the
> Faith of the Jews entered into the Sacrifices and Offerings, and God's
> Imagination entered into the Covenant: And the Offering was a Figure of the
> Restitution of that which Adam had lost; and so God did expiate his Anger in
> the human Property, through the Offering in the Limit of the Covenant. In
> which Covenant the most holy sweet name JESUS proceeding out of the
> holy Name and great Power of JEHOVAH, had incorporated itself; so that
> he would again move and manifest himself in the Substance of the heavenly
> World which disappeared in Adam, and kindle the holy divine Life therein
> again.

> This Mark or Limit of the Covenant was propagated from Adam and his Children, from Man to Man, and did go through from one upon all; as Sin also and the awakened Vanity did go through from one upon all.

Blake, likewise, insists in more than one passage that the limits stand "in every Individual Man."

Just as Eve came into being at the limit of the Fall, so it is the especial blessing bestowed upon woman—"Contraction's Limit"—that the birth of the Saviour shall be from the woman: the limit of the Covenant stands in the woman's seed, and through Mary is restored the virginity that in Eve was lost. The birth of the Saviour from this limit is thus explained by Boehme:

> And it stood in the promise of the Covenant at the End, in the root of David in the Virgin Mary, who was, in the inward Kingdom of the hidden Humanity (*viz.* of the Essentiality that disappeared as to the Kingdom of God) the Daughter of God's Covenant, but in the outward, according to the natural Humanity, she was begotten by her true bodily father Joachim and her true mother Anna, out of the Essences and Substance of their Souls and Bodies, like all other Children of Adam; a true Daughter of Eve. In this Mary from the Virgin (*viz.* the Wisdom of God) in the promised Limit of the Covenant of which the Prophets have prophesied—the eternal Speaking Word, which created all things, did in the Fulness of Time move itself in the Name JESUS.

This statement Blake certainly had in mind when he wrote, in the passage quoted above, of the birth of the Saviour from "Contraction's Limit," formed into the woman.

The "Limit," as Blake uses the word, has a double sense: it is at once the restricted state reached by man in his fall and at the same time the term set to that process of restriction "in mercy" by the Saviour. There are uses of the word by Boehme that sanction the former meaning as well as the latter. "The wicked souls," he writes "have lost their Image [that is, the Image of God in which they were formed] in the Limit, for it is entered into a Limit, and that Limit is the End of the Image; the *Turba* destroys the first Image" (*Forty Questions concerning the Soul*, ques. 19; *Works*, II, 74).

The limits were laid down, according to Boehme, before the foundation of the world or the creation of man, in the divine foresight:

> the Word of the Love of God came and spake itself again into the faded Ens. Signifying thereby, that it is an Aim, Mark, or Limit, of an Eternal Gracious Covenant, wherein God's Love, in the Name JESU, would destroy the works of the Devil. . . . which was done in Christ's Incarnation, or becoming Man: Here now we are to understand the Foreseeing Prevision, or Inspection, whereby the Spirit of God, before the Foundation of the World, has seen this Fall. . . . and has foreseen or provided the holy Name JESU, with the highest love Ens therein, for a new Regenerator. For the one only Root of the Divine Ens out of the Divine Love, *viz.* the heavenly World's Substance, faded, vanished, or disappeared in Adam . . . And in that one only Image which in Adam disappeared as to God, hath God pre-inspected

and foreseen the Scope, Time, Mark, or Limit, of his Eternal Holy Will in Christ.

In similar terms Blake writes of the fixing of the limits from the beginning, when

> . . . *All Eden was darken'd.*
> *The Corse of Albion lay on the Rock* . . .

Then,

> *The Saviour mild & gentle bent over the corse of Death,*
> *Saying, "If ye will Believe, your Brother shall rise again."*
> *And first he found the Limit of Opacity, & nam'd it Satan,*
> *In Albion's bosom, for in every human bosom these limits stand.*
> *And next he found the Limit of Contraction, & nam'd it Adam,*
> *While yet those beings were not born nor knew of good or evil.*
> [*F.Z.* IV; K. 304, 264–74]

Both Blake and Boehme see in the setting of the limits an act of mercy of the Saviour; and both see in that limit the meeting point of Eve's fall and the restitution through Mary.

41. *J.* 90; K. 736, 1–2.
42. *J.* 7; K. 626, 62–70.
43. *Blake and Modern Thought*, p. 27.
44. *G.P.;* K. 771, 21–24.
45. Notebook 109; K. 171.
46. *S.E.;* K. 215.
47. Notebook 115; K. 161.
48. *In a Mirtle Shade*, Notebook 111; K. 169.
49. *F.Z.* IX; K. 378, 791.
50. 1792 edn. The introduction was rewritten for the later editions and no longer contains the passages quoted in this chapter.
51. Pp. 71–72.
52. *S.E.;* K. 215.
53. *Banquet*, 203C.
54. *Anthroposophia Theomagica*, p. 25; *Works*, p. 29.
55. Taylor, *O.H.* (1792 edn.), p. 72.
56. Quoted ibid., pp. 74–76. Italics mine.
57. *B.U.* 18; K. 231, 11.
58. P. 53 of *Jerusalem* shows in its accompanying design a large and splendidly golden sunflower, floating lotus-like upon water. This most unnaturalistic detail is symbolic of the material condition of the flower. In the flower sits Vala, Psyche-winged, in an attitude of grief; her posture of hopeless inactivity recalls the mood of long waiting, powerless to act, of *Ah! Sun-flower*, and even of Clyte who, vegetated, can only watch from afar her beloved sun-god as he crosses the sky. The text of the page describes Los weeping by the waters of the Thames. Vala is the goddess Nature herself, bound to the terrene or vegetated condition of the sunflower, which can only "aspire," in the lowest of the four worlds, to a spiritual condition.

59. *M.* 29; K. 517, 23–24.
60. *O.H.* (1824 edn.) VIII, p. 22.
61. Ibid.
62. Cf. Taylor, introduction to *Timaeus*, in *Plato's Works*, II, p. 420.
63. See our I, pp. 280, 306–8.
64. Vaughan, *Anima Magica Abscondita*, p. 29; *Works*, p. 94.
65. *Of the Chymical Transmutation*, p. 18.
66. Cf. Henry Vaughan's image of the soul as "a star confin'd into a Tomb": "They all are gone into the world of light."
67. *Lumen de Lumine*, p. 41; *Works*, p. 266–67.
68. *Signature of All Things*, Chap. 8, § § 19–20; *Works*, IV, 53. Every herb is under the influence of one or another of the seven planets.
69. *D.L.W.*, § § 157–62, p. 127.
70. *Three Principles*, Chap. 8, § 19; *Works*, I, 51.
71. Nov. 22, 1802; K. 816–19.
72. *M.* 22; K. 505, 4–14.
73. In the possession of Sir Geoffrey Keynes. See *Blake's Pencil Drawings* (2nd ser.), ed. Keynes, No. 22.
74. Morley, *Blake, Coleridge, etc.*, p. 7.
75. *B.L.* IV; K. 260, 27–50.
76. *D.L.W.*, § 157, p. 128.
77. *Vala* 48ᵛ, 9–15 (*F.Z.* VIIb; K. 333, 29–35).
78. D. K. Sethna has written a fine exposition of this theme, still unpublished at the time of writing.

    The symbol of the Sun is in itself so all-embracing that it is impossible to set limits to Blake's solar imagery or its possible sources. Yet there is a scale of cabalistic correspondences in Agrippa (*Three Books of Occult Philosophy*, p. 176) that, whether Blake worked from it or no, fits well his system of four worlds, each dependent upon that immediately above, in which the most significant correspondences of the sun are set forth. This table is the

Scale of the Number of One

The exemplary world	Unity	One divine Essence, the fountain of all virtues and power
The intellectual world	The soul of the world	One supreme intelligence, the first creature, the fountain of lives.
The celestial world	The Sun	One king of stars, fountain of life.
The elemental world	The philosopher's stone	One subject, and instrument of all virtues, natural and supernatural.

| The lesser world | The heart | One first living, and last dying. |
| The infernal world | Lucifer | One prince of Rebellion, of Angels, and Darkness. |

Agrippa's scale corresponds, as we should expect, to the Platonic tradition, as perpetuated in the Hermetica, where we also have the same series of dependent causes: "The Image therefore of God, is Eternity; of Eternity, the World; of the World, the Sun; of the Sun, Man" (*Pym.* x. 103; p. 66).

9.   *Gates of Birth and Death*

1. *F.Z.* viii; K. 342, 36–40.
2. *J.* 59; K. 691, 22–25.
3. iii, 2.
4. *F.Z.* viii; K. 341, 28–31.
5. *F.Z.* viii; K. 345, 183–84.
6. *Cave of the Nymphs,* § 12; *Works,* pp. 190–91.
7. A passage in *The Four Zoas* viib (not in the original *Vala*) suggests that Blake was familiar with Agrippa's writings on the occult nature of the element of air:

> "*Hast thou forgot that the air listens thro' all its districts, telling*
> *The subtlest thoughts shut up from light in chambers of the Moon?*"
>
> "*Tharmas, The Moon has chambers where the babes of love lie hid,*
> *And whence they never can be brought in all Eternity*
> *Unless expos'd by their vain parents. . . .*"
>
> [K. 339, 242–46]

Agrippa calls the air "the resounding spirit of the worlds instrument. It immediately receives into it self the influencies of all Celestiall bodies, and then communicates them to the other Elements, as also to all mixt bodies: Also it receives into it self, as if it were a divine Looking-glass, the species of all things. . . . as also of all manner of speeches, and retains them" (*Three Books of Occult Philosophy,* Bk. i, Chap. 6, p. 14). Agrippa expands at length this notion of the air as a sounding board and looking glass, the medium of dreams and telepathy.

8. *F.Z.* vii; K. 332, 471–75.
9. K. 309, 177–81.
10. *P.L.* ii. 890–92.
11. *F.Z.* vii; K. 328, 323–28. The phrase "a Cloud she grew & grew" may relate, once more, to the Hermetic myth of the "moist cloud" of matter that is described as growing and spreading (*Pym.* ii. 5; p. 8).
12. *P.L.* ii. 871–84.
13. Ibid. 1026–31.
14. *F.Z.* viib; K. 340, 298–301.
15. *F.Z.* i; K. 279, 561–66.

16. *P.L.* II. 645–48.
17. *F.Z.* VII; K. 330, 412–16.
18. *J.* 7; K. 626, 63–65.
19. Pl. 3.
20. *J.* 57; K. 688, 5–16.
21. *Aurora*, Chap. 7, § 49; *Works*, I, 59.
22. *J.* 63; K. 697, 16–17.
23. *J.* 63; K. 697, 20–21.
24. *B.L.* 4; K. 258–59, 47 ff.
25. The episode is similar to the entanglement of Tharmas in Enion's "filmy woof."
26. *The Botanic Garden*, IV.423–30; p. 195.
27. Ibid., Additional Note 36; p. 98.
28. *M.* 35; K. 525, 19–25.
29. *Laocoön;* K. 776.
30. *M.* 24; K. 509, 37–38.
31. *M.* 29; K. 517, 30–31.
32. *F.Z.* IV; K. 304, 265–68. This self-propagating organism is, according to occult tradition, the Adam or *Adamah*, the natural man, which ramifies throughout nature as a single organism, and of which all the natural bodies of mankind are a part.
33. *M.* 34; K. 524, 24–30.
34. *F.Z.* IV; K. 300, 101–103.
35. Did another passage that he had illustrated in *The Gates of Paradise* also haunt Blake's imagination, "the globe of life blood trembling" (*B.V.* 17; K. 231, 13) that vegetates into life?—From Dryden's *Palamon and Arcite*, Bk. III, lines 1066–70, quoted in n. 28 to Chap. 23 (our II, p. 312).
36. *M.* 26; K. 512, 13–18. Plutarch, in *On Isis and Osiris*, p. 42, says that Osiris "was born on the right side of the world, and perished on the left. For it must be observed, that the Egyptians look upon the east as the front or face of the world, upon the north as its right side, and upon the south as its left." This may explain Los's orientation with his back to the east.
37. *J.* 38–39; K. 665–66, 55–9, 1–4.
38. *Auguries of Innocence;* K. 432, 42.
39. Letter to Linnell, June 7, 1825; K. 868.
40. Princeton University Press, 1953.
41. *Three Principles*, Chap. 13, §§ 21–25; *Works*, I, 96–97. Boehme uses the story of the men of Sodom who could not find the door of the house of Lot to illustrate this secret gate; and Blake's "watch-fiends" seeking for the door in blood-guilty London are the same citizens of an evil city, seeking to destroy the just man. The symbol had a personal meaning for Boehme, who had suffered persecution:

> *The Men of the City pressed sore upon the Man Lot, and when they drew near together to break the Door, the Men put forth their Hand and pulled Lot into the House to them, and shut too [sic] the Door: And the Men which were before the Door of the House were smitten with Blindness, both small and great; so that they wearied themselves, and could not find the Door.*

This Figure was acted thus externally. . . . but in the Spirit the FIGURE stands thus . . . they cannot find the Door, wherein they would break in to him, and do him Mischief; for *These* two Angels shut him up in themselves, that they cannot see the Door of *Revenge;* as it may be seen here in *Lot,* how God delivers the Messengers of his Mouth, and hides them from the Enemies; and this *Pen* has so found it by good Experience.

[*Mysterium Magnum,* Chap. 43, § § 58–63; *Works,* III, 259]

Blake must have warmed to this courageous personal word from a fellow-prophet, who, like himself, had in his day been the fearless and outspoken opponent of tyranny both temporal and spiritual. Blake cannot have forgotten that he himself had, in his trial for sedition, been in danger of the fate of those who go to "Tyburn's deathful shades."

42. *F.Z.* VI; K. 319, 279–80.
43. *F.Z.* VI; K. 318, 268–69.
44. *J.* 39; K. 666, 7–9.
45. *S.L.;* K. 159.
46. *America* I; K. 196, 15–18.
47. *Cath-Loda; Works,* II, 248.
48. *Carric-Thura; Works,* I, 277.
49. Ibid., p. 279.
49a. *F.Z.* IV; K. 299, 76–78.
50. *Carric-Thura; Works,* I, 278.
51. *O.H.* (1792 edn.), p. 142.
52. Ibid., pp. 142–43.
53. *On Providence; P.F.B.,* pp. 174–75; *Ennead* III.2.15.
54. *F.Z.* IX; K. 367, 375–77.
55. *F.Z.* IX; K. 358, 26–31.
56. *Europe* 9; K. 241, 6–7.
57. *Europe* 3; K. 239, 4.
58. St. 26.
59. *F.Z.* VI; K 319, 294–301.

10. *Specters and Watchers*

1. *F.Z.* VIII; K. 344, 110.
2. *F.Z.* I; K. 266, 64–65.
3. Milton, *Il Penseroso,* lines 91–92.
4. *P.F.B.,* p. 102; *Ennead* I.8.14.
5. See, for example, *The Tibetan Book of the Dead,* tr. W. Y. Evans-Wentz.
6. Ellis and Yeats thought so. Northrop Frye (among others) thinks not. On such a question I would rather follow Yeats, who, while he may have been mistaken in many points of detail, perfectly understood the kind of thought that we find in Blake. However, the question remains open.
7. *M.* 26; K. 512, 25–29.
8. See our I, pp. 352 ff.
9. *F.Z.* VIIa; K. 328, 330.
10. The soul of Orpheus enters the body of a swan, in the myth in the tenth book

of the *Republic* (620A); but this is usually understood in a symbolic sense, the swan being the emblem of the poet.

11. *F.Z.* viii; K. 344, 110–28.
12. Tr. Shri Purohit Swami, Bk. xvi, p. 83.
13. *M.* 28; K. 515, 23–28.
14. P. 300. See addendum, below, p. 428.
15. *Republic* 617D–620E; *Works*, i, 474, 477.
16. Ibid., 621A–B; *Works*, i, 477–78.
17. *F.Z.* viii; K. 346, 210–17.
18. *M.* 34; K. 524, 29–30.
19. Taylor, *Select Works of Porphyry*, p. 183.
20. *F.Z.* v; K. 308, 113.
21. *H.H.*, § 277, p. 168.
22. *On the Descent of the Soul; P.F.B.*, pp. 282–83; *Ennead* iv.8.8.
23. *J.* 42; K. 671, 66–70.
24. *J.* 42; K. 671, 71–75.
25. *F.Z.* vi; K. 318, 252–53.
26. *M.* 20; K. 502, 10–14.
27. *M.* 15; K. 496, 1–7.
28. *M.* 15; K. 496, 8–16.
29. Socrates, in his *Apology*, rejects the inspiration of poets as a form of *knowledge*: "I discovered this, therefore, in a short time concerning the poets, that they did not effect by wisdom that which they did, but by a certain genius and from enthusiastic energy, like prophets and those that utter oracles. For these also say many and beautiful things, but they understand nothing of what they say. . . . I departed, therefore, also from them, thinking that I surpassed them" (22A–C; *Works*, iv, 204–205). It is probably of this passage that Blake pertinently wrote: "Plato has made Socrates say that Poets & Prophets do not know or Understand what they write or Utter; this is a most Pernicious Falsehood. If they do not, pray is an inferior kind to be call'd Knowing? Plato confutes himself" (*V.L.J.* 68; K. 605). It is easy to understand his ambiguous attitude to Plato. Socrates claimed to have "human" wisdom: "For I, O Athenians, have acquired this name through nothing else than a certain wisdom. But of what kind is this wisdom? Perhaps it is human wisdom. For this in reality I appear to possess. Those indeed whom I just now mentioned possessed perhaps more than human wisdom, which I know not how to denominate; for I have no knowledge of it" (*Apology* 20D–E; *Works*, iv, 202–203). Plato's own attitude to inspired knowledge seems strangely ambiguous; for his Socrates would seem to agree with Blake that the "inferior kind" cannot be called "knowing."

Blake saw very clearly what had happened as a result of Plato's trend toward "human wisdom"; the Greek Muses became the Daughters of Memory in the sense not of reminiscence of eternity but of the ratio: "Jupiter usurped the Throne of his Father, Saturn, & brought on an Iron Age and Begat on Mnemosyne, or Memory, The Greek Muses, which are not Inspiration as the Bible is. Reality was Forgot, & the Vanities of Time & Space only Remember'd & call'd Reality" (Notebook 71–72; K. 605). What Plato has done is to make a distinction between the human and the daemonic, between "human wisdom" and what is given by the gods. Humanity curtailed of its highest faculty has relied ever-increasingly upon the lower kind of wisdom. Blake sought to restore to man what Plato assigned to the gods by the realization that "all deities reside in the human breast." Yet there is no finer statement of the traditional view of poetic inspiration than that of Plato:

> For the best epic poets, and all such as excel in the composing of any kind of verse to be recited, frame not those their admirable poems from the rules of art; but possessed by the Muse, they write from divine inspiration. Nor is it otherwise with the best lyric poets, and all other fine writers of verses to be sung. For as the priests of Cybele perform not their dances, while they have the free use of their intellect; so these melody poets pen those beautiful songs of theirs only when they are out of their sober minds . . . and, possessed by some divine power, are like the priestesses of Bacchus, who, full of the god, no longer draw water, but honey and milk out of the springs and fountains; though unable to do anything like it when they are sober. And in fact there passes in the souls of these poets that very thing which they pretend to do. For they assure us, that out of certain gardens and flowery vales belonging to the Muses, from fountains flowing there with honey, gathering the sweetness of their songs, they bring it to us, like the bees; and in the same manner withal, flying. Nor do they tell us any untruth. For a poet is a thing light, and volatile, and sacred; nor is he able to write poetry, till the Muse entering into him, he is transported out of himself, and has no longer the command of his intellect. . . . they write not what is taught them by art, but what is suggested to them by some divine power, on whose influence they depend. . . . But for this reason it is, that the god, depriving them of the use of their intellect, employs them as his ministers, his oracle singers, and divine prophets; that when we hear them, we may know, it is not these men who deliver things so excellent; these, to whom intellect is not present; but the god himself speaking, and through these men publishing his mind to us . . . those beautiful poems are not human, nor the compositions of men; but divine, and the work of gods.
>
> [*Ion* 533E–34E; *Works*, v, 458–63]

30. *P.A.* 39; K. 602–603.
31. *Annotations to Reynolds* xlvii; K. 449.
32. Letter to Butts, July 6, 1803; K. 825.
33. Plato, *Meno* 81C–D; *Works*, v, 61.
34. Letter to Flaxman, Sept. 21, 1800; K. 802.
35. *M.* 28; K. 516, 48–49.
36. *Annotations to Reynolds*, 50; K. 457.
37. "Noah is seen in the Midst of these, Canopied by a Rainbow, on his right hand Shem & on his Left Japhet; these three Persons represent Poetry, Painting & Music, the three Powers in Man of conversing with Paradise, which the flood did not Sweep away" (*V.L.J.* 78; K. 609). The rainbow is one of Blake's most beautiful symbols of anamnesis. In *Jerusalem* the rainbow is given not to Noah but to a Daughter of Beulah, Erin, who corresponds to the earlier figure of Eno, or Juno, the possessor of the rainbow in Greek mythology. Erin's rainbow has "windows into Eden"—that is, into eternity. Yeats believed that Blake's color scheme was based upon Boehme's ("I am now convinced that Blake's colour

scheme is founded on Boehme's scheme. March 1902." This note is written in the margin of his own copy of Ellis and Yeats, Vol. I, published in 1893. See our I, p. 380, n. 8.) The rainbow is a correspondence and manifestation of the Three Principles of the Divine Essence, shining through the opacity of the temporal world. Mrs. Sita Chari has suggested to me that Wordsworth's rainbow imagery may perhaps also have derived some of its potency from this tradition, even perhaps from Boehme. It is, besides, especially associated with the Last Judgment:

> This Bow is a Figure of the *last Judgment*, showing how the inward spiritual World will again manifest itself, and swallow up into itself this outward World of four Elements.
>
> And this is even the *Sign* or Token of the Covenant of *Grace*, which Sign in the Covenant denotes the Judge of the World, *viz. Christ*, who at the End of Days will *appear* in all the three Principles, *viz.* according to the Fire-sign as a severe Judge over the *Turba*, and all whatsoever shall be found therein; he will manifest the fiery Judgment, and enkindle the *Turba*, so that the first Principle shall appear in its fiery Property: For *all Things* of this World's Being *must be tried* or purified *in the Fire* of the first Principle, *viz.* in the Center of the Eternal Nature; and even then the *Turba* of all Beings shall be swallowed up in the Fire.
>
> And according to the Light's Sign he shall appear as a pleasant *Visage* to all the *Saints*, even in the Midst of the Fire, and defend His in his Love and Meekness from the *Flames* of the Fire.
>
> And according to the Kingdom of the outward Nature of this World, he shall appear in his *assumed Humanity*.
>
> [Boehme, *Mysterium Magnum*, Chap. 33, §§ 28–31; *Works*, III, 178–79]

This beautiful symbolic vision is revealing both of Blake's understanding and use of the rainbow, and of his vision of the Last Judgment. The appearance of the rainbow in that great image, and in many paintings on the theme of death—"The Death of the Virgin," "The Death of St. Joseph," and one version of Ugolino and his sons—symbolizes a divine epiphany that swallows up the temporal and reveals the eternal; for every death is a Last Judgment, in the sense in which both Blake and Boehme understood that spiritual event as a vanishing of the temporal in the light of eternity, a "burning up" of the unreal in the light of reality.

38. *F.Z.* VIII; K. 347, 254.
39. See our I, pp. 18, 22.
40. *M.* 40–41; K. 533, 35–37, 1.
41. *D.C.* V; K. 579–80.
42. *D.C.* IV; K. 576.
43. Notebook 59; K. 594–95.
44. *Timaeus* 27D–28B; *Works*, IV, 472–73.
45. *F.Z.* VIIa; K. 331, 439–41.
46. *J.* 43; K. 672, 19–21.
47. Taylor, *D.E.*, p. 6.
48. *F.Z.* VIIa; K. 331, 451–55.
49. *J.* 95; K. 742, 20.

50. Following here is a deleted line that confirms the nature of Los's activity as that of the artist, and recalls the adorning of the cavern in the printing house (*M.H.H.* 15–17; K. 154): "To hew the cavern'd rocks of Dranthon into forms of beauty."
51. Vulcan needed the cooperation of Venus to fabricate his works; and so perhaps Blake is acknowledging his debt to Mrs. Blake.
52. *F.Z.* vii; K. 331–32, 456–74.
53. *Midsummer Night's Dream* v.i.
54. Gilchrist, *Life*, i, 364.
55. *M.* 28; K. 514–15, 1–9.
56. *M.* 28; K. 515, 13–18.
57. Blake's favorite painter was Fra Angelico. Dürer he greatly admired, but found his line less pure than that of "the ancients."
58. *D.C.* xv; K. 585.
59. *The Ghost of Abel;* K. 779.
60. *On Nature, Contemplation and the One; P.F.B.*, pp. 201–203; *Ennead* iii.8.2.
61. Ibid., pp. 206–207; *Ennead* iii.8.3.

11. A Hermetic Myth

1. This Text F is, of course, hypothetical: it no longer exists as such, and it is presumed, by Margoliouth, from the textual evidence of *Vala*. See Margoliouth's *Vala*, Note on Night i, p. 156.
2. 1795. *S.L.* iii; K. 246, 18–19.

> To Trismegistus, Palamabron gave an abstract Law:
> To Pythagoras, Socrates & Plato.

3. *Pym.* ii. 5; p. 8.
4. *Aula Lucis*, pp. [30–31]; *Works*, p. 330. See also *Anthroposophia Theomagica; Works*, p. 19: "the darkness was thrust downwards, partly confused and dejected, and tortuously circumscribed, so that I appeared to behold it transformed into a certain humid substance and more agitated than words could express, vomiting forth smoke as from fire and emitting an inexpressible and lugubrious sound."
5. *Mysteries of Creation*, Bk. i, text 1, pp. 1–2.
6. Ibid., text 8, p. 7.
7. *F.Z.* ix; K. 366, 361.
8. *J.* 5; K. 624, 48–52.
9. *Europe* 1; K. 238, 6–13.
10. Nature, Vaughan writes, "hath two Extremes":

> and of the lower and darker . . . example enough wee have in the Creation. The first Extreme was that cloud or darkness whereof we have spoken formerly: Some call it the Remote Matter and the Invisible Chaos, but very improperly, for it was not invisible. This is the Jewish Ensoph outwardly, and it is the same with that Orphic night;
>> O Night, thou black nurse of the golden stars.
> Out of this Darkness all things that are in this world came, as out of their

fountain or matrix: Hence that Position of all famous Poets and Philosophers, *Omnia ex Nocte Prodiisse.* [*Coelum Terrae*, p. 114; *Works*, p. 216]

11. Not necessarily so in this case. "Crystall spheres" (Milton's *Hymn on the Morning of Christ's Nativity*) in the sense of the spheres of the planets might sufficiently explain this use of the phrase, especially in a poem (*Europe*) bearing so many other traces of this poem.

12. *Aula Lucis*, pp. [27]–28; *Works*, p. 329.

13. *Anima Magica Abscondita*, p. 11; *Works*, p. 79.

14. *Magia Adamica; Works*, p. 146.

15. Ibid.; *Works*, p. 168.

16. *Anthroposophia Theomagica; Works*, p. 27.

17. P. 11; *Works*, p. 79.

18. *J.* 70; K. 709, 20–30.

19. *F.Z.* I; K. 264, 24.

20. *Pym.* II.18; p. 10.

21. Ibid. The Harmony is, again, the revolving circles. In the Platonic myth given in the tenth book of the *Republic* (617B) the seven circles are revolved by sirens, each uttering a single note that together make a "harmony."

22. See our I, pp. 108 f. In *The Four Zoas* an added line describes the Spectre as issuing "from the feet" of Tharmas. This line is interpolated between lines 8 and 9 of *Vala* 3ᴿ: "His spectre issuing from his feet in flames of fire" (*F.Z.* I; K. 266, 78). This is an optical image of a reflection seen in water, joining the body that casts the image *at the feet*, as all reflections do. The bent specter of Los may, similarly, have been suggested by a shadow:

> *A shadow blue obscure & dismal. like a statue of lead*
> *Bent by its fall from a high tower. . . .*
> [*Vala* 25ᴿ, 13–14; *F.Z.* IV; K. 299, 65–6]

Shadows are blue and leaden in color, and can appear bent if cast on a surface that is not flat.

23. *P.C.B.*, pp. 11–12 n.; *Ennead* VI.3.2.

24. *Pym.* II.24–26; p. 11.

25. *Ques.* 1, §§ 280–81; *Works*, II, 40.

26. *Vala* 3ᴿ, 3–11 (*F.Z.* I; K. 266, 71–81). Margoliouth's restored text.

27. *Pym.* II.29; p. 11.

28. In Hesiod, Thaumas is a sea god. Blake knew Cooke's Hesiod, in which he would have found him described (*Theogony*, lines 357–64, 415–17; *Works*, II, 39, 43):

> *Of Ocean born,* Electre *plights her Word*
> *To* Thaumas, *and obeys her rightful Lord,*
> Iris *to whom, a Goddess swift, she bears.*

and

> *Old* Nereus *to the* Sea *was born of* Earth,
>
> .   .   .
>
> Thaumas *the great from the same Parents came*
> Phorcys *the strong, and* Ceto *beauteous dame.*

Northrop Frye first pointed out the Hesiod source, and suggested Eione as the source of Enion. In finding sources of Blake's names, however, we often find more than one association united in a single name.

Blake's Thaumas, in his later appearances, certainly does unite in his person the aspects and attributes of more than one sea-god. Phorcys, the Old Man of the Sea, is the shepherd of seals and the god of generation. Thaumas also has his "flocks" and his shepherd's crook, and he is also a "parent power." He likewise has attributes of Nereus and of Glaucus, another symbol of an immortal nature immersed in the waters of matter, unable to die and yet oppressed with mortality (we remember Samuel Palmer's recollection that Blake's mind "found room" for many fables of antiquity): "the antient members of his body are partly broken off, and others are worn away; and he is altogether damaged by the waves: and besides this, other things are grown to him, such as shell fish, sea weed, and stones: so that he in every respect resembles a beast, rather than what he naturally was" (*Republic* x.611D; *Works*, I, 464). So Tharmas complains:

> *O Enion my weary head is on the bed of death*
> *For weeds of death have wrapd around my limbs in the hoary deeps.*
> *I sit in the place of shells & mourn . . .*
>   [*Vala* 65ᴿ, 20–23; *F.Z.* IX, 487–89; K. 370]

He is also, perhaps, Oceanus himself, with his sea horses and conches:

> *. . . Tharmas on his furious chariots of the Deep*
> *Departed far into the Unknown & left a wondrous void*
> *Round Los. afar his waters bore on all sides round. with noise*
> *Of wheels & horses hoofs & trumpets Horns & Clarions.*
>   [*Vala*, 26ᵛ, 7–10; *F.Z.* IV, 157–60; K. 301]

He combines in his person many water-gods, but his name points clearly to his origin as the *Thaumas* of the Hermetica.

29. *F.Z.*, canceled fragment 11–16; K. 380.
30. Margoliouth, *Blake's Vala*, p. 160 (Notes on 2ᵛ); K. 381.
31. Ibid.
32. *Vala* 3ᴿ, 29; 3ᵛ, 1–8 (*F.Z.* I; K. 267, 126–33). Margoliouth's restored text.
33. *F.Z.* I; K. 266, 90.
34. *J*. 64; K. 699, 25–33.
35. A passage in Bryant's *Mythology* ties together many threads of the Tharmas myth, including perhaps the tendency of the Spectre to reveal the colors of the rainbow. In a chapter entitled "Of Juno, Iris, Eros, Thamuz" (II, 343) Bryant tells us that Eros (who is also called Thaumas) is the rainbow in the heavens: "This beautiful phaenomenon in the heavens was by the Egyptians stiled *Thamuz*, and seems to have signified *the wonder*. The Greeks expressed it *Thaumas*. . . . This Thaumas they did not immediately appropriate to the bow; but supposed them to be two personages, and Thaumas the parent" (II, 346). This is evidently an allusion to Hesiod, who makes Thaumas the father of Iris.
36. *V.L.J.*, Notebook 79; K. 607.
37. *Metamorphoses*, Bk. IV; ed. Garth, tr. Addison, pp. 118–19. This was probably the translation that Blake read.

38.   *Vala* 4ᴿ, 16–21 (*F.Z.* I; K. 269, 179–84). Margoliouth's restored text.

39.   K. 381.

40.   *F.Z.*, canceled fragment; K. 381. Also *F.Z.* I; K. 269, 185–86.

41.   *Vala* 4ᴿ, 23–26 (*F.Z.* I; K. 269, 186–89).

42.   K. 381, 8.

43.   Hermes and Aphrodite. (The quotation is from the *Metamorphoses;* see above. n. 37.)

44.   *Vala* 4ᵛ, 1–4 (*F.Z.* I; K. 269, 191–92). Margoliouth's restored text.

45.   *Pym.* VIII.7–8; p. 52.

46.   *Vala* 3ᴿ, 1–2 (*F.Z.* I; K̇. 266, 69–70).

47.   See our I, p. 387, n. 15. See also *Vala* 3ᴿ, 8–11 (*F.Z.* I; K. 266, 76–81).

48.   *F.Z.* I; K. 266, 83–85.

49.   *F.Z.* VIII; K. 346, 220–23.

50.   *F.Z.* I; K. 265, 47–48.

51.   Josh. 2:6. See our I, p. 385, n. 15.

52.   *F.Z.* VIII; K. 347, 230–36.

53.   *Vala* 71ᴿ (*F.Z.*, Additional Fragments; K. 380).

54.   *Blake's Vala*, p. xix. This, Margoliouth points out, settles the pronunciation—*a* as in "veil."

55.   *G.P.* 1–2, 13; K. 770.

12. Enion

1.   *F.Z.* III; K. 297, 195–201.

2.   *F.Z.* VIIb; K. 339, 237–38.

3.   *P.C.B.*, p. 11 n.; *Ennead* III.6.7.

4.   Ino, or Leucothea of the sea-veil, and Ino (Juno) no doubt also enter into her composition. Northrop Frye suggests Hesiod's Tharmas and Eione as models for Tharmas and Enion.

5.   *F.Z.* II; K. 291, 422–23. The "bright Female" is Ahania, Earth; the line that follows, "And never from that moment could she rest upon her pillow," is very much to the point, philosophically; for when the Earth has perceived the non-entity of matter, she must know her own existence threatened, since it is only as a consort or emanation of the intelligible world that she is upheld. Ahania is, in fact, thrown out by Urizen, and wanders with Enion in "Non Entity."

6.   *F.Z.* III; K. 296, 188–89.

7.   *F.Z.* III; K. 297, 208–11.

8.   *On the Nature and Origin of Evil; P.F.B.*, p. 63; *Ennead* I.8.3.

9.   *P.C.B.*, pp. 11–12 n.; *Ennead* III.6.7.

10.   *F.Z.* III; K. 296, 182–93.

11.   *On the Nature and Origin of Evil; P.F.B.*, p. 104; *Ennead* I.8.14.

12.   *F.Z.* I; K. 265, 35–42.

13.   *F.Z.* I; K. 265, 44–45.

14.   Her guilt has produced the specter, the hermaphrodite monster of soul ensnared in matter.

15.   *F.Z.* I; K. 267, 109–12.

16.   *F.Z.* I; K. 268, 137–42.

17.   *P.C.B.*, p. 36; *Ennead* I.6.8.

18. *F.Z.* II; K. 290, 385–86.
19. *F.Z.* III; K. 296, 178–81. An article by Thomas Taylor in *The Monthly Magazine* (London), III, suppl. no. XIX (June 1797), "A Concise Exposition of the Chaldaic Dogmas, by Psellus," contains the following: "They assert that there are seven corporeal worlds, one Empyrean and the first; after this, three ethereal, and then three material worlds, the last of which is said to be terrestrial, and the hater of life: and this is the sublunary place, containing likewise in itself matter, which they call a profundity."
20. *F.Q.* III.vi.36–37.
21. *P.L.* II.890 ff.
22. Gen. 3:17–19.
23. The dog, according to Taylor, symbolizes "material demons."
24. *F.Z.* II; K. 290, 387–90.
25. Cf. Eliot's "Fear death by water" (*The Waste Land* 1.55).
26. *Mysteries of Creation*, Bk. II, text 6, p. 33. The probability of an allusion in Blake is often cumulative. I would not have mentioned this suggestion but for the preceding sentence, "That which nourisheth, is from the Element of aire." The far from self-evident image of "the nourishing air" appears in *Vala* 63^v, 33.
27. *F.Z.* VIII; K. 354–55, 536–44.
28. *F.Z.* VIII; K. 355–56, 555–83.
29. *F.Z.* VIII; K. 356, 593–96.
30. *Aula Lucis*, p. 29; *Works*, p. 330.
31. *F.Z.* VIIb; K. 334, 65.
32. *F.Z.* VIIb; K. 334, 71.
33. *F.Z.* IX; K. 370–71, 517–21.
34. *F.Z.* IX; K. 371, 525–26.
35. *F.Z.* IX; K. 371, 530–31.
36. *F.Z.* IX; K. 372, 554–56.
37. *F.Z.* IX; K. 373, 594–616.

13.   Tharmas and the Mental Traveller

1. See Margoliouth's text of *Vala*.
2. *F.Z.* III; K. 296, 153–68.
3. *Mythology*, II, 353–56.
4. Ezek. 37:1–10. Blake's illustration to this subject is in the Fogg Art Museum.
5. *F.Z.* IV; K. 299, 54.
6. *F.Z.* IV; K. 297–98, 10–20.
7. *F.Z.* IV; K. 301, 131–36.
8. One of the cult objects of Bacchus is the winnowing fan. The God was named "him of the winnowing-fan," for in this fan he was carried as in a cradle; and his power of arousing ecstatic energy was likened to the wind stirred by the winnowing fan. Blake may have found this in Bryant, in Plutarch, or in Vergil's first *Georgic*, which is most likely, because Blake certainly took from this poem the vermin of the threshing floor: "The fan of Bacchus, with the flying sail." Not surprisingly, therefore, we find this attributed to Tharmas:

> *Then Tharmas took the Winnowing fan; the winnowing wind furious*
> *Above, veer'd round by violent whirlwind, driven west & south,*
> *Tossed the Nations like chaff into the seas of Tharmas.*
>
> [F.Z. IX; K. 374, 654–56]

In Plutarch also, the close connection of Bacchus with the element of water is stressed:

> The *Thyades*, or priestesses of *Bacchus*, with their hymns endeavour to raise their God, whom they at that time distinguish by the name of the *Winnower*. Now that the Greeks themselves do not look upon *Bacchus* as the Lord or President of wine only, but of all kind of humidity in general, may be sufficiently proved from the testimony of *Pindar*, where he says "May bountiful *Bacchus*, the bright glory of the year, make all my trees fruitful."
>
> [*On Isis and Osiris*, tr. Squire, pp. 46–47]

He is also, according to Plutarch, the same as Osiris, and, as such, called *Hyes* (or the *wetter*), signifying thereby his being the "Lord of the humid nature" (ibid.).

9. The words spoken by Jesus at the Last Supper, and retained in the Sacrament of Holy Communion, include this ancient tradition, as does, even more explicitly, the breaking of the bread that accompanies the words, "Take, eat; this is my body" (Mark 14:22).

10. Quoted by Taylor in *D.E.*, pp. 135–36. Here no doubt is the origin of the personified "Odors" that rise from Blake's wine presses:

> *The blood of life flow'd plentiful. Odors of life arose*
> *All round the heavenly arches, & the Odors rose singing this song:*
>
> *"O terrible wine presses of Luvah! O caverns of the Grave!*
> *How lovely the delights of those risen again from death!"*
>
>   .   .   .
>
> *So sang the Human Odors round the wine presses of Luvah*
>
> [F.Z. IX; K. 376, 726–30]

11. *D.E.*, pp. 147–48.
12. Ques. 1, §§ 87–89; *Works*, II, 16.
13. Pickering MS; K. 424.
14. By Northrop Frye, among others.
15. P. 134.
16. *Politicus* 269C–D; *Works*, IV, 121.
17. Ibid. 270E; *Works*, p. 123.
18. F.Z. I; K. 266, 79–81.
19. F.Z. I; K. 265, 47–50.
20. J. 22; K. 645, 28–29.
21. J. 66; K. 702, 20–34.
22. "Notes on Blake," *Review of English Studies*, XXIV (Oct. 1948), 303. Blake might also have read an English translation of Bernal Diaz, which also describes the flint knives used for sacrifices.

23. For evidence of Yeats's knowledge of Thomas Taylor, see F. A. C. Wilson, *W. B. Yeats and Tradition*.
24. *D.E.*, p. 138.
25. Sallust, *On the Gods and the World*, tr. Taylor, pp. 41–42.
26. *A Vision* (1st edn.), p. 133.
27. Dr. F. A. C. Wilson suggests that Yeats here is not so much commenting on Blake as looking forward to his own use of the Dionysus myth in *A Full Moon in March*.
28. *Politicus* 270A; *Works*, IV, 122.
29. *Pastoral* IV.5–10; *Works*, tr. Dryden, p. 15.
30. See our II, p. 327.
31. Ellis and Yeats, *Works of Blake*, II, 35–36.
32. Another source of Yeats's poem is the last chorus of Shelley's *Hellas*, also upon the theme of the historic cycles; but the passages quoted relate directly to Blake.
33. *F.Z.* VIIb; K. 339, 232–38.
34. *F.Z.* IX; K. 371, 538–44.
35. *M.* 29; K. 516, 8–11.
36. *M.* 29; K. 516, 15–16.
37. Notebook 7; K. 418.
38. It seems likely that Blake read Newton's *Opticks* during his residence at Felpham. The passage about Ozoth in *Milton* is evidence that the question of optics had particularly interested him; and within a month of his arrival he wrote a verse epistle to Thomas Butts (Oct. 2, 1800; K. 804) on the subject of light:

> *To my Friend Butts I write*
> *My first Vision of Light,*
> *On the yellow sands sitting.*
> *The Sun was Emitting*
> *His Glorious beams*
> *From Heaven's high Streams. . . .*
> *In particles bright*
> *The jewels of Light*
> *Distinct shone & clear.*

What follows is the Swedenborgian vision of each particle of light and each grain of sand as "Men Seen Afar." But the *distinct particles* of light are Newtonian. Newton believed "particles" to be the component units of color in the solar spectrum; and the separation of the particles into "distinct" categories, each according to size and color, was the object of the experiments. No wonder that Blake should write: "I each particle gazed, / Astonish'd, Amazed;" and his reverie on the shores of Felpham took flight from these "jewels of light" that Newton describes, violet, blue, green, yellow, and red. Blake's poem goes on to link the "particles bright" of the light with the grains of sand on the seashore—all are living, and all are human.

A similar linking of particles of light and grains of sand suggests that another poem harks back to the same "vision," and here Newton is mentioned by name:

> *Mock on, Mock on Voltaire, Rousseau:*
> *Mock on, Mock on: 'tis all in vain!*

You throw the sand against the wind,
And the wind blows it back again.

And every sand becomes a Gem
Reflected in the beams divine;
Blown back they blind the mocking Eye,
But still in Israel's paths they shine.

The Atoms of Democritus
And Newton's Particles of light
Are sands upon the Red sea shore,
Where Israel's tents do shine so bright.
[Notebook 7; K. 418]

Perhaps Blake had read Voltaire's *The Metaphysics of Sir Isaac Newton: Or a comparison between the Opinions of Sir Isaac Newton and Mr. Leibnitz* (1747). In any case the comparison of the particles of light to grains of sand is perfectly just; for Newton wrote:

> it seems probable to me, that God in the Beginning form'd Matter in solid, massy, hard, impenetrable, moveable Particles, of such Sizes and Figures, and with such other Properties, and in such Proportion to Space, as most conduced to the End for which he form'd them; and that these primitive Particles being Solids, are incomparably harder than any porous Bodies compounded of them; even so very hard, as never to wear or break in pieces; No ordinary Power being able to divide what God himself made one in the first Creation. [*Opticks* (1721 edn.), Bk. III, Pt. I, pp. 375–76]

These have "the petrific hardness" of Urizen's "wide world of solid construction"; but for Blake they are first jewels of light, then "Men Seen Afar," living visions of the human imagination:

I each particle gazed,
Astonish'd, Amazed;
For each was a Man
Human-form'd. Swift I ran,
For they beckon'd to me
Remote by the Sea,
Saying: Each grain of Sand,
Every Stone on the Land,
Each rock & each hill,
Each fountain & rill,
Each herb & each tree,
Mountain, hill, earth & sea,
Cloud, Meteor & Star,
Are Men Seen Afar.

According to Swedenborgian doctrine, all material particles are human-formed, in consequence of heaven's being "in its greatest and least parts like itself." The physical *corpus* of the universe is contained within the body of the

Grand Man: all is human. The "whole Heaven, and every part of it, resembles a Man, because it exists from the Divine Human of the Lord." Heaven "consists of innumerable societies, and each society is heaven in a less form; and each angel in the least." The whole heaven, viewed collectively, resembles one man, and every society in the heavens, also, resembles a man: "Hence every angel is in a perfect human form" (*H.H.*, § 78, p. 47). Nothing exists outside the Divine Humanity; nothing exists that is not human. The influence of this Swedenborgian anthropomorphism is to be seen on almost every page of Blake's designs, where animate human figures spring to life at every touch of calligraphy, from tendril and spray. Tiny insects, caterpillars, midges, moths, and ants become "Men Seen Afar," because all are in truth living cells within the greater organism of the Grand Man.

The "desert" of Enion is, on the contrary, the world of "particles" postulated by Newton, collectively conceived as a waste of sands.

39. *P.C.B.*, p. vii.

40. *F.Z.* I; K. 265, 35–43.

41. *F.Z.* I; K. 266, 75.

42. *F.Z.* I; K. 265, 28.

43. *A Vision* (2nd edn.), p. 277. Yeats's reference to the "barbers" is an echo of Gibbon.

44. 533; K. 82.

45. 2 Sam. 6:6.

46. 1 Kings 13:2–4.

47. *A.C.*, I, § 878, pp. 387–88.

48. The more so perhaps for the fine visual image of the Hand of God that follows, one likely to appeal to his pictorial sense: "That hand signifies and represents ability, may appear from representatives in the world of spirits, where a kind of bare arm sometimes is presented to view, which hath such strength in it, that it can break bones to pieces, and bruise as it were to nothing the inmost marrow contained therein, and hence so great terror is excited, that all who see it are ready to melt at heart; nay, such strength is actually in it."

I am indebted to Mr. Hillel Halkin for the reference to Jeroboam.

49. Rev. 6:13.

50. Yeats, *The Second Coming*.

51. In *The Little Girl Lost* the "beasts" are tamed by the presence of the soul in their "dens."

52. See our I, p. 327.

53. *J.* 75; K. 716, 24.

54. Sir William Jones, *Works*, I, 281. The text is slightly different in the version published in *Asiatick Researches*, II (1790), 111 ff.

55. *The Bhagvat-Geeta*, tr. Wilkins, p. 75.

56. *M.* 37; K. 528, 35–45.

57. *J.* 75; K. 716, 10–20.

58. *J.* 13; K. 634, 62–63.

59. *T.C.R.*, Vol. II, § 753, pp. 388–89.

60. Ibid., § 756, pp. 391–92.

61. Ibid., § 760, p. 395.

62. I, 288 ff.

63. Ezek. 28:13–16.
64. *J.* 49; K. 680, 73.
65. *J.* 89; K. 734, 9–12.
66. *Mysterium Magnum*, Chap. 30, § § 40–42; *Works*, III, 158.
67. *Mysterium Magnum*, Chap. 30, § 34; *Works*, III, 157.
68. See our II, pp. 114–15.
69. See also our II, pp. 49 ff.
70. *M.H.H.* 14; K. 154.
71. *Treatise on the Incarnation*, Pt. I, Chap. 6, § 92; *Works*, II, 47.
72. *Three Principles*, Chap. 20, §§ 40–41; *Works*, I, 203.
73. Gen. 3:24.
74. *J.* 77; K. 717–18, 1–19.
75. *Three Principles*, Chap. 20, § 42; *Works*, I, 204.

14. The Demon Red

1. *M.H.H.* 3; K. 149.
2. *M.* 22; K. 506, 50.
3. "Heaven" is the subjective and spiritual world, earth the external, following the scriptural teaching that "heaven" is within. The "heavens" or "heaven" is used by Blake also in this sense.
4. A. L. Morton, in *The Everlasting Gospel*, makes some interesting suggestions of other channels through which the teaching of the new Reign of the Spirit, originating with Joachim of Flora, may have reached Blake through such surviving Antinomian sects as the Muggletonians, Ranters, and Seekers, which had held this doctrine in the seventeenth century.
5. *Last Judgment*, §§ 45–46, pp. 86 ff.
6. Ibid., § 38, p. 63.
7. *M.H.H.* 2; K. 149.
8. *M.H.H.* 2; K. 148.
9. Notebook 105; K. 178.
10. *A.C.*, Vol. IV, § 3576, p. 446.
11. Ibid.
12. Ibid., Vol. VI, § 4640, p. 297.
13. *M.H.H.* 2; K. 148, 12–13.
14. Angels who belong to the principle of love always, in Swedenborg's "Relations," wear red garments, those of wisdom, blue. In Blake's Dante drawings Dante (a bodily man) wears red, Vergil (an intelligence), blue—and here also the colors of the two poets appropriately signify the devotion of Dante to the principle of love, that of Vergil to wisdom.
15. Blake engraved a plate for Hoole's translation of this work, published in 1785.
16. *America* 11; K. 196, 14. He is the "Leviathan" of *M.H.H.*
17. *P.L.* XI.825–31.
18. *M.H.H.* 25–27; K. 159.
19. *America* 10; K. 200, 5–10. Wicksteed (*William Blake's "Jerusalem,"* pp. 48–51) relates this group of symbols to Bacon's *New Atlantis*. A ship sailing in the South Seas, near Peru, discovers the Island of Bensalem, where lives an

innocent race descended from the Atlanteans, survivors of the flood that destroyed all but the mountain tops of that continent—as described by Plato in the *Critias* (108E ff.).

Mr. Wicksteed points out that the Latin phrase, *scala coeli*, may have caught Blake's eye in Bacon's account, and suggested the image "from their bright summits you may pass to the Golden world." Nevertheless, there is evidence that Blake also knew Plato's account of Atlantis. The city was built for a stolen bride, and this Blake did not find in Bacon's *New Atlantis*. Poseidon, according to the *Critias* (113C–D), received for his portion Atlantis; and he stole a mortal woman for his bride—Cleito, daughter of Evenor: "But when the virgin arrived at maturity, and her father and mother were dead, Neptune being captivated with her beauty had connection with her, and enclosed the hill on which she dwelt with spiral streams of water" (*Works*, tr. Taylor, II, 583). Their sons were the ten kings of Atlantis, who lived together in peace and made good laws. Why Blake has changed the name of Neptune for that of Ariston it is impossible to say; but Ariston certainly stole a bride. Blake seems to have read Herodotus (*The History*, tr. Littlebury, Vol. II, Bk. VI, p. 103). Ariston, King of Sparta, fell in love with the wife of Agetus, who was a woman of miraculously bestowed beauty: "Pleas'd with the Beauty of this Woman, *Ariston* contriv'd the following Design. He acquainted *Agetus*, who was her Husband and his familiar Friend, that he would make him a Present of any one thing he should chuse out of all his Possessions, on Condition he would oblige himself to do the like to him. *Agetus* not suspecting any Design upon his Wife, because he knew *Ariston* had one already, accepted the Proposal"—and so Ariston came, through a trick amounting to theft, into possession of Agetus' wife. Ariston and his stolen bride is no invention of Blake's. But the relevance of the story to the myth of Atlantis passes my comprehension.

20. Notebook 113; K. 166.
21. *F.Q.* II.ii.2.
22. *B.U.* 19; K. 232, 44–46.
23. *B.U.* 20; K. 233, 3–5.
24. *F.Z.* v; K. 306, 36–42.
25. *F.Z.* v; K. 307, 70–71.
26. *F.Z.* v; K. 311, 240–41.
27. *V.D.A.* 6; K. 193, 4–7.
28. *S.E.;* K. 218–19, 17–24.
29. *B.U.* 20; K. 233, 3–24.
30. *F.Z.* v; K. 307–308, 97–106.
31. Mallet's *Northern Antiquities*, II, 90–94.
31a. Yeats must have been consciously or unconsciously aware of his identification of Orc with the wolf Fenris; for in his *Blake's Works* (I. 96) he tells of how he performed "some curious experiments" with "persons who, on receiving a symbol, have the power of seeing and conversing with visionary forms raised by that symbol. Some of these seers have beheld personages that are recognizably identical with those of Blake's myth, though differing a little, as Blake himself says visions differ with the eye of the visionary. Orc, for instance, was viewed by one seer as black, instead of glowing, and by another as a wolf in armour." Dr.

F. A. C. Wilson has pointed out to me that Yeats's appreciation of the Orc-Fenris relationship is evidently more than superficial, for Yeats elsewhere has said that "the *wolf* is but a more violent symbol of longing than the hound"—and Orc is of course desire itself. Shelley in *Alastor* uses the wolf as the symbol of sexual passion.

32. *F.Z.* v; K. 309, 155–70.
33. *F.Z.* v; K. 307, 84.
34. *Europe* 3; K. 239, 26.
35. Isa. 63:1–6.
36. Rev. 14:14–16.
37. *F.Z.* ix; K. 372, 573–76.
38. He keeps his sickle "deep in the south." Is this an allusion to the southern gate of the Zodiac, the sign of Capricorn, through which souls leave this life?
39. *F.Z.* ix; K. 372, 579–84.
40. *F.Z.* ix; K. 374–75, 659–68.
41. *M.* 25; K. 510, 9–11.
42. *Bhagvat-Geeta*, tr. Wilkins, Bk. xi, pp. 92–93.
43. Published in 1785.
44. Sir William Jones is probably the source of this information: " 'among other *Indian* curiosities, which Callisthenes transmitted to his uncle, was *a technical system of logick*, which the Brahmans had communicated to the inquisitive Greek,' and which the *Mohammedan* writer supposes to have been the ground work of the famous *Aristotelean* method: if this be true, it is one of the most interesting facts, that I have met with in Asia" (*Asiatick Researches*, iv (1794), 170–71).
45. Brama is of course God and not a prophet. But Brama is named as if a prophet in Burnet's *Archaeologiae Philosophicae*—the work from which Coleridge extracted the passage that prefaces his *Ancient Mariner*. Blake may have read this work in its English (abridged) translation.
46. *S.L.* 3; K. 245, 11–14.
47. *Geeta*, tr. Wilkins, Bk. ii, pp. 36–37.
48. *F.Z.* ix; K. 376–77, 732–42.
49. See our i, pp. 55–56.
50. *P.F.B.*, pp. 173–74; *Ennead* iii.2.15.
51. *F.Z.* ix; K. 376, 723–31.
52. *F.Z.* ix; K. 372, 577.
53. *F.Z.* ix; K. 373, 619–20.
54. *D.E.*, p. 137.
55. *D.E.*, p. 35. See quotation our i, pp. 306 f.
56. *M.* 25; K. 510, 17–21.
57. *Works*, tr. Dryden, p. 57.
58. *F.Z.* ix; K. 377, 755–66.
59. *M.* 27; K. 513, 7–29.
60. *F.Z.* ix; K. 376, 713–21.
61. *F.Z.* iv; K. 377, 743–46.
62. *J.* 72; K. 712, 50–52.
63. *D.C.*; K. 565.

15.   Energy Is the Only Life

1. Sept. 12, 1800; K. 799.
2. *Archidoxis* x.viii; p. 154.
3. Ibid.
4. "*Origen*'s opinion concerning the devils, is: The spirits who act of their own free will, left the service of God with their Prince the devil; if they began to repent a little, are clothed with humane flesh; That further by this repentance, after the resurrection, by the same means by the which they came into the flesh, they might at the last return to the vision of God . . . and then all knees are to be bowed to God, of Celestiall, Terrestriall, and Infernall things, that God may be all in all: . . . there are many of the devils who are fallen, who hope for their salvation" (Agrippa, *Three Books of Occult Philosophy*, Bk. III, p. 401).
5. See our I, p. 274.
6. Tr. from Latin in Vaughan, *Anthroposophia Theomagica; Works*, I, 16. Italics mine.
7. *Mysterium Magnum*, Chap. 8, § 24; *Works*, III, 33.
8. *Threefold Life of Man*, Chap. 2, § 8; *Works*, II, 9.
9. Blake also had access to the root of all such thought—the philosophy of Heraclitus and Empedocles—through the writings of Fludd (*Mosaicall Philosophy*). Fludd quotes Heraclitus as saying "that all things were composed of strife and friendship; and *Empedocles*, That the soul was made of amity and enmity." The dark forces are "the divine puissance" and their place is in the center, of which the God of Light is the circumference. Fludd's exposition of the cabala is full of this duality reconciled in unity. God first created light and darkness, and Satan is the "first born" of darkness—that is, he originates in God. "And as his darkness, such is his light."

    Of the ten Sefiroth, "evil" originates in three—Binah, Geburah, and Malkuth. Fludd gives a full and clear exposition of how this duality was understood by the alchemists:

    > Here you may see the two principles of concord and discord, of love and hatred, and consequently of sympathy and antipathy, of the effects whereof all the Scripture and each member of Philosophy, is full. The catholick matter which was originally extracted out of darkness, namely, the waters, which was made the materiall substance, (of which the heavens and the earth were framed by the divine word, doth occupy all that space which the world containeth) was by the celestiall Alchimy, or spagerick vertue of the divine illuminating emanation, divided according unto the contrary and discordant natures of the said two principles, into the upper waters, and the lower waters: whereof the first or higher waters were good, and obedient unto the bright Divinity, and were converted into a fiery nature, being thereupon tearmed the Emperiall nature, for their obedience unto the bright emanation, & were full of intellectual fire, and angelicall light. And therefore this portion of the waters was ordained for the seat of the good Angells. The lower waters contrariwise, as being fecall, gross, impure, and therefore more rebellious unto light, and obedient by participation unto darknesse,

were placed next unto their dark beginning, namely, the earth; and did possess all that space between the starry heaven and the earth, which is called Elementary, and for this cause is subject to all changes of generation and corruption: And this was ordained to be the seat of Satan and his angels. . . . Lo here the two extreams in the created nature! from the upper whereof, a generall sympathy and love, or a Symphoniacall content of things, is made and effected in this world: by the other, namely the lower, an universal Antipatheticall jar, is by turns effected, and intruded into the Symphoniacall accord of things in the lower world, namely when the severe Attributes of God, do rain down into the starry world, influences of a contrary nature.

[*Mosaicall Philosophy*, Sec. II, Bk. II, Chap. 5, pp. 192–93]

10. *Works*, V, 125.
11. *Threefold Life of Man*, Chap. 2, § 9; *Works*, II, 9.
12. *Aurora*, Chap. 18, § 143; *Works*, I, 183.
13. *Annotations to Berkeley's Siris* 219; K. 775.
14. *Threefold Life of Man*, Chap. 2, §§ 57–58; *Works*, II, 15.
15. *Three Principles*, Chap. 9, § 7; *Works*, I, 57.
16. *M.H.H.* 6–7; K. 150. Doubtless Milton's Satan, who attempts to cross that same great gulf, was also in Blake's mind:

> *. . . he then survey'd*
> *Hell and the Gulf between, and* Satan *there*
> *Coasting the wall of Heav'n on this side Night*
> *In the dun Air sublime, and ready now*
> *To stoop with wearied wings, and willing feet*
> *On the bare outside of this World.*
>
> [*P.L.* III, 69–74]

17. *Mysterium Magnum*, Chap. 8, §§ 19–28; *Works*, III, 33.
18. Graham Robertson has described this picture, and identifies the child as the newborn Orc, the "devil" as Los. He refers to a passage in *The Four Zoas* V (K. 306–307, 37–67):

> *. . . a terrible child sprang forth*
>
> . . .
>
> *Soon as his burning Eyes were open'd on the Abyss,*
>
> . . .
>
> *The Enormous Demons woke & howl'd around the new born King,*
> *Crying* . . .
>
> . . .
>
> *"Let loose the Enormous Spirit on the darkness of the deep,"*
>
> . . .
>
> *Sweat & blood stood on the limbs of Los in globes; his fiery Eyelids*
> *Faded* . . .

It is more likely that Blake conceived the design at first without reference to Los and the later elaborations of the myth of the birth of Orc.

19. *Forty Questions*, ques. 1, § 104; *Works*, II, 18.

20. *Treatise on the Incarnation*, Chap. I, § 35; *Works*, II, 15.

21. *Mysterium Magnum*, Chap. 3, § 7; *Works*, III, 15.

22. *M.H.H.* 5–6; K. 150.

23. *Aurora*, Chap. 3, § 52; *Works*, I, 36.

24. *T.C.R.*, Vol. II, § 570, pp. 183–84.

25. *M.H.H.* 6; K. 150.

26. *M.H.H.* 6–7; K. 150.

27. *Mysterium Magnum*, Chap. 4, §§ 11–12; *Works*, III, 20.

28. Ibid., Chap. 5, § 3; *Works*, III, 22.

29. *O.H.* (1792 edn.), p. 167.

30. The Titans are called "Our fathers' sires" because mankind was made from the dust and ashes of the Titans, when these were destroyed by Zeus. See our I, p. 306.

31. *M.H.H.* 15–17; K. 155. See also below, the myth of Fenris overcome by "cunning," our I, p. 348.

32. Tr. Potter, p. 65.

ADDENDUM

Ad p. 411, n. 14: Another passage relating to the cock, which Blake might have seen, is from Proclus' Dissertation on Magic, quoted by Thomas Taylor in his notes to Plato's "First Alcibiades," *Works*, I, 65:

> . . . there are many solar animals, such as lions and cocks, which participate, according to their nature, of a certain solar divinity; whence it is wonderful how much inferiors yield to superiors in the same order, though they do not yield in magnitude and power. Hence, they report that a cock is very much feared, and as it were reverenced, by a lion; the reason of which we cannot assign from matter or sense, but from the contemplation alone of a supernal order: for thus we shall find that the presence of the solar virtue accords more with a cock than a lion. This will be evident from considering that the cock, as it were, with certain hymns, applauds and calls to the rising sun, when he bends his course to us from the antipodes; and that solar angels sometimes appear in forms of this kind, who, though they are without shape, yet present themselves to us, who are connected with shape, in some sensible form. Sometimes too, there are dæmons with a leonine front, who, when a cock is placed before them, unless they are of a solar order, suddenly disappear; and this, because those natures which have an inferior rank in the same order, always reverence their superiors. . . .